PRODUCT NAME: Fullmetal Alchemist
INGREDIENTS: Alchemy (non-genetically modified)
AMOUNT PER SERVING: 192 pages
STORAGE GUIDELINES: Store in a cool, dry place.
HANDLING PRECAUTIONS: If any of it gets in your eyes, quickly purchase every volume of the series.

—*Hiromu Arakawa, 2003*

Born in Hokkaido (northern Japan), Hiromu Arakawa first attracted national attention in 1999 with her award-winning manga *Stray Dog*. Her series *Fullmetal Alchemist* debuted in 2001 in Square Enix's monthly manga anthology *Shonen Gangan*.

FULLMETAL ALCHEMIST VOL. 5

VIZ Media Edition

Story and Art by Hiromu Arakawa

Translation/Akira Watanabe
English Adaptation/Jake Forbes
Touch-up Art & Lettering/Wayne Truman
Design/Amy Martin
Editor/Jason Thompson

Hagane no RenkinJutsushi vol. 5 © 2003 Hiromu Arakawa/SQUARE ENIX. First published in Japan in 2003 by SQUARE ENIX CO., LTD. English translation rights arranged with SQUARE ENIX CO., LTD. and VIZ Media, LLC.

Printed in the U.S.A.

Published by VIZ Media, LLC
P.O. Box 77010
San Francisco, CA 94107

11
First printing, December 2005
Eleventh printing, May 2013

www.viz.com

鋼の錬金術師

FULLMETAL ALCHEMIST

5

荒川弘

HIROMU ARAKAWA

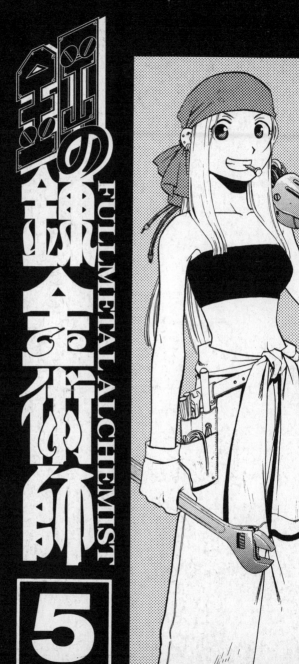

アルフォンス・エルリック

Alphonse Elric

エドワード・エルリッ

Edward Elric

アレックス・ルイ・アームストロング

Alex Louis Armstrong

ロイ・マスタング

Roy Mustang

Using a forbidden alchemical ritual, the Elric brothers attempted to bring their dead mother back to life. But the ritual went wrong, consuming Edward Elric's leg and Alphonse Elric's entire body. At the cost of his arm, Edward was able to graft his brother's soul into a suit of armor. Equipped with mechanical "auto-mail" to replace his missing limbs, Edward becomes a state alchemist, serving the military on deadly missions. Now, the two brothers roam the world in search of a way to regain what they have lost…

In search of the Philosopher's Stone, the Elric brothers break into a top-secret government laboratory, only to meet the mysterious Lust and Envy, who blow up the lab to hide the evidence. Uncertain of the extent of the Philosopher's Stone conspiracy, Edward and Al decide to return to their old alchemy teacher for advice, taking their mechanic Winry along for the ride…

鋼の錬金術師
FULLMETAL ALCHEMIST

CHARACTERS
FULLMETAL ALCHEMIST

□ ウィンリィ・ロックベル

Winry Rockbell

□ 傷の男（スカー）

Scar

□ グラトニー

Gluttony

□ ラスト

Lust

□ ピナコ・ロックベル

Pinako Rockbell

□ エンヴィー

Envy

CONTENTS

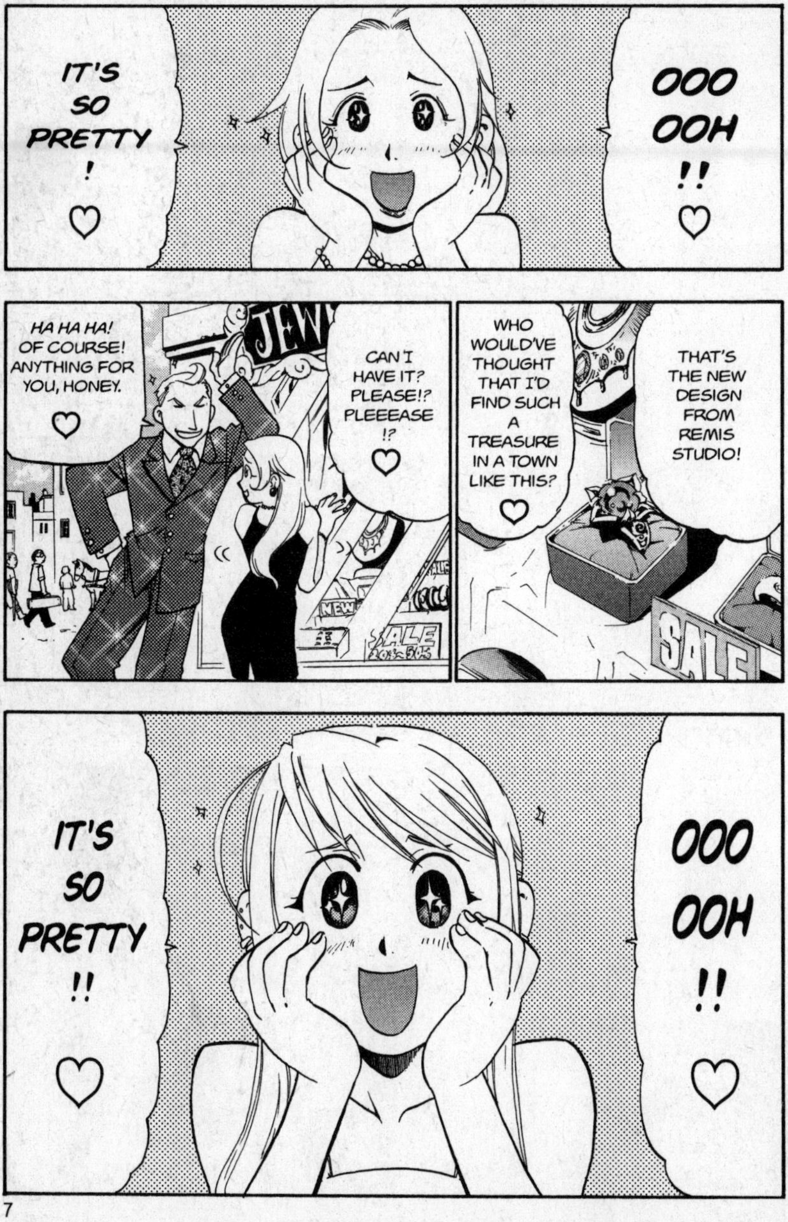
OOOOOH!! ♡
IT'S SO PRETTY! ♡
THAT'S THE NEW DESIGN FROM REMIS STUDIO!
WHO WOULD'VE THOUGHT THAT I'D FIND SUCH A TREASURE IN A TOWN LIKE THIS? ♡
CAN I HAVE IT? PLEASE!? PLEEEASE!? ♡
HA HA HA! OF COURSE! ANYTHING FOR YOU, HONEY. ♡
SALE
OOOOOH!! ♡
IT'S SO PRETTY!! ♡

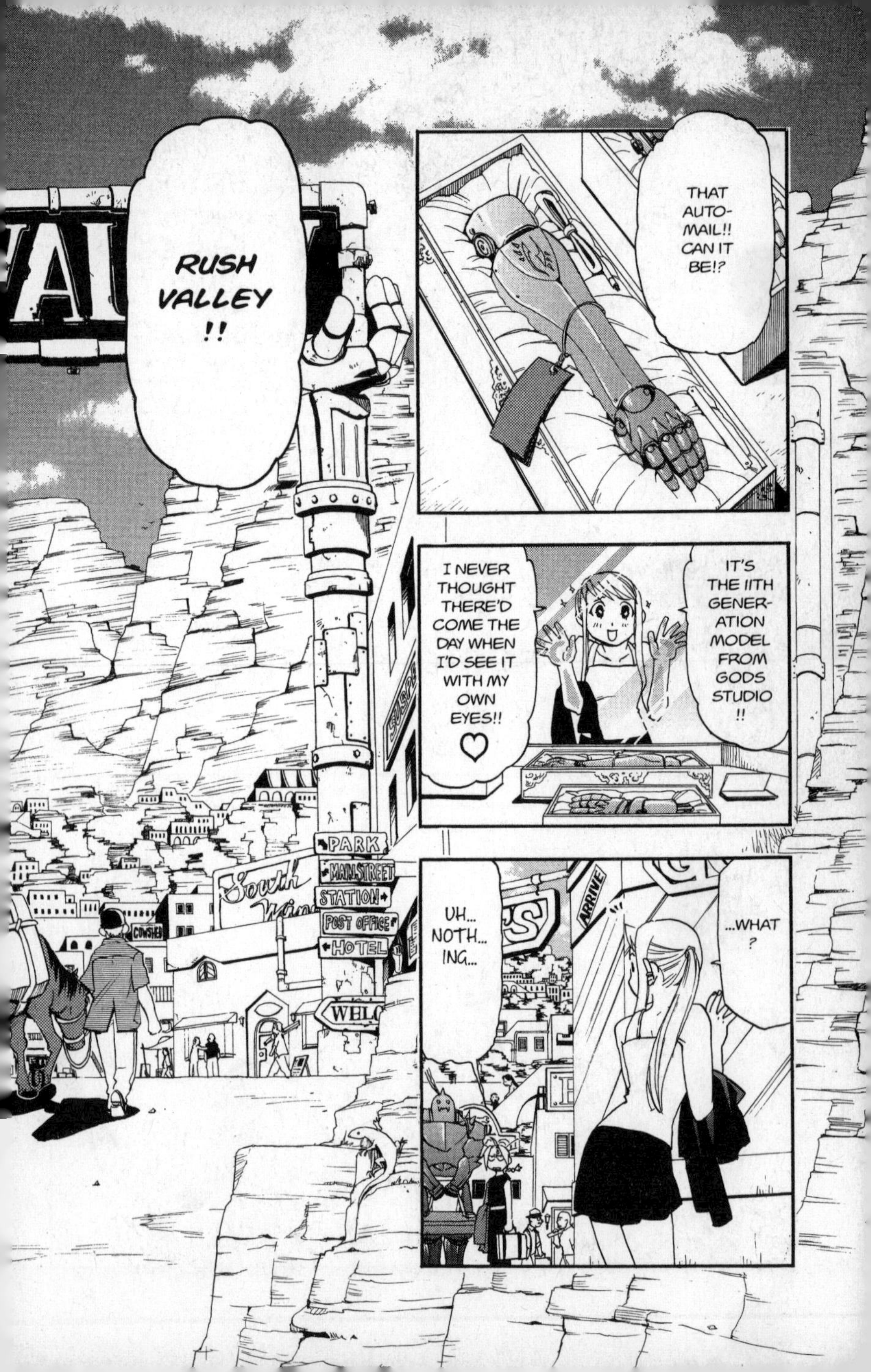
THAT AUTO-MAIL!! CAN IT BE!?
IT'S THE 11TH GENER-ATION MODEL FROM GODS STUDIO !!
I NEVER THOUGHT THERE'D COME THE DAY WHEN I'D SEE IT WITH MY OWN EYES!! ♡
...WHAT ?
UH... NOTH... ING...
RUSH VALLEY !!
PARK
MAIN STREET
STATION
POST OFFICE
HOTEL
COWSHED

Chapter 17: The Boomtown of the Broken Down

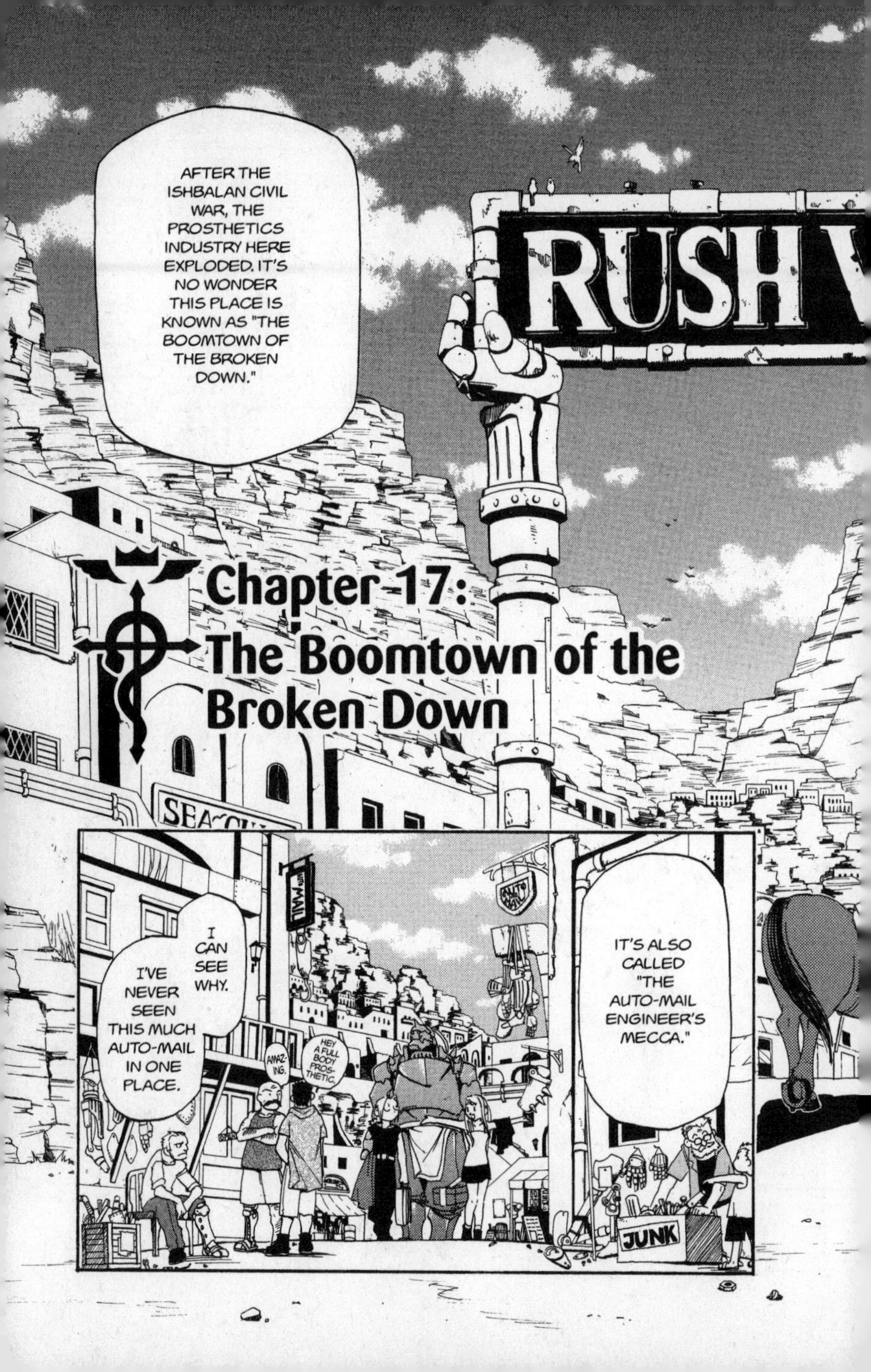
AFTER THE ISHBALAN CIVIL WAR, THE PROSTHETICS INDUSTRY HERE EXPLODED. IT'S NO WONDER THIS PLACE IS KNOWN AS "THE BOOMTOWN OF THE BROKEN DOWN."
RUSH
IT'S ALSO CALLED "THE AUTO-MAIL ENGINEER'S MECCA."
I CAN SEE WHY.
I'VE NEVER SEEN THIS MUCH AUTO-MAIL IN ONE PLACE.
HEY A FULL BODY PROS-THETIC.
AMAZ-ING.
JUNK

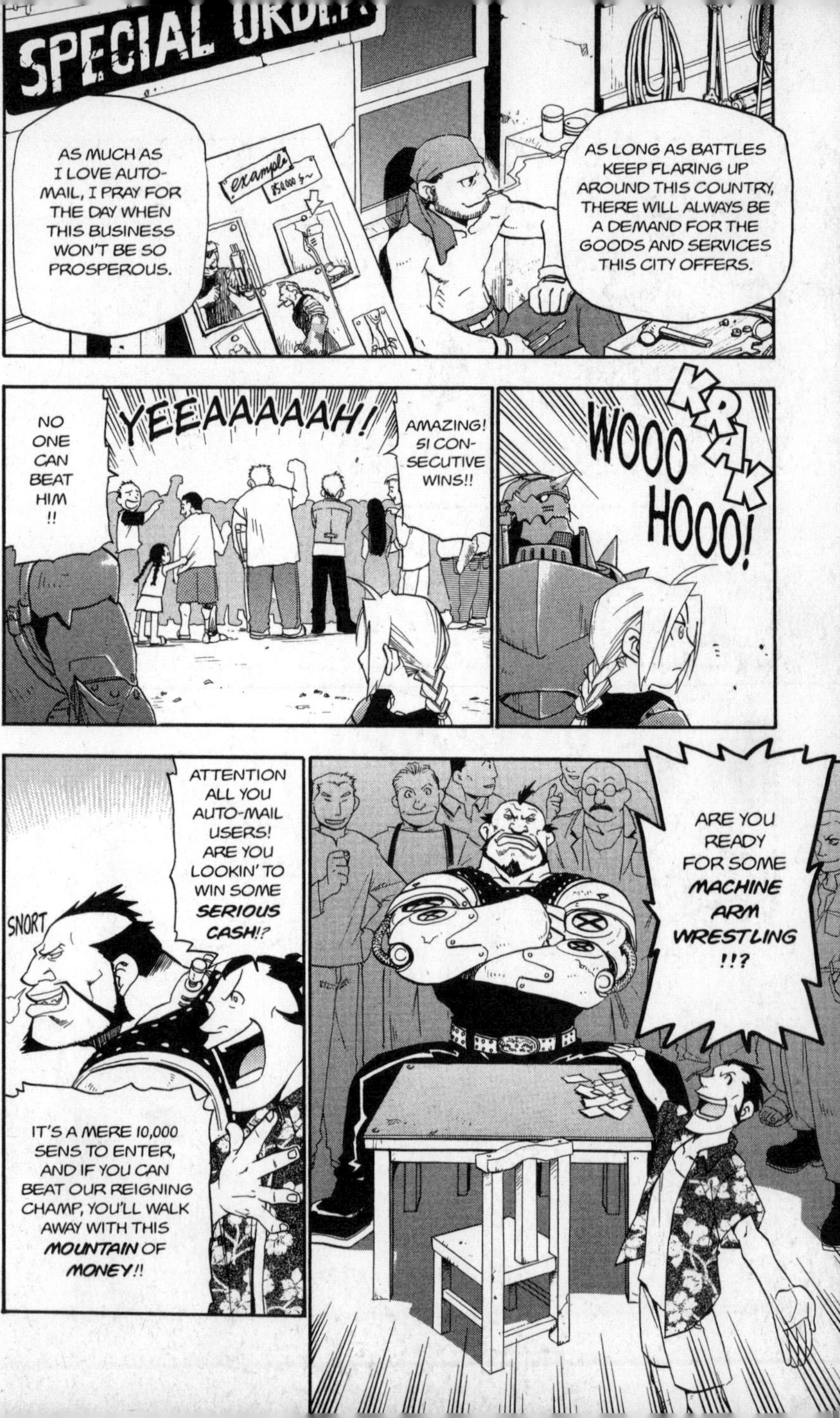
AS LONG AS BATTLES KEEP FLARING UP AROUND THIS COUNTRY, THERE WILL ALWAYS BE A DEMAND FOR THE GOODS AND SERVICES THIS CITY OFFERS.
example
AS MUCH AS I LOVE AUTO-MAIL, I PRAY FOR THE DAY WHEN THIS BUSINESS WON'T BE SO PROSPEROUS.
KRAK
WOOO HOOO!
AMAZING! 51 CON-SECUTIVE WINS!!
YEEAAAAAH!
NO ONE CAN BEAT HIM !!
ARE YOU READY FOR SOME ***MACHINE ARM WRESTLING*** !!?
ATTENTION ALL YOU AUTO-MAIL USERS! ARE YOU LOOKIN' TO WIN SOME ***SERIOUS CASH***!?
SNORT
IT'S A MERE 10,000 SENS TO ENTER, AND IF YOU CAN BEAT OUR REIGNING CHAMP, YOU'LL WALK AWAY WITH THIS ***MOUNTAIN*** OF ***MONEY***!!

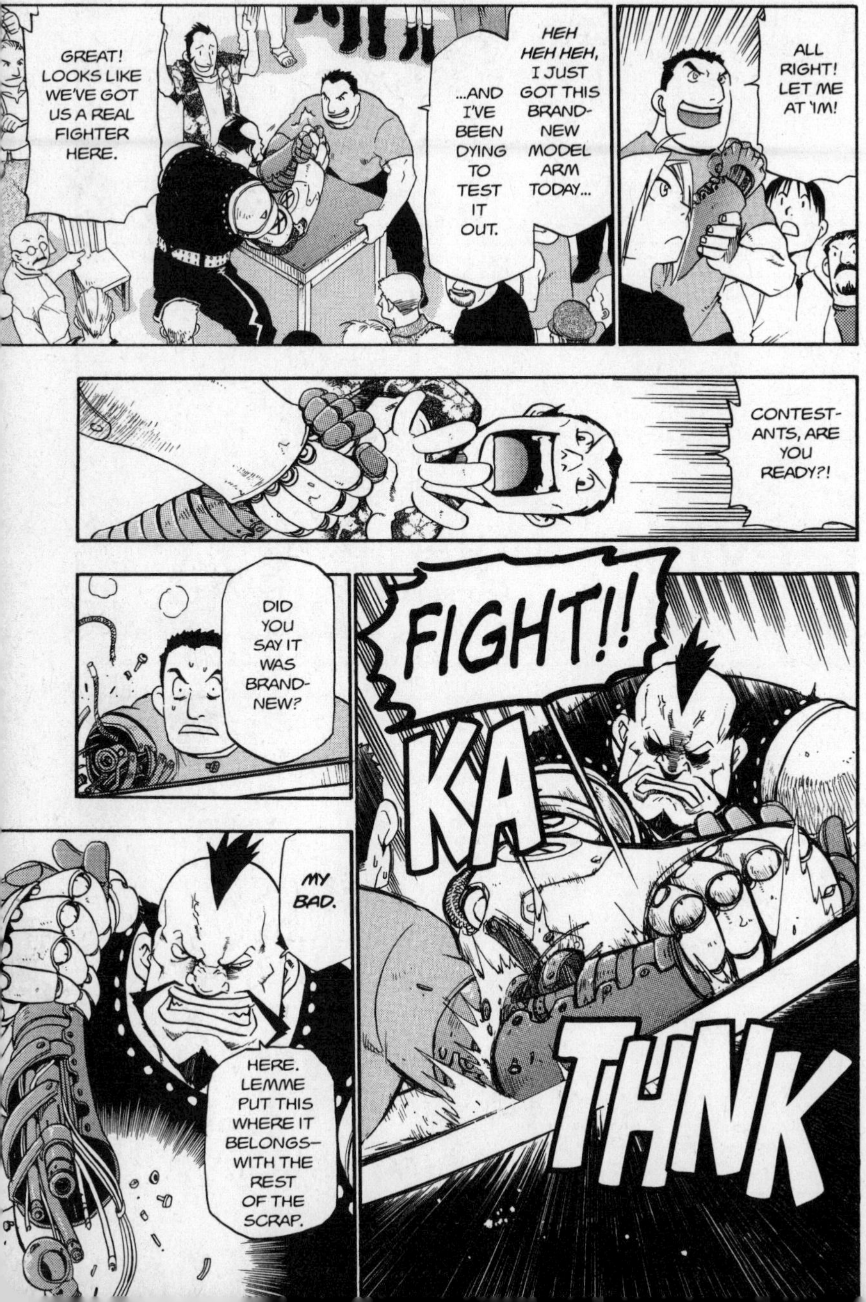
ALL RIGHT! LET ME AT 'IM!
HEH HEH HEH, I JUST GOT THIS BRAND-NEW MODEL ARM TODAY...
...AND I'VE BEEN DYING TO TEST IT OUT.
GREAT! LOOKS LIKE WE'VE GOT US A REAL FIGHTER HERE.
CONTEST-ANTS, ARE YOU READY?!
FIGHT!!
KA
THNK
DID YOU SAY IT WAS BRAND-NEW?
MY BAD.
HERE. LEMME PUT THIS WHERE IT BELONGS— WITH THE REST OF THE SCRAP.

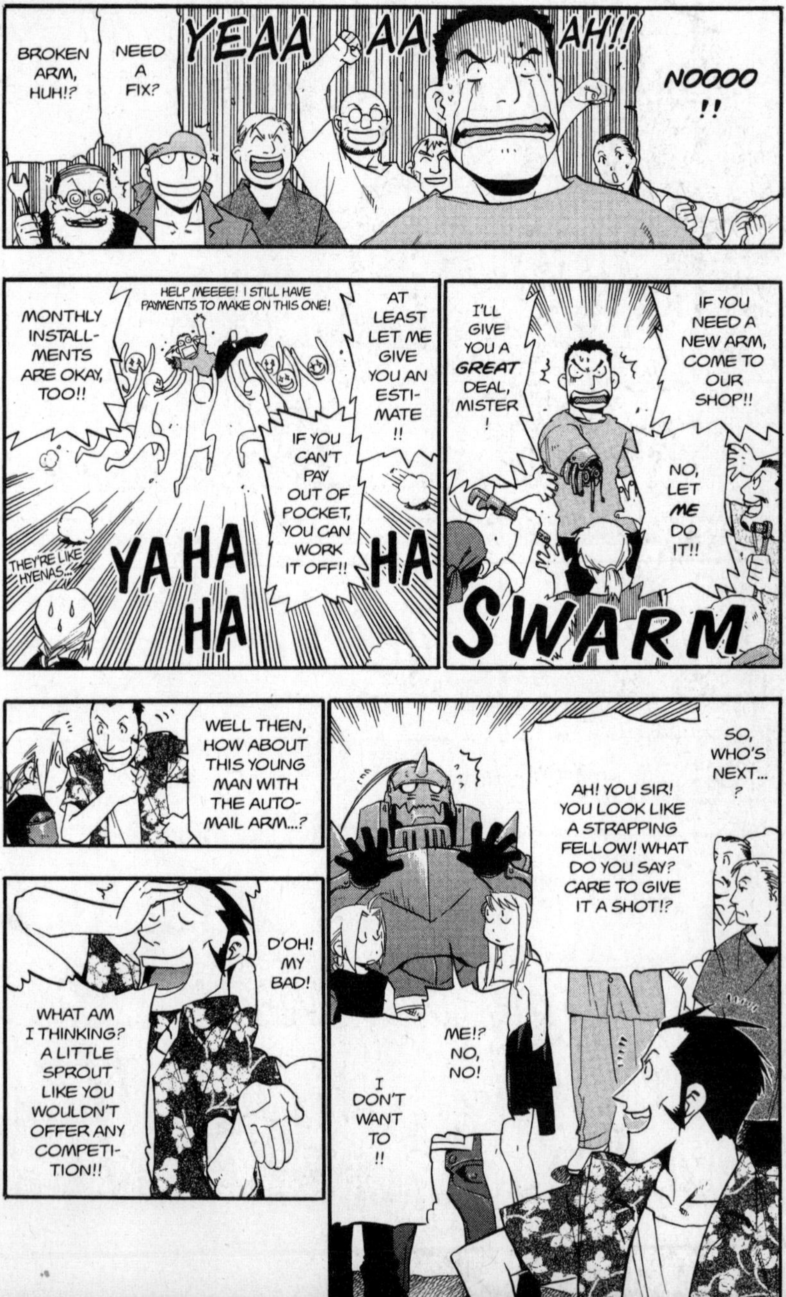
NOOOO!!
YEAAAAAH!!
NEED A FIX?
BROKEN ARM, HUH!?
IF YOU NEED A NEW ARM, COME TO OUR SHOP!!
I'LL GIVE YOU A GREAT DEAL, MISTER!
NO, LET ME DO IT!!
SWARM
AT LEAST LET ME GIVE YOU AN ESTIMATE!!
HELP MEEEE! I STILL HAVE PAYMENTS TO MAKE ON THIS ONE!
MONTHLY INSTALLMENTS ARE OKAY, TOO!!
IF YOU CAN'T PAY OUT OF POCKET, YOU CAN WORK IT OFF!!
YAHAHAHA
HA
THEY'RE LIKE HYENAS...
SO, WHO'S NEXT...?
AH! YOU SIR! YOU LOOK LIKE A STRAPPING FELLOW! WHAT DO YOU SAY? CARE TO GIVE IT A SHOT!?
ME!? NO, NO!
I DON'T WANT TO!!
WELL THEN, HOW ABOUT THIS YOUNG MAN WITH THE AUTO-MAIL ARM...?
D'OH! MY BAD!
WHAT AM I THINKING? A LITTLE SPROUT LIKE YOU WOULDN'T OFFER ANY COMPETITION!!

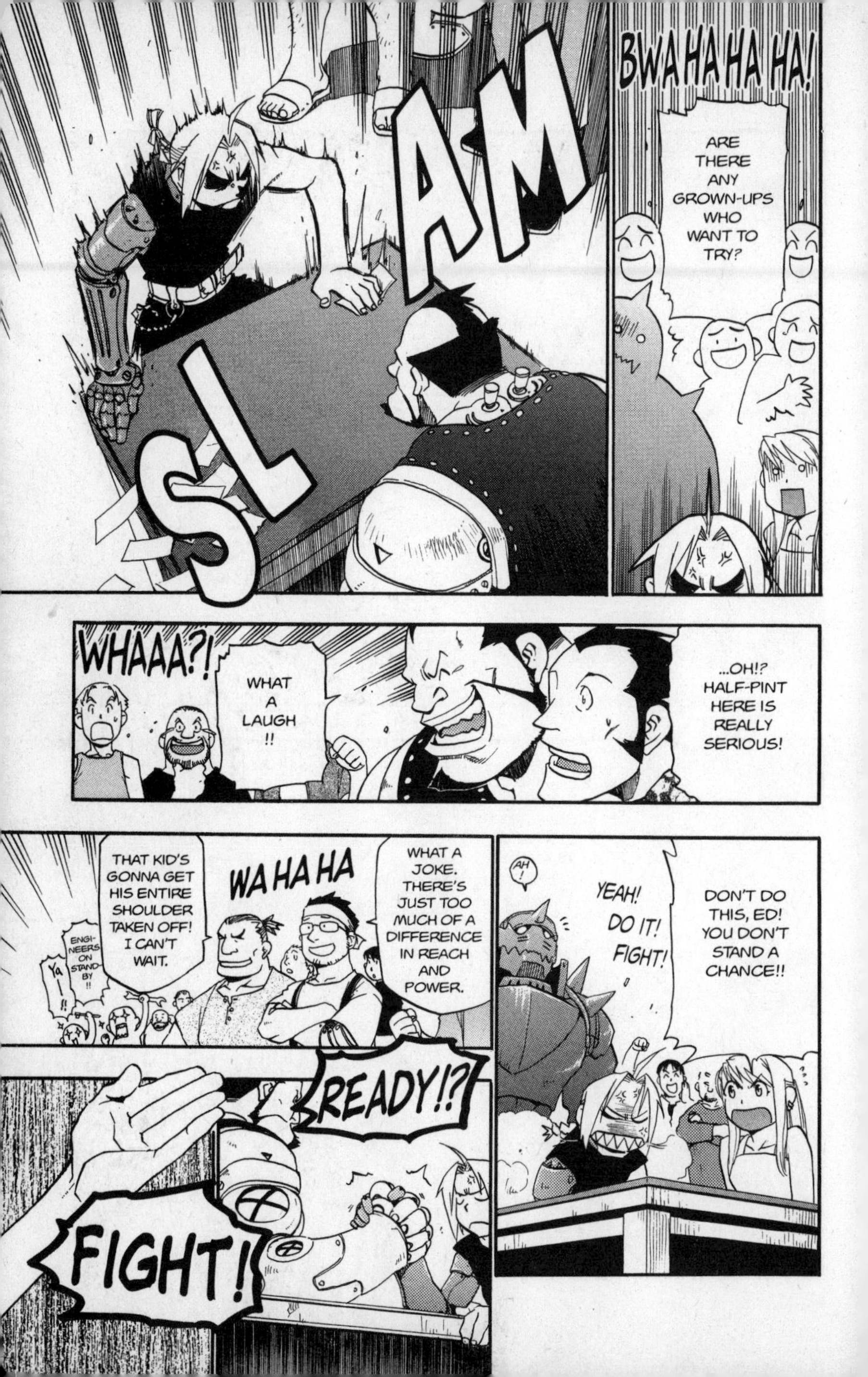
BWAHA HA HA HA!
ARE THERE ANY GROWN-UPS WHO WANT TO TRY?
SLAM
...OH!? HALF-PINT HERE IS REALLY SERIOUS!
WHAT A LAUGH!!
WHAAA?!
DON'T DO THIS, ED! YOU DON'T STAND A CHANCE!!
YEAH! DO IT! FIGHT!
AH!
WHAT A JOKE. THERE'S JUST TOO MUCH OF A DIFFERENCE IN REACH AND POWER.
WA HA HA
THAT KID'S GONNA GET HIS ENTIRE SHOULDER TAKEN OFF! I CAN'T WAIT.
ENGINEERS ON STANDBY!!
Ya!!
READY!?
FIGHT!

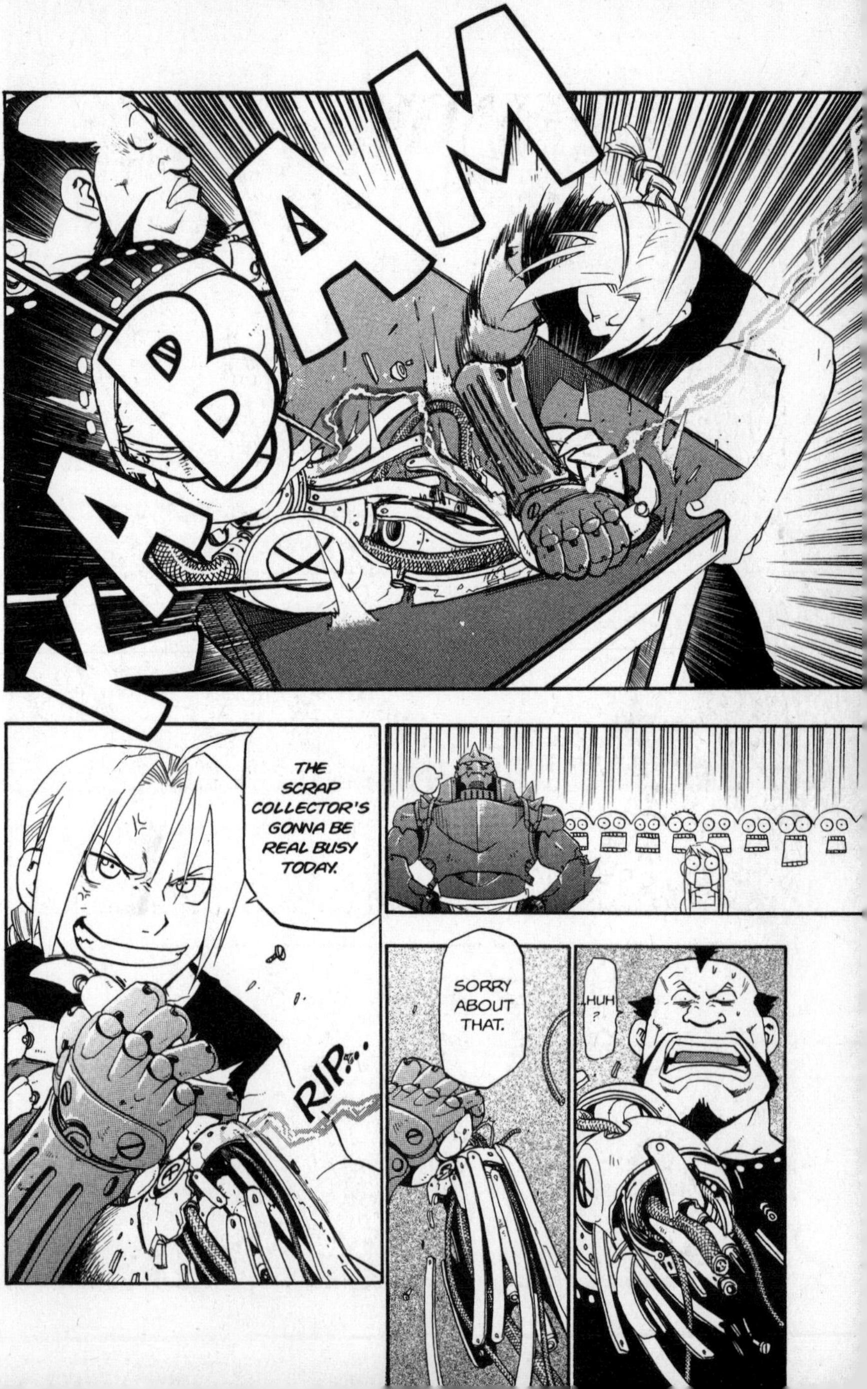
KABAM
..HUH?
SORRY ABOUT THAT.
THE SCRAP COLLECTOR'S GONNA BE REAL BUSY TODAY.
RIP...

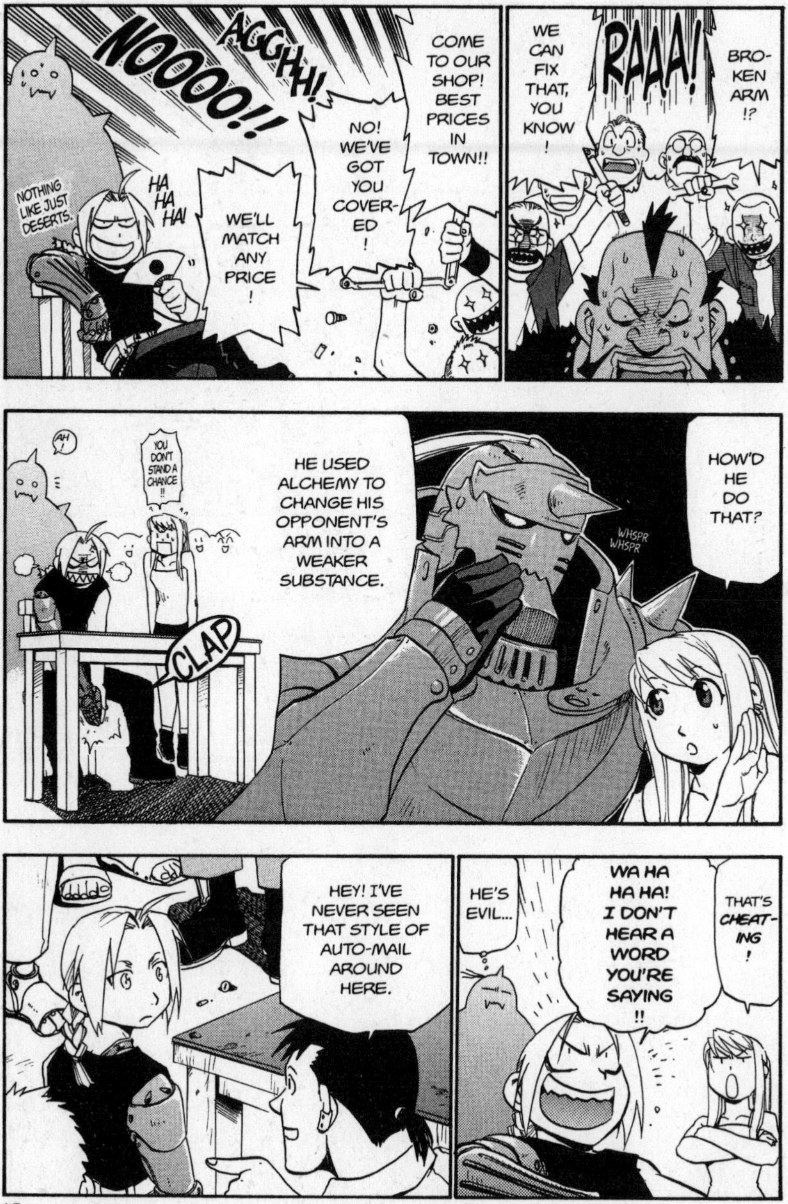
BROKEN ARM!?
RAAA!
WE CAN FIX THAT, YOU KNOW!
COME TO OUR SHOP! BEST PRICES IN TOWN!!
AGGHH!
NO! WE'VE GOT YOU COVERED!
NOOOO!!
WE'LL MATCH ANY PRICE!
HA HA HA!
NOTHING LIKE JUST DESERTS.
HOW'D HE DO THAT?
WHSPR WHSPR
HE USED ALCHEMY TO CHANGE HIS OPPONENT'S ARM INTO A WEAKER SUBSTANCE.
YOU DON'T STAND A CHANCE!!
AH!
CLAP
THAT'S CHEATING!
WA HA HA HA! I DON'T HEAR A WORD YOU'RE SAYING!!
HE'S EVIL...
HEY! I'VE NEVER SEEN THAT STYLE OF AUTO-MAIL AROUND HERE.

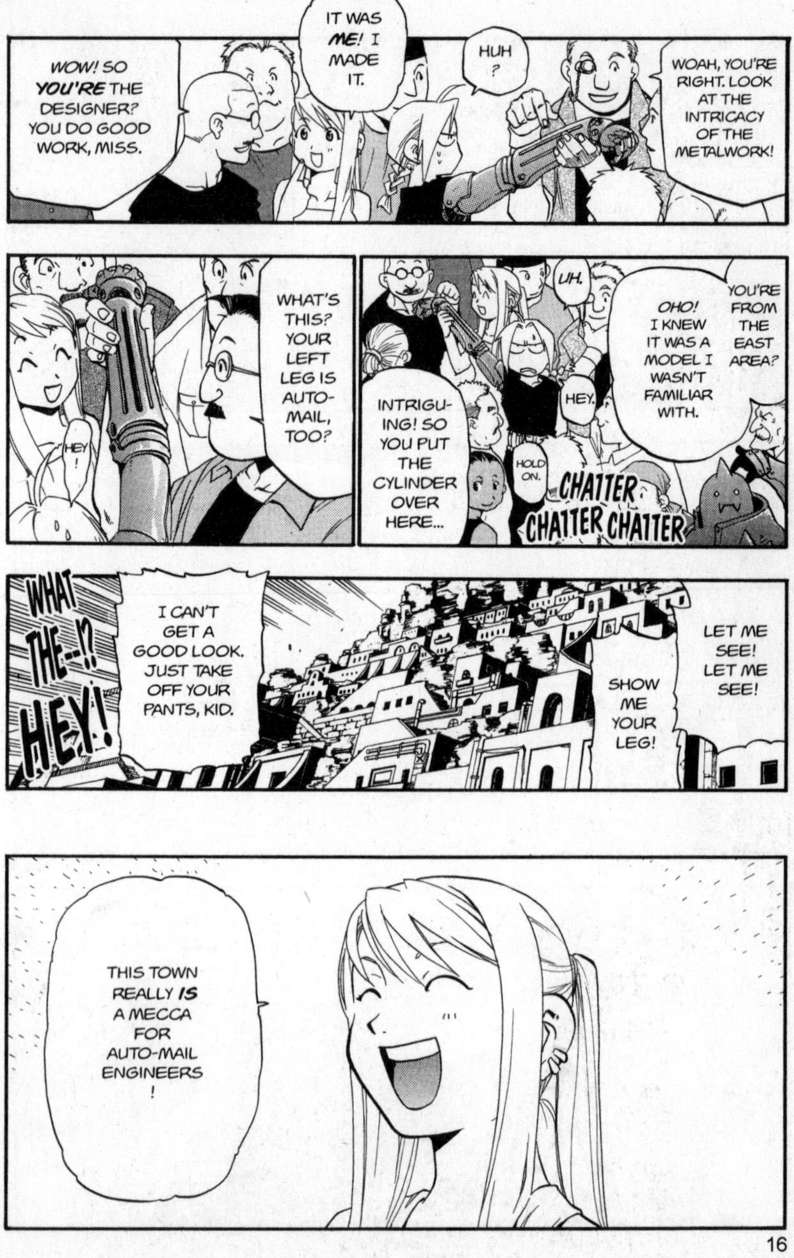
WOAH, YOU'RE RIGHT. LOOK AT THE INTRICACY OF THE METALWORK!
HUH?
IT WAS *ME*! I MADE IT.
WOW! SO ***YOU'RE*** THE DESIGNER? YOU DO GOOD WORK, MISS.
YOU'RE FROM THE EAST AREA?
OHO! I KNEW IT WAS A MODEL I WASN'T FAMILIAR WITH.
UH.
HEY.
INTRIGUING! SO YOU PUT THE CYLINDER OVER HERE...
HOLD ON.
CHATTER CHATTER CHATTER
WHAT'S THIS? YOUR LEFT LEG IS AUTO-MAIL, TOO?
HEY!
LET ME SEE! LET ME SEE!
SHOW ME YOUR LEG!
I CAN'T GET A GOOD LOOK. JUST TAKE OFF YOUR PANTS, KID.
WHAT THE--!? HEY!
THIS TOWN REALLY ***IS*** A MECCA FOR AUTO-MAIL ENGINEERS!

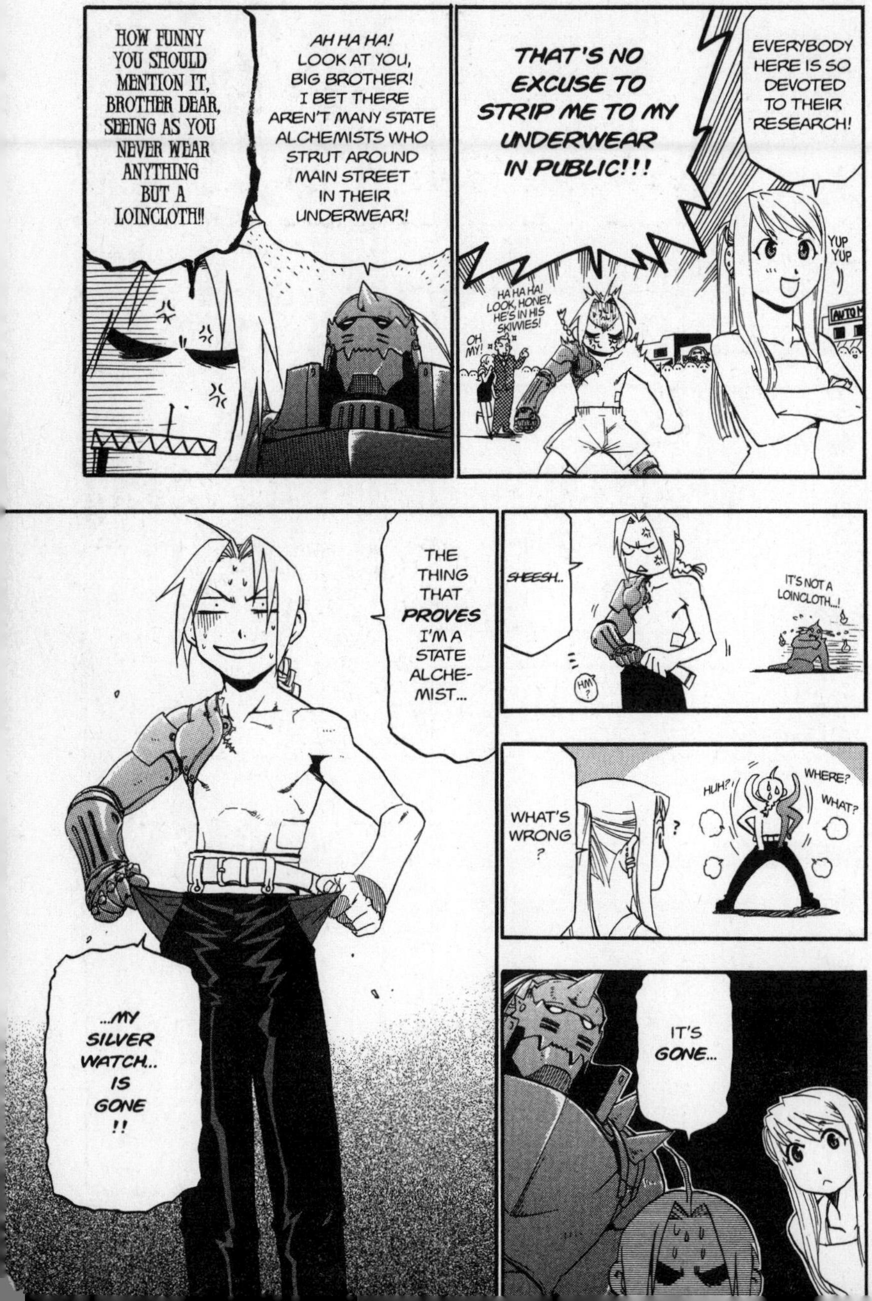
EVERYBODY HERE IS SO DEVOTED TO THEIR RESEARCH!
YUP YUP
THAT'S NO EXCUSE TO STRIP ME TO MY UNDERWEAR IN PUBLIC!!!
HA HA HA! LOOK, HONEY, HE'S IN HIS SKIVVIES!
OH MY!
AH HA HA! LOOK AT YOU, BIG BROTHER! I BET THERE AREN'T MANY STATE ALCHEMISTS WHO STRUT AROUND MAIN STREET IN THEIR UNDERWEAR!
HOW FUNNY YOU SHOULD MENTION IT, BROTHER DEAR, SEEING AS YOU NEVER WEAR ANYTHING BUT A LOINCLOTH!!
IT'S NOT A LOINCLOTH...!
SHEESH..
HM?
WHERE?
WHAT?
HUH?
WHAT'S WRONG?
IT'S GONE...
THE THING THAT PROVES I'M A STATE ALCHEMIST...
...MY SILVER WATCH.. IS GONE!!

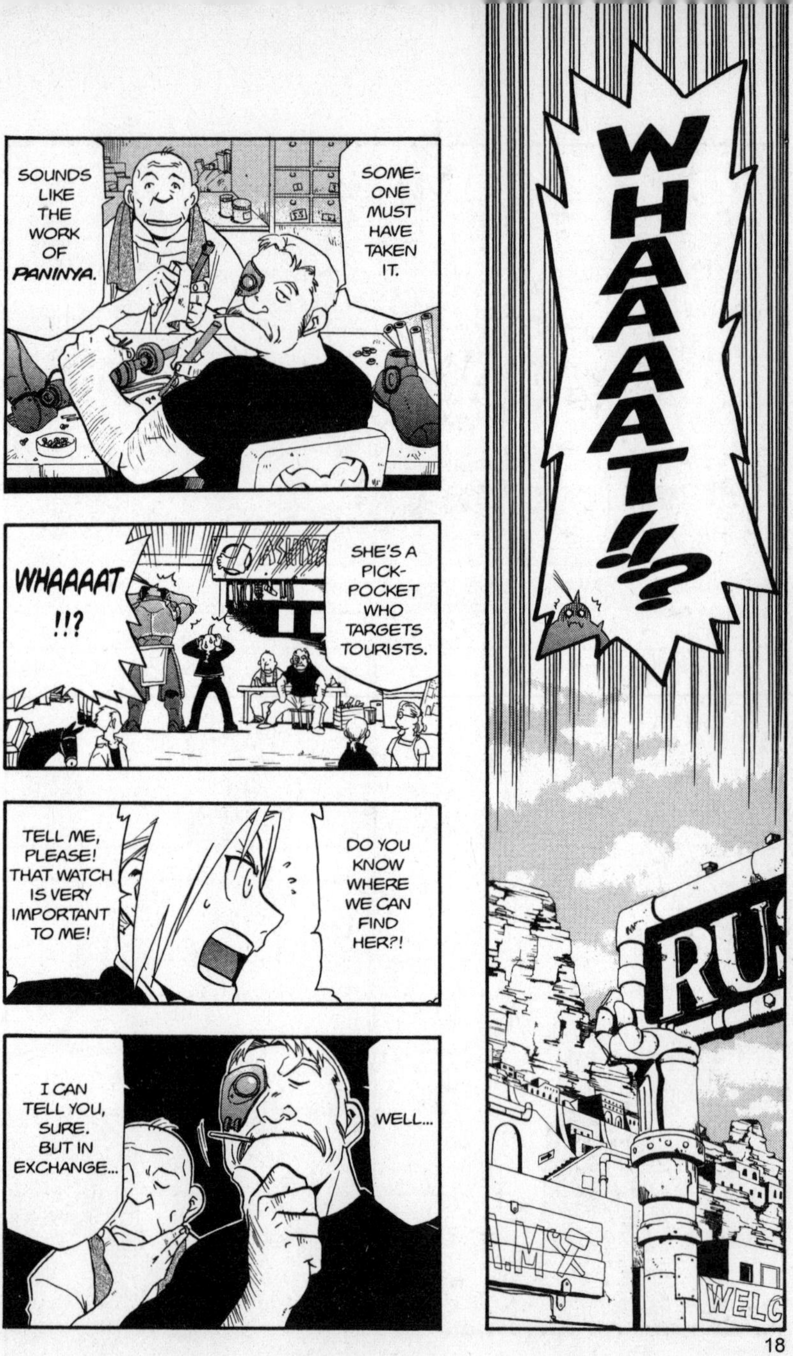
WHAAAT!!?
SOMEONE MUST HAVE TAKEN IT.
SOUNDS LIKE THE WORK OF PANINYA.
SHE'S A PICKPOCKET WHO TARGETS TOURISTS.
WHAAAAT!!?
DO YOU KNOW WHERE WE CAN FIND HER?!
TELL ME, PLEASE! THAT WATCH IS VERY IMPORTANT TO ME!
WELL...
I CAN TELL YOU, SURE. BUT IN EXCHANGE...

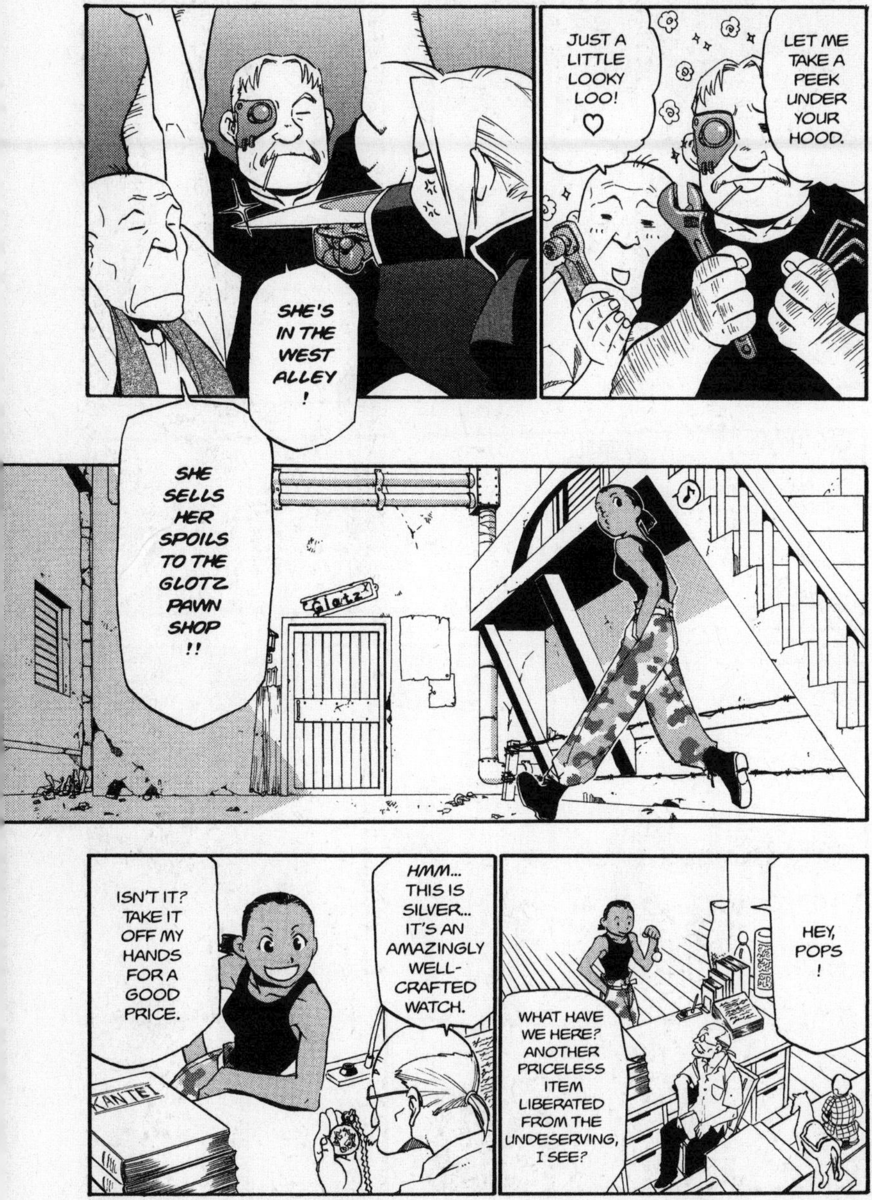
LET ME TAKE A PEEK UNDER YOUR HOOD.
JUST A LITTLE LOOKY LOO! ♡
SHE'S IN THE WEST ALLEY!
SHE SELLS HER SPOILS TO THE GLOTZ PAWN SHOP!!
Glotz
HEY, POPS!
WHAT HAVE WE HERE? ANOTHER PRICELESS ITEM LIBERATED FROM THE UNDESERVING, I SEE?
HMM... THIS IS SILVER... IT'S AN AMAZINGLY WELL-CRAFTED WATCH.
ISN'T IT? TAKE IT OFF MY HANDS FOR A GOOD PRICE.
KANTEI

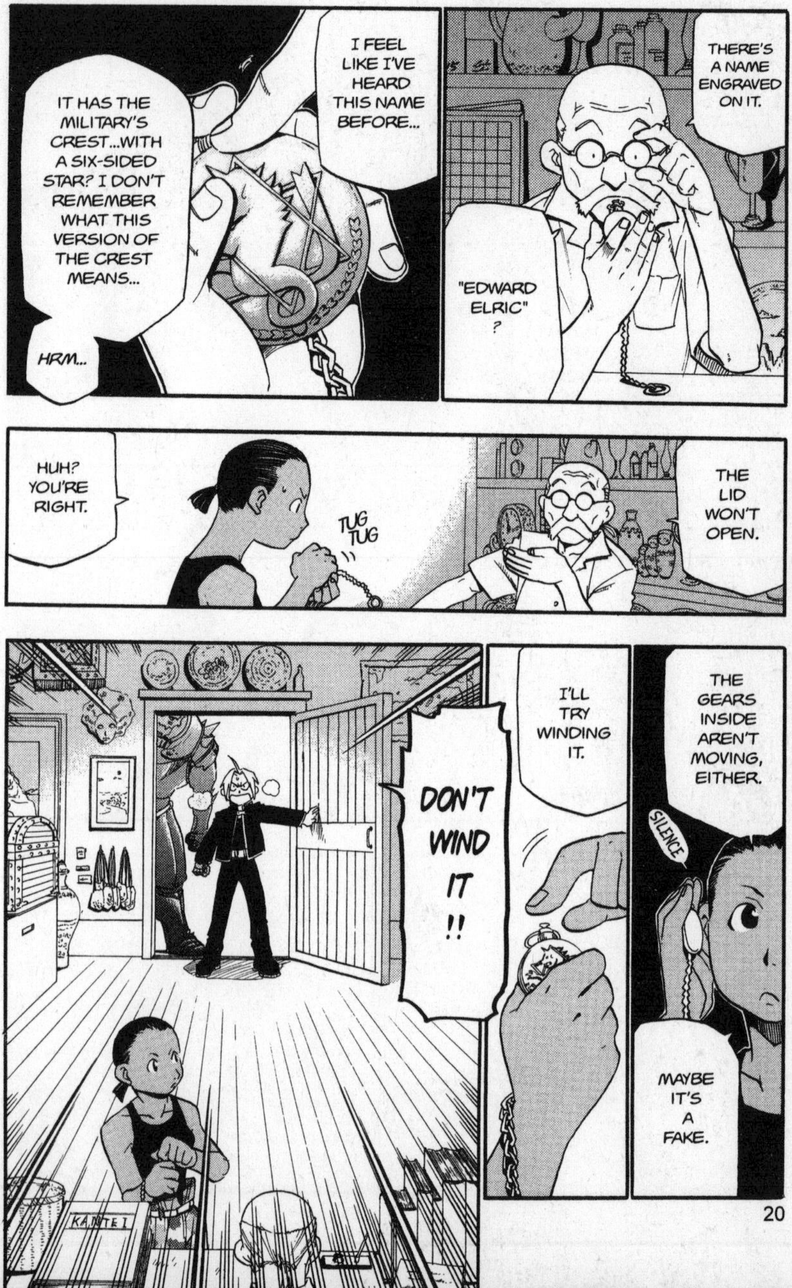
THERE'S A NAME ENGRAVED ON IT.
"EDWARD ELRIC"?
I FEEL LIKE I'VE HEARD THIS NAME BEFORE...
IT HAS THE MILITARY'S CREST...WITH A SIX-SIDED STAR? I DON'T REMEMBER WHAT THIS VERSION OF THE CREST MEANS...
HRM...
THE LID WON'T OPEN.
TUG TUG
HUH? YOU'RE RIGHT.
THE GEARS INSIDE AREN'T MOVING, EITHER.
SILENCE
MAYBE IT'S A FAKE.
I'LL TRY WINDING IT.
DON'T WIND IT!!

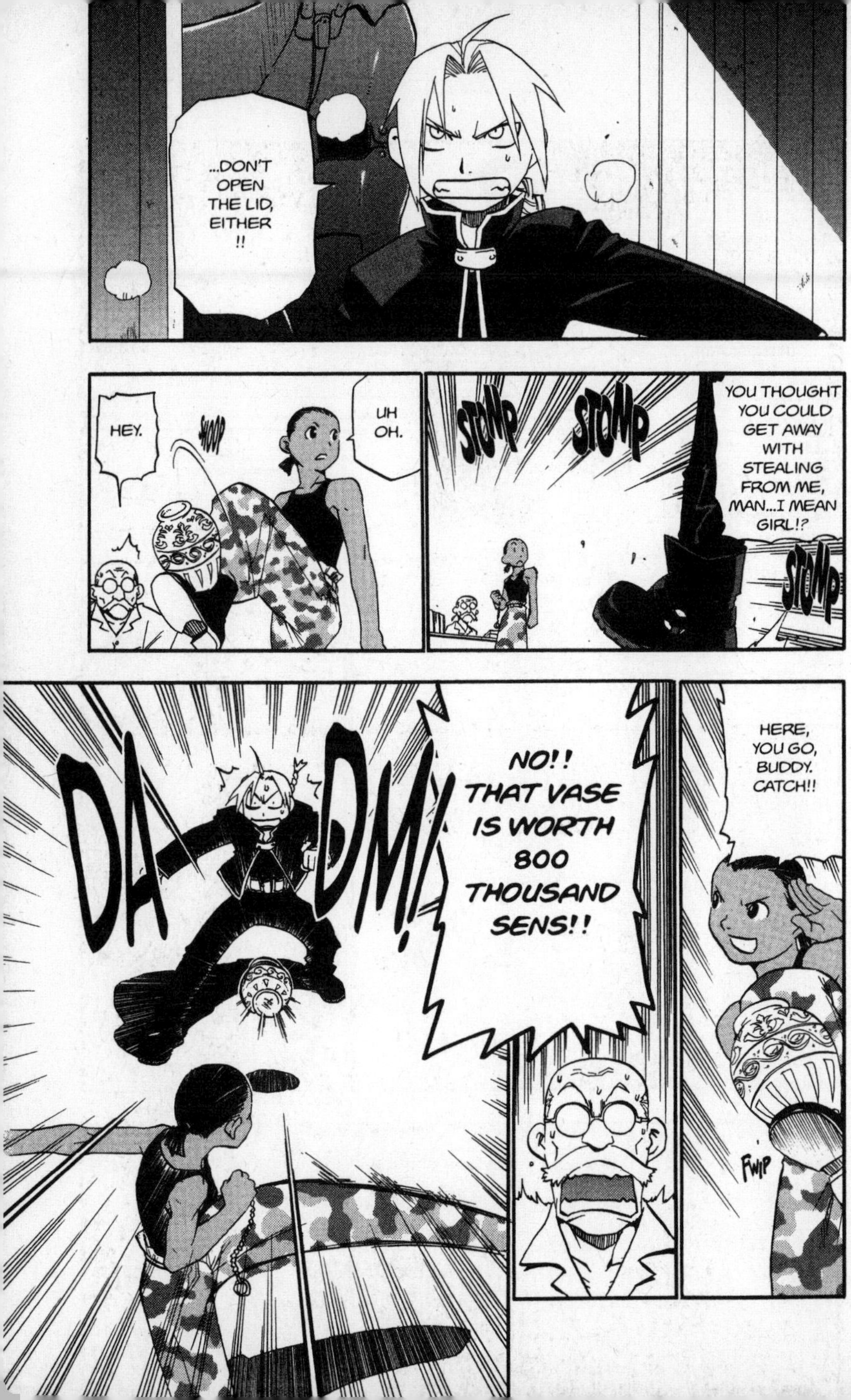
...DON'T OPEN THE LID, EITHER !!
STOMP
STOMP
YOU THOUGHT YOU COULD GET AWAY WITH STEALING FROM ME, MAN...I MEAN GIRL!?
STOMP
UH OH.
HEY.
SHOOP
HERE, YOU GO, BUDDY. CATCH!!
FWIP
NO!! THAT VASE IS WORTH 800 THOUSAND SENS!!
DA DM!!

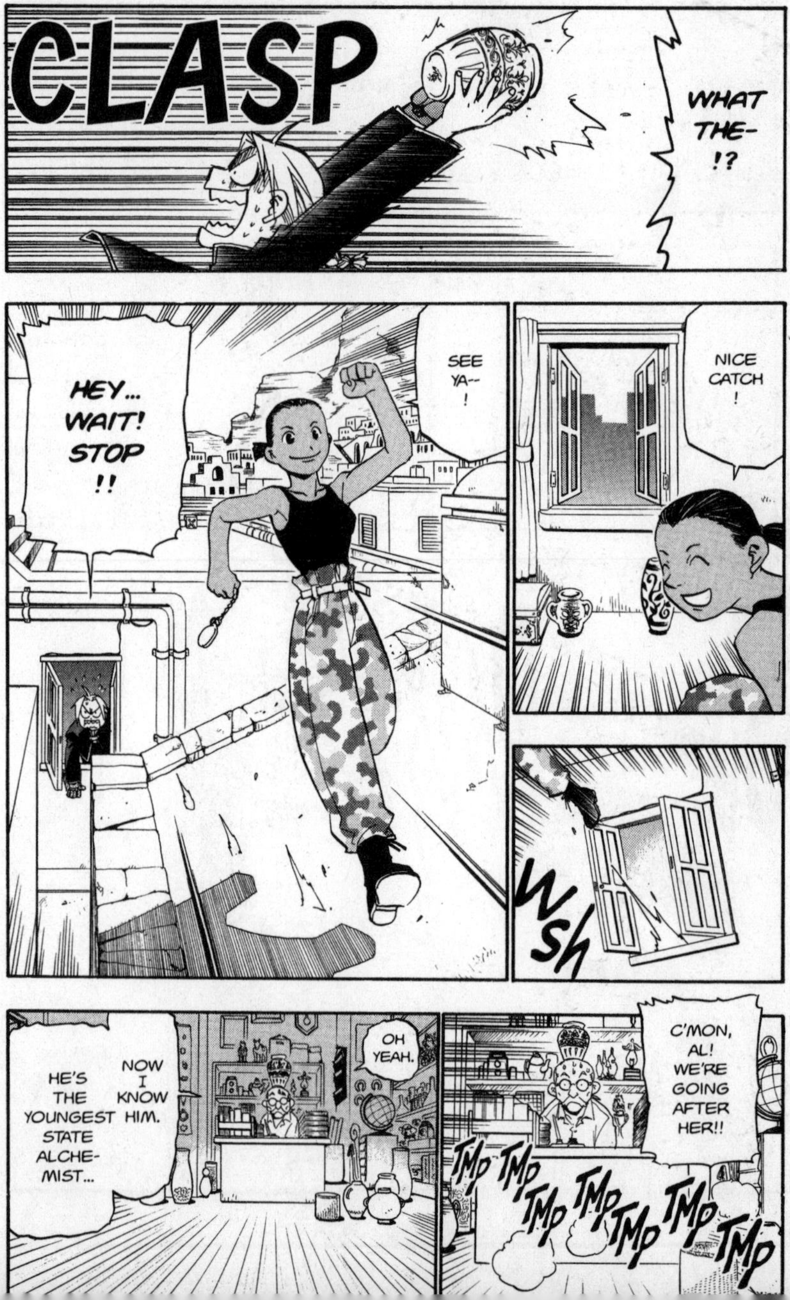
WHAT THE- !?
CLASP
NICE CATCH !
Wsh
SEE YA-- !
HEY... WAIT! STOP !!
C'MON, AL! WE'RE GOING AFTER HER!!
TMP TMP TMP TMP TMP TMP TMP
OH YEAH.
NOW I KNOW HIM.
HE'S THE YOUNGEST STATE ALCHE-MIST...

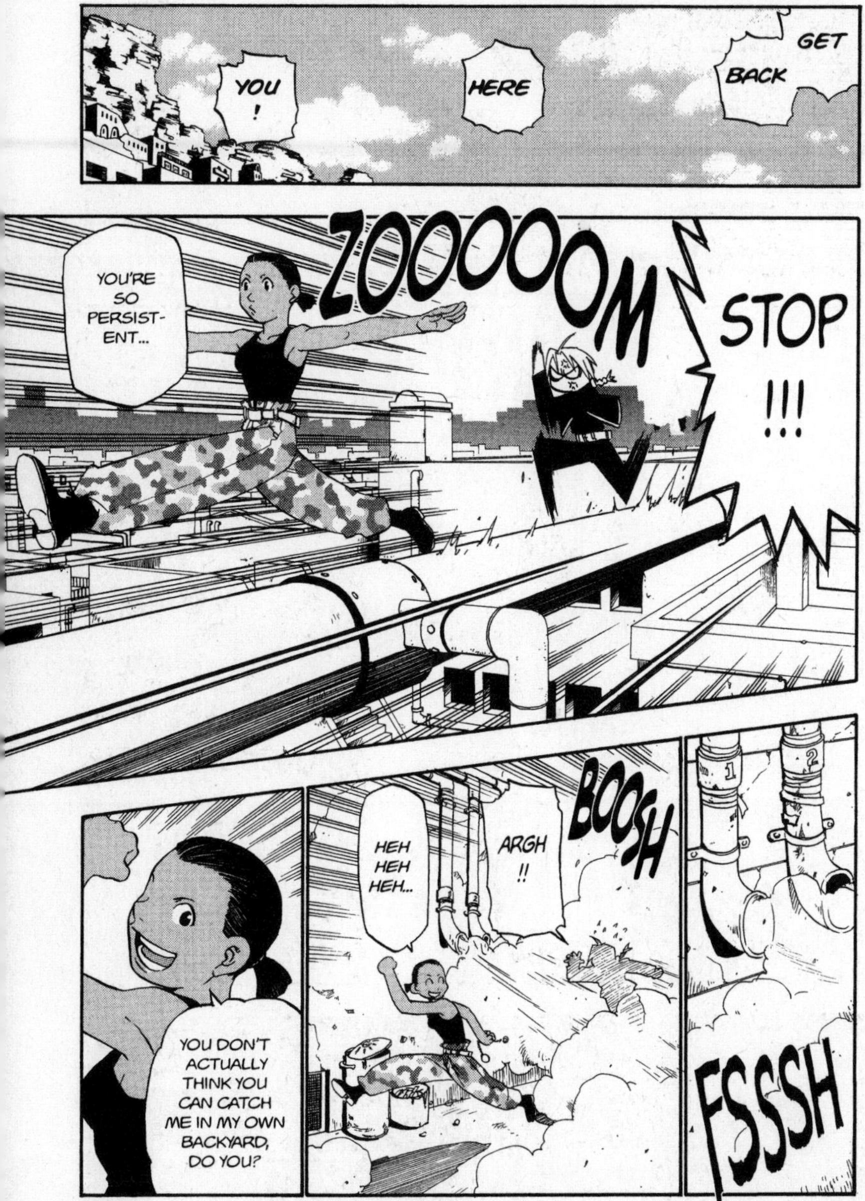
GET BACK
HERE
YOU !
STOP !!!
ZOOOOOM
YOU'RE SO PERSIST-ENT...
FSSSH
BOOSH
ARGH !!
HEH HEH HEH...
YOU DON'T ACTUALLY THINK YOU CAN CATCH ME IN MY OWN BACKYARD, DO YOU?

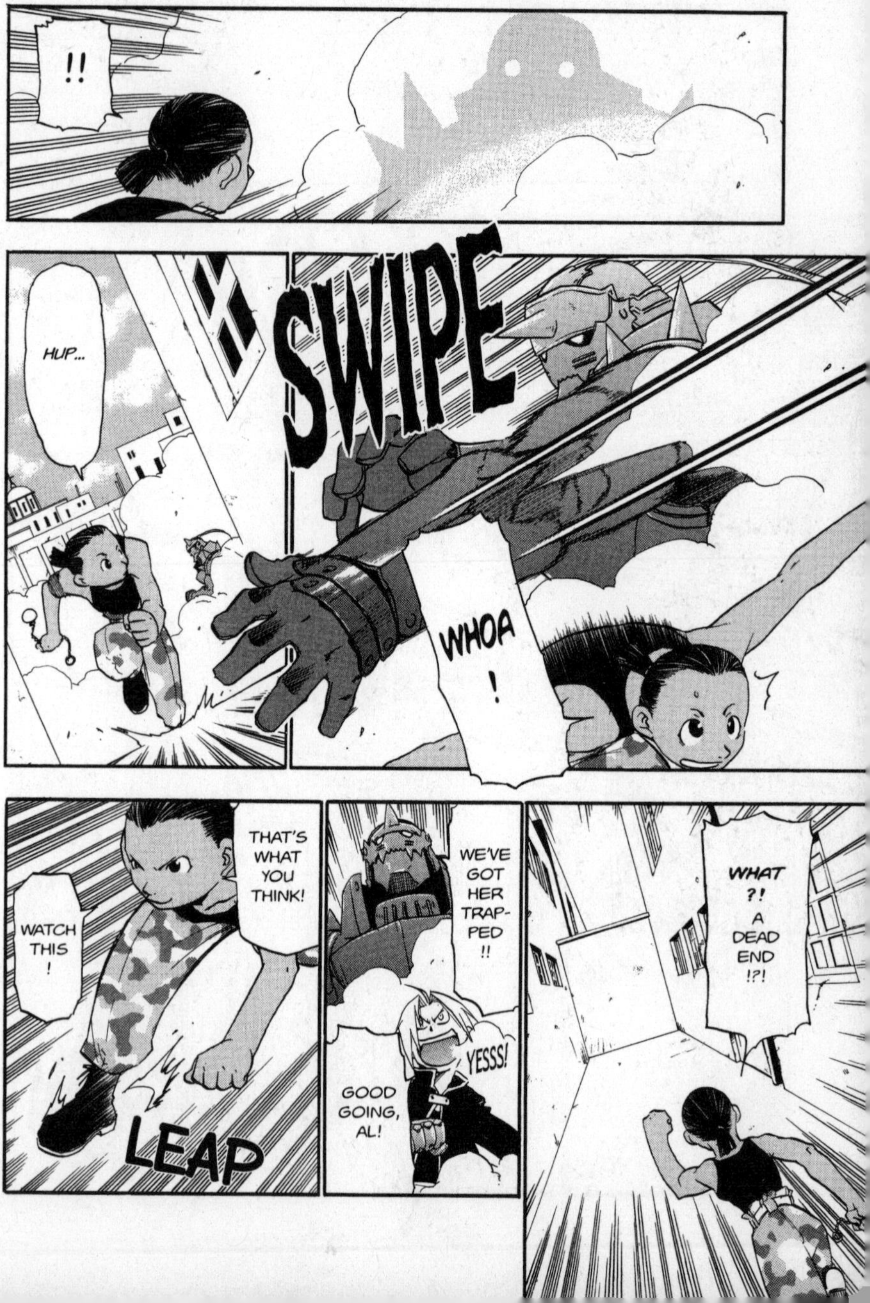
!!
SWIPE
WHOA!
HUP...
WHAT?! A DEAD END!?!
WE'VE GOT HER TRAP-PED!!
YESSS!
GOOD GOING, AL!
THAT'S WHAT YOU THINK!
WATCH THIS!
LEAP

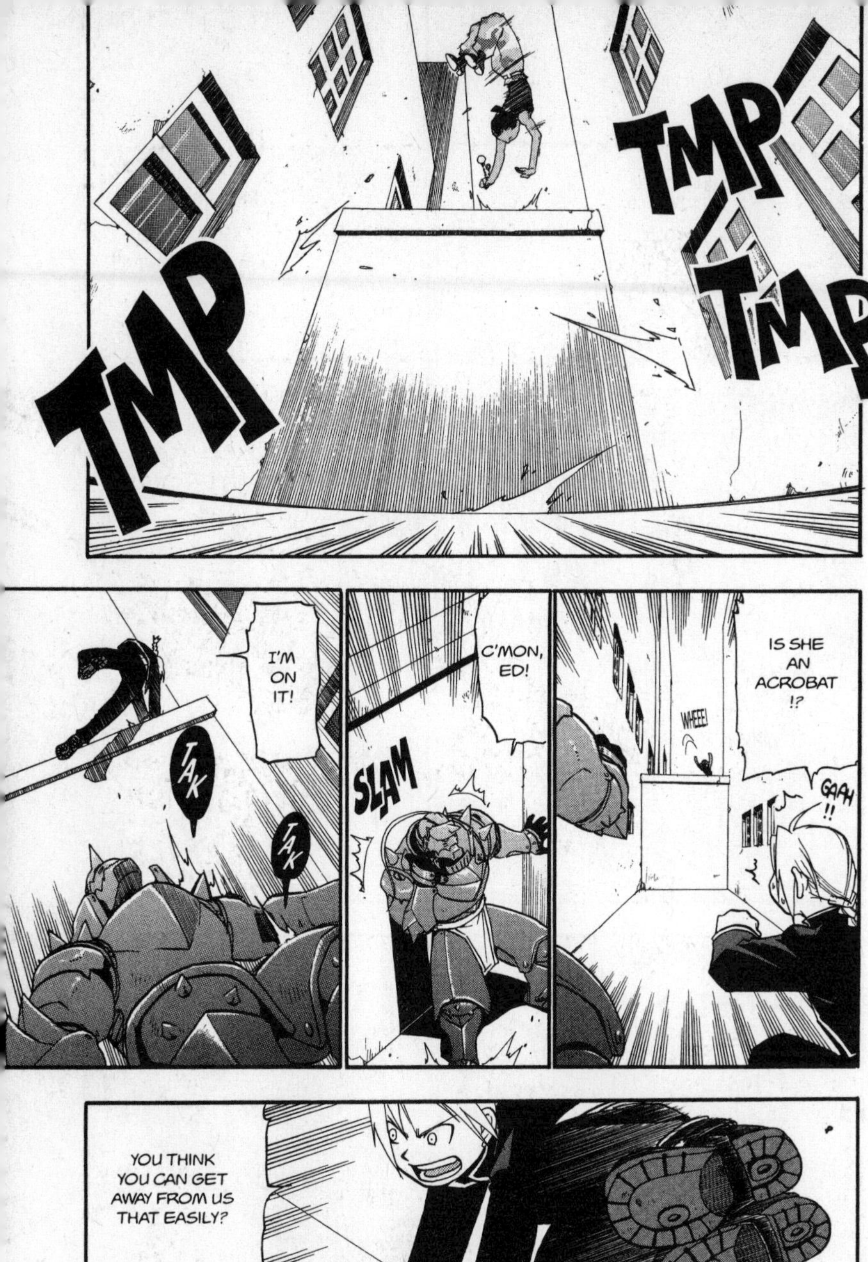
TMP
TMP
TMP
IS SHE AN ACROBAT!?
WHEEE!
GAAH!!
C'MON, ED!
SLAM
I'M ON IT!
TAK
TAK
YOU THINK YOU CAN GET AWAY FROM US THAT EASILY?

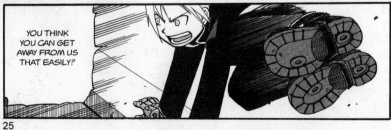

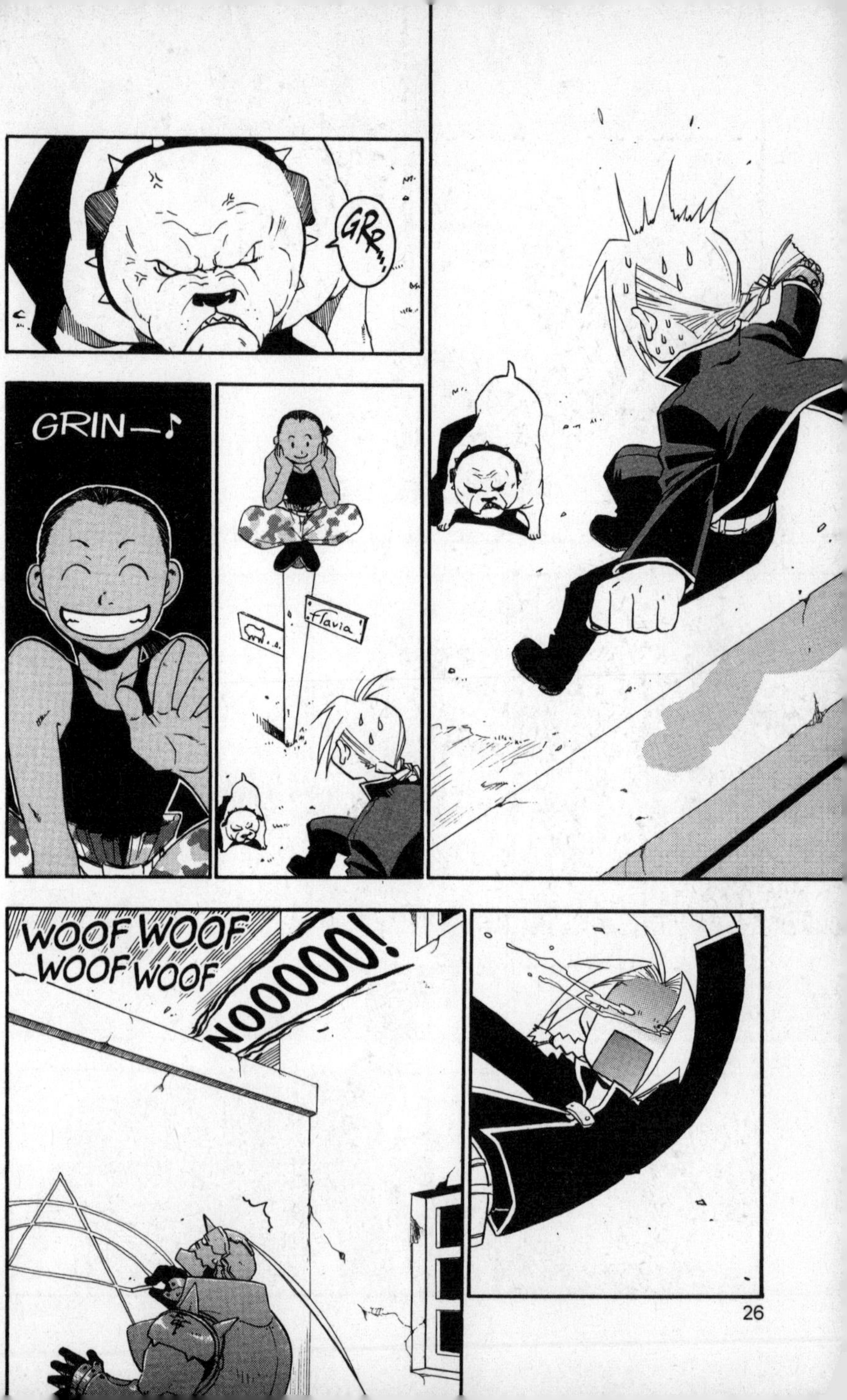
GRR...
Flavia
GRIN—♪
NOOOOO!
WOOF WOOF
WOOF WOOF

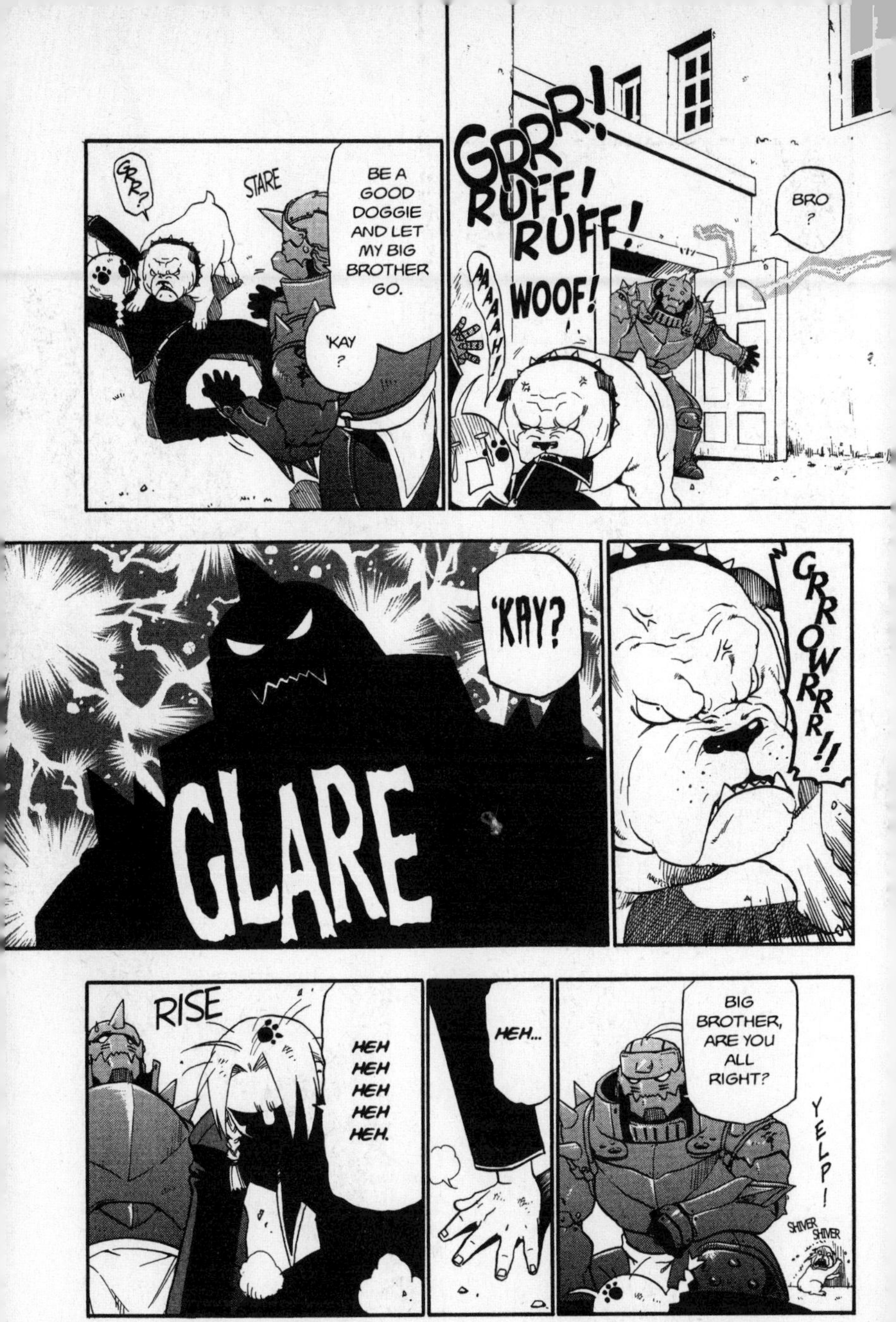
BRO?
GRRR!
RUFF! RUFF!
WOOF!
AAAAAAH!
GRR?
STARE
BE A GOOD DOGGIE AND LET MY BIG BROTHER GO.
'KAY?
GRRROWRRR!!
'KAY?
GLARE
BIG BROTHER, ARE YOU ALL RIGHT?
YELP!
SHIVER SHIVER
HEH...
RISE
HEH HEH HEH HEH HEH.

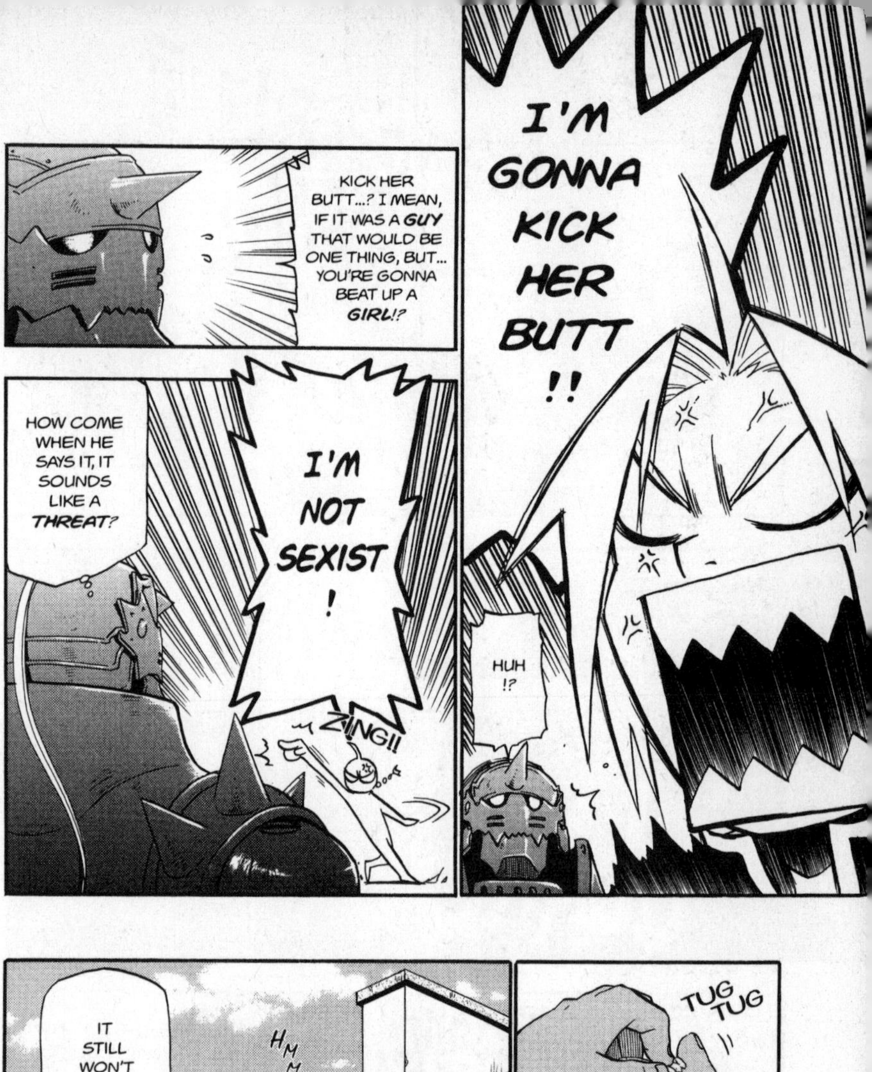
I'M GONNA KICK HER BUTT!!
HUH!?
KICK HER BUTT...? I MEAN, IF IT WAS A GUY THAT WOULD BE ONE THING, BUT... YOU'RE GONNA BEAT UP A GIRL!?
I'M NOT SEXIST!
HOW COME WHEN HE SAYS IT, IT SOUNDS LIKE A THREAT?
ZING!!
TUG TUG
IT STILL WON'T OPEN.
HMM

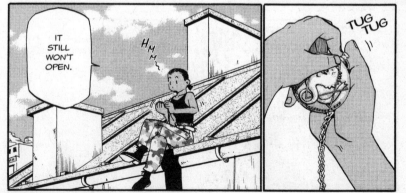

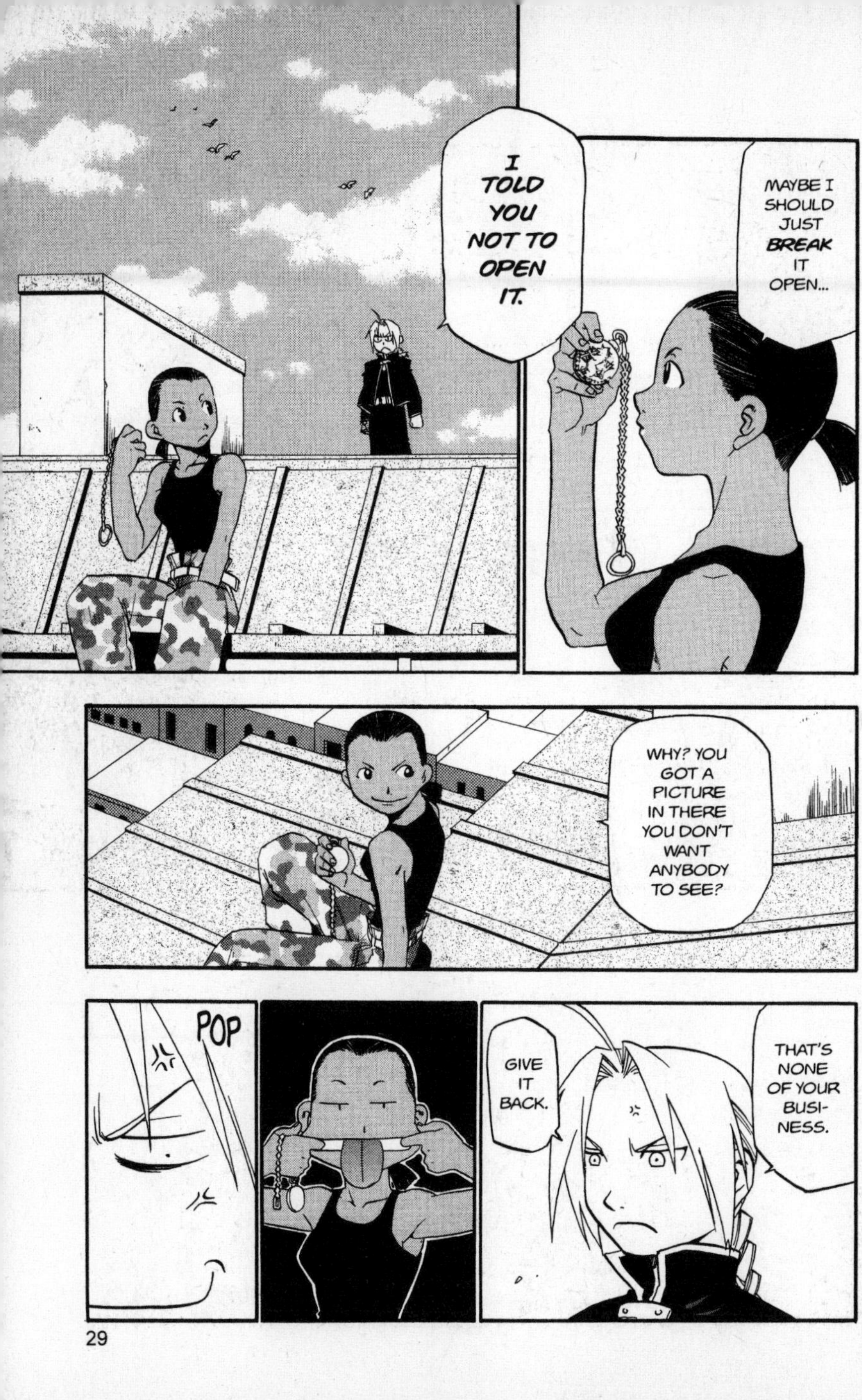
MAYBE I SHOULD JUST **BREAK** IT OPEN...
I TOLD YOU NOT TO OPEN IT.
WHY? YOU GOT A PICTURE IN THERE YOU DON'T WANT ANYBODY TO SEE?
THAT'S NONE OF YOUR BUSI-NESS.
GIVE IT BACK.
POP

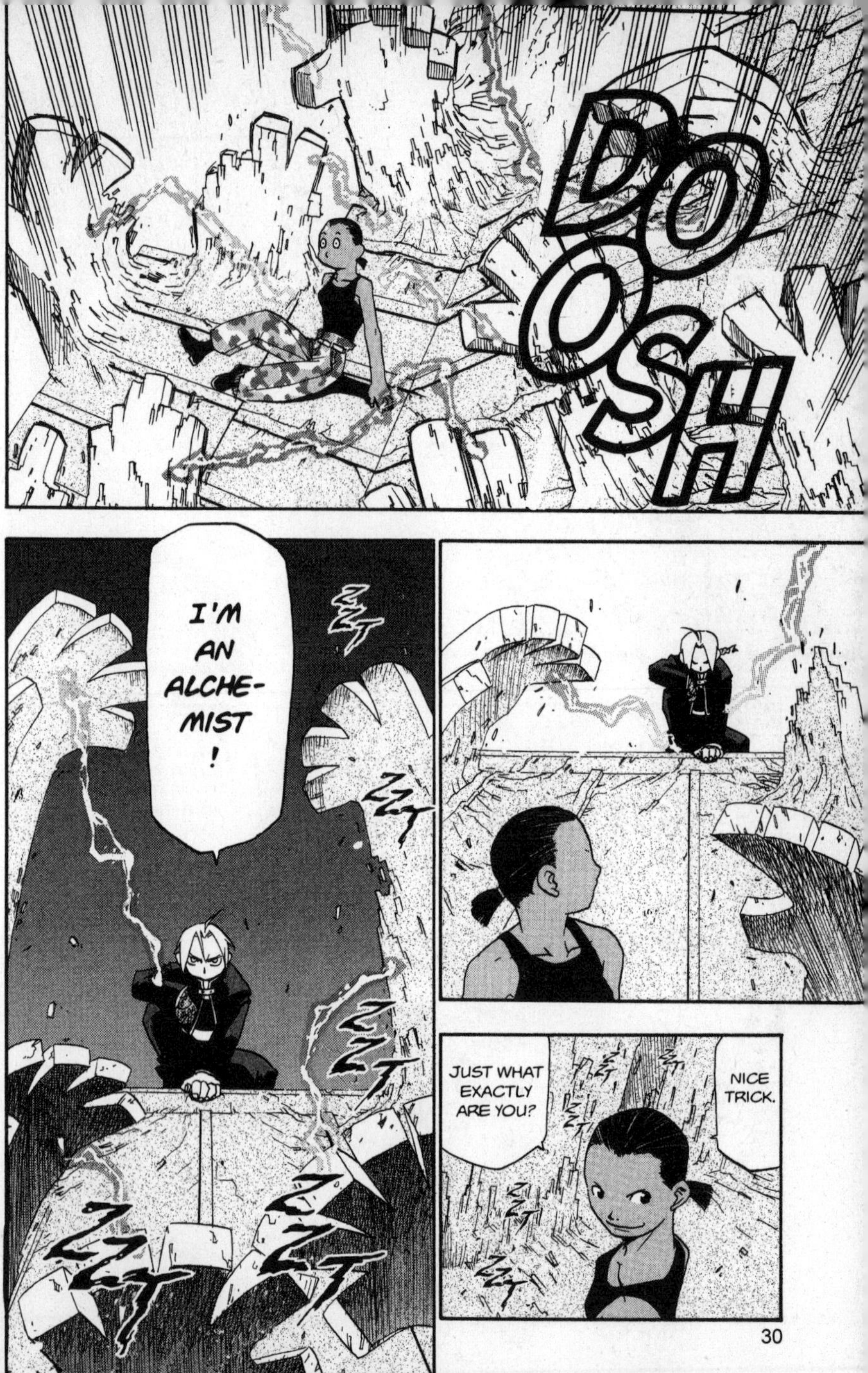
DOOOSH
NICE TRICK.
JUST WHAT EXACTLY ARE YOU?
I'M AN ALCHEMIST!

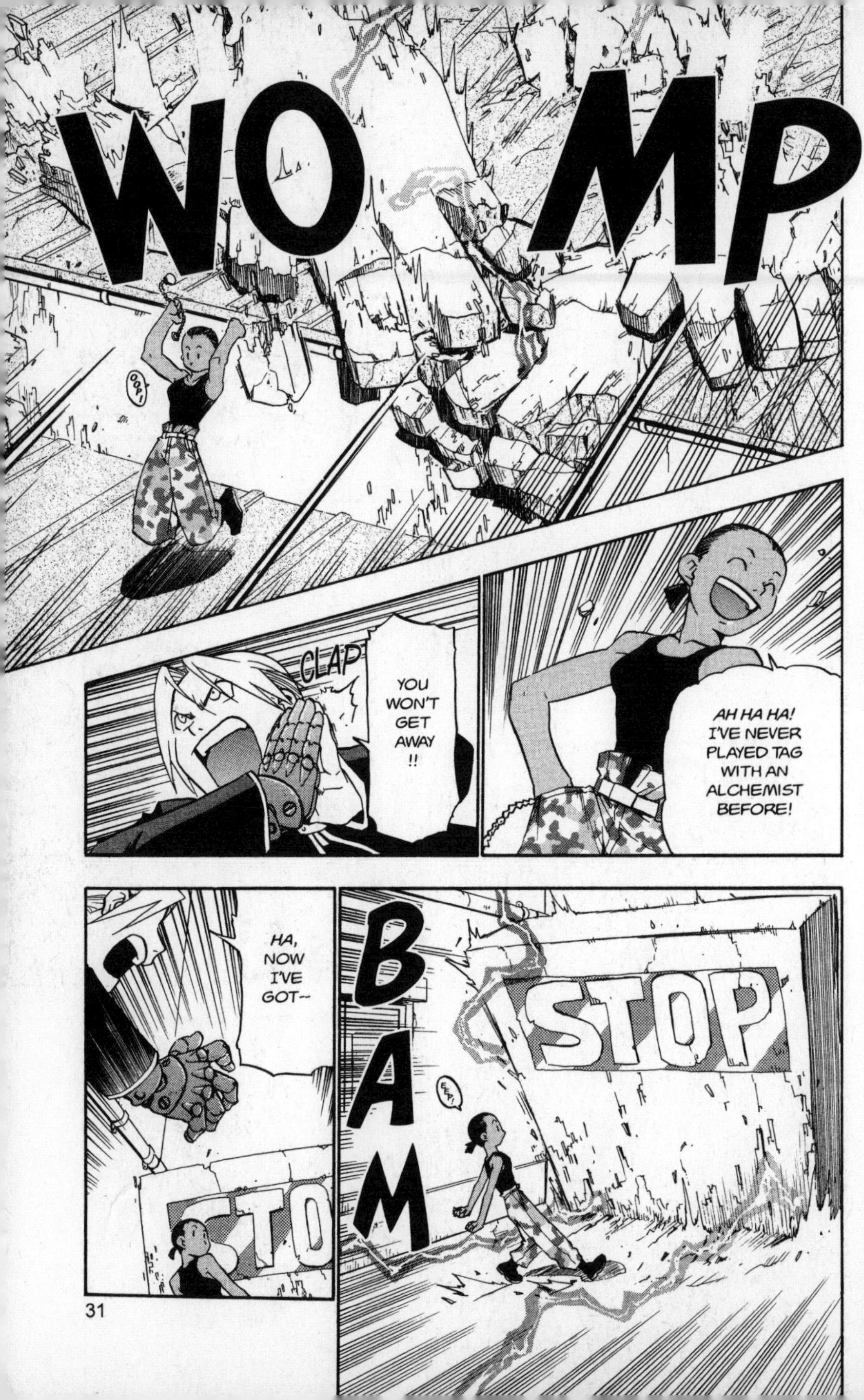
WOMP
OOP!
AH HA HA! I'VE NEVER PLAYED TAG WITH AN ALCHEMIST BEFORE!
CLAP
YOU WON'T GET AWAY !!
BAM
STOP
EEP!
HA, NOW I'VE GOT--
TO

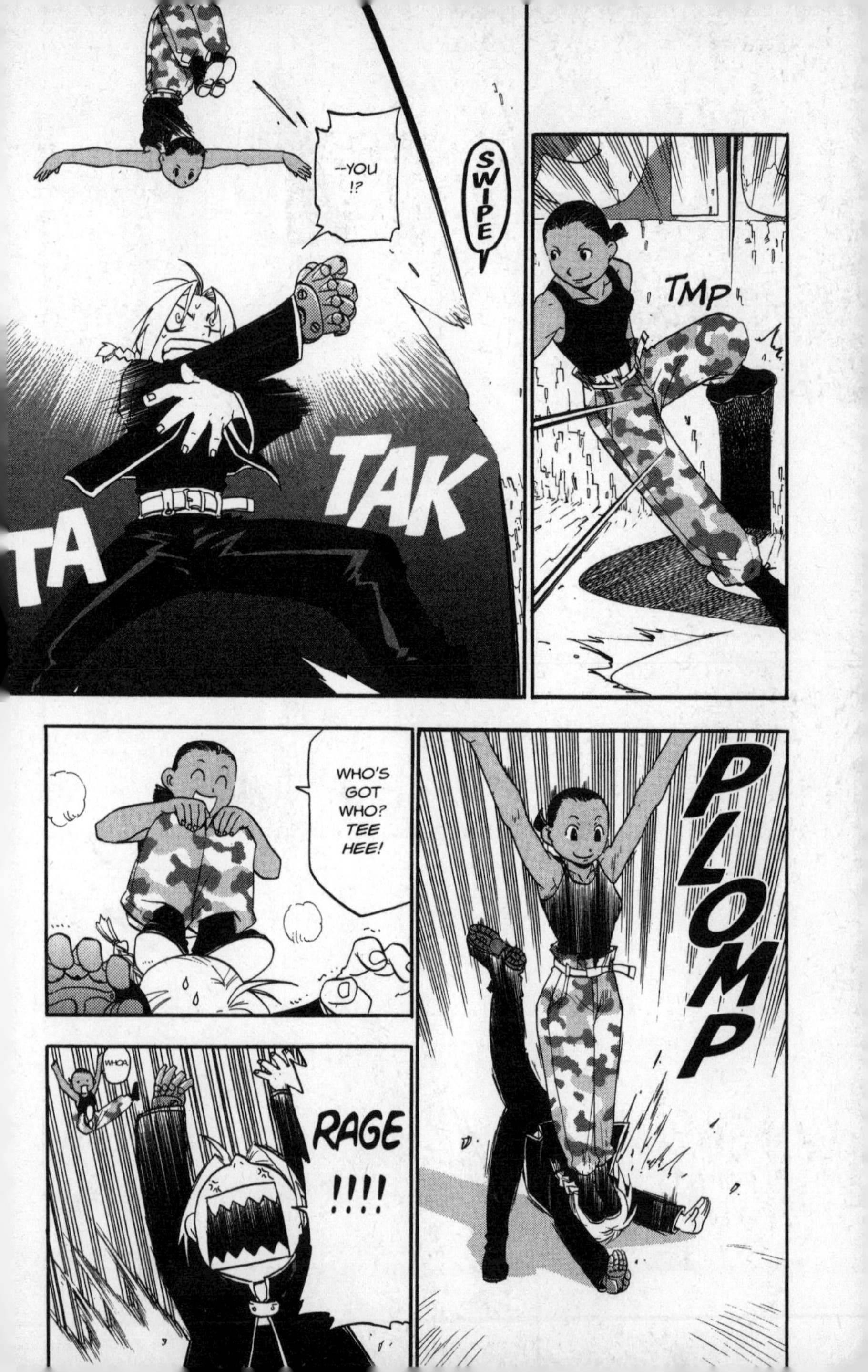
SWIPE
TMP
--YOU !?
TA TAK
PLOMP
WHO'S GOT WHO? TEE HEE!
WHOA
RAGE !!!!

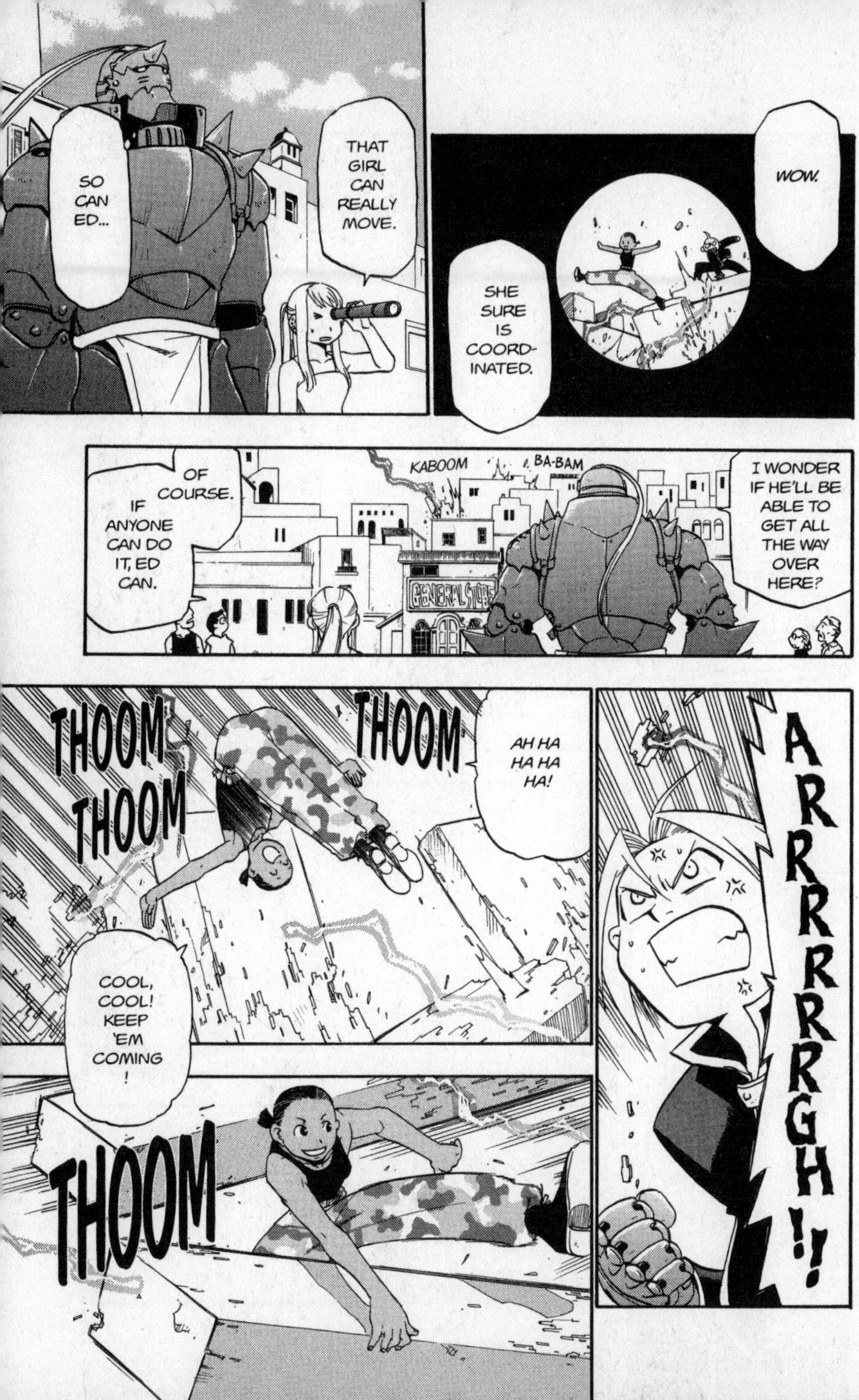
WOW.
SHE SURE IS COORDINATED.
THAT GIRL CAN REALLY MOVE.
SO CAN ED...
I WONDER IF HE'LL BE ABLE TO GET ALL THE WAY OVER HERE?
BA-BAM
KABOOM
OF COURSE. IF ANYONE CAN DO IT, ED CAN.
GENERAL STORE
ARRRRRRGH!!
THOOM
AH HA HA HA HA!
THOOM THOOM
COOL, COOL! KEEP 'EM COMING!
THOOM

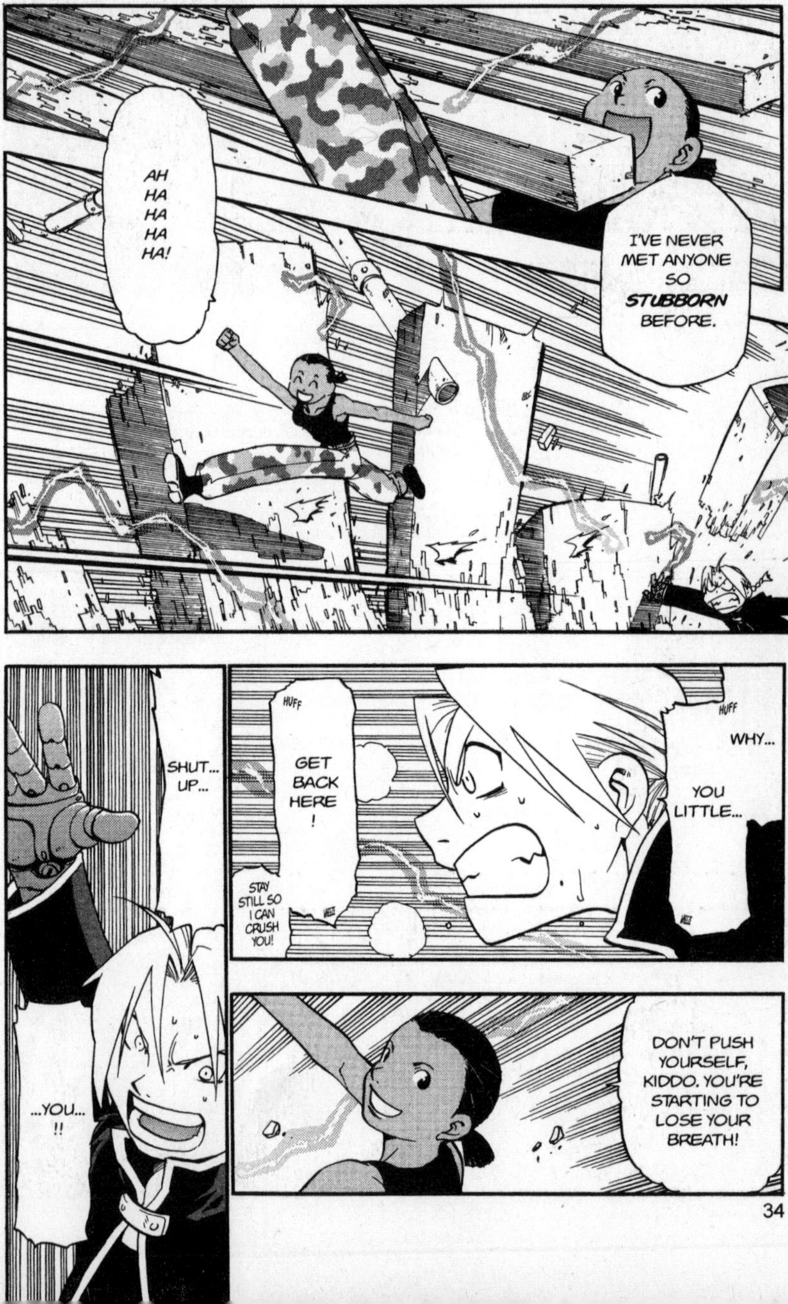
I'VE NEVER MET ANYONE SO STUBBORN BEFORE.
AH HA HA HA HA!
HUFF
WHY...
YOU LITTLE...
HUFF
GET BACK HERE!
STAY STILL SO I CAN CRUSH YOU!
DON'T PUSH YOURSELF, KIDDO. YOU'RE STARTING TO LOSE YOUR BREATH!
SHUT... UP...
...YOU... !!

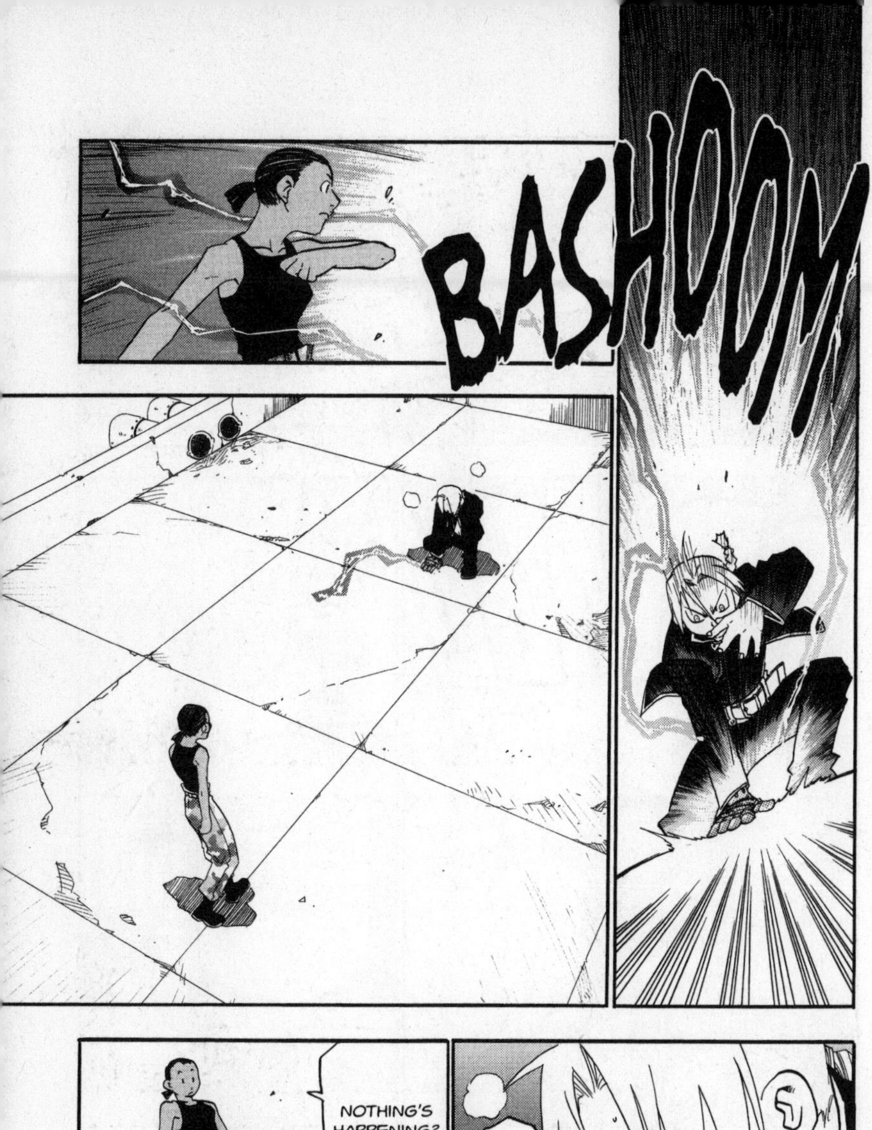
BASHOOM
...!!
NOTHING'S HAPPENING?

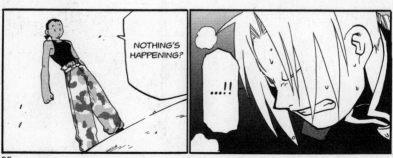

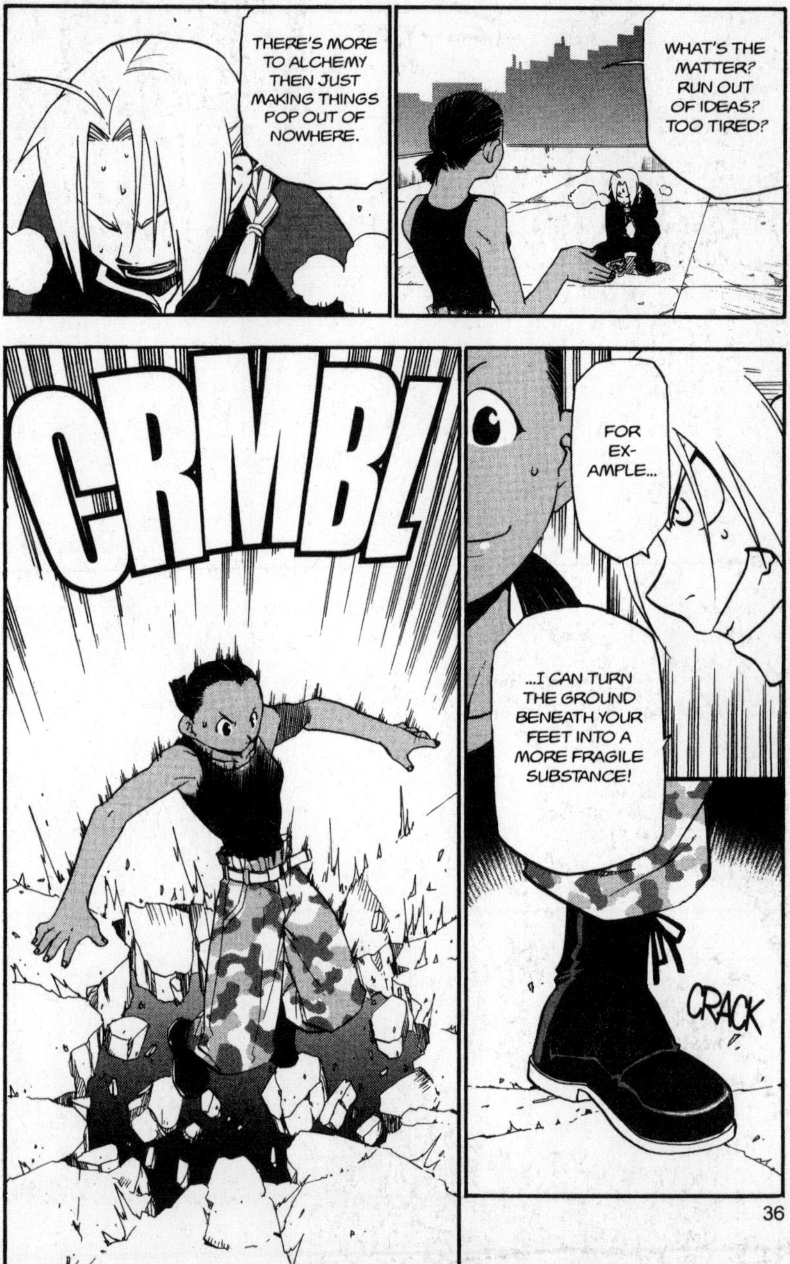
WHAT'S THE MATTER? RUN OUT OF IDEAS? TOO TIRED?
THERE'S MORE TO ALCHEMY THEN JUST MAKING THINGS POP OUT OF NOWHERE.
FOR EX- AMPLE...
...I CAN TURN THE GROUND BENEATH YOUR FEET INTO A MORE FRAGILE SUBSTANCE!
CRACK
CRMBL

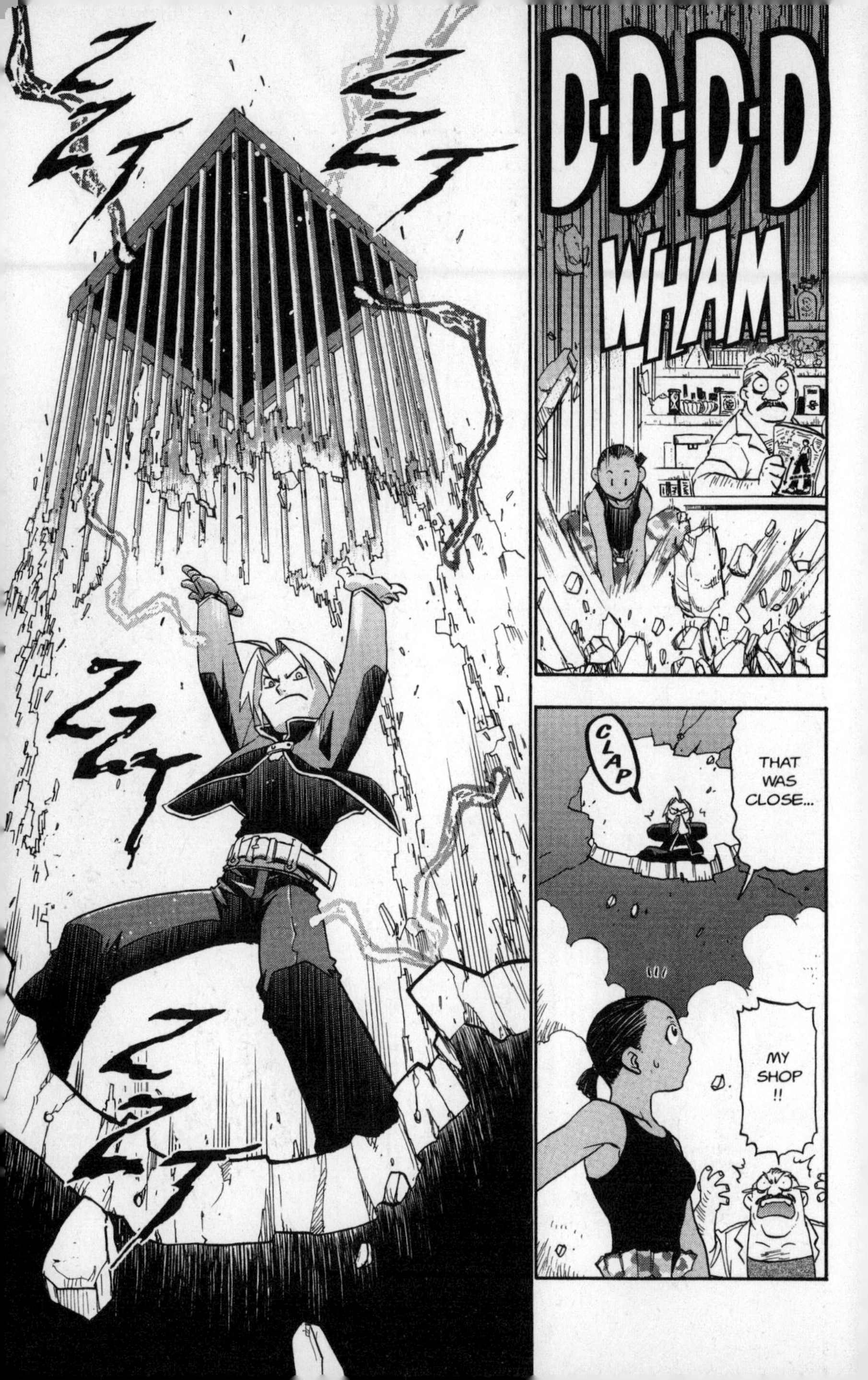
D-D-D-D
WHAM
CLAP
THAT WAS CLOSE...
MY SHOP !!

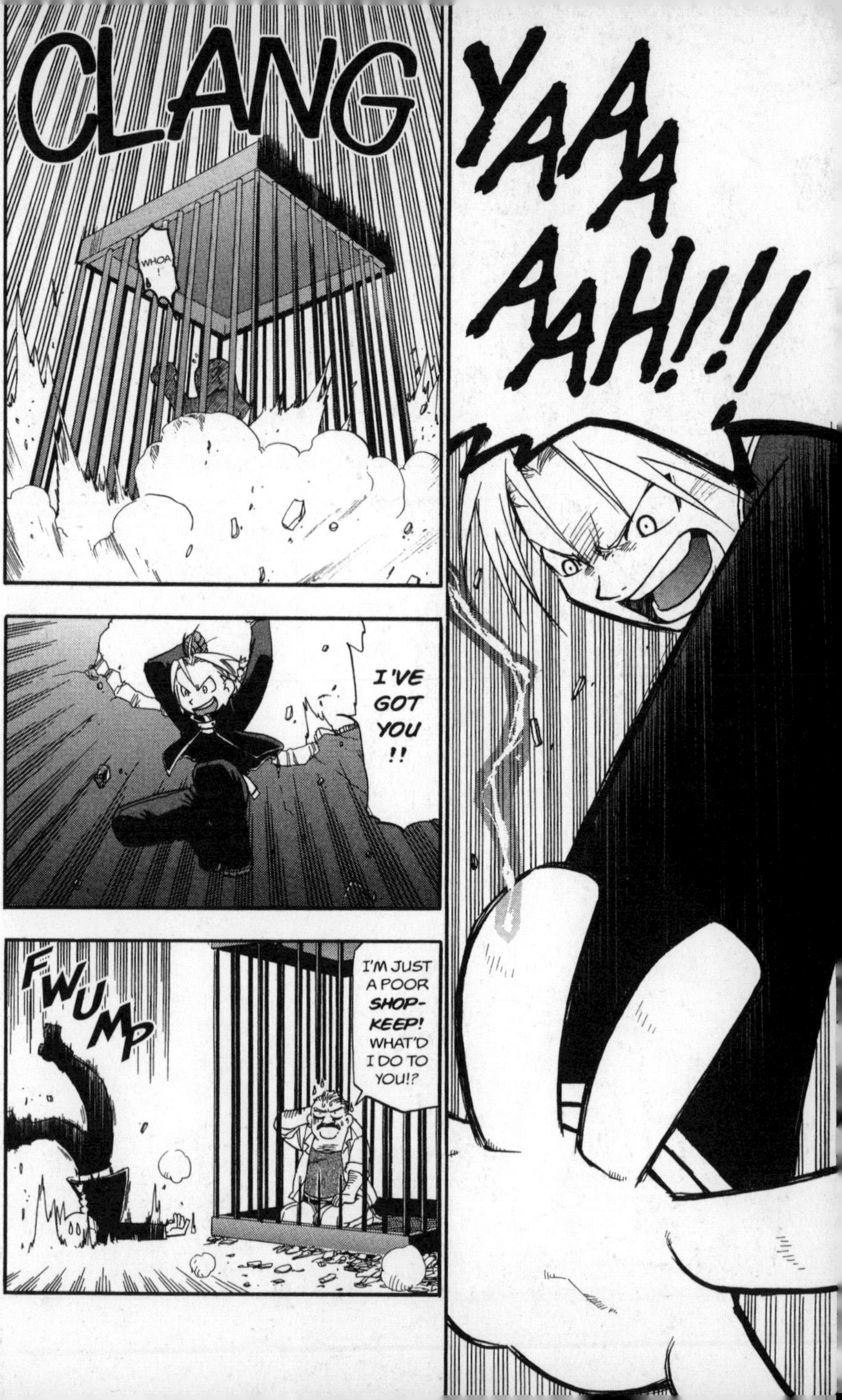
YAAAAAH!!!
CLANG
WHOA!
I'VE GOT YOU!!
FWUMP
I'M JUST A POOR SHOP-KEEP! WHAT'D I DO TO YOU!?

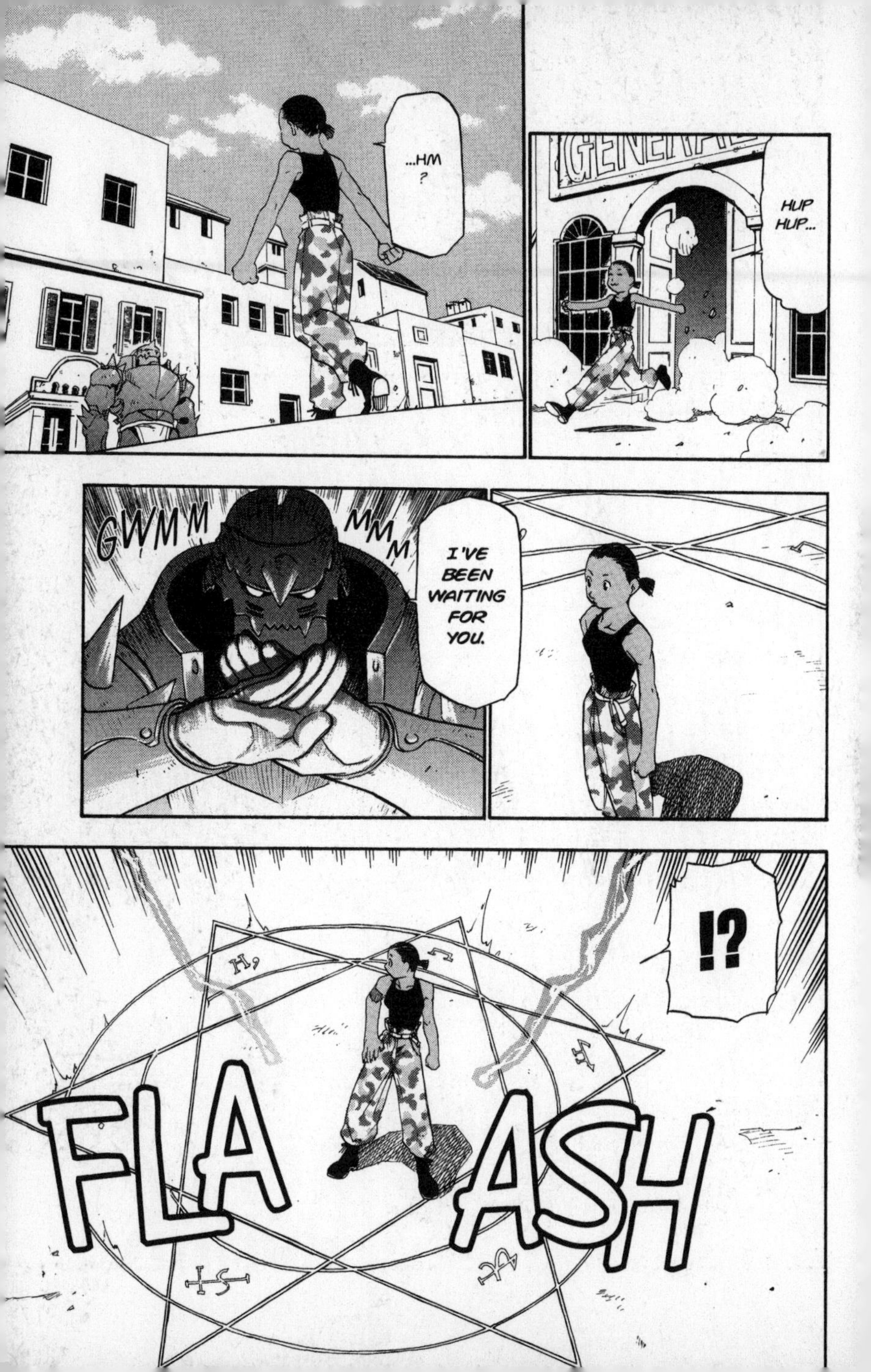
HUP HUP...
...HM ?
I'VE BEEN WAITING FOR YOU.
GWMMMMM
!?
FLA ASH

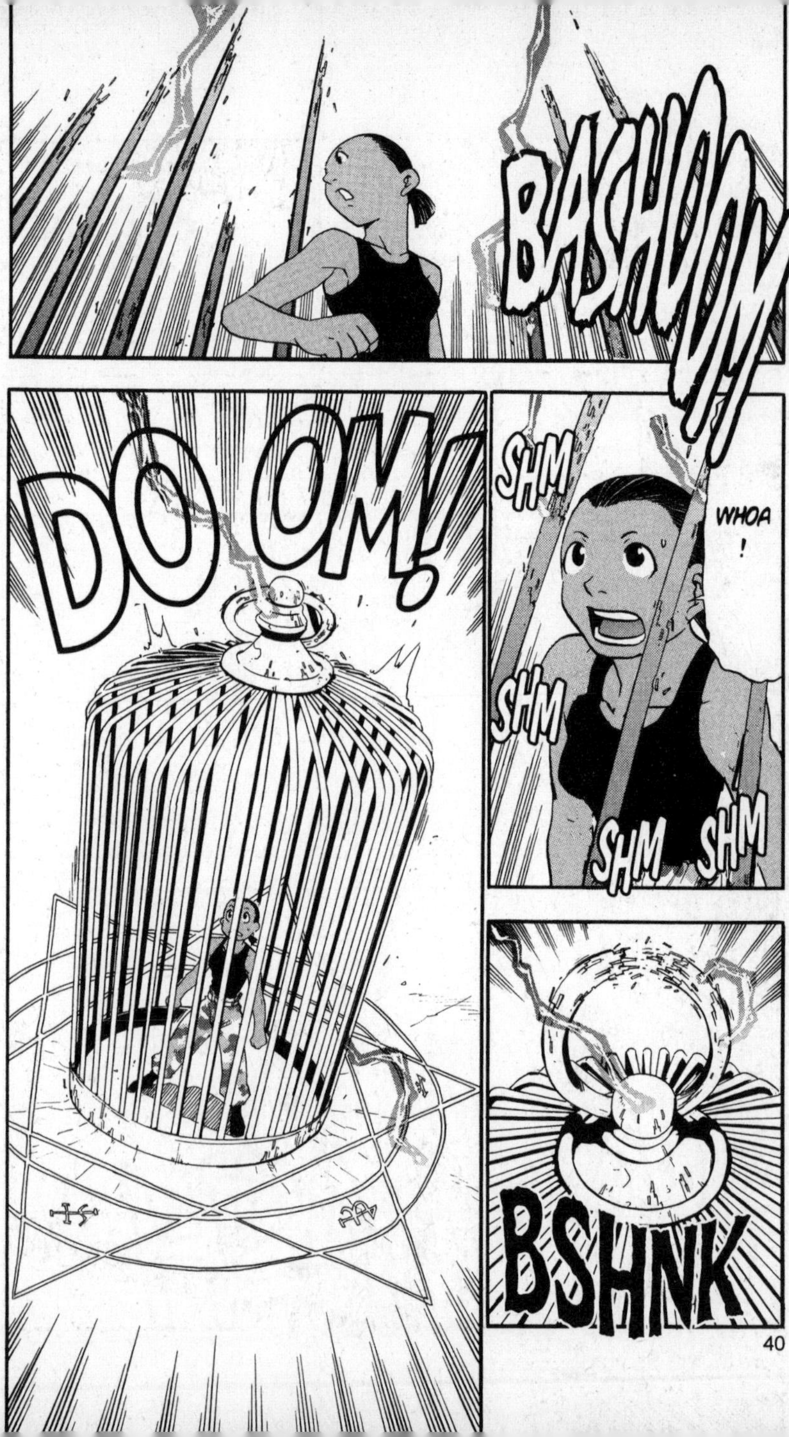
BASHOOM
SHM
WHOA!
SHM
SHM
SHM
BSHNK
DOOM!

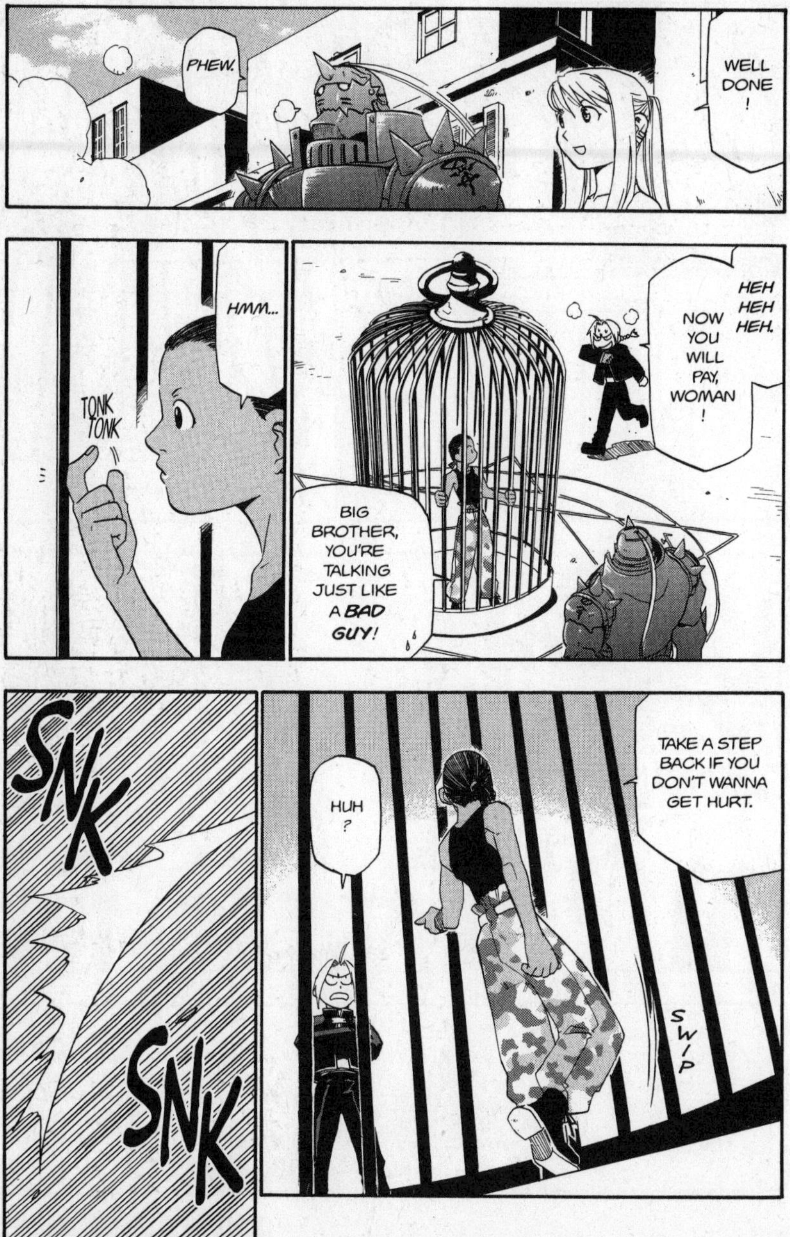
WELL DONE!
PHEW.
HEH HEH HEH.
NOW YOU WILL PAY, WOMAN!
BIG BROTHER, YOU'RE TALKING JUST LIKE A BAD GUY!
HMM...
TONK TONK
TAKE A STEP BACK IF YOU DON'T WANNA GET HURT.
HUH?
SWIP
SNK
SNK

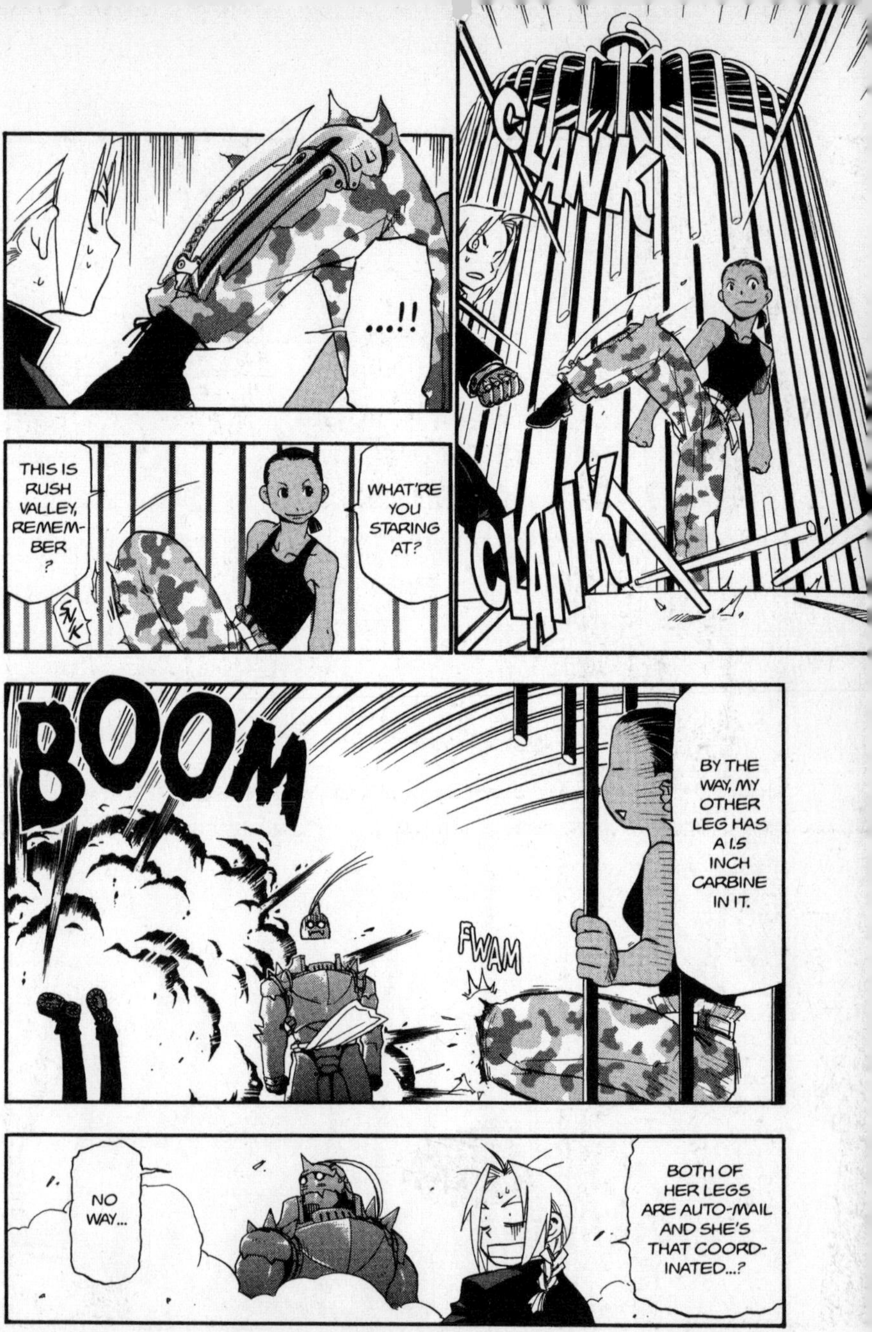
CLANK
CLANK
...!!
WHAT'RE YOU STARING AT?
THIS IS RUSH VALLEY, REMEMBER?
SNIK
BY THE WAY, MY OTHER LEG HAS A 1.5 INCH CARBINE IN IT.
FWAM
BOOM
BOTH OF HER LEGS ARE AUTO-MAIL AND SHE'S THAT COORDINATED...?
NO WAY...

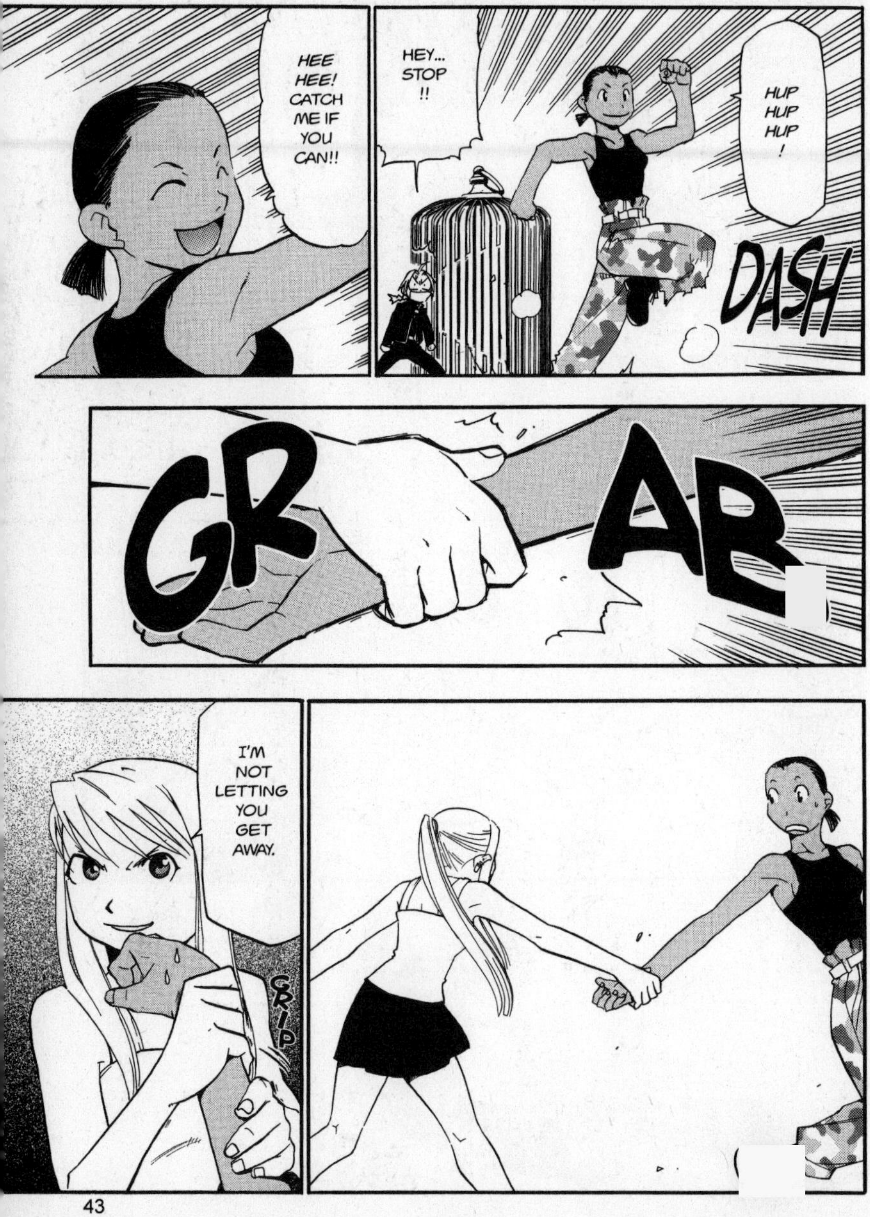
HUP HUP HUP !
HEY... STOP !!
DASH
HEE HEE! CATCH ME IF YOU CAN!!
GRAB
I'M NOT LETTING YOU GET AWAY.
GRIP

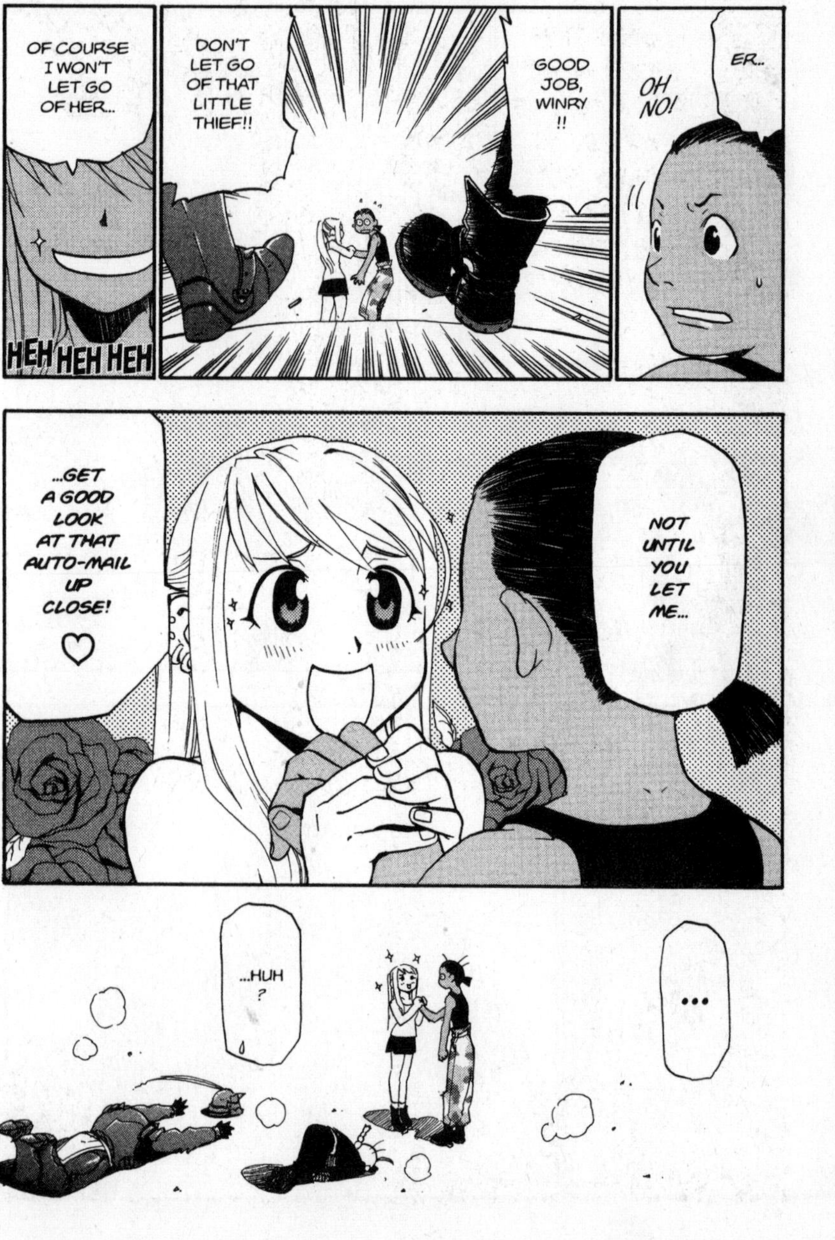
ER...
OH NO!
GOOD JOB, WINRY !!
DON'T LET GO OF THAT LITTLE THIEF!!
OF COURSE I WON'T LET GO OF HER...
HEH HEH HEH
NOT UNTIL YOU LET ME...
...GET A GOOD LOOK AT THAT AUTO-MAIL UP CLOSE! ♡
...
...HUH ?

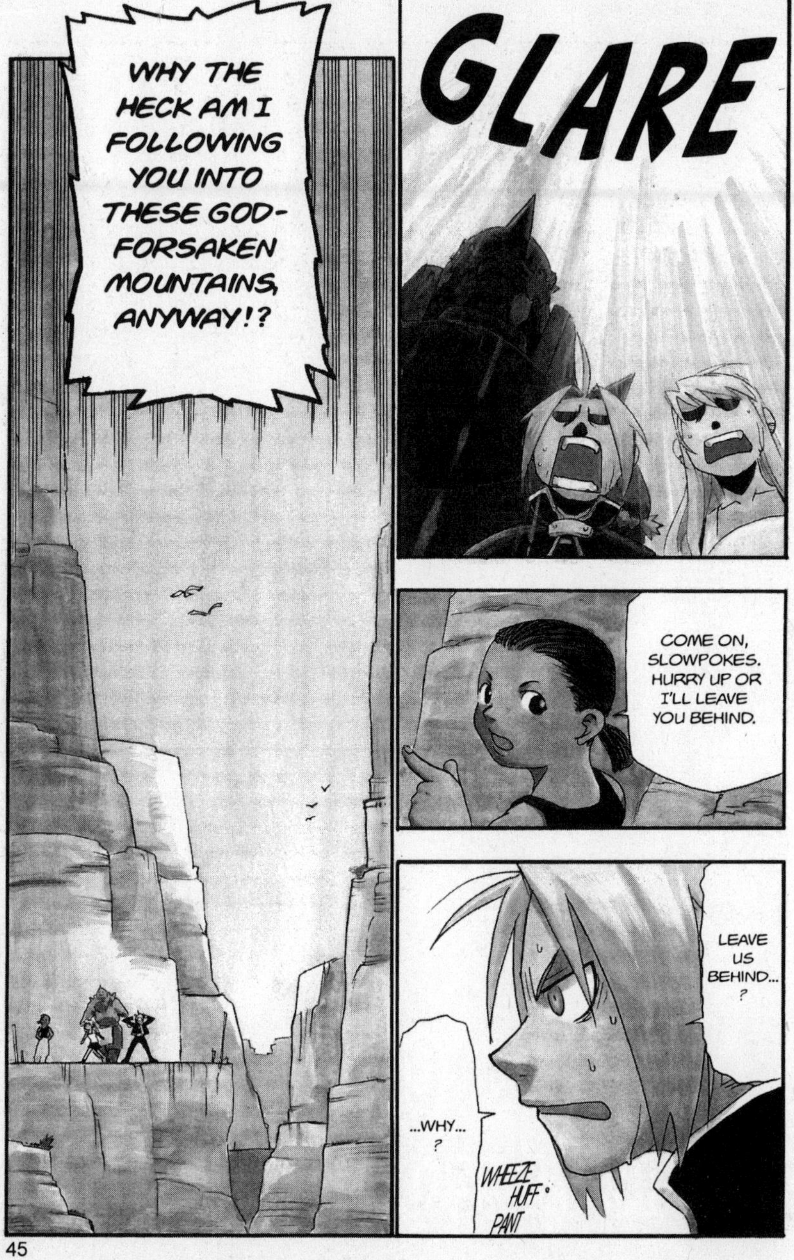
GLARE
COME ON, SLOWPOKES. HURRY UP OR I'LL LEAVE YOU BEHIND.
LEAVE US BEHIND... ?
...WHY... ?
WHEEZE HUFF PANT
WHY THE HECK AM I FOLLOWING YOU INTO THESE GOD-FORSAKEN MOUNTAINS, ANYWAY!?

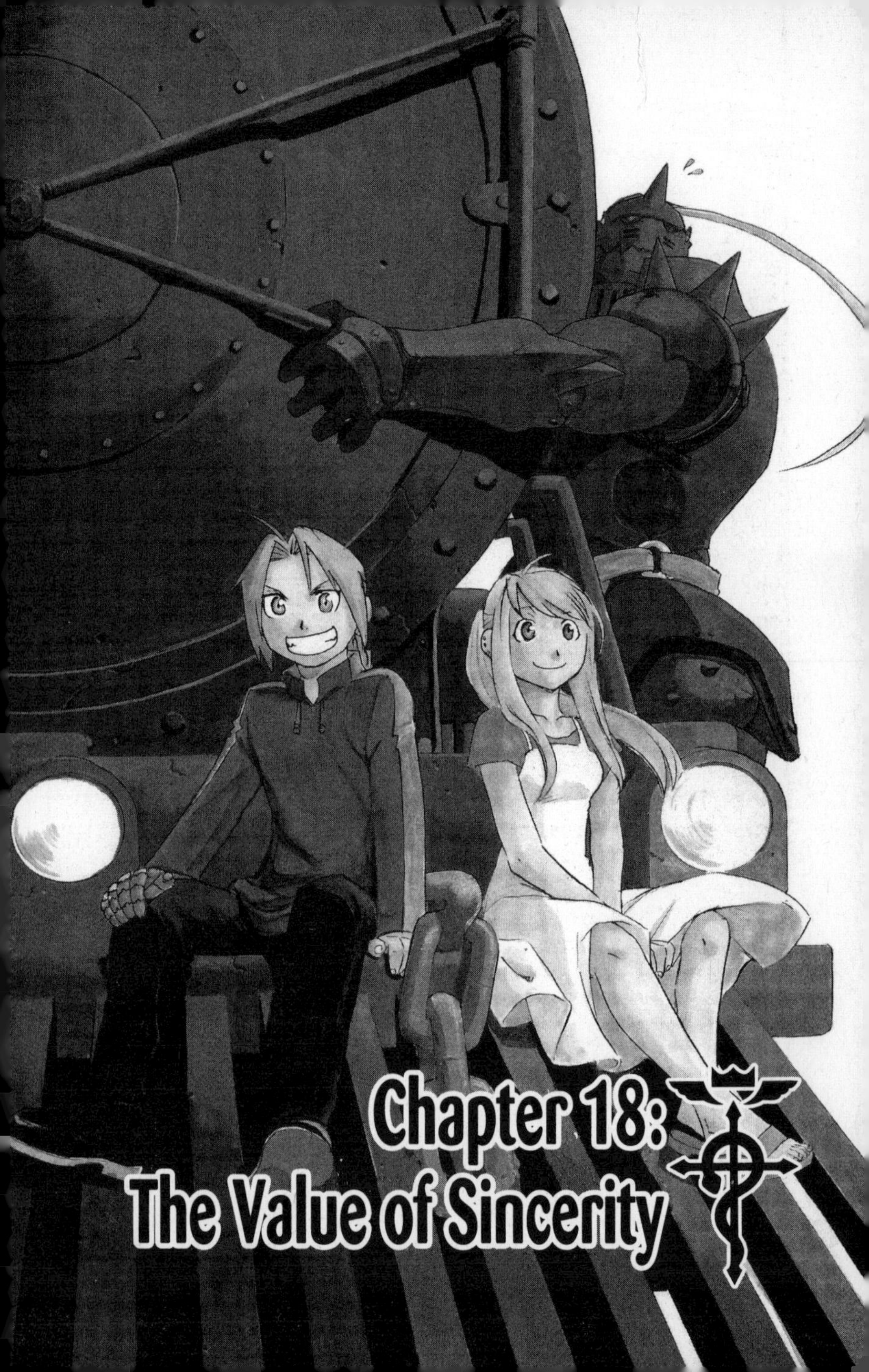
Chapter 18:
The Value of Sincerity

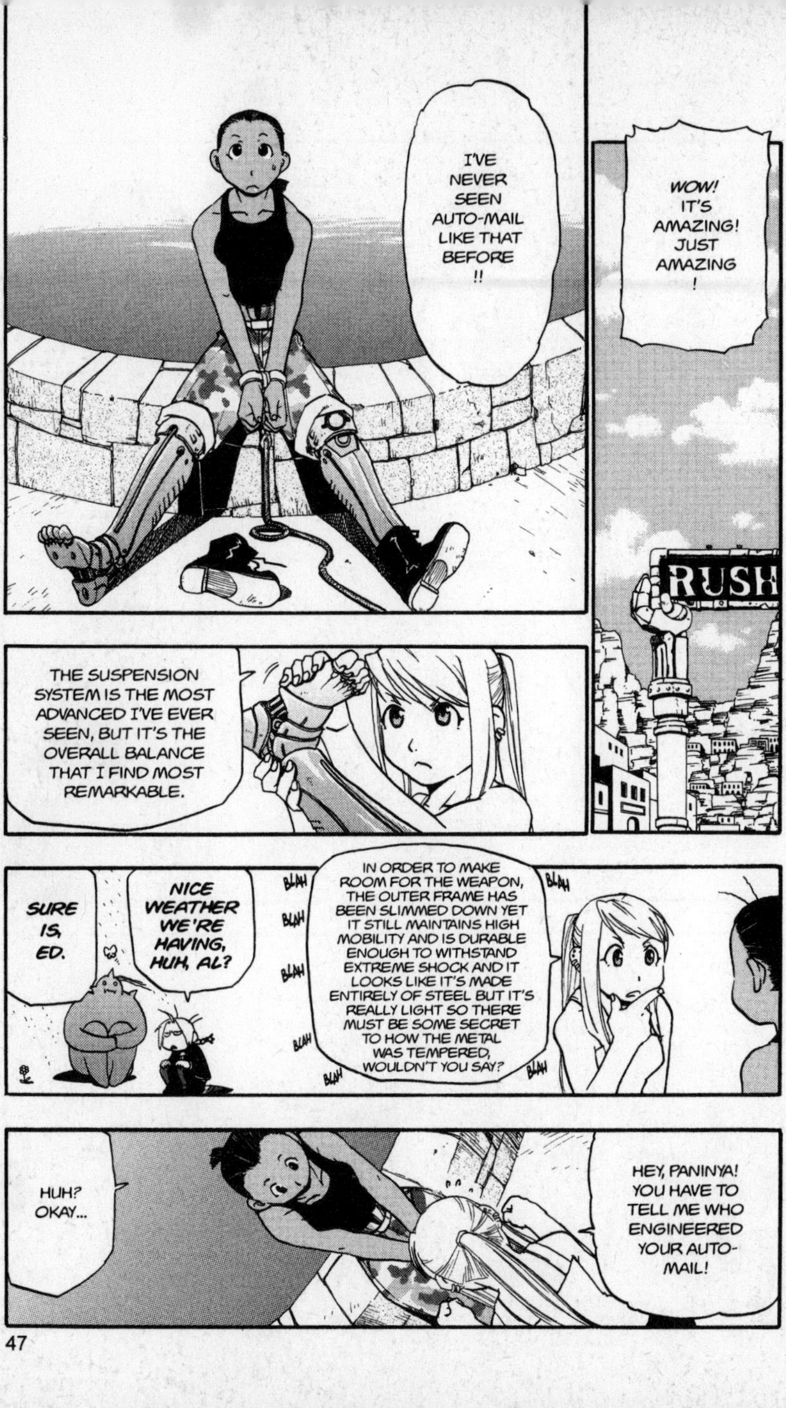
WOW! IT'S AMAZING! JUST AMAZING!
RUSH
I'VE NEVER SEEN AUTO-MAIL LIKE THAT BEFORE !!
THE SUSPENSION SYSTEM IS THE MOST ADVANCED I'VE EVER SEEN, BUT IT'S THE OVERALL BALANCE THAT I FIND MOST REMARKABLE.
BLAH
BLAH
IN ORDER TO MAKE ROOM FOR THE WEAPON, THE OUTER FRAME HAS BEEN SLIMMED DOWN YET IT STILL MAINTAINS HIGH MOBILITY AND IS DURABLE ENOUGH TO WITHSTAND EXTREME SHOCK AND IT LOOKS LIKE IT'S MADE ENTIRELY OF STEEL BUT IT'S REALLY LIGHT SO THERE MUST BE SOME SECRET TO HOW THE METAL WAS TEMPERED, WOULDN'T YOU SAY?
BLAH
BLAH
BLAH
BLAH
BLAH
NICE WEATHER WE'RE HAVING, HUH, AL?
SURE IS, ED.
HEY, PANINYA! YOU HAVE TO TELL ME WHO ENGINEERED YOUR AUTO-MAIL!
HUH? OKAY...

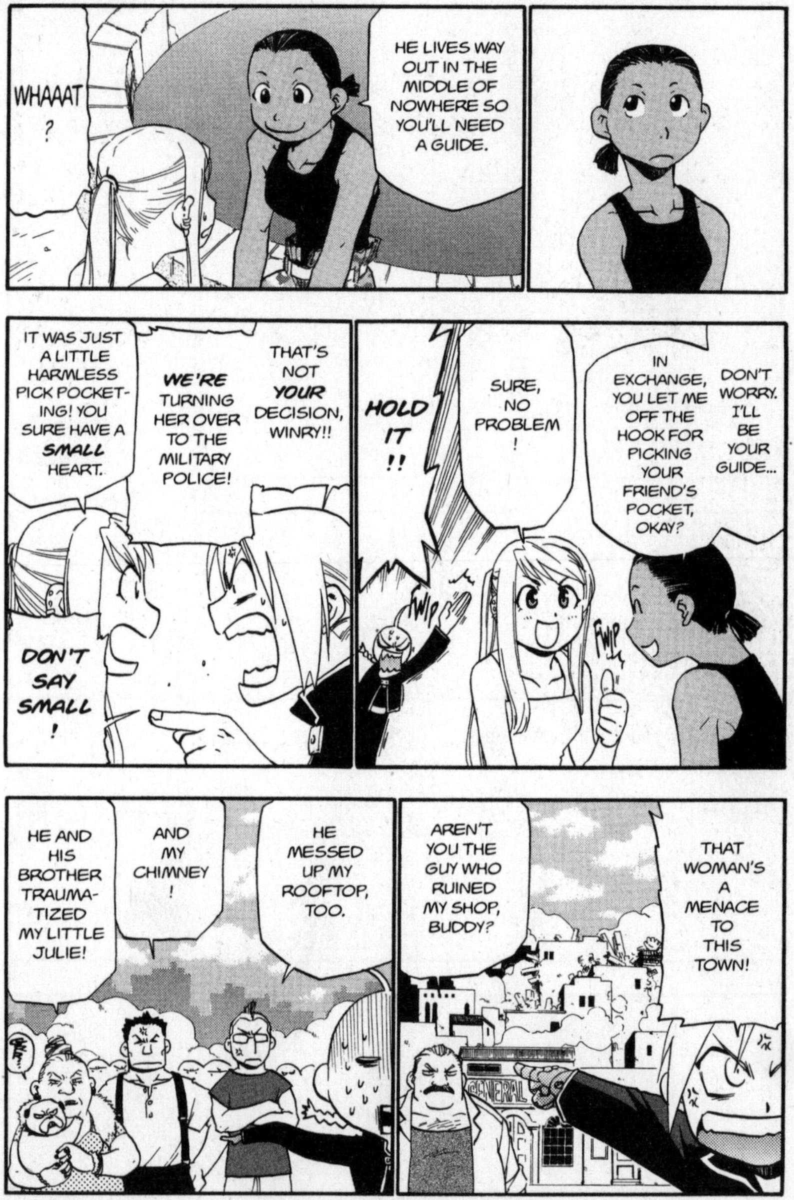
HE LIVES WAY OUT IN THE MIDDLE OF NOWHERE SO YOU'LL NEED A GUIDE.
WHAAAT ?
DON'T WORRY. I'LL BE YOUR GUIDE...
IN EXCHANGE, YOU LET ME OFF THE HOOK FOR PICKING YOUR FRIEND'S POCKET, OKAY?
FWIP
SURE, NO PROBLEM !
FWIP
HOLD IT !!
THAT'S NOT YOUR DECISION, WINRY!!
WE'RE TURNING HER OVER TO THE MILITARY POLICE!
IT WAS JUST A LITTLE HARMLESS PICK POCKETING! YOU SURE HAVE A SMALL HEART.
DON'T SAY SMALL !
THAT WOMAN'S A MENACE TO THIS TOWN!
AREN'T YOU THE GUY WHO RUINED MY SHOP, BUDDY?
GENERAL
HE MESSED UP MY ROOFTOP, TOO.
AND MY CHIMNEY !
HE AND HIS BROTHER TRAUMATIZED MY LITTLE JULIE!

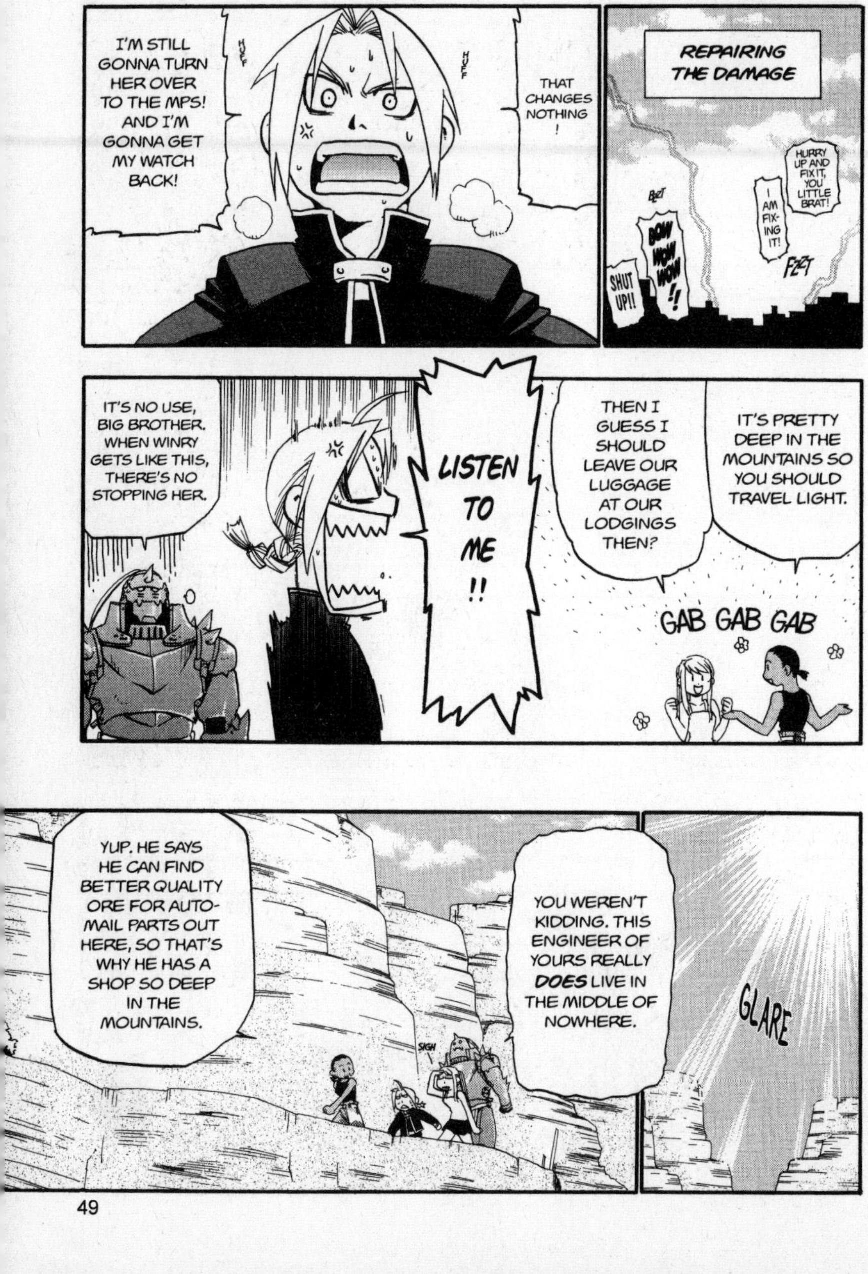
REPAIRING THE DAMAGE
HURRY UP AND FIX IT, YOU LITTLE BRAT!
I AM FIX-ING IT!
FZZT
BZZT
BOW WOW WOW!!
SHUT UP!!
THAT CHANGES NOTHING!
HUFF
HUFF
I'M STILL GONNA TURN HER OVER TO THE MPS! AND I'M GONNA GET MY WATCH BACK!
IT'S PRETTY DEEP IN THE MOUNTAINS SO YOU SHOULD TRAVEL LIGHT.
THEN I GUESS I SHOULD LEAVE OUR LUGGAGE AT OUR LODGINGS THEN?
GAB GAB GAB
LISTEN TO ME!!
IT'S NO USE, BIG BROTHER. WHEN WINRY GETS LIKE THIS, THERE'S NO STOPPING HER.
GLARE
YOU WEREN'T KIDDING. THIS ENGINEER OF YOURS REALLY ***DOES*** LIVE IN THE MIDDLE OF NOWHERE.
YUP. HE SAYS HE CAN FIND BETTER QUALITY ORE FOR AUTO-MAIL PARTS OUT HERE, SO THAT'S WHY HE HAS A SHOP SO DEEP IN THE MOUNTAINS.
SIGH

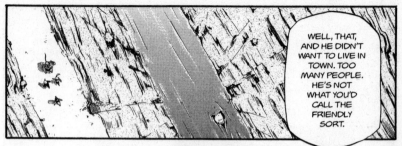

WELL, THAT, AND HE DIDN'T WANT TO LIVE IN TOWN. TOO MANY PEOPLE. HE'S NOT WHAT YOU'D CALL THE FRIENDLY SORT.

WILL YOU JUST GIVE ME BACK MY WATCH, ALREADY!?

WE MADE A *DEAL*, REMEMBER? I GUIDE YOU TO THE ENGINEER AND YOU LET ME OFF THE HOOK.

I'M KEEPING THIS WATCH HOSTAGE UNTIL THEN. ♥

I'M NOT THE ONE WHO MADE A DEAL WITH YOU...!

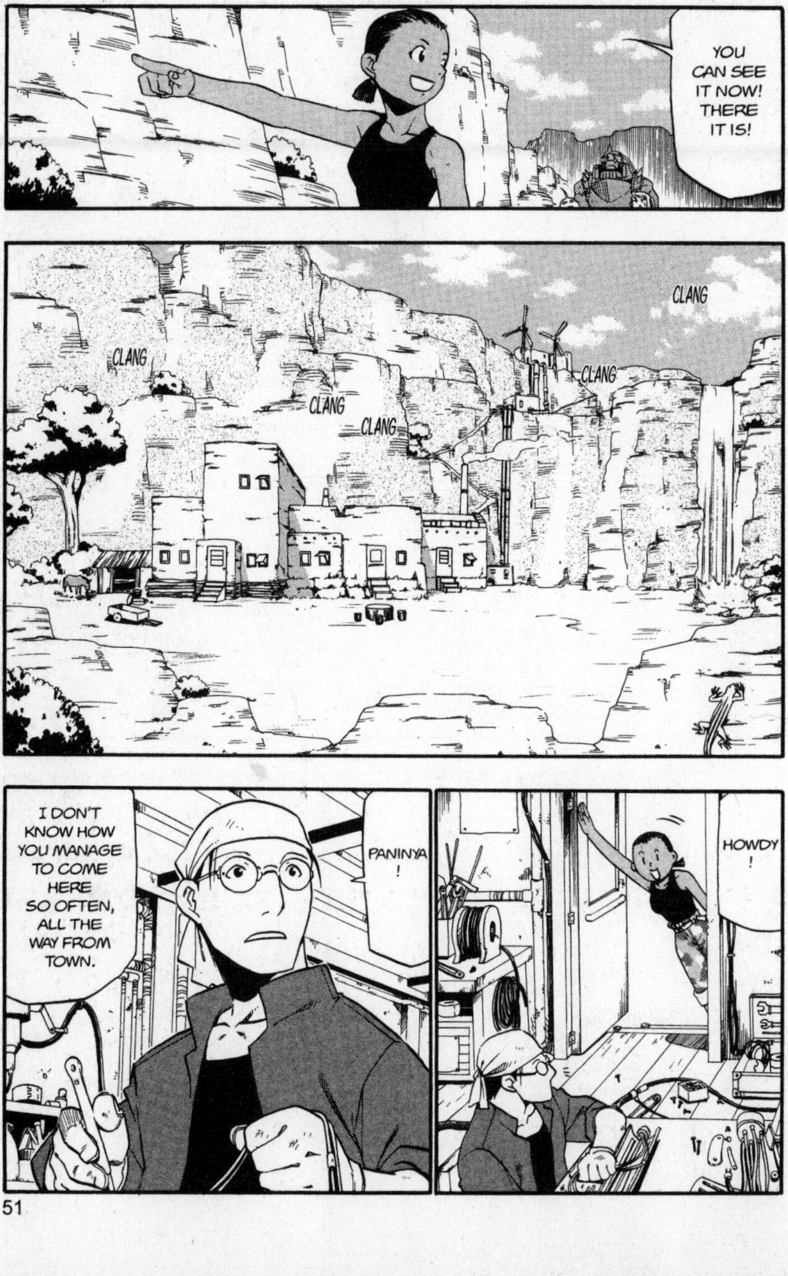
YOU CAN SEE IT NOW! THERE IT IS!
CLANG
CLANG
CLANG
CLANG
CLANG
HOWDY!
PANINYA!
I DON'T KNOW HOW YOU MANAGE TO COME HERE SO OFTEN, ALL THE WAY FROM TOWN.

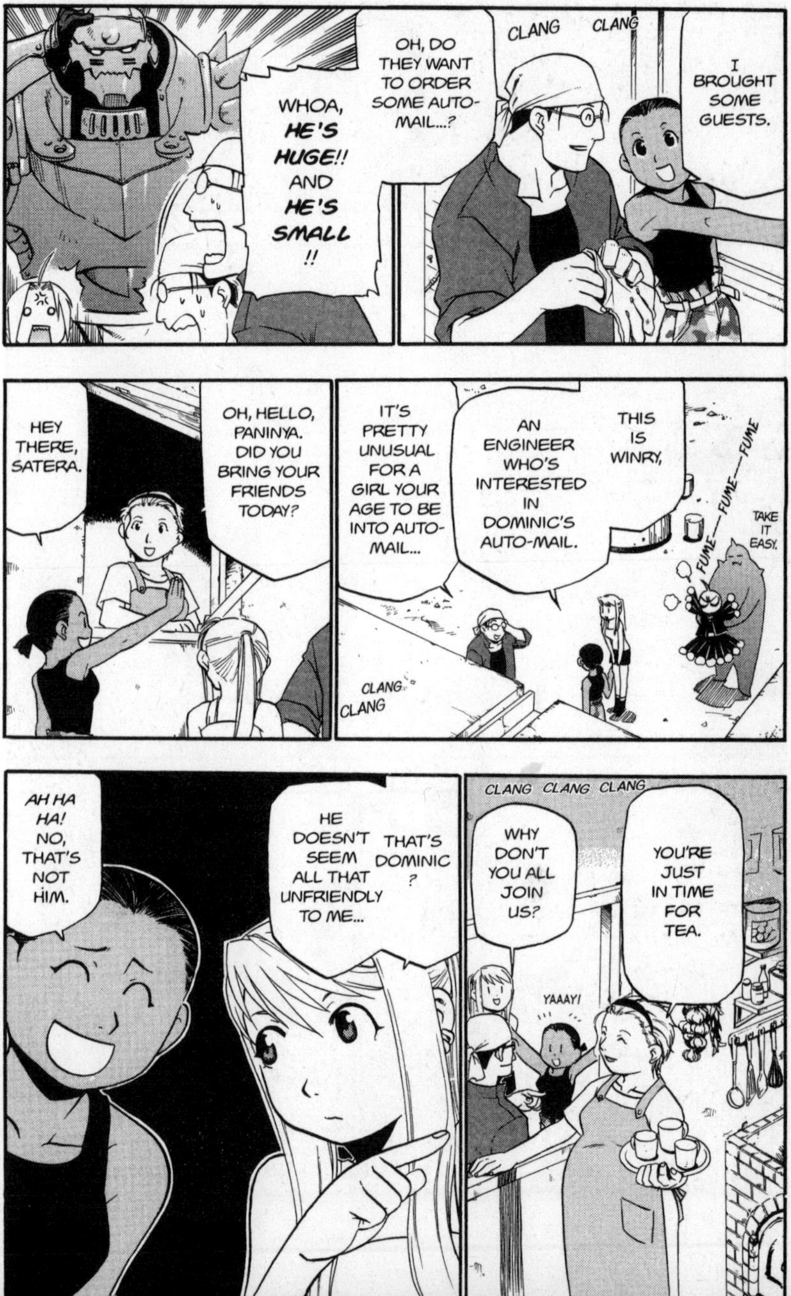
I BROUGHT SOME GUESTS.
CLANG CLANG
OH, DO THEY WANT TO ORDER SOME AUTO-MAIL...?
WHOA, **HE'S HUGE!!** AND **HE'S SMALL** !!
THIS IS WINRY,
AN ENGINEER WHO'S INTERESTED IN DOMINIC'S AUTO-MAIL.
IT'S PRETTY UNUSUAL FOR A GIRL YOUR AGE TO BE INTO AUTO-MAIL...
FUME FUME FUME
TAKE IT EASY.
CLANG CLANG
OH, HELLO, PANINYA. DID YOU BRING YOUR FRIENDS TODAY?
HEY THERE, SATERA.
CLANG CLANG CLANG
YOU'RE JUST IN TIME FOR TEA.
WHY DON'T YOU ALL JOIN US?
YAAAY!
THAT'S DOMINIC?
HE DOESN'T SEEM ALL THAT UNFRIENDLY TO ME...
AH HA HA! NO, THAT'S NOT HIM.

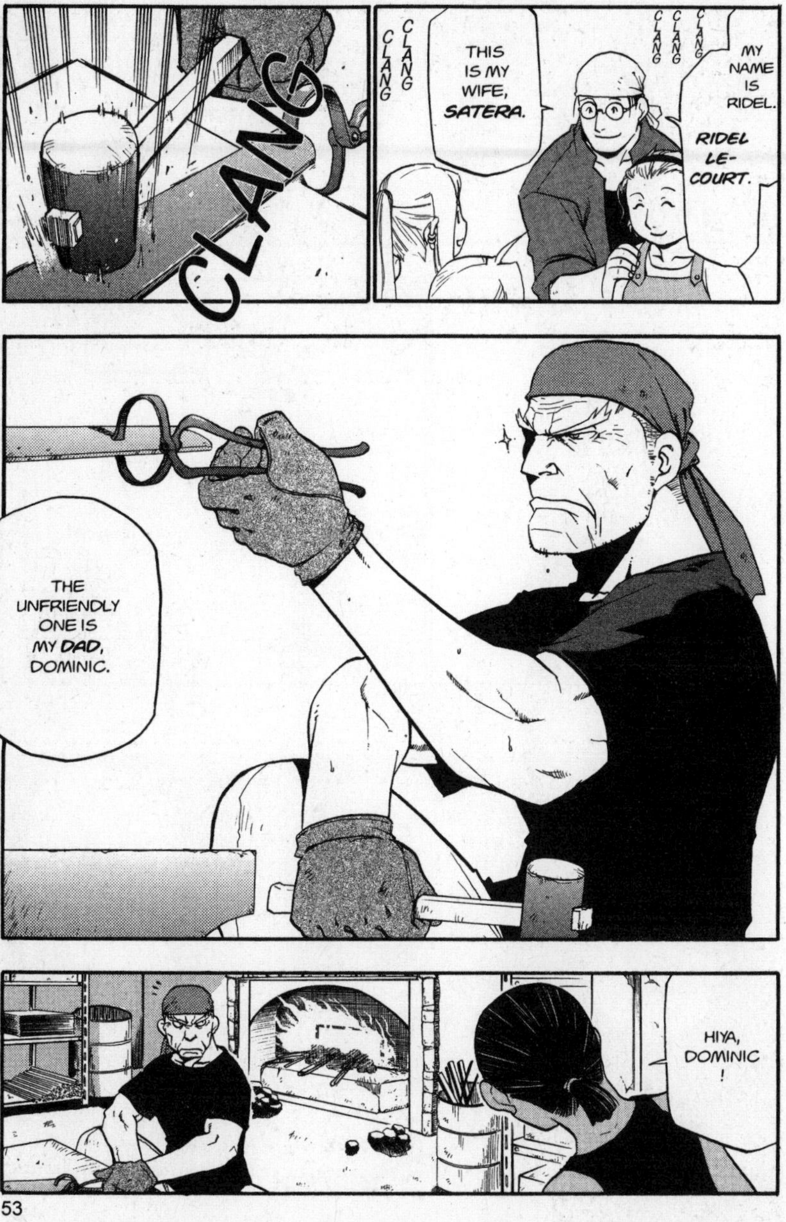
MY NAME IS RIDEL.
RIDEL LE-COURT.
CLANG CLANG CLANG
THIS IS MY WIFE, SATERA.
CLANG CLANG
CLANG
THE UNFRIENDLY ONE IS MY DAD, DOMINIC.
HIYA, DOMINIC!

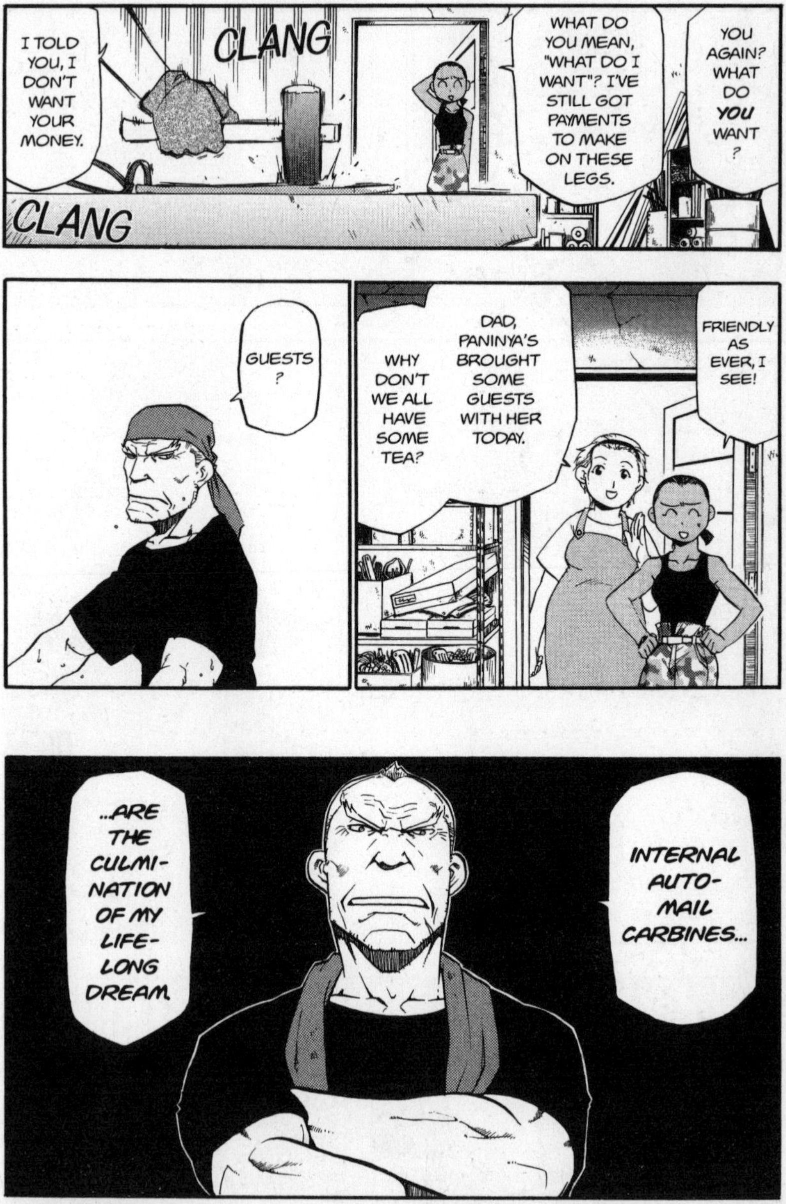
YOU AGAIN? WHAT DO *YOU* WANT?
WHAT DO YOU MEAN, "WHAT DO I WANT"? I'VE STILL GOT PAYMENTS TO MAKE ON THESE LEGS.
CLANG
I TOLD YOU, I DON'T WANT YOUR MONEY.
CLANG
FRIENDLY AS EVER, I SEE!
DAD, PANINYA'S BROUGHT SOME GUESTS WITH HER TODAY.
WHY DON'T WE ALL HAVE SOME TEA?
GUESTS?
INTERNAL AUTO-MAIL CARBINES...
...ARE THE CULMINATION OF MY LIFE-LONG DREAM.

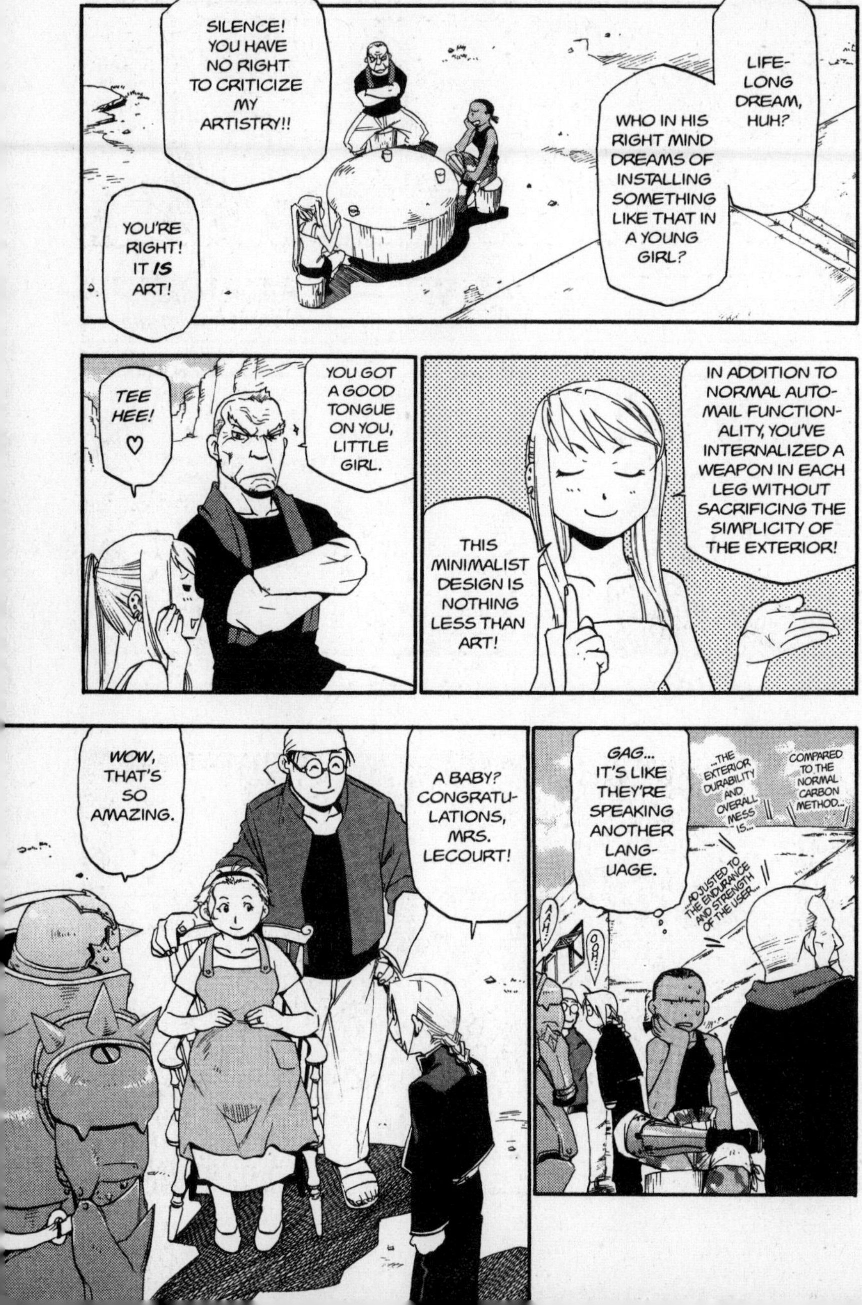
LIFE-LONG DREAM, HUH?
WHO IN HIS RIGHT MIND DREAMS OF INSTALLING SOMETHING LIKE THAT IN A YOUNG GIRL?
SILENCE! YOU HAVE NO RIGHT TO CRITICIZE MY ARTISTRY!!
YOU'RE RIGHT! IT *IS* ART!
IN ADDITION TO NORMAL AUTO-MAIL FUNCTION-ALITY, YOU'VE INTERNALIZED A WEAPON IN EACH LEG WITHOUT SACRIFICING THE SIMPLICITY OF THE EXTERIOR!
THIS MINIMALIST DESIGN IS NOTHING LESS THAN ART!
YOU GOT A GOOD TONGUE ON YOU, LITTLE GIRL.
TEE HEE! ♡
COMPARED TO THE NORMAL CARBON METHOD...
...THE EXTERIOR DURABILITY AND OVERALL MESS IS...
GAG... IT'S LIKE THEY'RE SPEAKING ANOTHER LANG-UAGE.
...ADJUSTED TO THE ENDURANCE AND STRENGTH OF THE USER...
AAH!
OOH...
A BABY? CONGRATU-LATIONS, MRS. LECOURT!
WOW, THAT'S SO AMAZING.

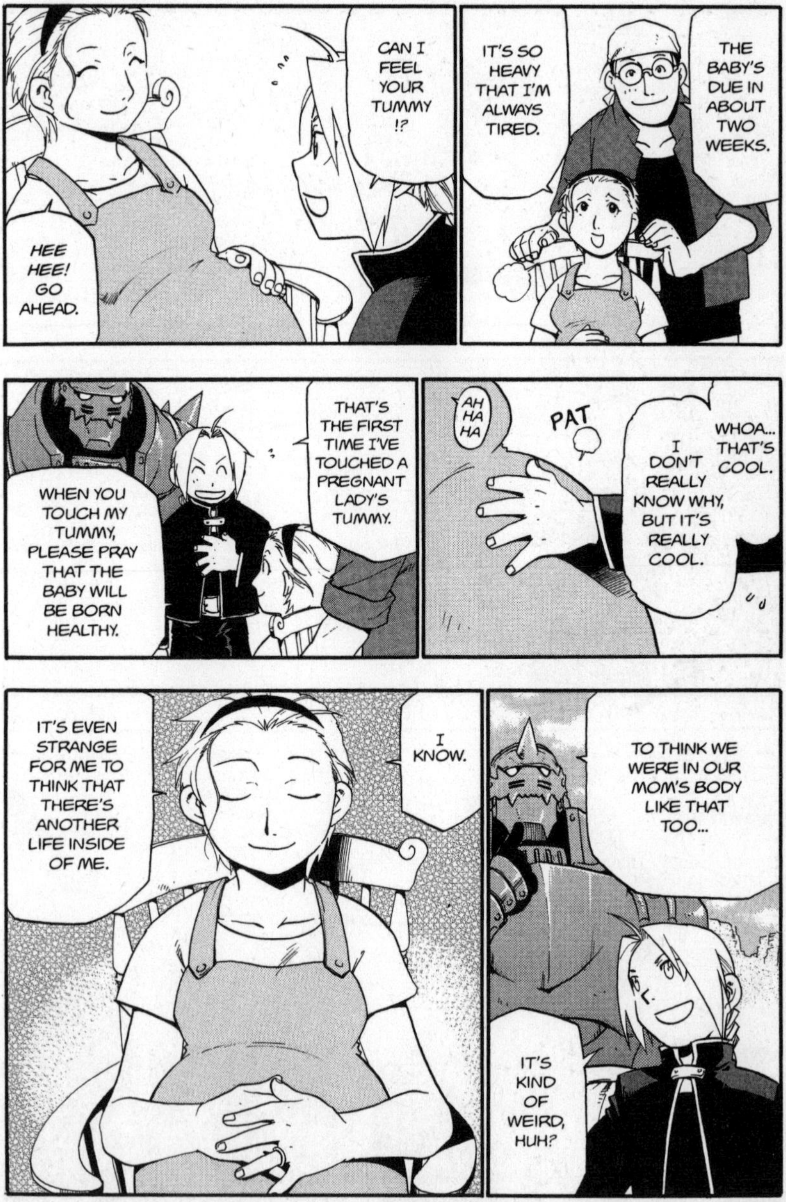
THE BABY'S DUE IN ABOUT TWO WEEKS.
IT'S SO HEAVY THAT I'M ALWAYS TIRED.
CAN I FEEL YOUR TUMMY !?
HEE HEE! GO AHEAD.
WHOA... THAT'S COOL.
I DON'T REALLY KNOW WHY, BUT IT'S REALLY COOL.
PAT
AH HA HA
THAT'S THE FIRST TIME I'VE TOUCHED A PREGNANT LADY'S TUMMY.
WHEN YOU TOUCH MY TUMMY, PLEASE PRAY THAT THE BABY WILL BE BORN HEALTHY.
TO THINK WE WERE IN OUR MOM'S BODY LIKE THAT TOO...
IT'S KIND OF WEIRD, HUH?
I KNOW.
IT'S EVEN STRANGE FOR ME TO THINK THAT THERE'S ANOTHER LIFE INSIDE OF ME.

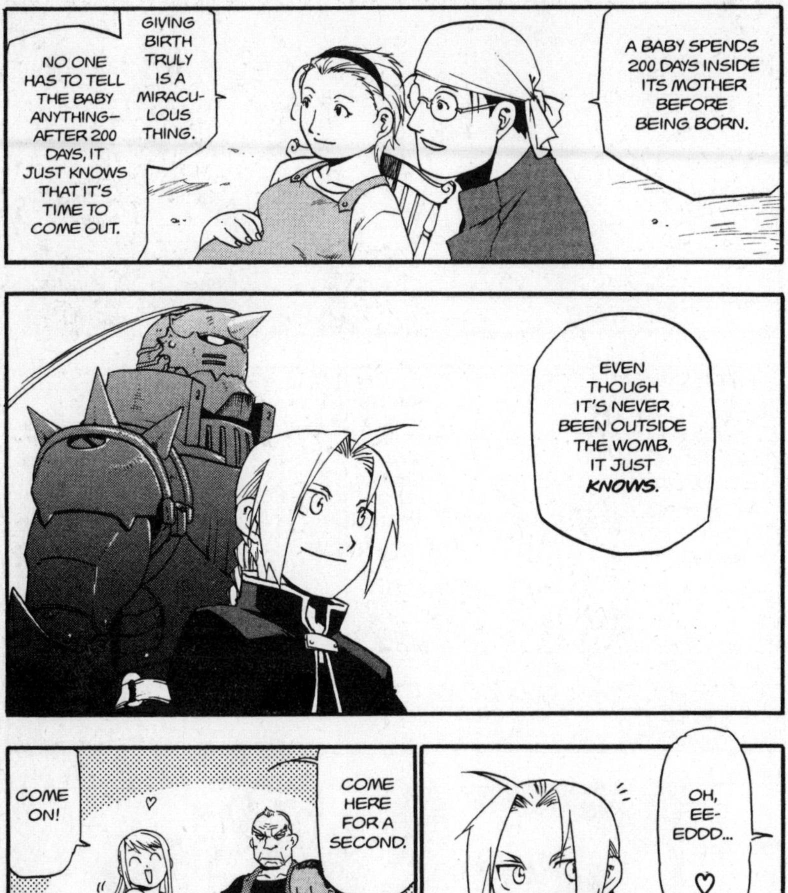
A BABY SPENDS 200 DAYS INSIDE ITS MOTHER BEFORE BEING BORN.
GIVING BIRTH TRULY IS A MIRACULOUS THING.
NO ONE HAS TO TELL THE BABY ANYTHING—AFTER 200 DAYS, IT JUST KNOWS THAT IT'S TIME TO COME OUT.
EVEN THOUGH IT'S NEVER BEEN OUTSIDE THE WOMB, IT JUST ***KNOWS.***
OH, EE-EDDD... ♡
COME HERE FOR A SECOND.
COME ON! ♡

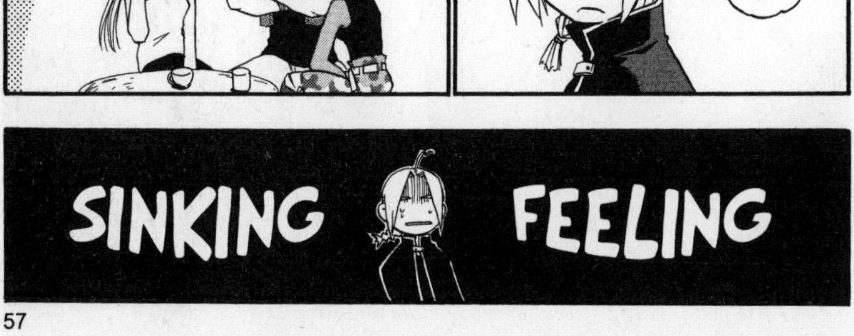
SINKING FEELING

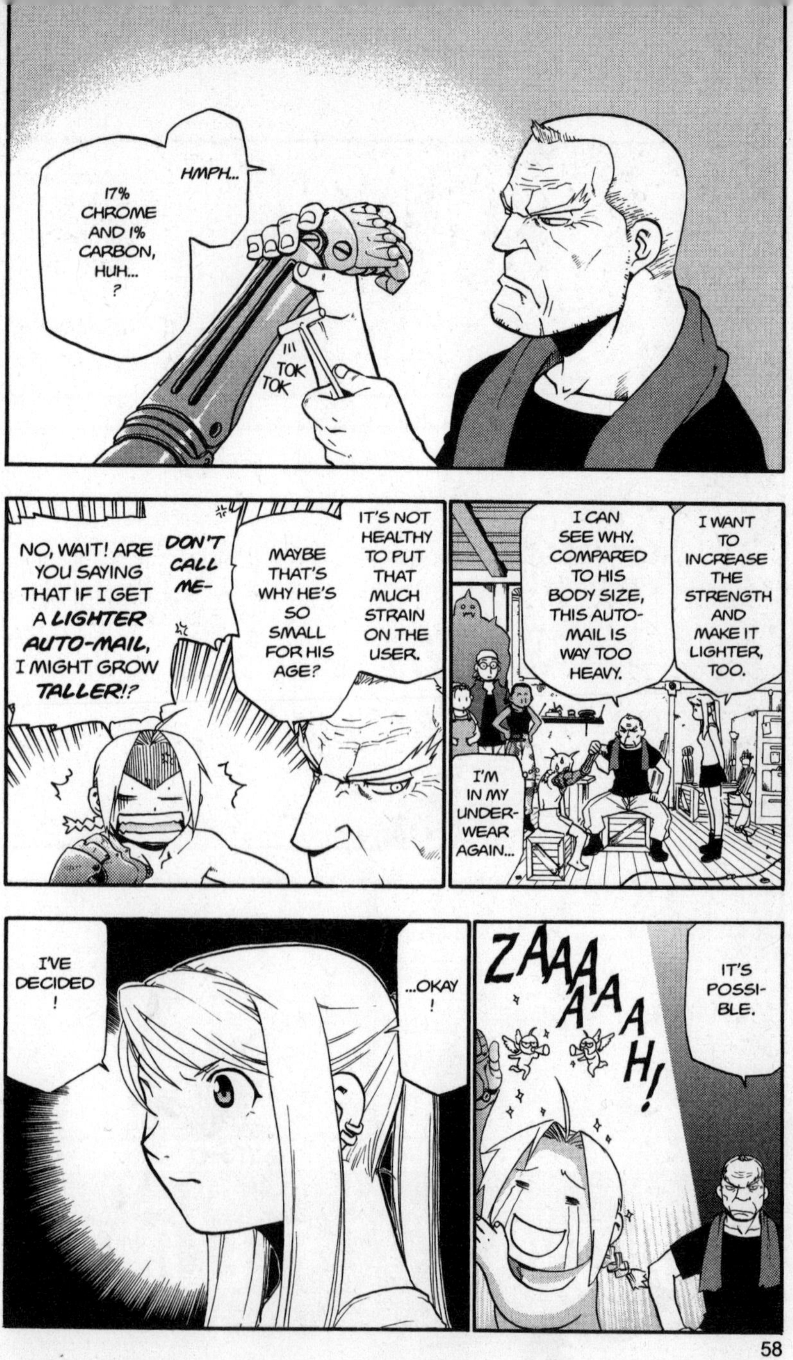
HMPH...
17% CHROME AND 1% CARBON, HUH...?
TOK TOK
I WANT TO INCREASE THE STRENGTH AND MAKE IT LIGHTER, TOO.
I CAN SEE WHY. COMPARED TO HIS BODY SIZE, THIS AUTO-MAIL IS WAY TOO HEAVY.
I'M IN MY UNDERWEAR AGAIN...
IT'S NOT HEALTHY TO PUT THAT MUCH STRAIN ON THE USER.
MAYBE THAT'S WHY HE'S SO SMALL FOR HIS AGE?
DON'T CALL ME-
NO, WAIT! ARE YOU SAYING THAT IF I GET A LIGHTER AUTO-MAIL, I MIGHT GROW TALLER!?
IT'S POSSIBLE.
ZAAAAAAAH!
...OKAY!
I'VE DECIDED!

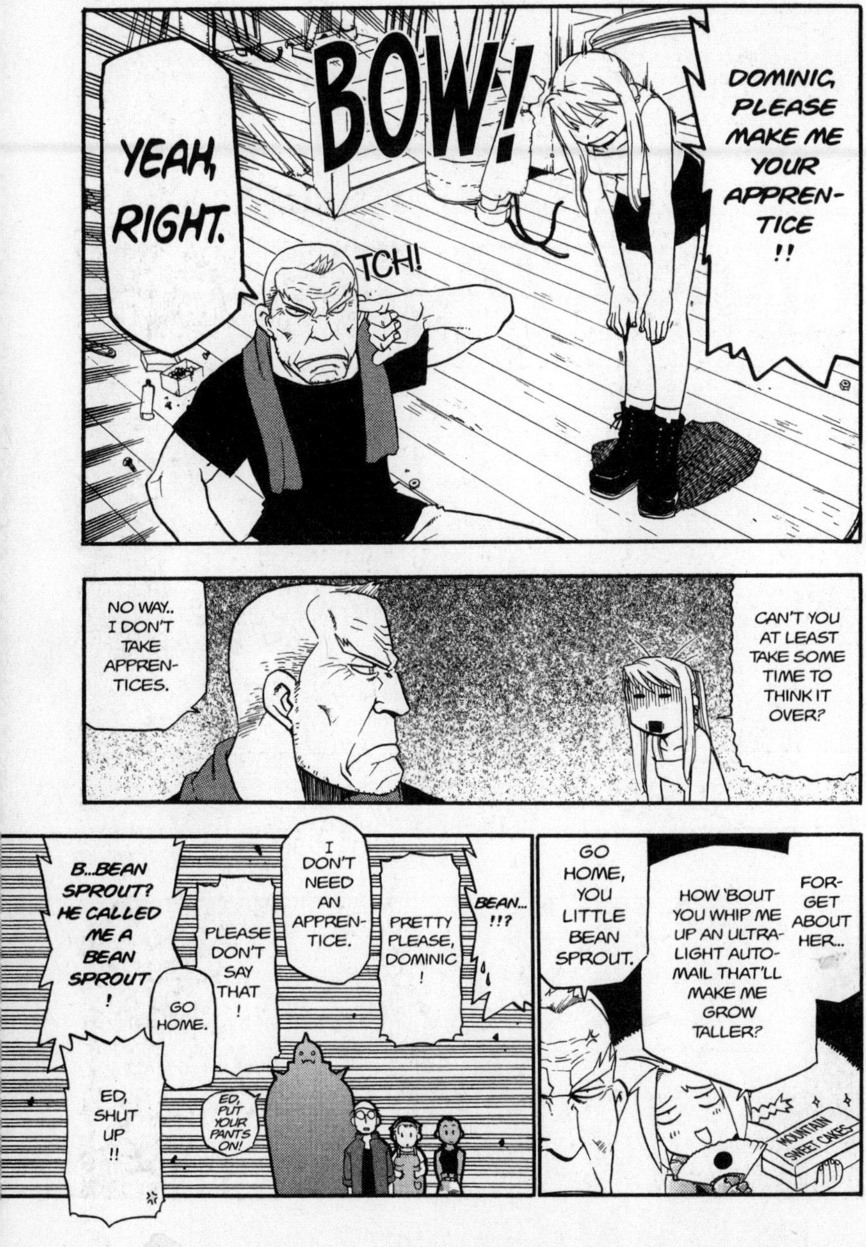
DOMINIC, PLEASE MAKE ME YOUR APPREN-TICE !!
BOW!
TCH!
YEAH, RIGHT.
CAN'T YOU AT LEAST TAKE SOME TIME TO THINK IT OVER?
NO WAY.. I DON'T TAKE APPREN-TICES.
FOR-GET ABOUT HER...
HOW 'BOUT YOU WHIP ME UP AN ULTRA-LIGHT AUTO-MAIL THAT'LL MAKE ME GROW TALLER?
GO HOME, YOU LITTLE BEAN SPROUT.
MOUNTAIN SWEET CAKES
BEAN... !!?
PRETTY PLEASE, DOMINIC !
I DON'T NEED AN APPREN-TICE.
PLEASE DON'T SAY THAT !
GO HOME.
B...BEAN SPROUT? HE CALLED ME A BEAN SPROUT !
ED, PUT YOUR PANTS ON!
ED, SHUT UP !!

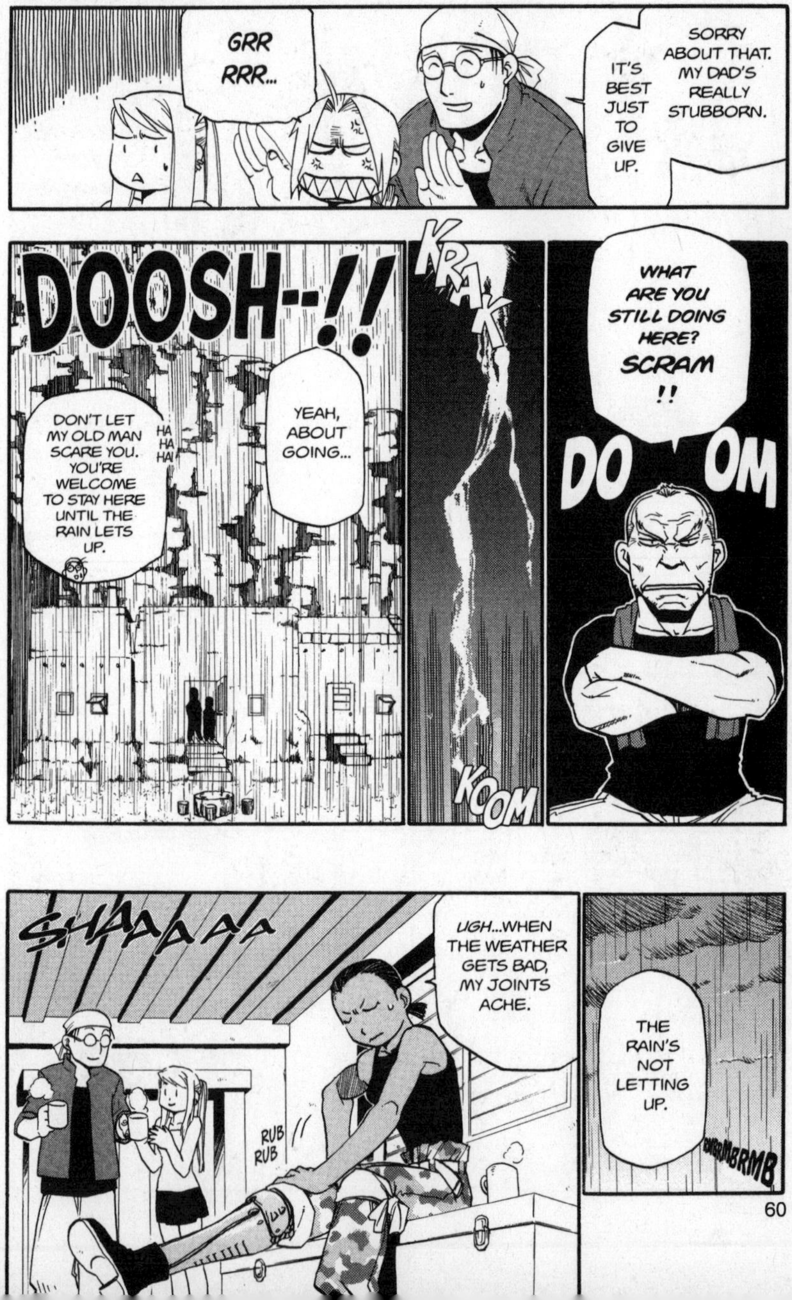
SORRY ABOUT THAT. MY DAD'S REALLY STUBBORN.
IT'S BEST JUST TO GIVE UP.
GRR RRR...
WHAT ARE YOU STILL DOING HERE? SCRAM!!
DO OM
KRAK
KOOM
DOOSH--!!
YEAH, ABOUT GOING...
DON'T LET MY OLD MAN SCARE YOU. YOU'RE WELCOME TO STAY HERE UNTIL THE RAIN LETS UP.
HA HA HA!
THE RAIN'S NOT LETTING UP.
UGH...WHEN THE WEATHER GETS BAD, MY JOINTS ACHE.
SHAAAAA
RUB RUB

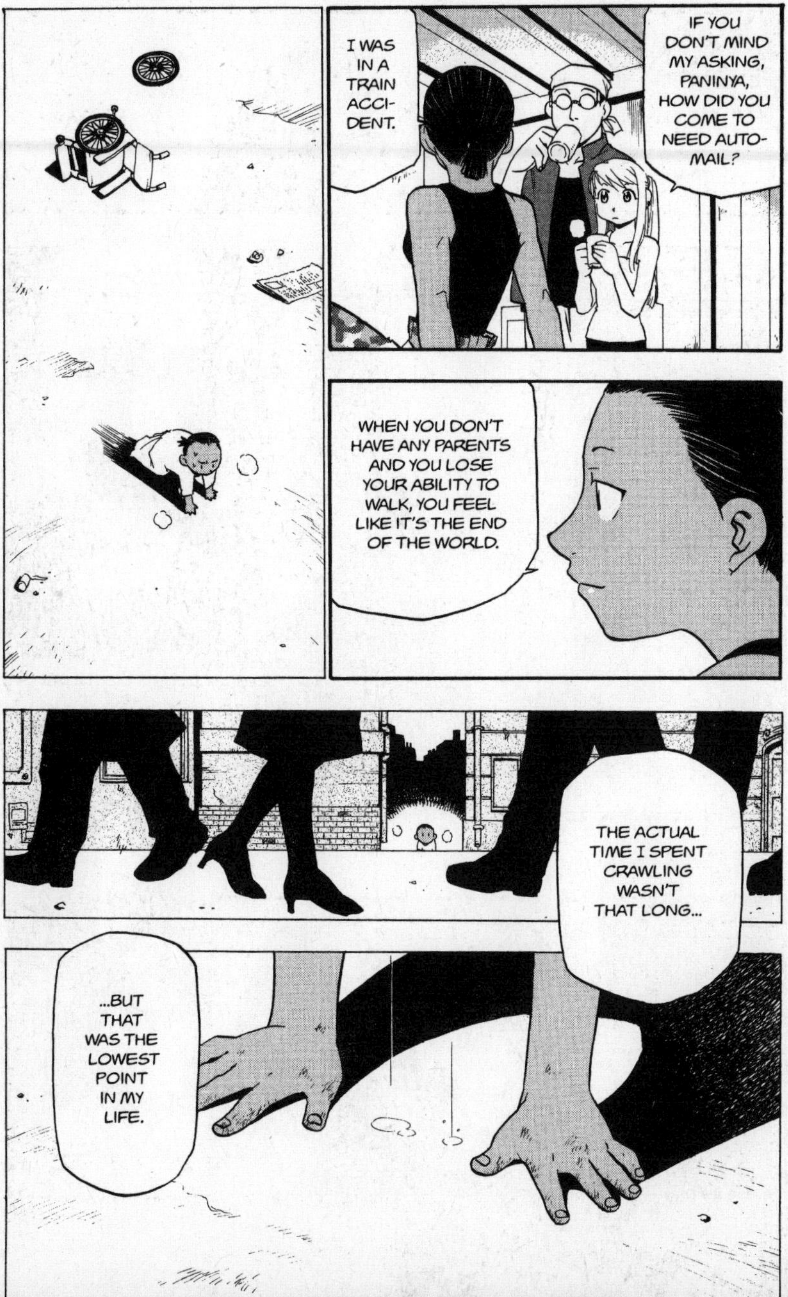
IF YOU DON'T MIND MY ASKING, PANINYA, HOW DID YOU COME TO NEED AUTO-MAIL?
I WAS IN A TRAIN ACCI-DENT.
WHEN YOU DON'T HAVE ANY PARENTS AND YOU LOSE YOUR ABILITY TO WALK, YOU FEEL LIKE IT'S THE END OF THE WORLD.
THE ACTUAL TIME I SPENT CRAWLING WASN'T THAT LONG...
...BUT THAT WAS THE LOWEST POINT IN MY LIFE.

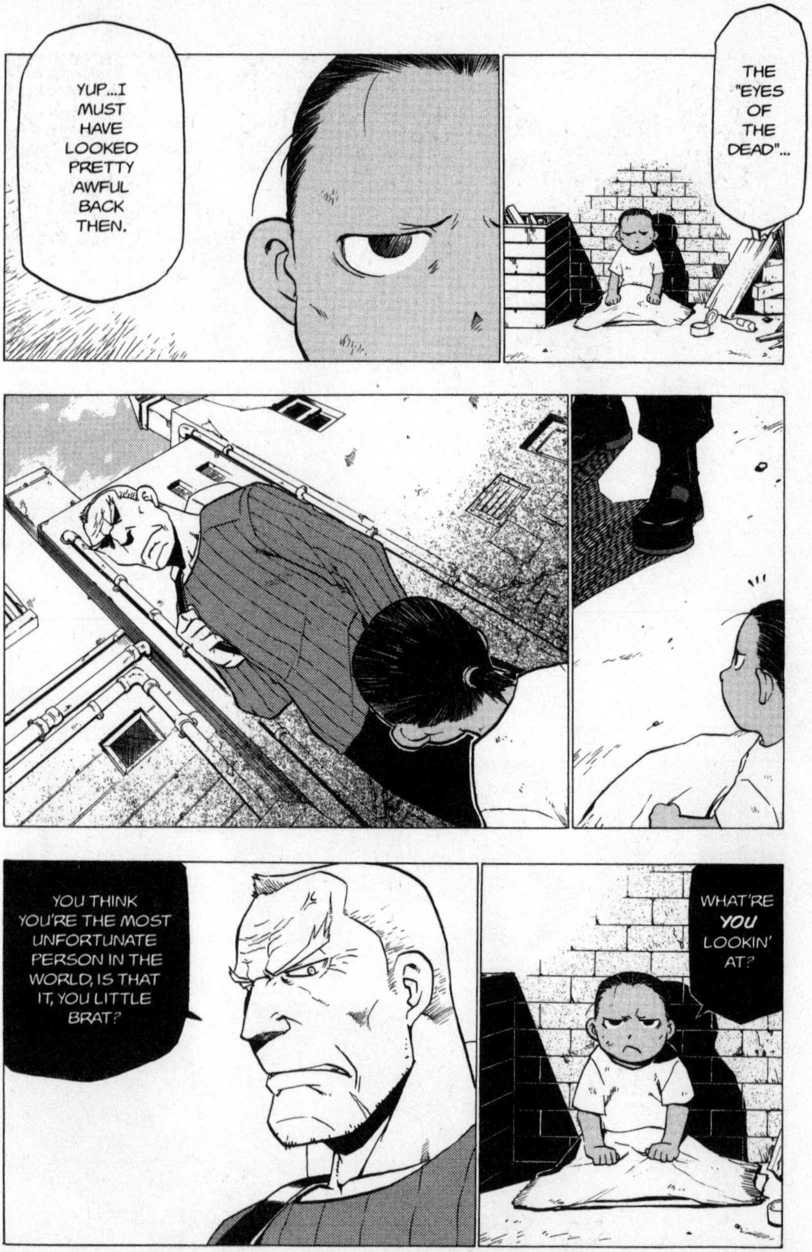
THE "EYES OF THE DEAD"...
YUP...I MUST HAVE LOOKED PRETTY AWFUL BACK THEN.
WHAT'RE *YOU* LOOKIN' AT?
YOU THINK YOU'RE THE MOST UNFORTUNATE PERSON IN THE WORLD, IS THAT IT, YOU LITTLE BRAT?

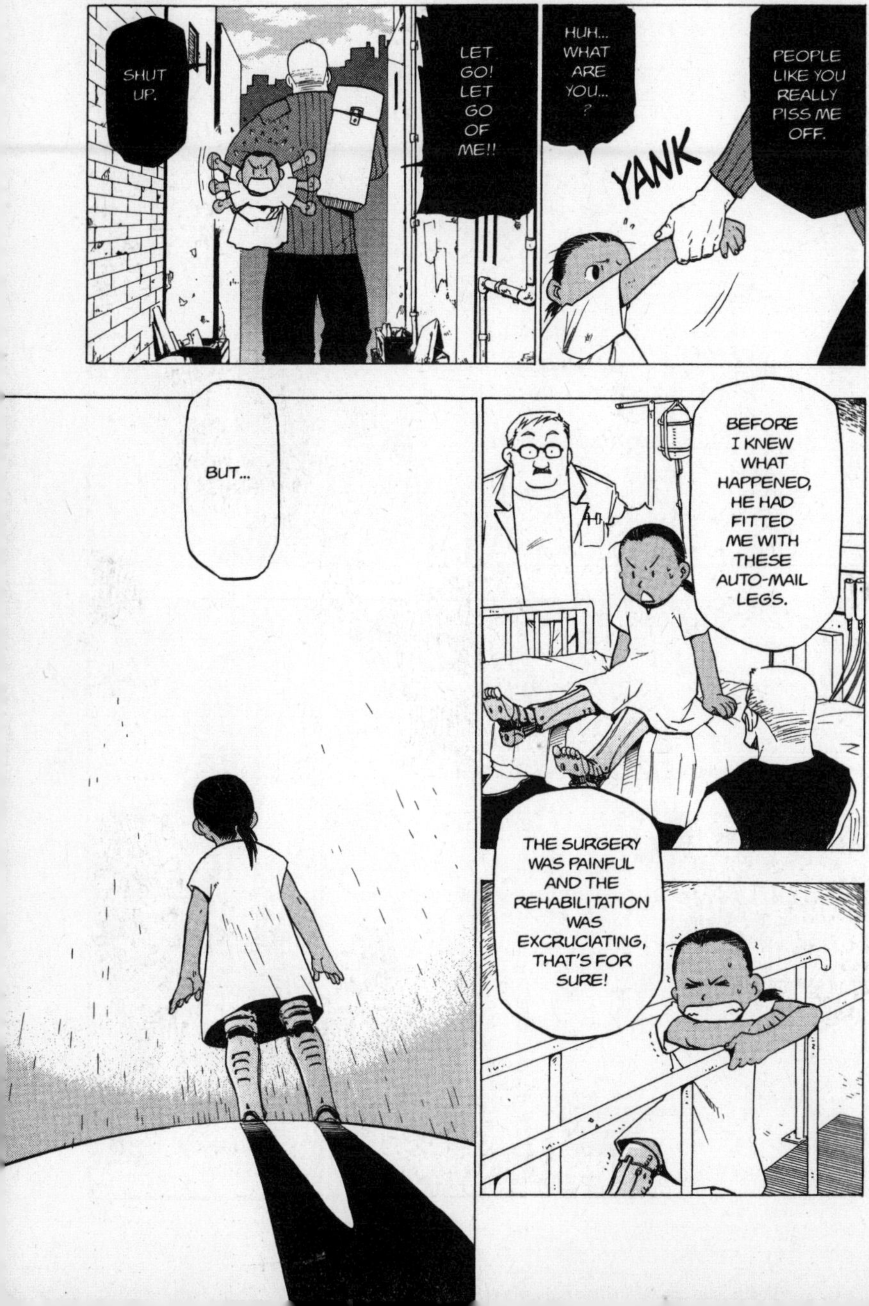
PEOPLE LIKE YOU REALLY PISS ME OFF.
HUH... WHAT ARE YOU...?
YANK
LET GO! LET GO OF ME!!
SHUT UP.
BEFORE I KNEW WHAT HAPPENED, HE HAD FITTED ME WITH THESE AUTO-MAIL LEGS.
THE SURGERY WAS PAINFUL AND THE REHABILITATION WAS EXCRUCIATING, THAT'S FOR SURE!
BUT...

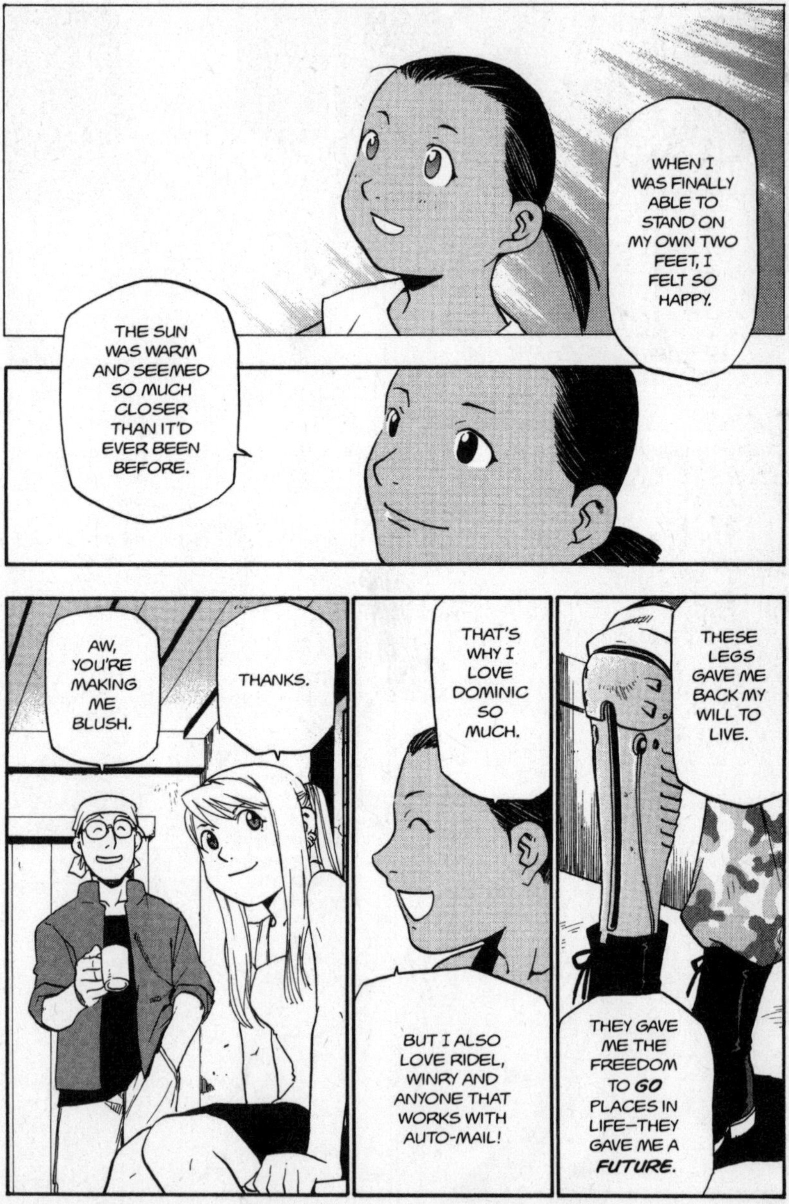
WHEN I WAS FINALLY ABLE TO STAND ON MY OWN TWO FEET, I FELT SO HAPPY.
THE SUN WAS WARM AND SEEMED SO MUCH CLOSER THAN IT'D EVER BEEN BEFORE.
THESE LEGS GAVE ME BACK MY WILL TO LIVE.
THEY GAVE ME THE FREEDOM TO **GO** PLACES IN LIFE—THEY GAVE ME A ***FUTURE***.
THAT'S WHY I LOVE DOMINIC SO MUCH.
BUT I ALSO LOVE RIDEL, WINRY AND ANYONE THAT WORKS WITH AUTO-MAIL!
THANKS.
AW, YOU'RE MAKING ME BLUSH.

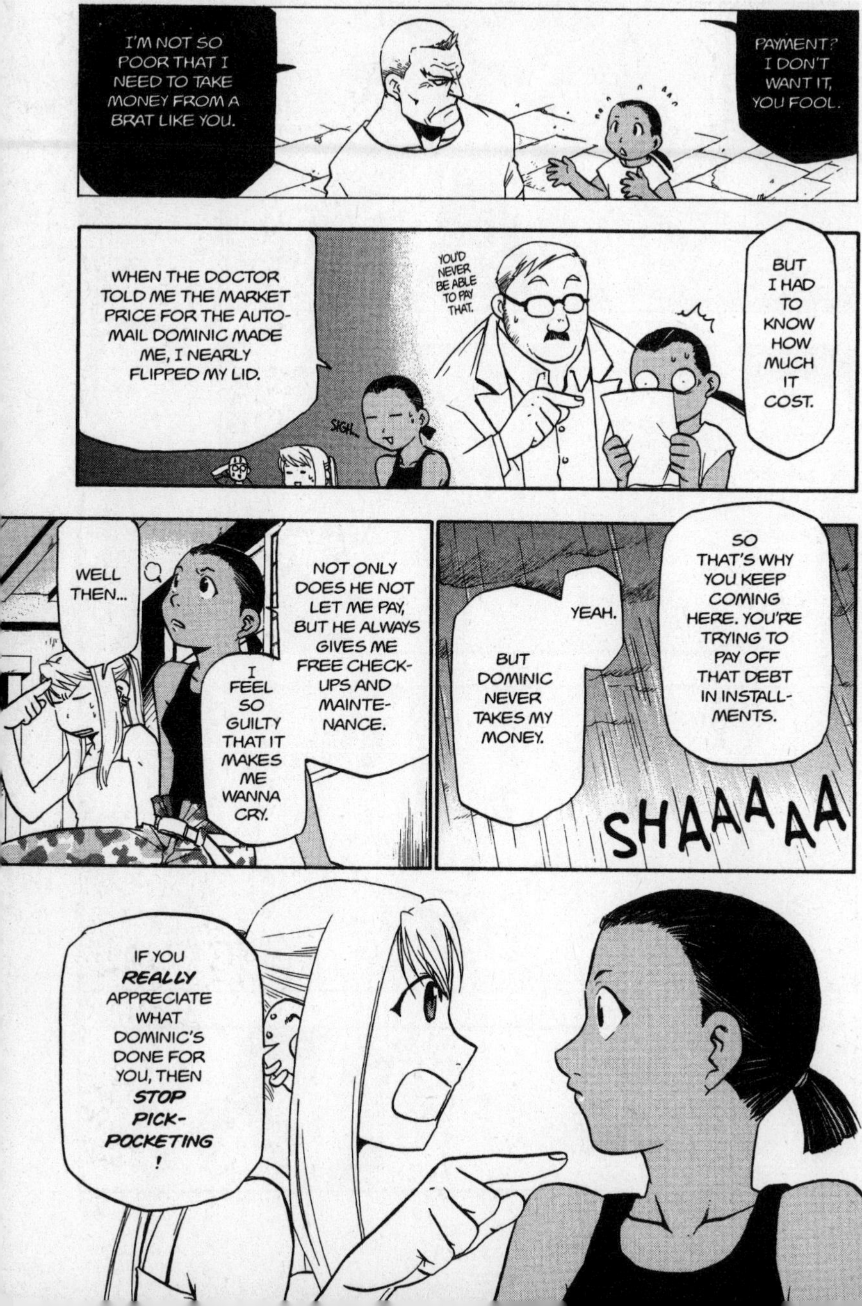
PAYMENT? I DON'T WANT IT, YOU FOOL.
I'M NOT SO POOR THAT I NEED TO TAKE MONEY FROM A BRAT LIKE YOU.
BUT I HAD TO KNOW HOW MUCH IT COST.
YOU'D NEVER BE ABLE TO PAY THAT.
WHEN THE DOCTOR TOLD ME THE MARKET PRICE FOR THE AUTO-MAIL DOMINIC MADE ME, I NEARLY FLIPPED MY LID.
SIGH.
SO THAT'S WHY YOU KEEP COMING HERE. YOU'RE TRYING TO PAY OFF THAT DEBT IN INSTALL-MENTS.
YEAH.
BUT DOMINIC NEVER TAKES MY MONEY.
SHAAAAA
NOT ONLY DOES HE NOT LET ME PAY, BUT HE ALWAYS GIVES ME FREE CHECK-UPS AND MAINTE-NANCE.
I FEEL SO GUILTY THAT IT MAKES ME WANNA CRY.
WELL THEN...
IF YOU REALLY APPRECIATE WHAT DOMINIC'S DONE FOR YOU, THEN STOP PICK-POCKETING!

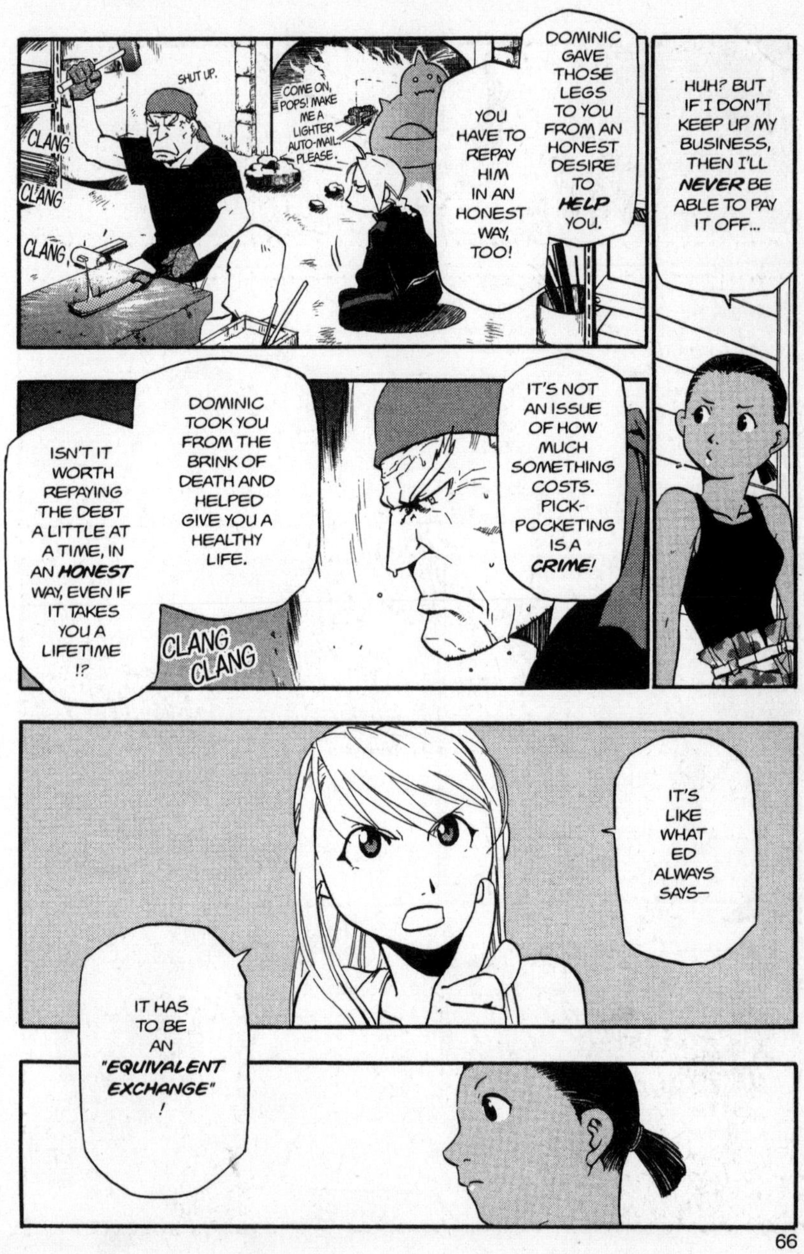
HUH? BUT IF I DON'T KEEP UP MY BUSINESS, THEN I'LL **NEVER** BE ABLE TO PAY IT OFF...
DOMINIC GAVE THOSE LEGS TO YOU FROM AN HONEST DESIRE TO **HELP** YOU.
YOU HAVE TO REPAY HIM IN AN HONEST WAY, TOO!
SHUT UP.
COME ON, POPS! MAKE ME A LIGHTER AUTO-MAIL. PLEASE.
CLANG
CLANG
CLANG
IT'S NOT AN ISSUE OF HOW MUCH SOMETHING COSTS. PICK-POCKETING IS A **CRIME**!
DOMINIC TOOK YOU FROM THE BRINK OF DEATH AND HELPED GIVE YOU A HEALTHY LIFE.
ISN'T IT WORTH REPAYING THE DEBT A LITTLE AT A TIME, IN AN **HONEST** WAY, EVEN IF IT TAKES YOU A LIFETIME !?
CLANG CLANG
IT'S LIKE WHAT ED ALWAYS SAYS—
IT HAS TO BE AN **"EQUIVALENT EXCHANGE"** !

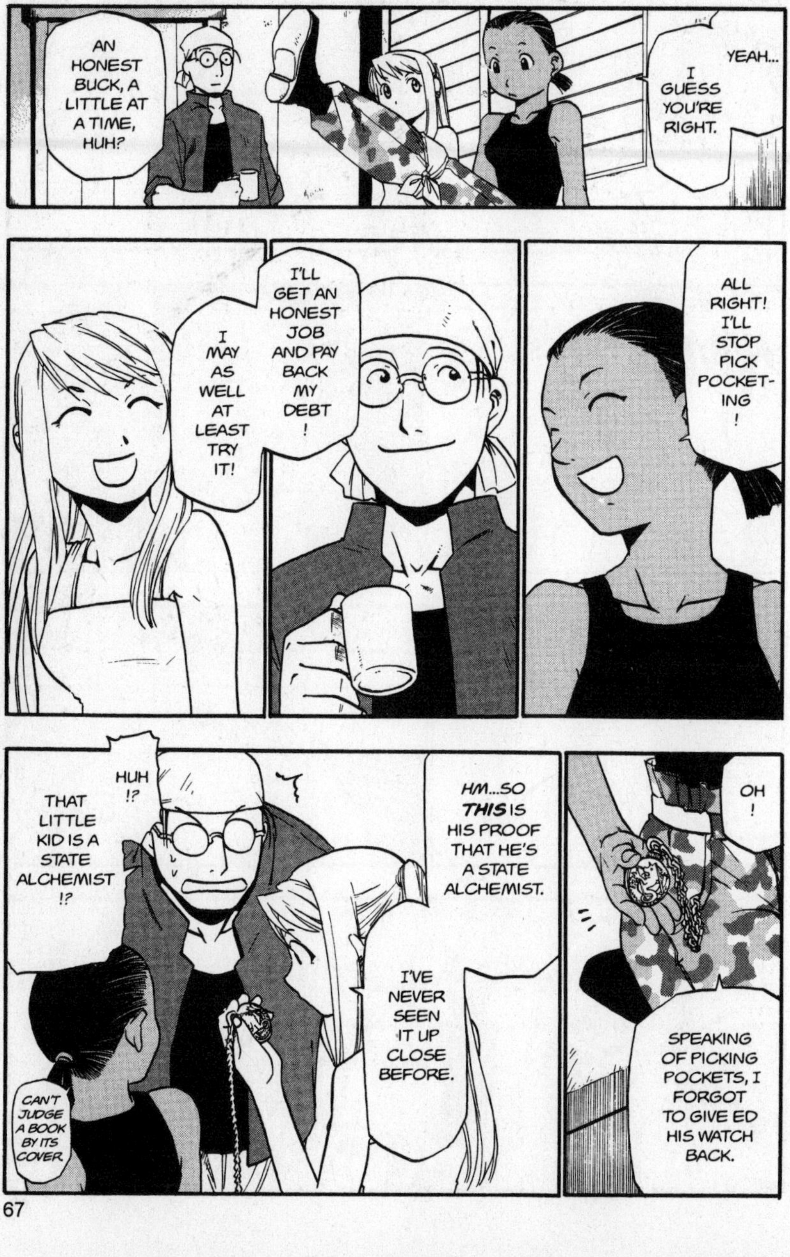
YEAH... I GUESS YOU'RE RIGHT.
AN HONEST BUCK, A LITTLE AT A TIME, HUH?
ALL RIGHT! I'LL STOP PICK POCKETING!
I'LL GET AN HONEST JOB AND PAY BACK MY DEBT!
I MAY AS WELL AT LEAST TRY IT!
OH!
SPEAKING OF PICKING POCKETS, I FORGOT TO GIVE ED HIS WATCH BACK.
HM...SO **THIS** IS HIS PROOF THAT HE'S A STATE ALCHEMIST.
I'VE NEVER SEEN IT UP CLOSE BEFORE.
HUH!?
THAT LITTLE KID IS A STATE ALCHEMIST!?
CAN'T JUDGE A BOOK BY ITS COVER

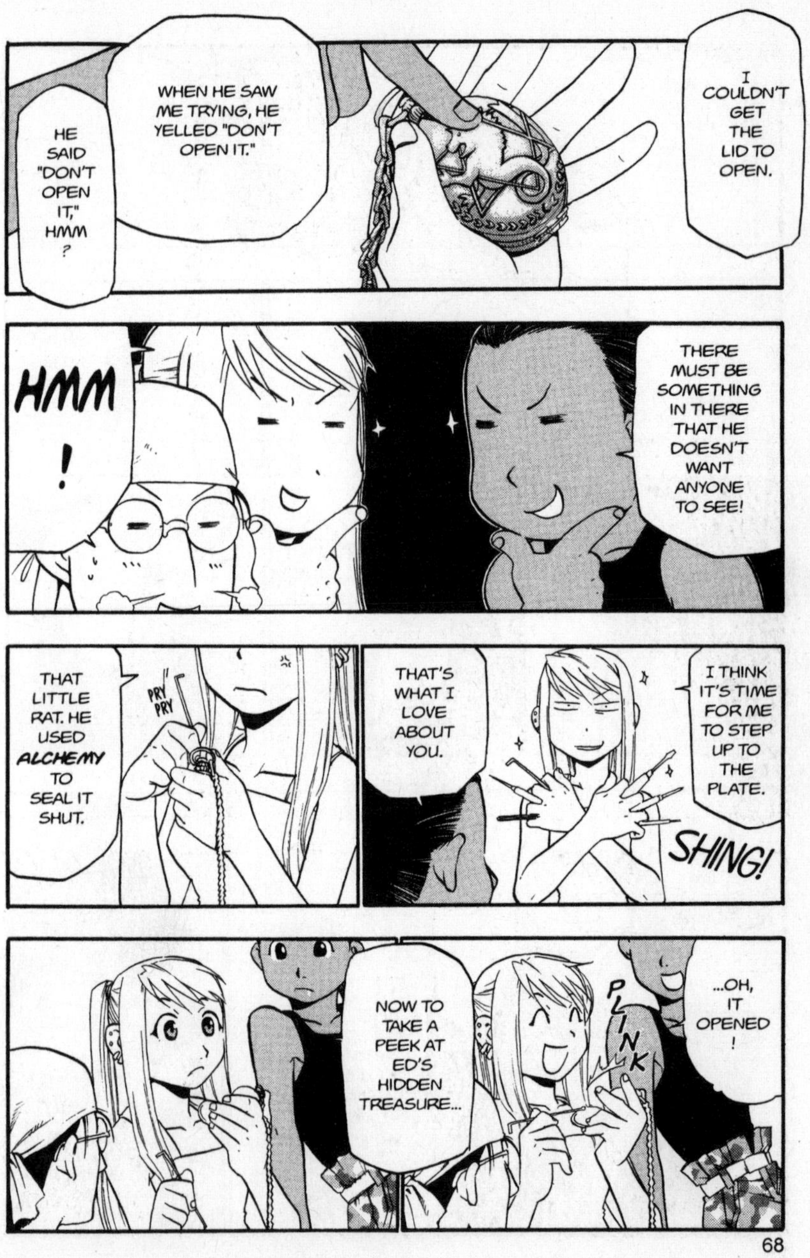
I COULDN'T GET THE LID TO OPEN.
WHEN HE SAW ME TRYING, HE YELLED "DON'T OPEN IT."
HE SAID "DON'T OPEN IT," HMM?
THERE MUST BE SOMETHING IN THERE THAT HE DOESN'T WANT ANYONE TO SEE!
HMM!
I THINK IT'S TIME FOR ME TO STEP UP TO THE PLATE.
SHING!
THAT'S WHAT I LOVE ABOUT YOU.
THAT LITTLE RAT. HE USED *ALCHEMY* TO SEAL IT SHUT.
PRY PRY
...OH, IT OPENED!
PLINK
NOW TO TAKE A PEEK AT ED'S HIDDEN TREASURE...

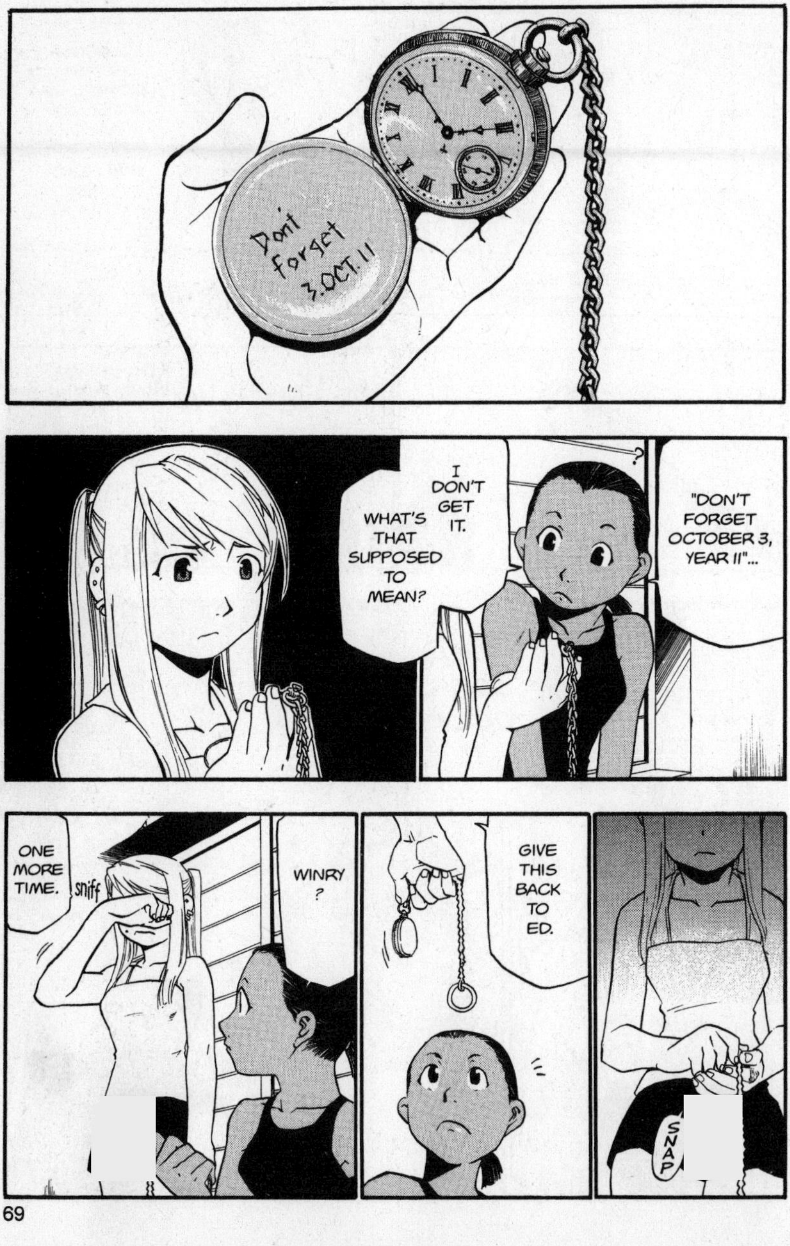
Don't forget 3.OCT.11
"DON'T FORGET OCTOBER 3, YEAR 11"...
I DON'T GET IT.
WHAT'S THAT SUPPOSED TO MEAN?
SNAP
GIVE THIS BACK TO ED.
WINRY?
ONE MORE TIME.
sniff

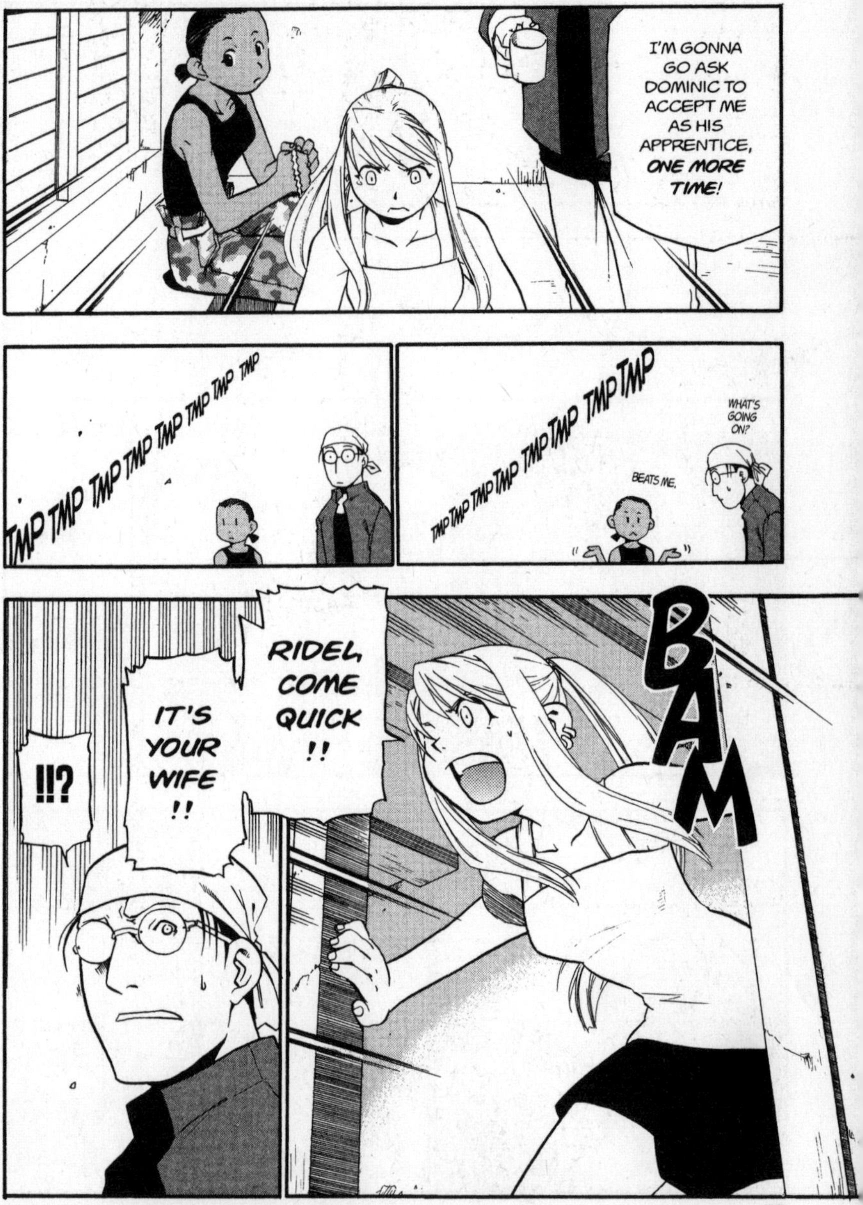
I'M GONNA GO ASK DOMINIC TO ACCEPT ME AS HIS APPRENTICE, ONE MORE TIME!
TMP TMP TMP TMP TMP TMP TMP TMP
WHAT'S GOING ON?
BEATS ME.
TMP TMP TMP TMP TMP TMP TMP TMP TMP
BAM
RIDEL, COME QUICK!!
IT'S YOUR WIFE!!
!!?

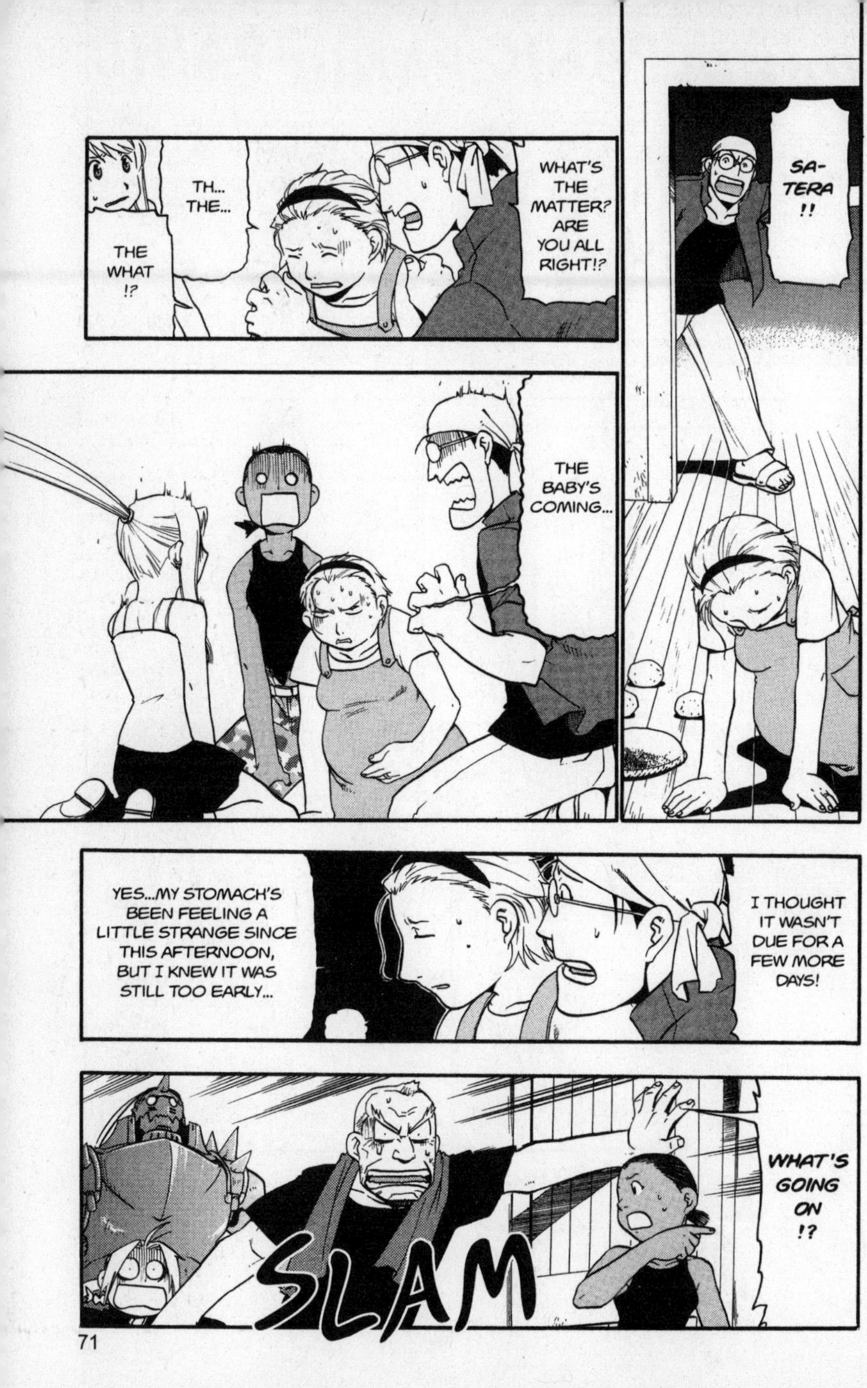
SA-TERA !!
WHAT'S THE MATTER? ARE YOU ALL RIGHT!?
TH... THE...
THE WHAT !?
THE BABY'S COMING...
I THOUGHT IT WASN'T DUE FOR A FEW MORE DAYS!
YES...MY STOMACH'S BEEN FEELING A LITTLE STRANGE SINCE THIS AFTERNOON, BUT I KNEW IT WAS STILL TOO EARLY...
WHAT'S GOING ON !?
SLAM

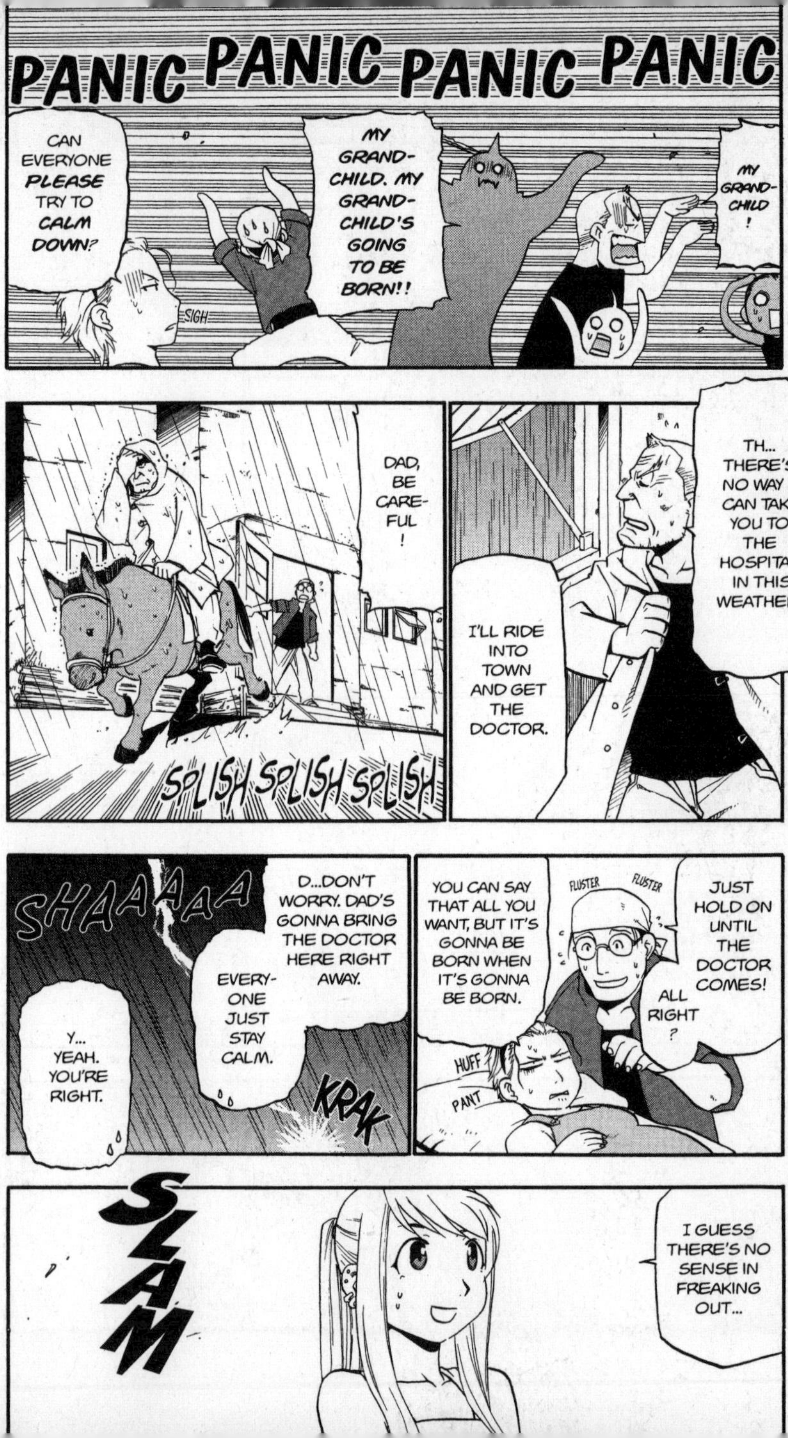
PANIC PANIC PANIC PANIC
MY GRANDCHILD!
MY GRANDCHILD. MY GRANDCHILD'S GOING TO BE BORN!!
CAN EVERYONE PLEASE TRY TO CALM DOWN?
SIGH
TH... THERE'S NO WAY I CAN TAKE YOU TO THE HOSPITAL IN THIS WEATHER.
I'LL RIDE INTO TOWN AND GET THE DOCTOR.
DAD, BE CAREFUL!
SPLISH SPLISH SPLISH
FLUSTER FLUSTER
JUST HOLD ON UNTIL THE DOCTOR COMES!
ALL RIGHT?
YOU CAN SAY THAT ALL YOU WANT, BUT IT'S GONNA BE BORN WHEN IT'S GONNA BE BORN.
HUFF
PANT
SHAAAAAA
D...DON'T WORRY. DAD'S GONNA BRING THE DOCTOR HERE RIGHT AWAY.
EVERYONE JUST STAY CALM.
Y... YEAH. YOU'RE RIGHT.
KRAK
I GUESS THERE'S NO SENSE IN FREAKING OUT...
SLAM

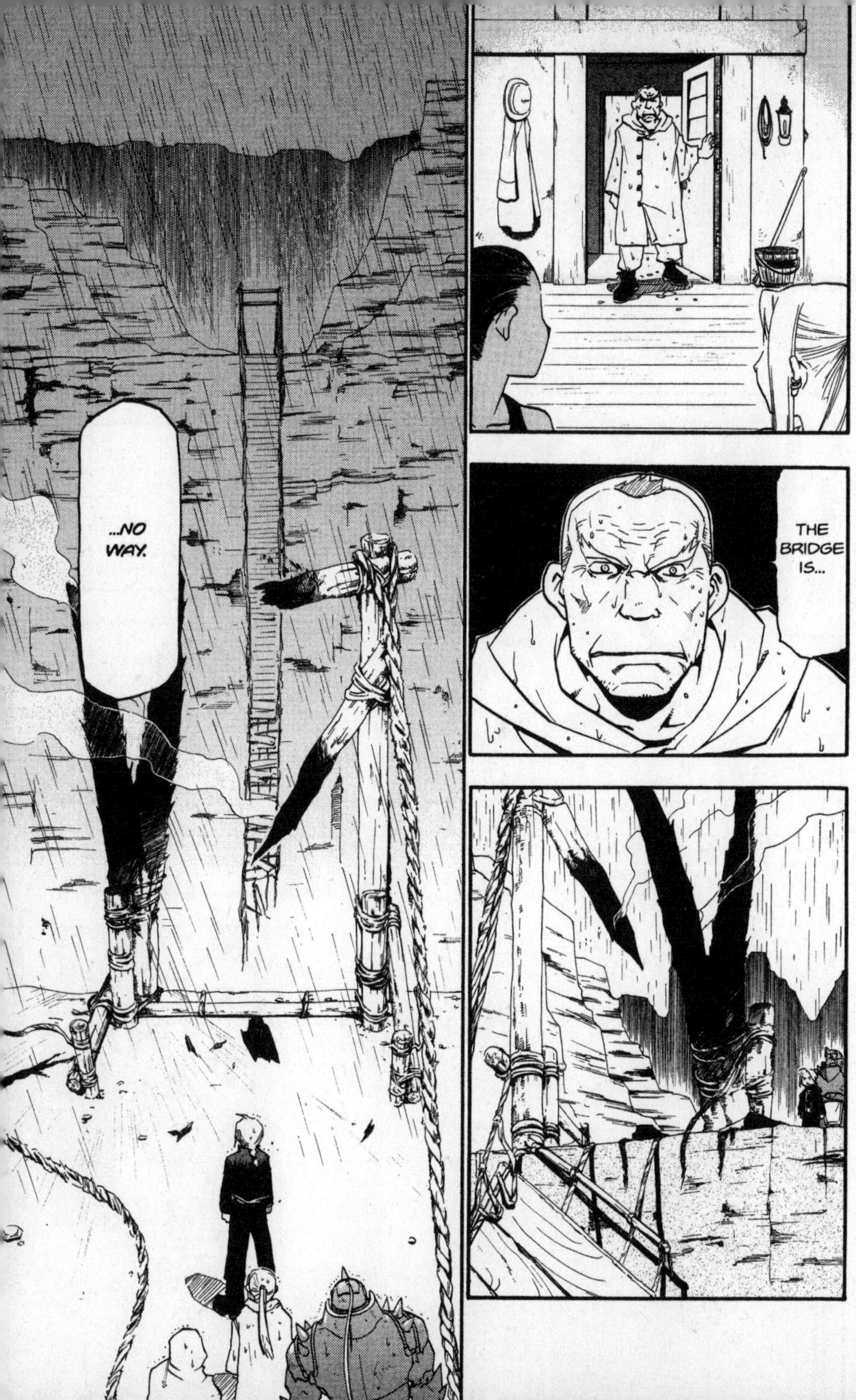
THE BRIDGE IS...
...NO WAY.

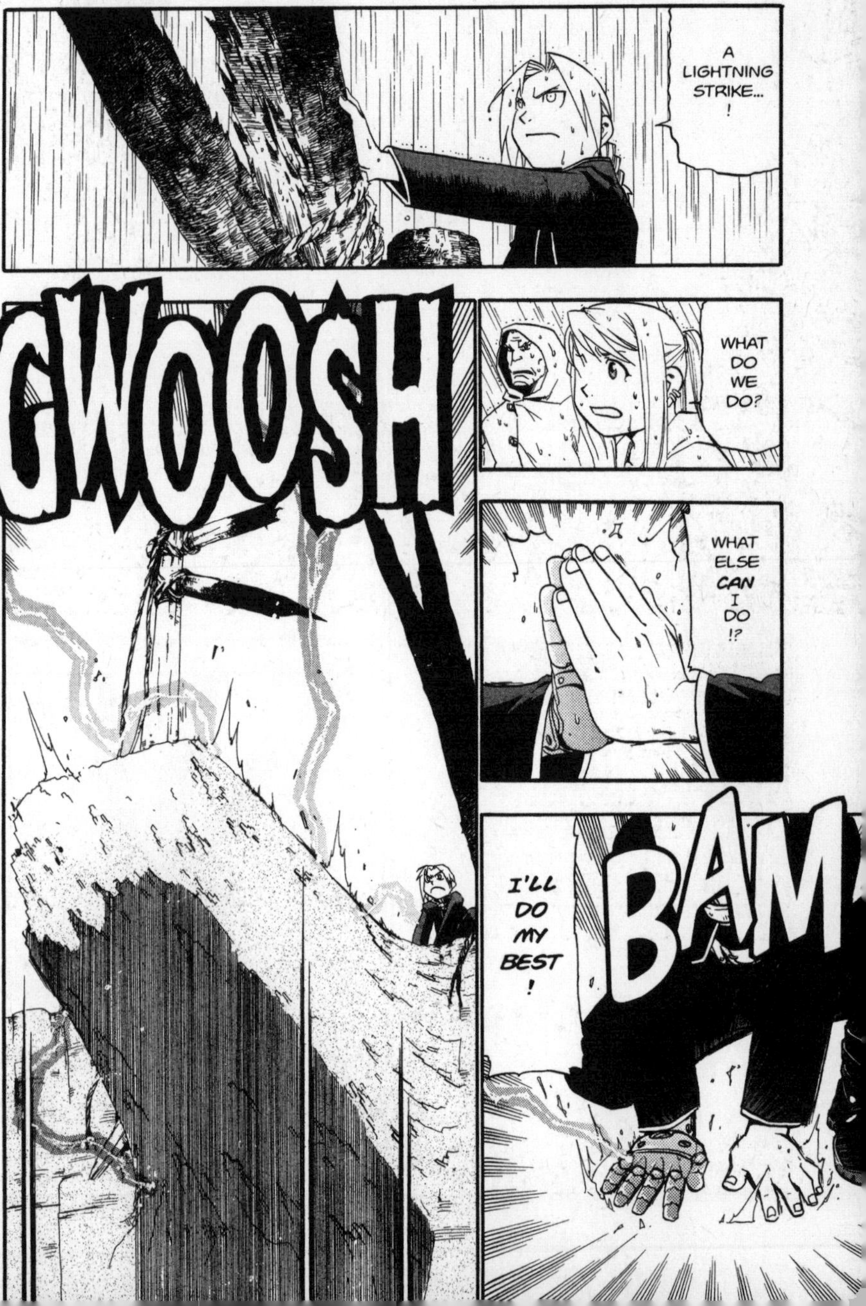
A LIGHTNING STRIKE...!
WHAT DO WE DO?
WHAT ELSE CAN I DO!?
BAM
I'LL DO MY BEST!
GWOOSH

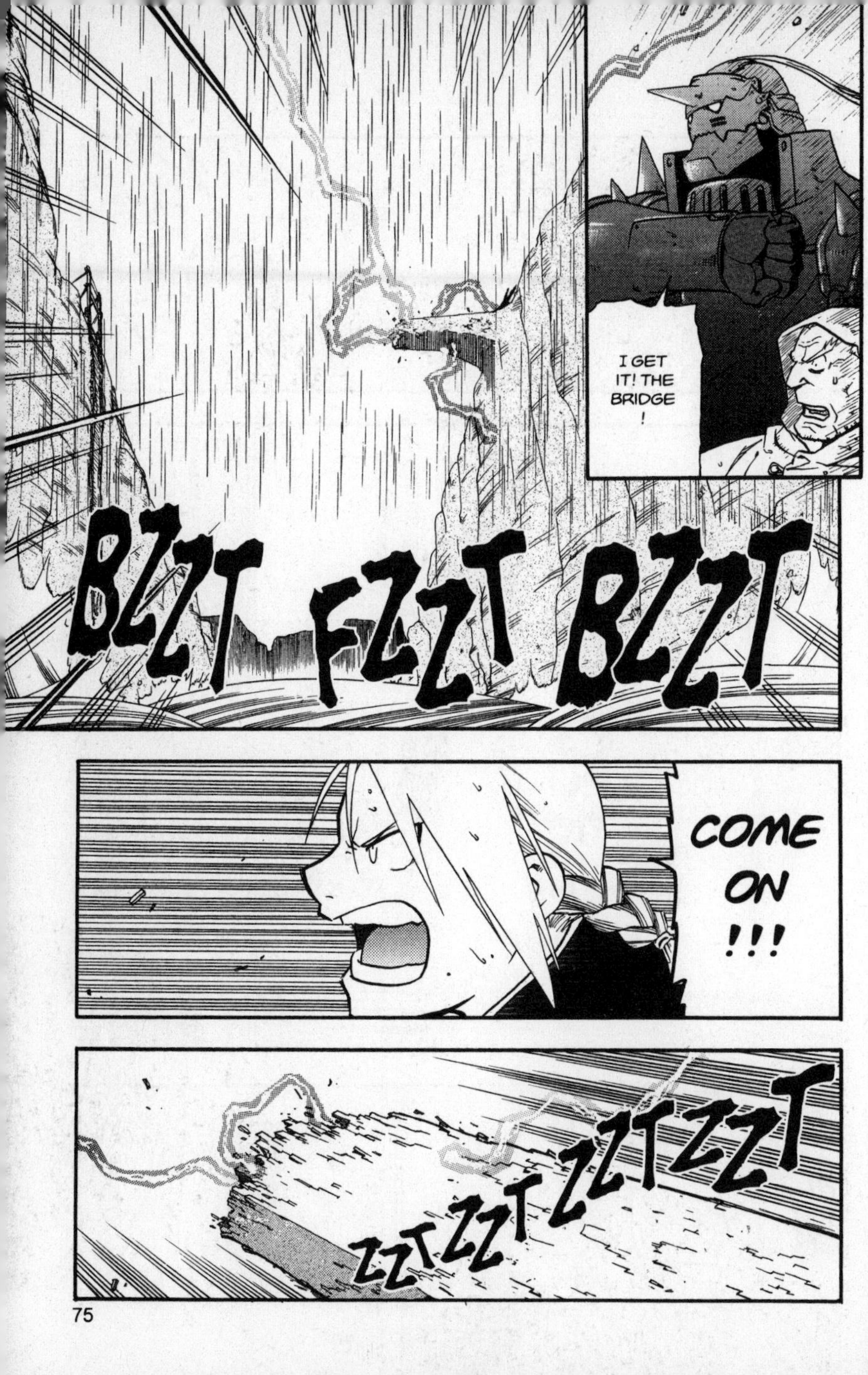
I GET IT! THE BRIDGE!
BZZT FZZT BZZT
COME ON!!!
ZZTZZTZZTZZT

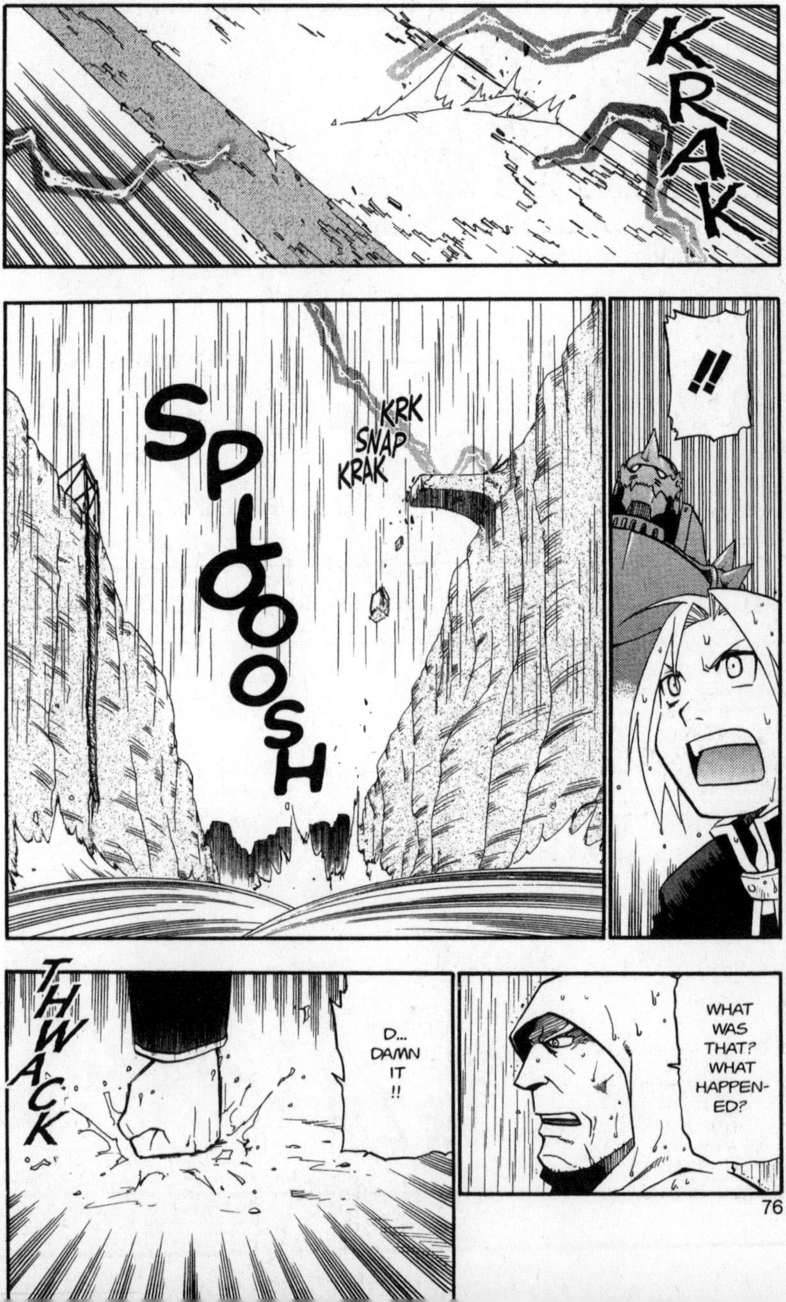
KRAK
!!
SPLOOOSH
KRK
SNAP
KRAK
WHAT WAS THAT? WHAT HAPPEN-ED?
D... DAMN IT !!
THWACK

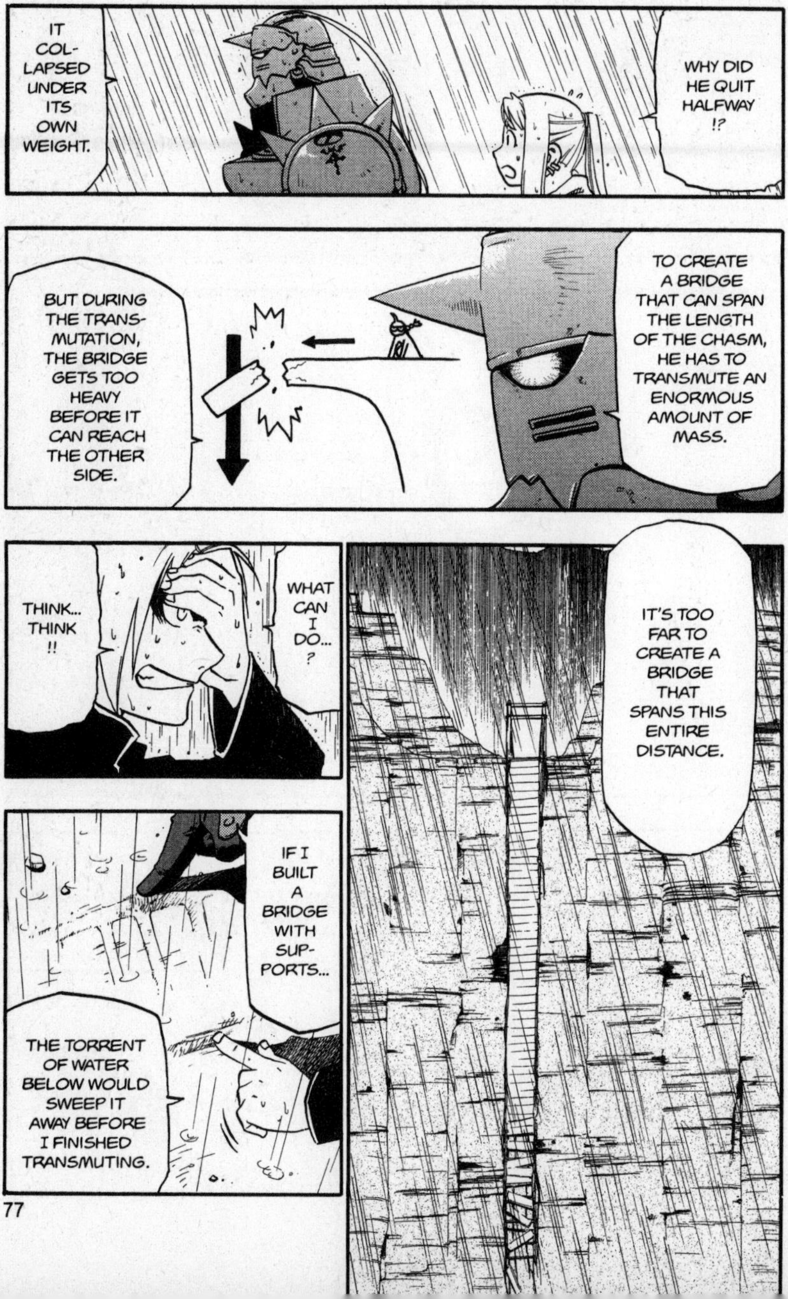
WHY DID HE QUIT HALFWAY !?
IT COL-LAPSED UNDER ITS OWN WEIGHT.
TO CREATE A BRIDGE THAT CAN SPAN THE LENGTH OF THE CHASM, HE HAS TO TRANSMUTE AN ENORMOUS AMOUNT OF MASS.
BUT DURING THE TRANS-MUTATION, THE BRIDGE GETS TOO HEAVY BEFORE IT CAN REACH THE OTHER SIDE.
IT'S TOO FAR TO CREATE A BRIDGE THAT SPANS THIS ENTIRE DISTANCE.
WHAT CAN I DO...?
THINK... THINK!!
IF I BUILT A BRIDGE WITH SUP-PORTS...
THE TORRENT OF WATER BELOW WOULD SWEEP IT AWAY BEFORE I FINISHED TRANSMUTING.

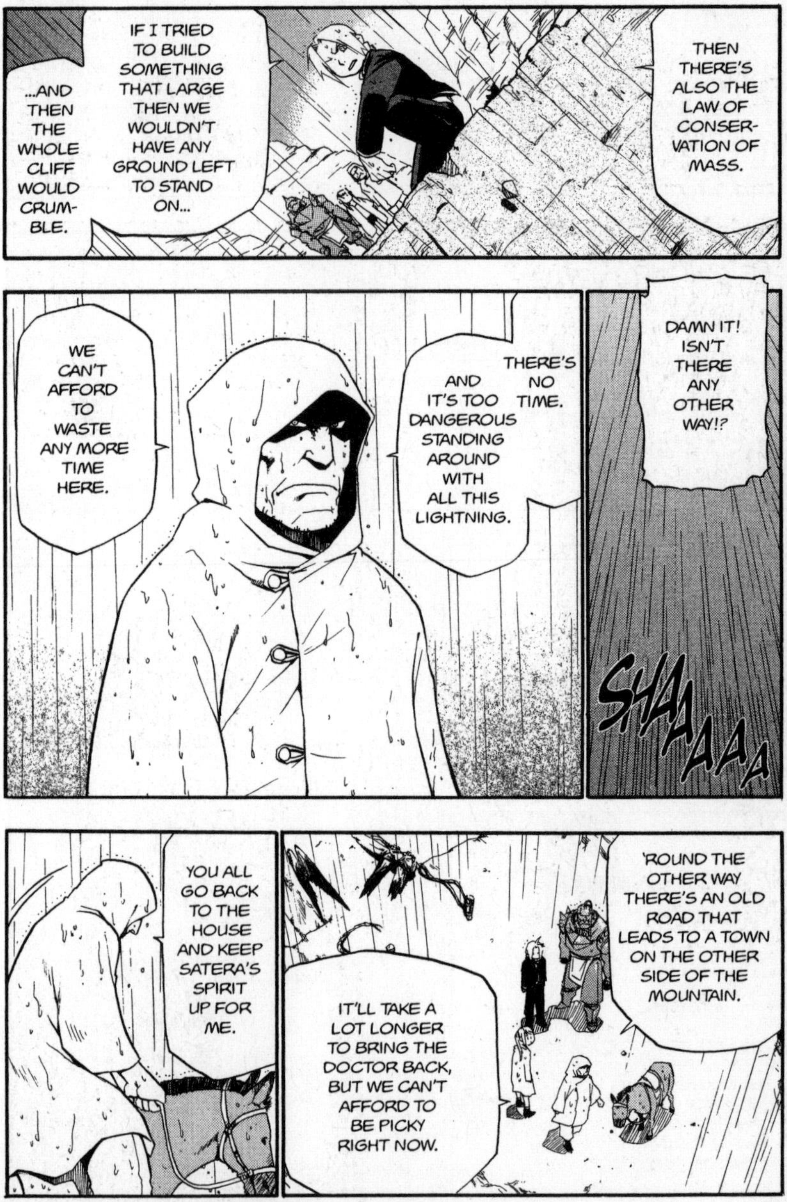
THEN THERE'S ALSO THE LAW OF CONSERVATION OF MASS.
IF I TRIED TO BUILD SOMETHING THAT LARGE THEN WE WOULDN'T HAVE ANY GROUND LEFT TO STAND ON...
...AND THEN THE WHOLE CLIFF WOULD CRUMBLE.
DAMN IT! ISN'T THERE ANY OTHER WAY!?
SHAAAAAA
THERE'S NO TIME.
AND IT'S TOO DANGEROUS STANDING AROUND WITH ALL THIS LIGHTNING.
WE CAN'T AFFORD TO WASTE ANY MORE TIME HERE.
'ROUND THE OTHER WAY THERE'S AN OLD ROAD THAT LEADS TO A TOWN ON THE OTHER SIDE OF THE MOUNTAIN.
IT'LL TAKE A LOT LONGER TO BRING THE DOCTOR BACK, BUT WE CAN'T AFFORD TO BE PICKY RIGHT NOW.
YOU ALL GO BACK TO THE HOUSE AND KEEP SATERA'S SPIRIT UP FOR ME.

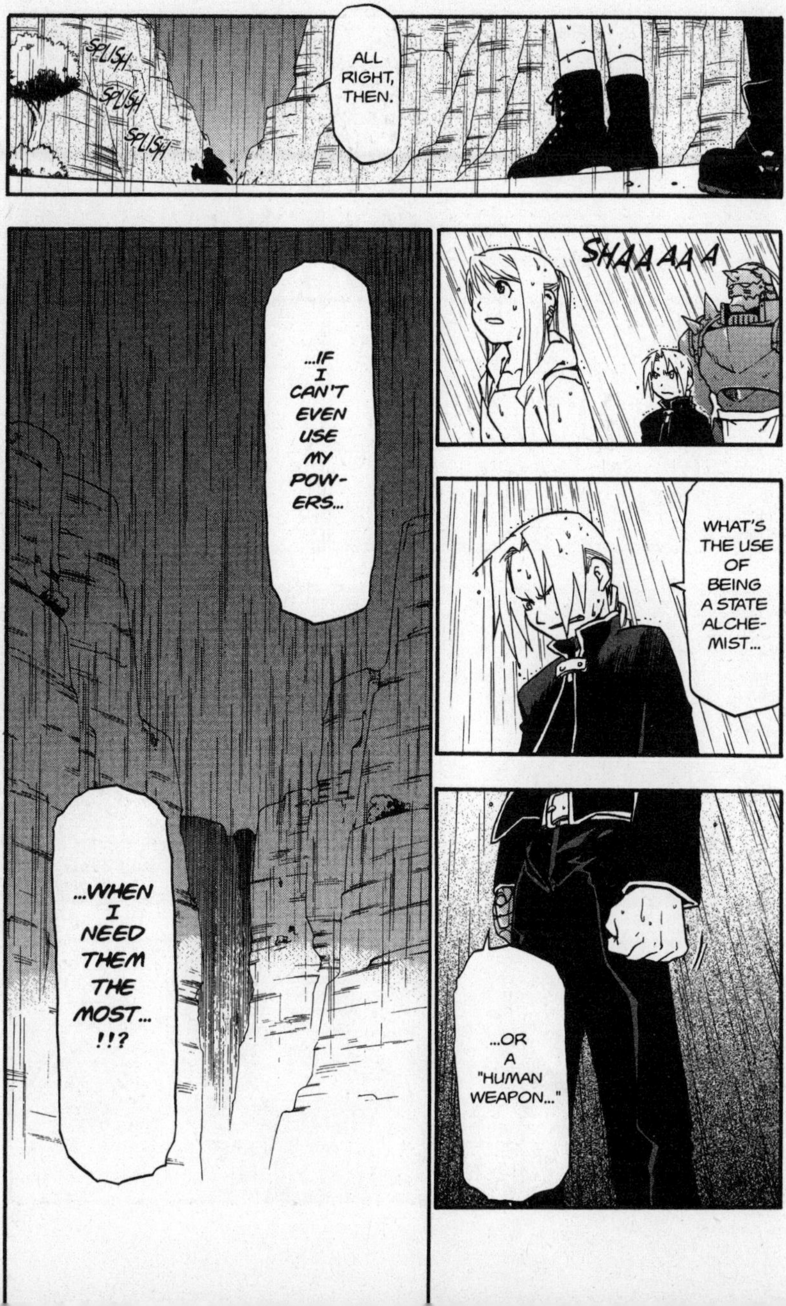
ALL RIGHT, THEN.
SPLISH
SPLISH
SPLISH
SHAAAAA
WHAT'S THE USE OF BEING A STATE ALCHEMIST...
...OR A "HUMAN WEAPON..."
...IF I CAN'T EVEN USE MY POWERS...
...WHEN I NEED THEM THE MOST...!!?

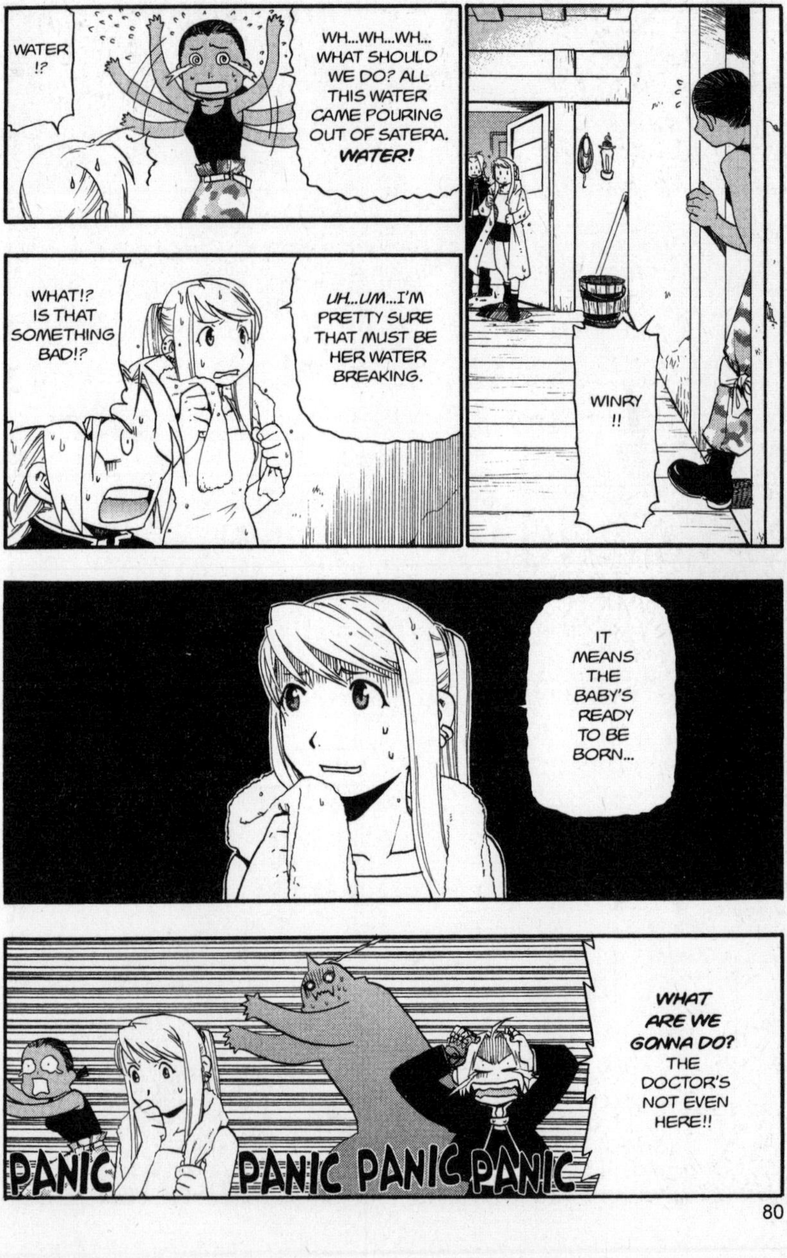
WINRY!!
WH...WH...WH... WHAT SHOULD WE DO? ALL THIS WATER CAME POURING OUT OF SATERA. **WATER!**
WATER!?
UH...UM...I'M PRETTY SURE THAT MUST BE HER WATER BREAKING.
WHAT!? IS THAT SOMETHING BAD!?
IT MEANS THE BABY'S READY TO BE BORN...
WHAT ARE WE GONNA DO? THE DOCTOR'S NOT EVEN HERE!!
PANIC PANIC PANIC PANIC

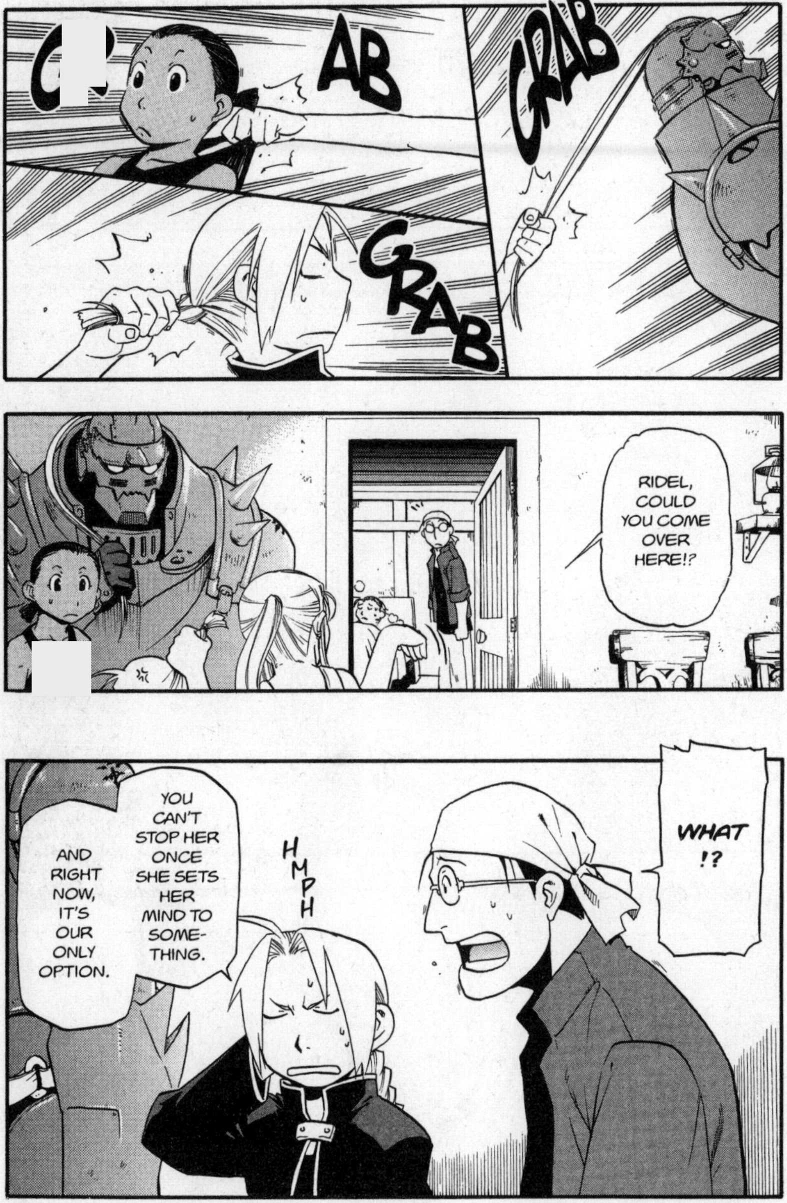
GRAB
GRAB
RIDEL, COULD YOU COME OVER HERE!?
WHAT !?
HMPH
YOU CAN'T STOP HER ONCE SHE SETS HER MIND TO SOMETHING.
AND RIGHT NOW, IT'S OUR ONLY OPTION.

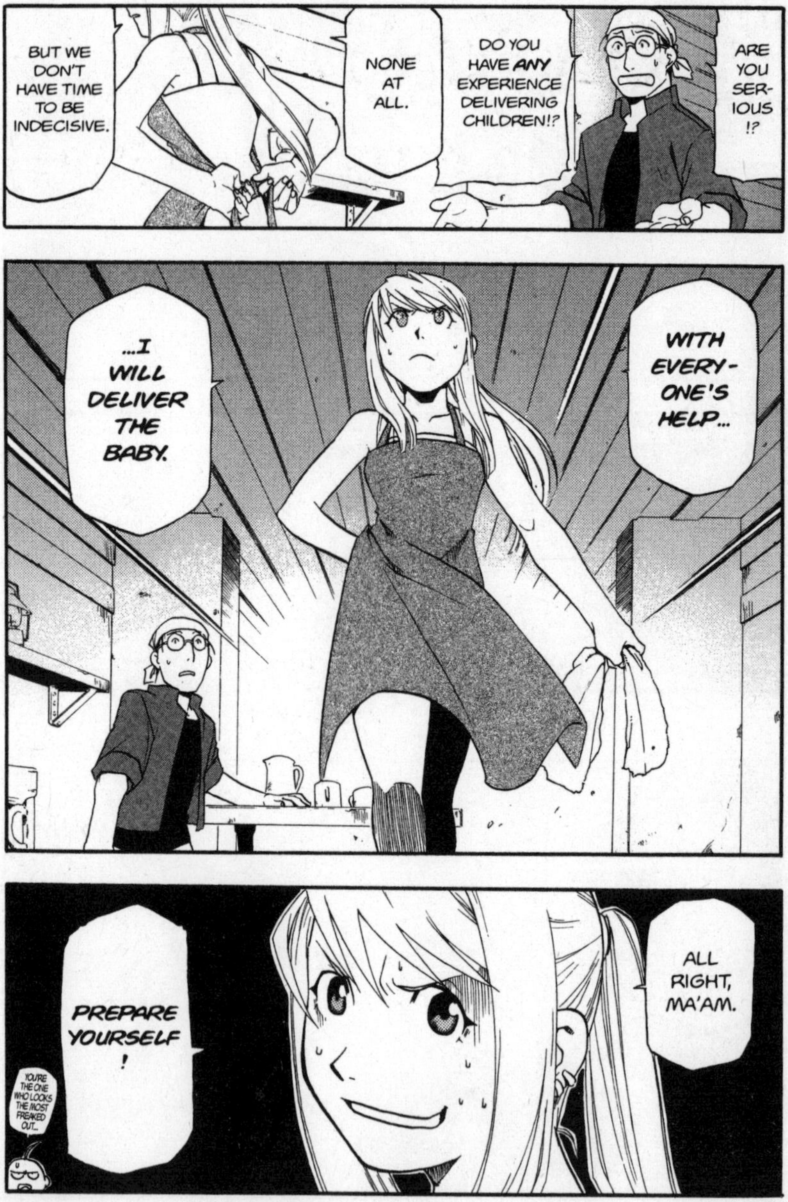
ARE YOU SERIOUS!?
DO YOU HAVE ANY EXPERIENCE DELIVERING CHILDREN!?
NONE AT ALL.
BUT WE DON'T HAVE TIME TO BE INDECISIVE.
WITH EVERY-ONE'S HELP...
...I WILL DELIVER THE BABY.
ALL RIGHT, MA'AM.
PREPARE YOURSELF!
YOU'RE THE ONE WHO LOOKS THE MOST FREAKED OUT...

Chapter 19: I'll Do It for You Guys!

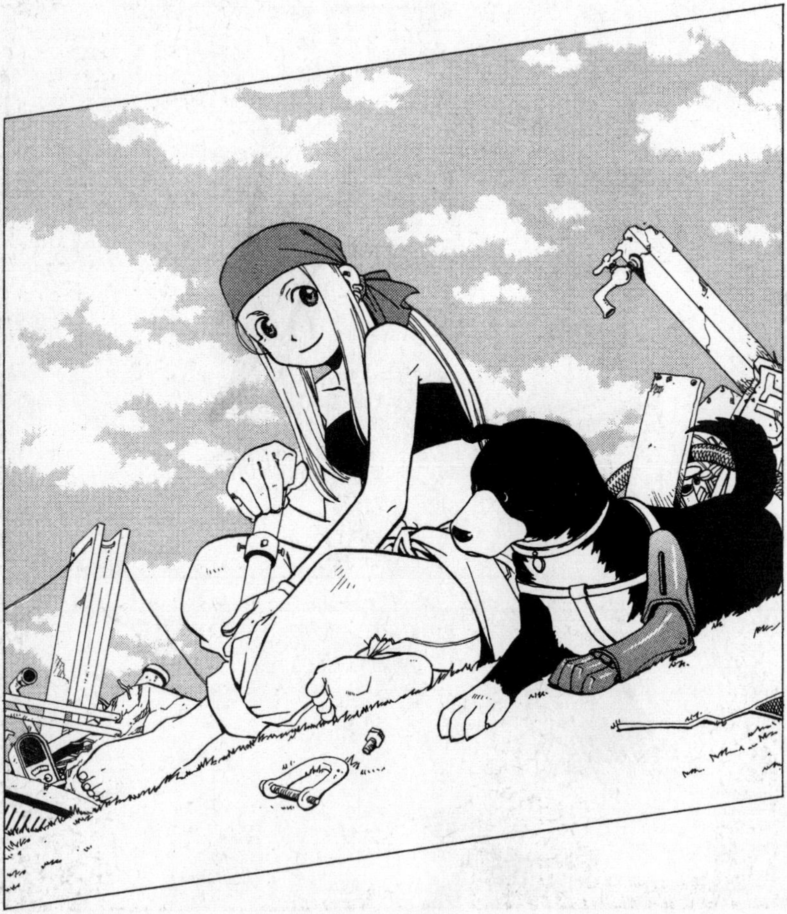

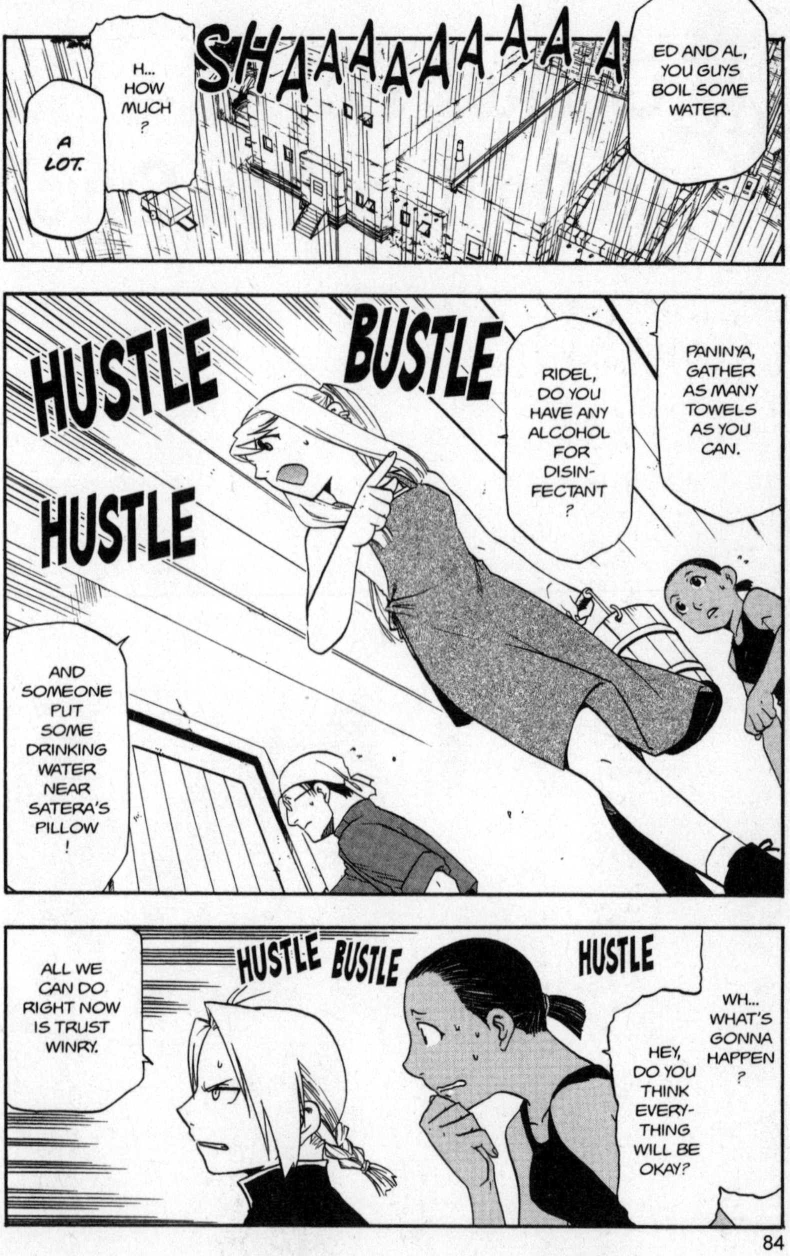
ED AND AL, YOU GUYS BOIL SOME WATER.
SHAAAAAAAAA
H... HOW MUCH?
A LOT.
PANINYA, GATHER AS MANY TOWELS AS YOU CAN.
RIDEL, DO YOU HAVE ANY ALCOHOL FOR DISIN-FECTANT?
BUSTLE
HUSTLE
HUSTLE
AND SOMEONE PUT SOME DRINKING WATER NEAR SATERA'S PILLOW!
WH... WHAT'S GONNA HAPPEN?
HEY, DO YOU THINK EVERY-THING WILL BE OKAY?
HUSTLE
BUSTLE
HUSTLE
ALL WE CAN DO RIGHT NOW IS TRUST WINRY.

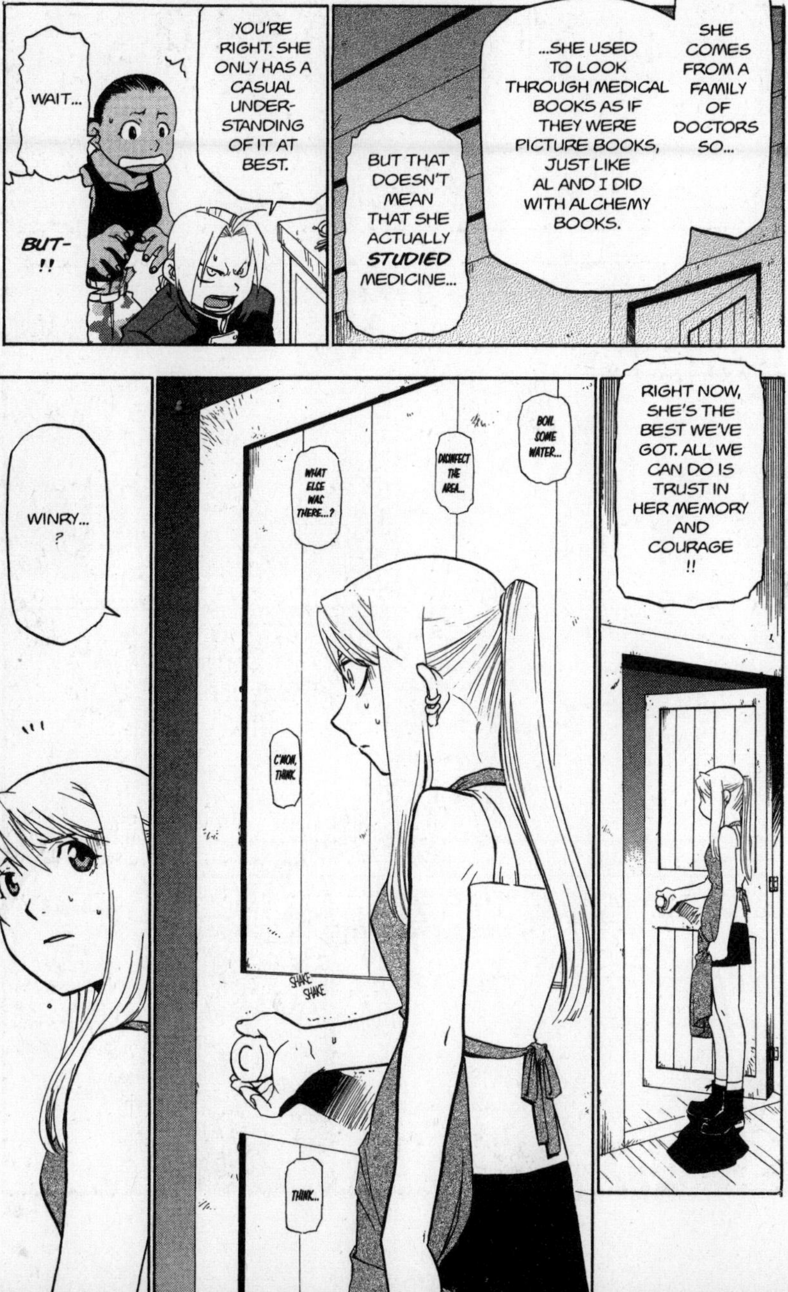
SHE COMES FROM A FAMILY OF DOCTORS SO...
...SHE USED TO LOOK THROUGH MEDICAL BOOKS AS IF THEY WERE PICTURE BOOKS, JUST LIKE AL AND I DID WITH ALCHEMY BOOKS.
BUT THAT DOESN'T MEAN THAT SHE ACTUALLY **STUDIED** MEDICINE...
YOU'RE RIGHT. SHE ONLY HAS A CASUAL UNDER-STANDING OF IT AT BEST.
WAIT...
BUT-!!
RIGHT NOW, SHE'S THE BEST WE'VE GOT. ALL WE CAN DO IS TRUST IN HER MEMORY AND COURAGE !!
BOIL SOME WATER...
DISINFECT THE AREA...
WHAT ELSE WAS THERE...?
C'MON, THINK.
SHAKE SHAKE
THINK...
WINRY...?

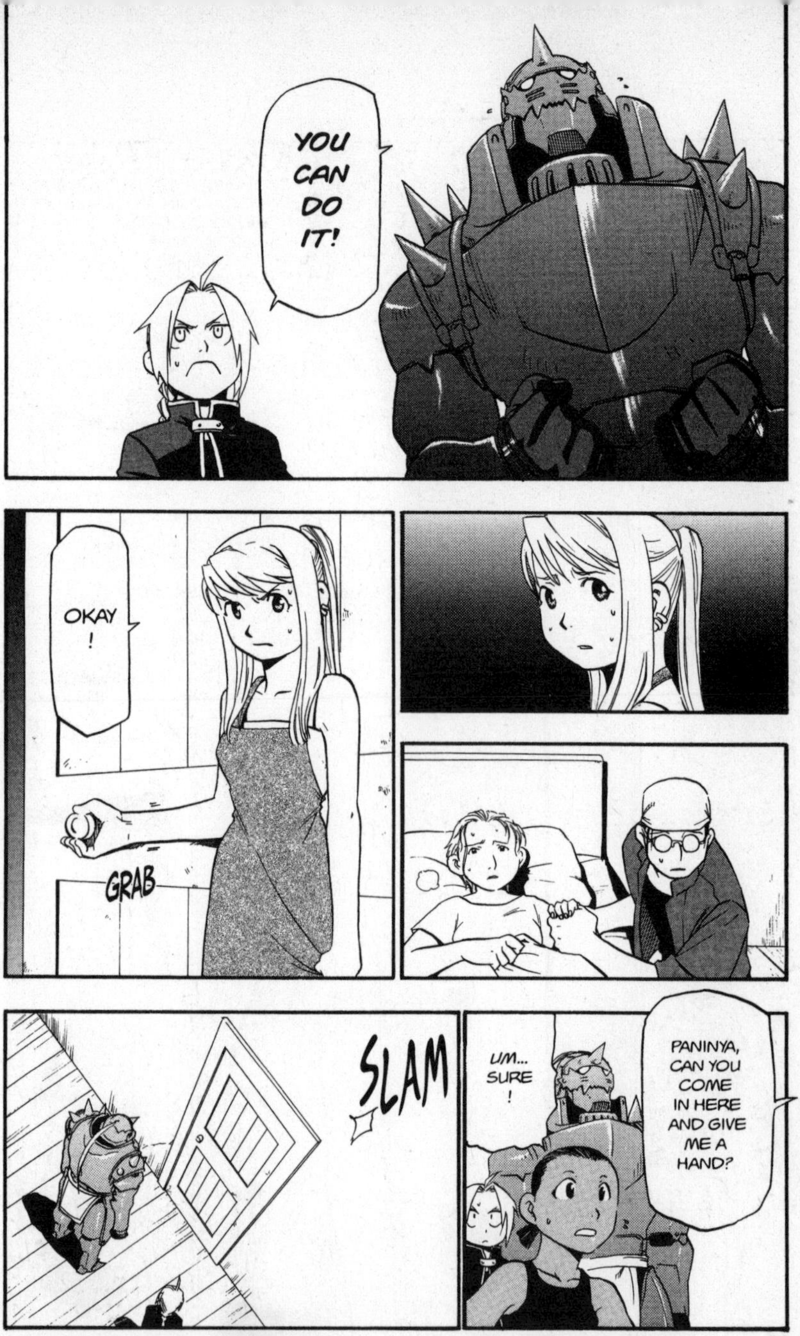
YOU CAN DO IT!
OKAY!
GRAB
PANINYA, CAN YOU COME IN HERE AND GIVE ME A HAND?
UM... SURE!
SLAM

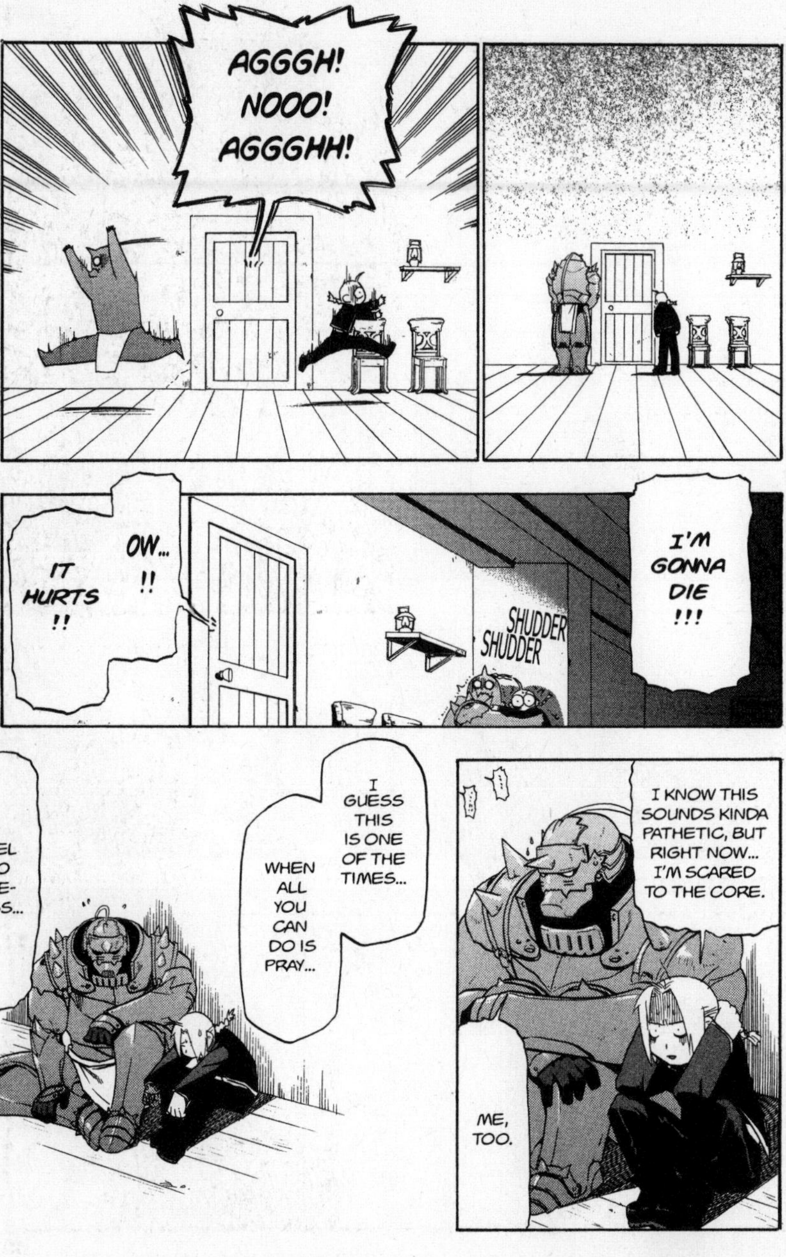
AGGGH! NOOO! AGGGHH!
I'M GONNA DIE!!!
SHUDDER SHUDDER
OW...!!
IT HURTS!!
I KNOW THIS SOUNDS KINDA PATHETIC, BUT RIGHT NOW... I'M SCARED TO THE CORE.
ME, TOO.
I GUESS THIS IS ONE OF THE TIMES...
WHEN ALL YOU CAN DO IS PRAY...
I FEEL SO USE-LESS...

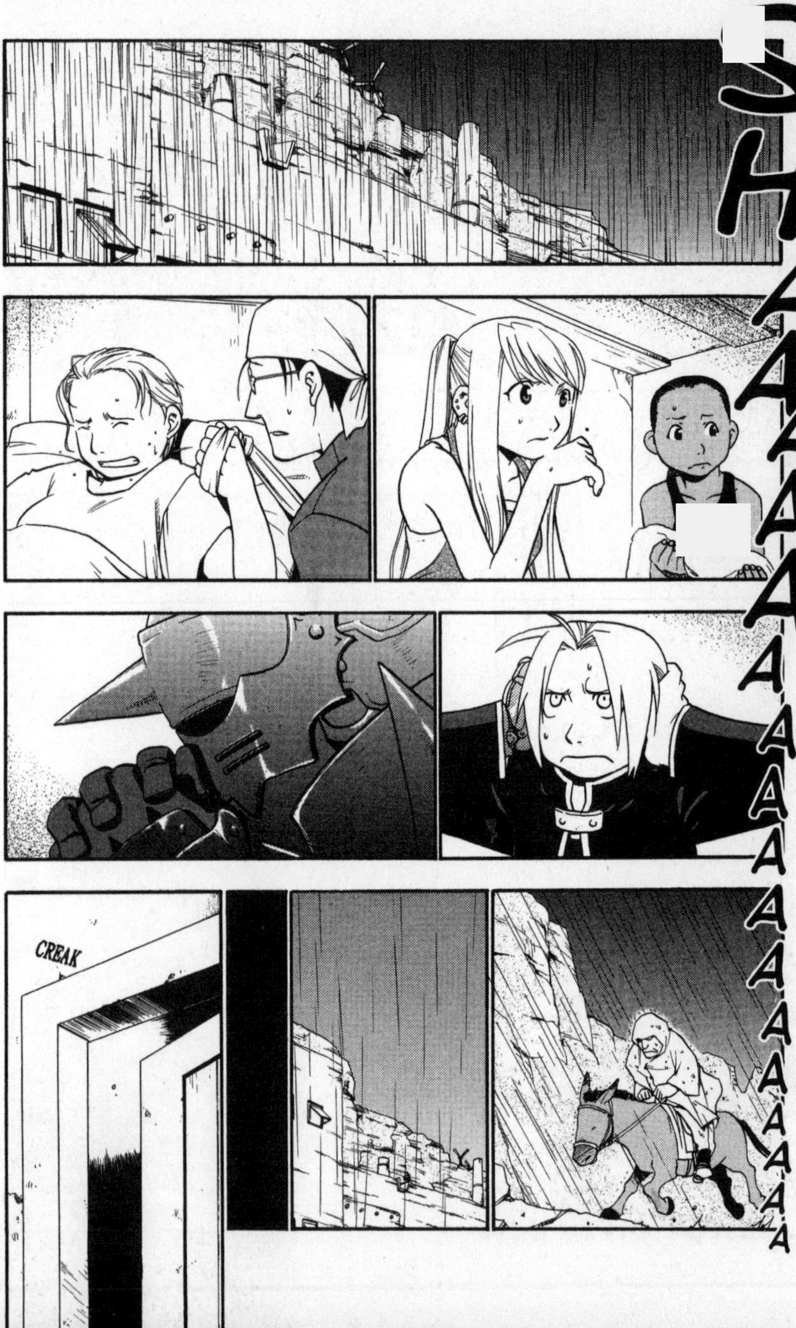
SHAAAAAAAAAAAAAAAAAAAA
CREAK

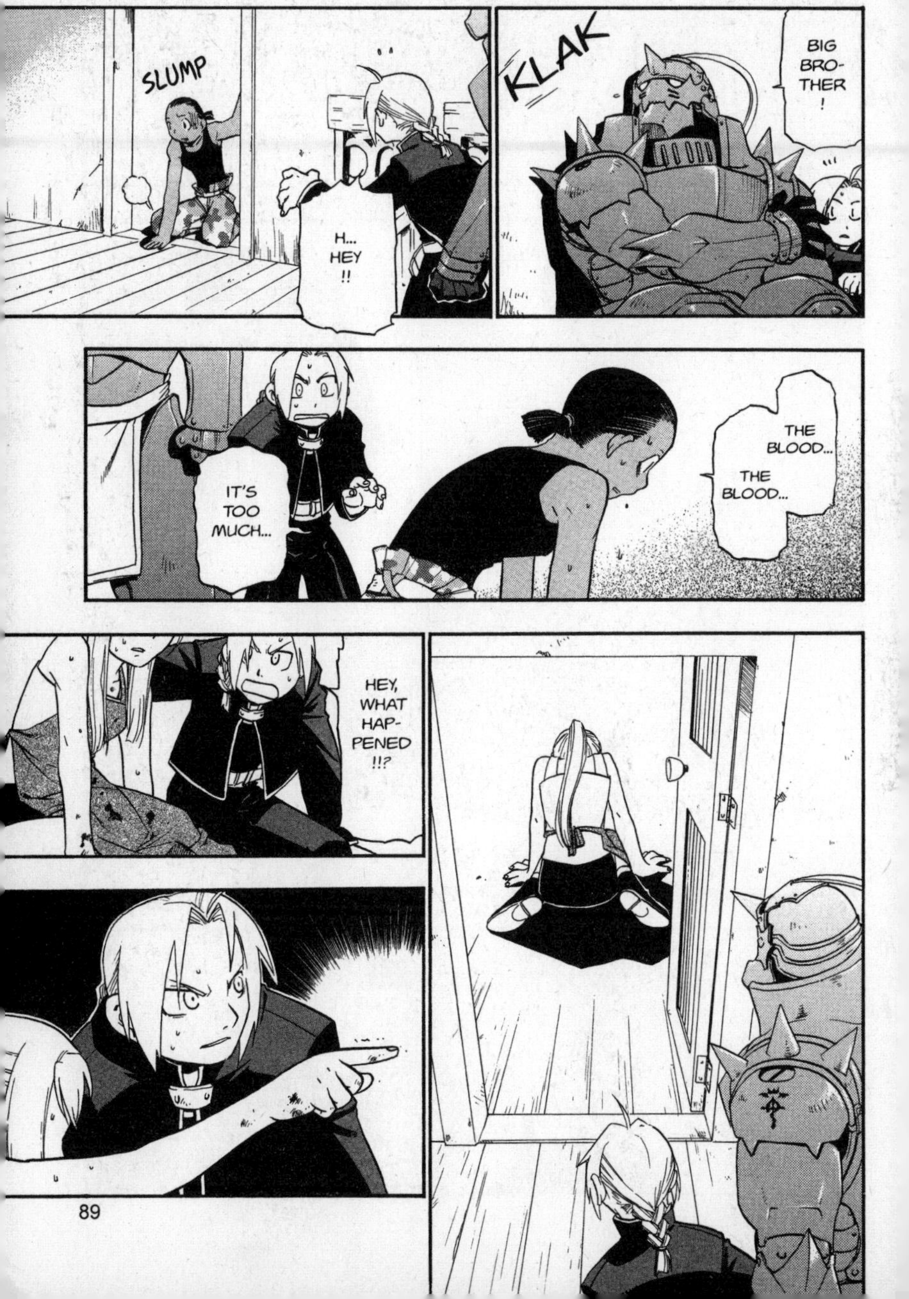
KLAK
BIG BRO-THER!
SLUMP
H... HEY!!
THE BLOOD... THE BLOOD...
IT'S TOO MUCH...
HEY, WHAT HAP-PENED!!?

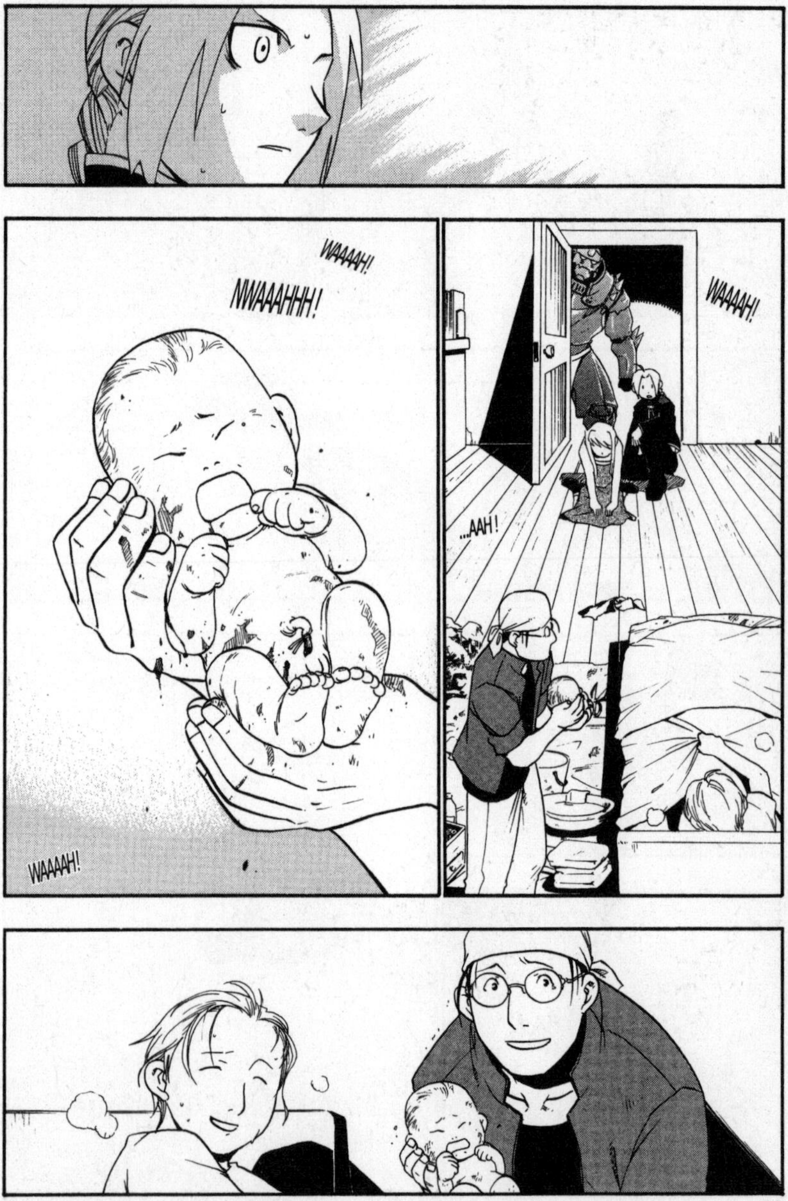
WAAAAH!
...AAH!
WAAAAH!
NWAAAHHH!
WAAAAH!

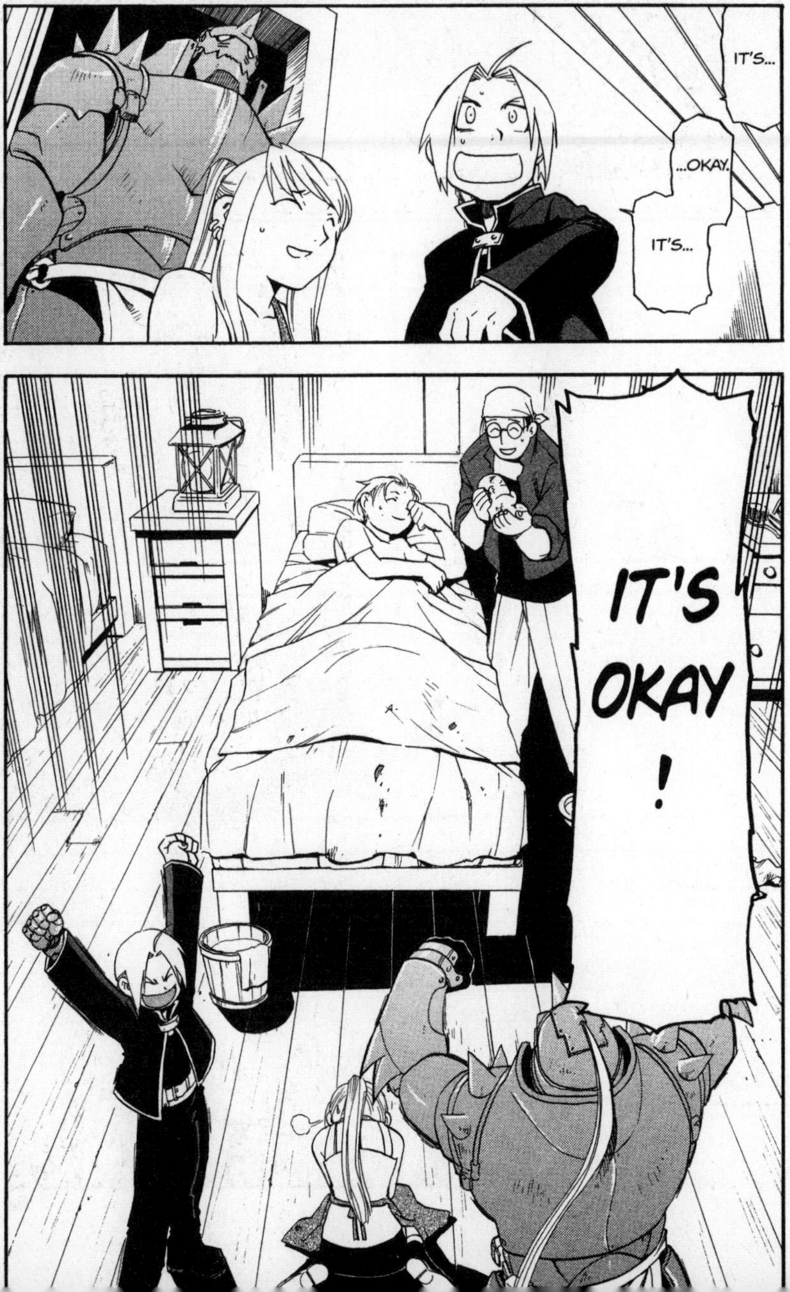
IT'S...
...OKAY.
IT'S...
IT'S OKAY!

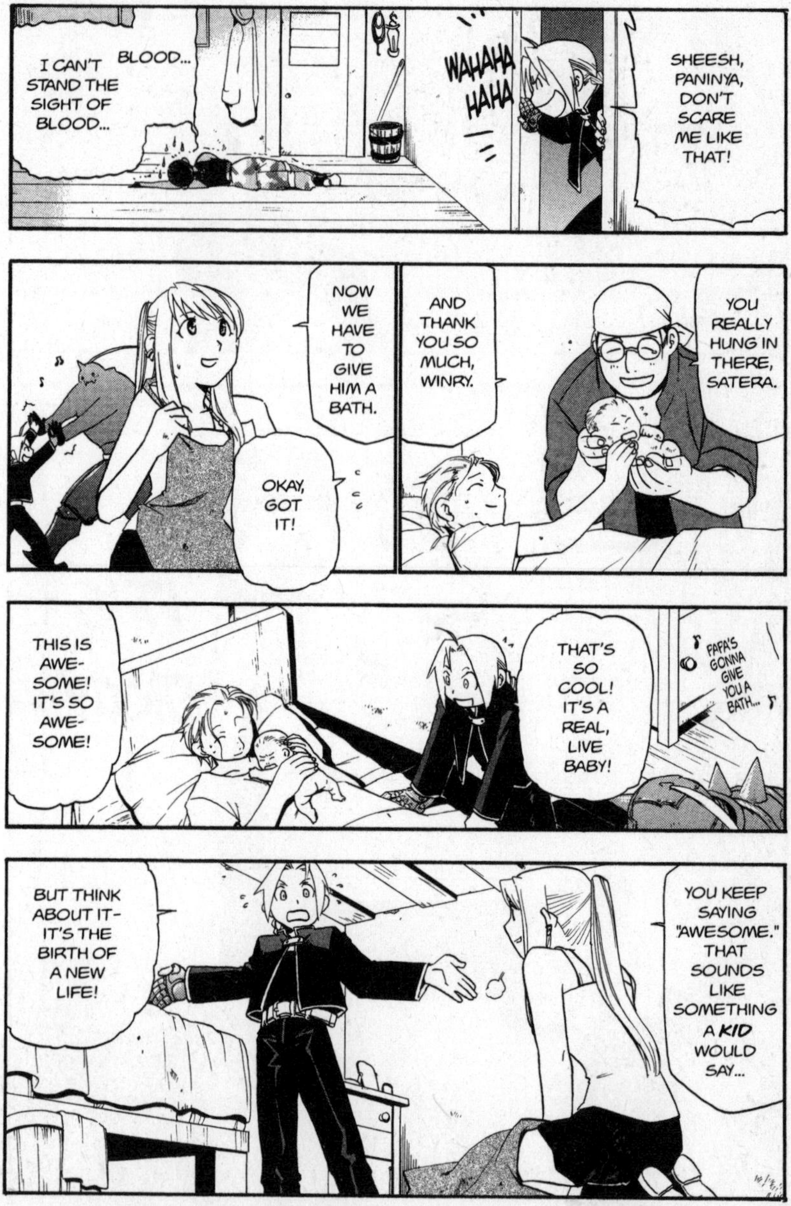
SHEESH, PANINYA, DON'T SCARE ME LIKE THAT!
WAHAHA HAHA
BLOOD...
I CAN'T STAND THE SIGHT OF BLOOD...
YOU REALLY HUNG IN THERE, SATERA.
AND THANK YOU SO MUCH, WINRY.
NOW WE HAVE TO GIVE HIM A BATH.
OKAY, GOT IT!
PAPA'S GONNA GIVE YOU A BATH...
THAT'S SO COOL! IT'S A REAL, LIVE BABY!
THIS IS AWESOME! IT'S SO AWESOME!
YOU KEEP SAYING "AWESOME." THAT SOUNDS LIKE SOMETHING A *KID* WOULD SAY...
BUT THINK ABOUT IT- IT'S THE BIRTH OF A NEW LIFE!

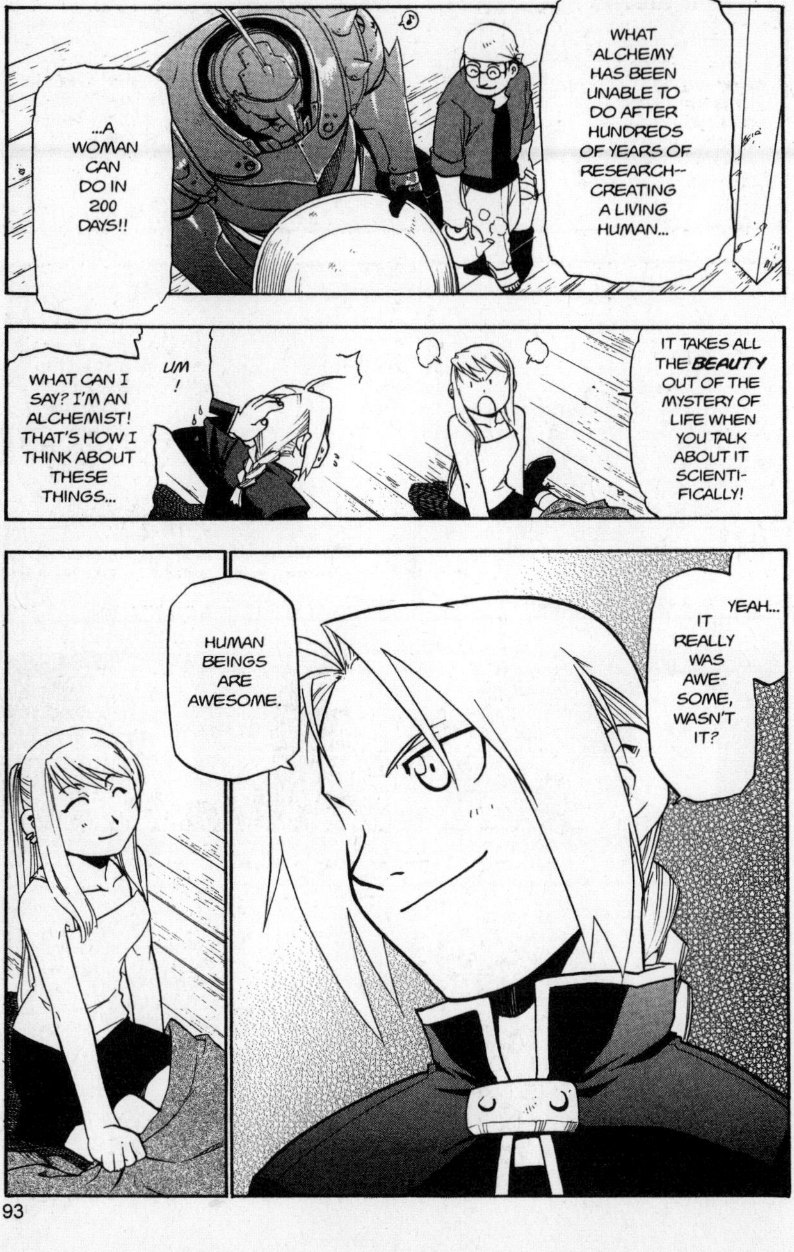
WHAT ALCHEMY HAS BEEN UNABLE TO DO AFTER HUNDREDS OF YEARS OF RESEARCH-- CREATING A LIVING HUMAN...
...A WOMAN CAN DO IN 200 DAYS!!
IT TAKES ALL THE ***BEAUTY*** OUT OF THE MYSTERY OF LIFE WHEN YOU TALK ABOUT IT SCIENTIFICALLY!
UM!
WHAT CAN I SAY? I'M AN ALCHEMIST! THAT'S HOW I THINK ABOUT THESE THINGS...
HUMAN BEINGS ARE AWESOME.
YEAH... IT REALLY WAS AWESOME, WASN'T IT?

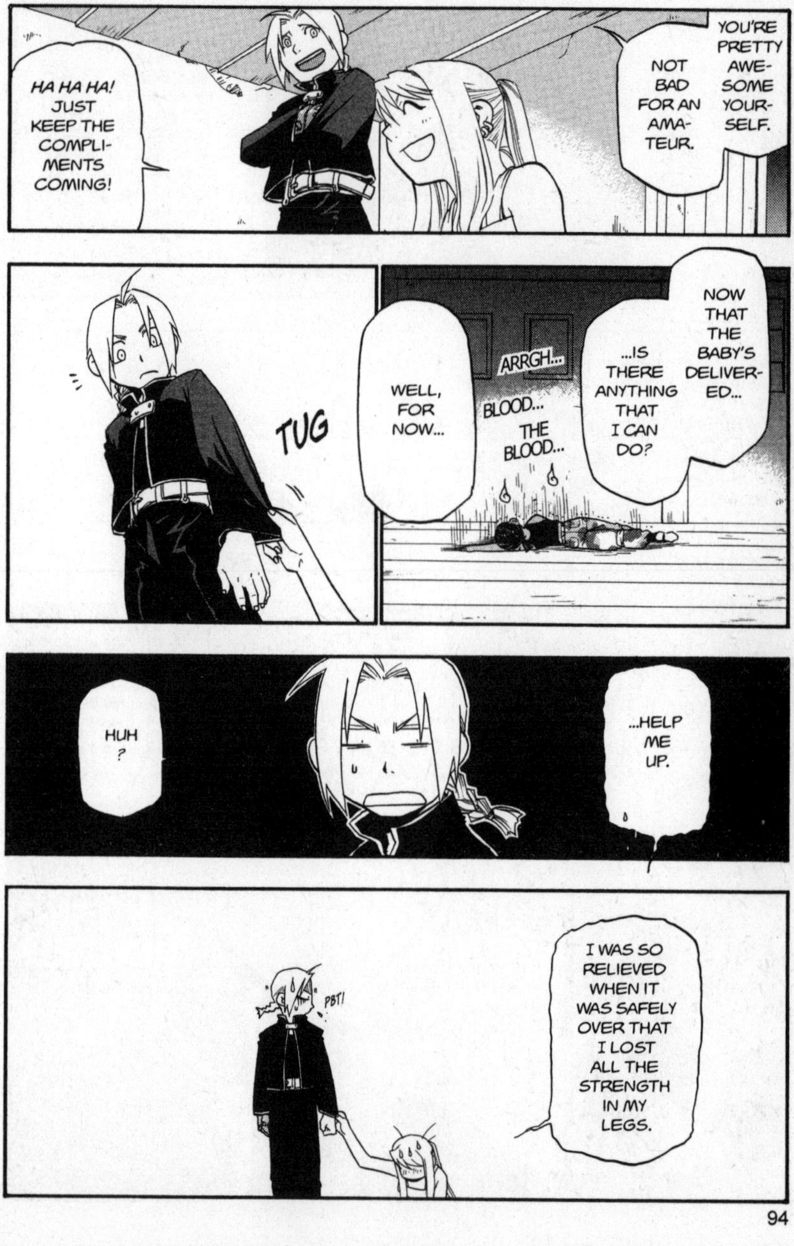
YOU'RE PRETTY AWE-SOME YOUR-SELF.
NOT BAD FOR AN AMA-TEUR.
HA HA HA! JUST KEEP THE COMPLI-MENTS COMING!
NOW THAT THE BABY'S DELIVER-ED...
...IS THERE ANYTHING THAT I CAN DO?
ARRGH...
BLOOD...
THE BLOOD...
WELL, FOR NOW...
TUG
...HELP ME UP.
HUH?
I WAS SO RELIEVED WHEN IT WAS SAFELY OVER THAT I LOST ALL THE STRENGTH IN MY LEGS.
PBT!

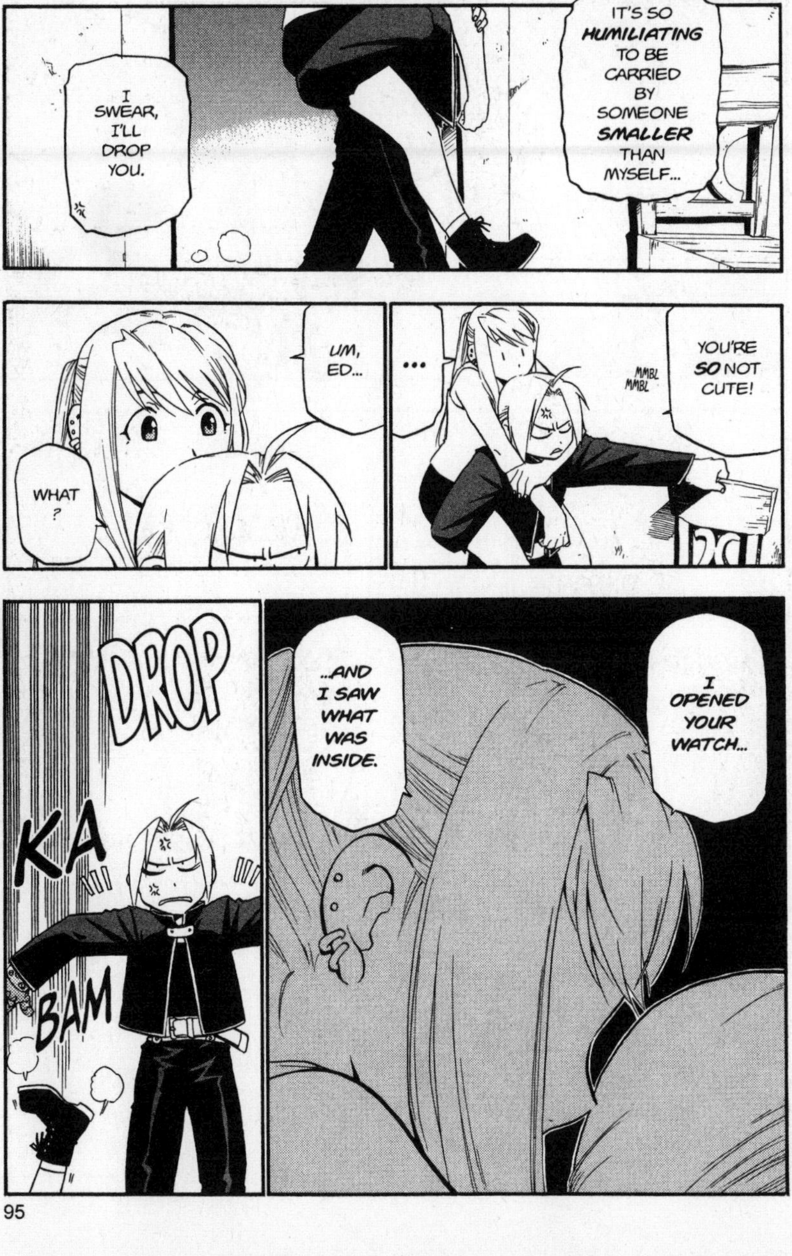
IT'S SO HUMILIATING TO BE CARRIED BY SOMEONE SMALLER THAN MYSELF...
I SWEAR, I'LL DROP YOU.
YOU'RE SO NOT CUTE!
MMBL MMBL
...
UM, ED...
WHAT?
I OPENED YOUR WATCH...
...AND I SAW WHAT WAS INSIDE.
DROP
KA
BAM

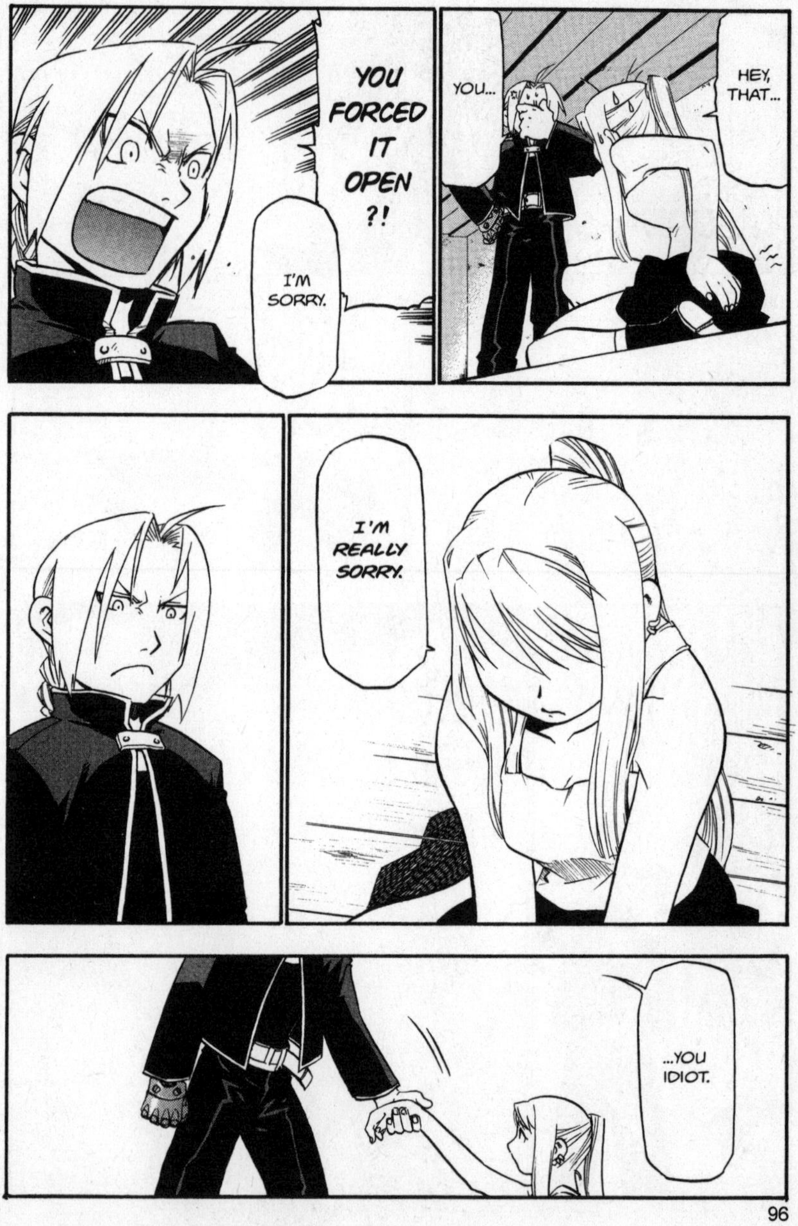

HEY, THAT...
YOU...
YOU FORCED IT OPEN ?!
I'M SORRY.
I'M REALLY SORRY.
...YOU IDIOT.

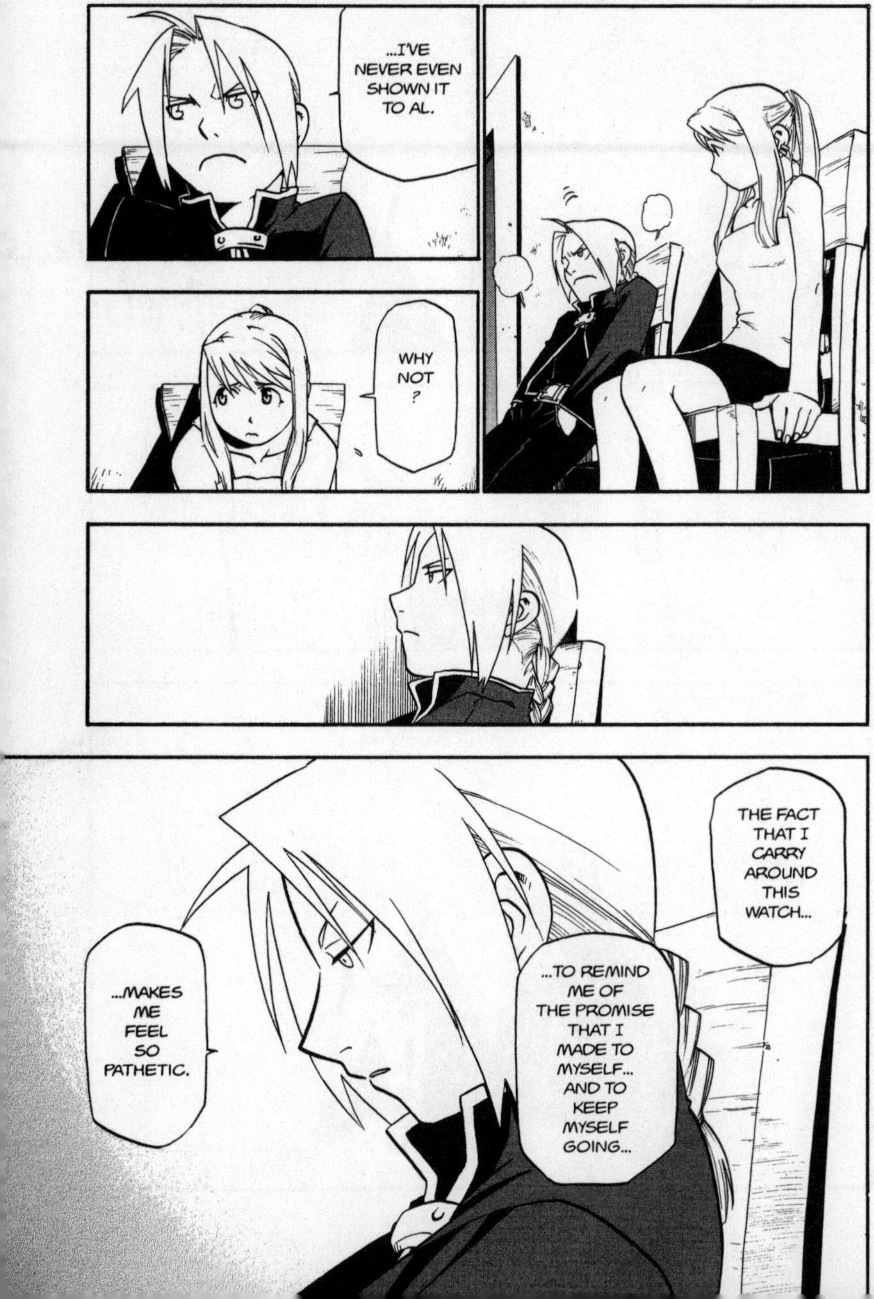
...I'VE NEVER EVEN SHOWN IT TO AL.
WHY NOT ?
THE FACT THAT I CARRY AROUND THIS WATCH...
...TO REMIND ME OF THE PROMISE THAT I MADE TO MYSELF... AND TO KEEP MYSELF GOING...
...MAKES ME FEEL SO PATHETIC.

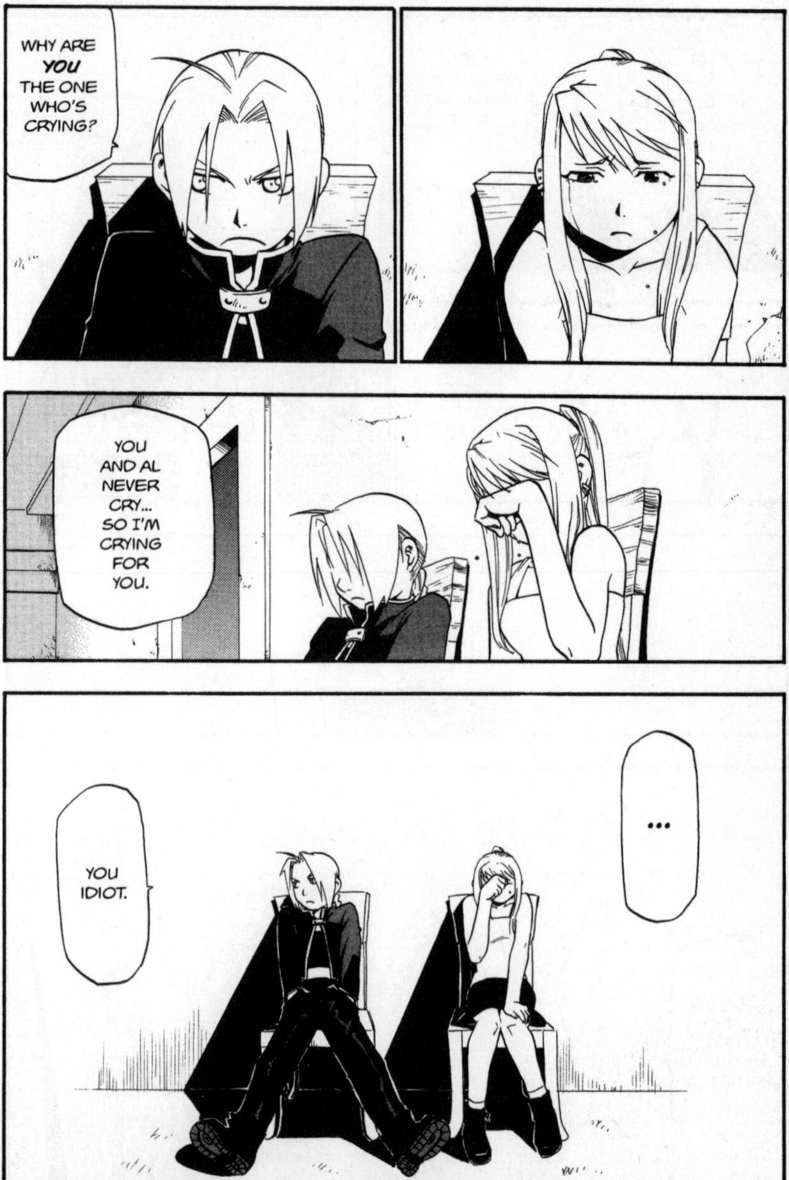
WHY ARE ***YOU*** THE ONE WHO'S CRYING?
YOU AND AL NEVER CRY... SO I'M CRYING FOR YOU.
...
YOU IDIOT.

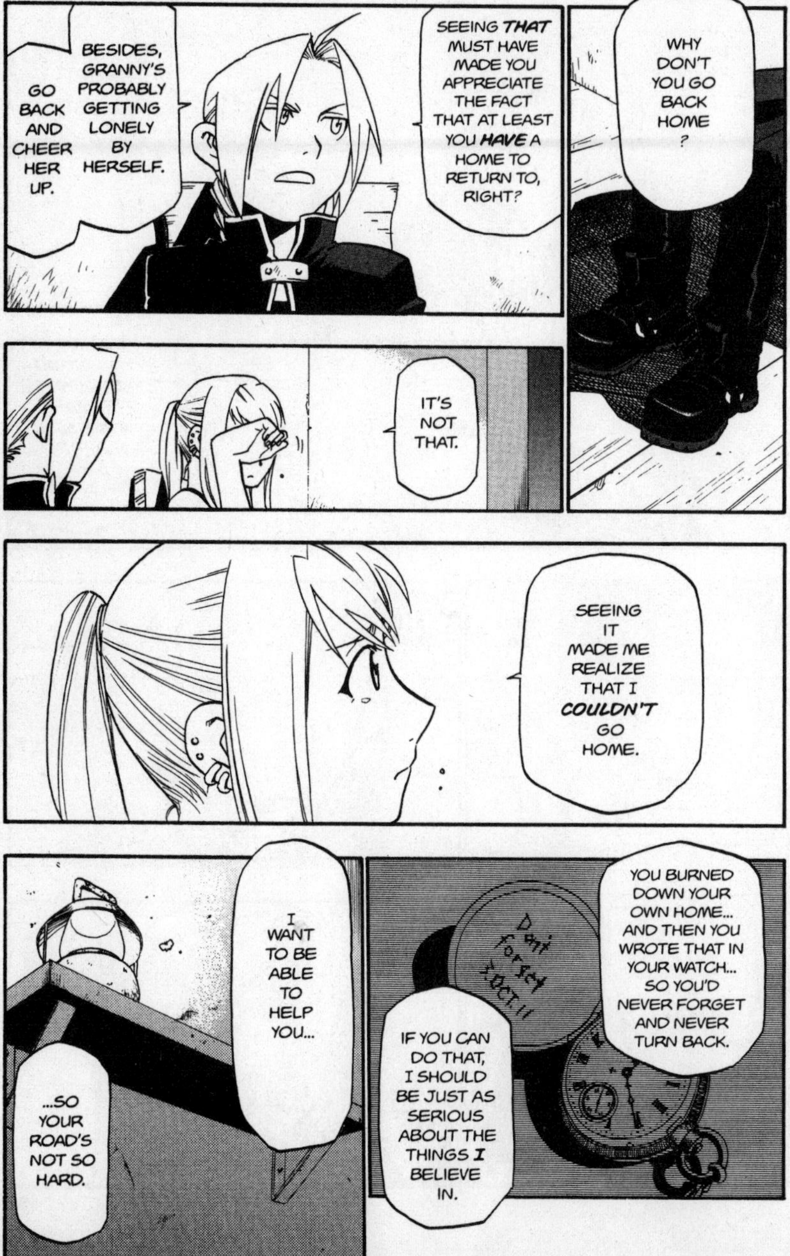
WHY DON'T YOU GO BACK HOME ?
SEEING **THAT** MUST HAVE MADE YOU APPRECIATE THE FACT THAT AT LEAST YOU **HAVE** A HOME TO RETURN TO, RIGHT?
BESIDES, GRANNY'S PROBABLY GETTING LONELY BY HERSELF.
GO BACK AND CHEER HER UP.
IT'S NOT THAT.
SEEING IT MADE ME REALIZE THAT I **COULDN'T** GO HOME.
YOU BURNED DOWN YOUR OWN HOME... AND THEN YOU WROTE THAT IN YOUR WATCH... SO YOU'D NEVER FORGET AND NEVER TURN BACK.
Don't forget 3.OCT.11
IF YOU CAN DO THAT, I SHOULD BE JUST AS SERIOUS ABOUT THE THINGS **I** BELIEVE IN.
I WANT TO BE ABLE TO HELP YOU...
...SO YOUR ROAD'S NOT SO HARD.

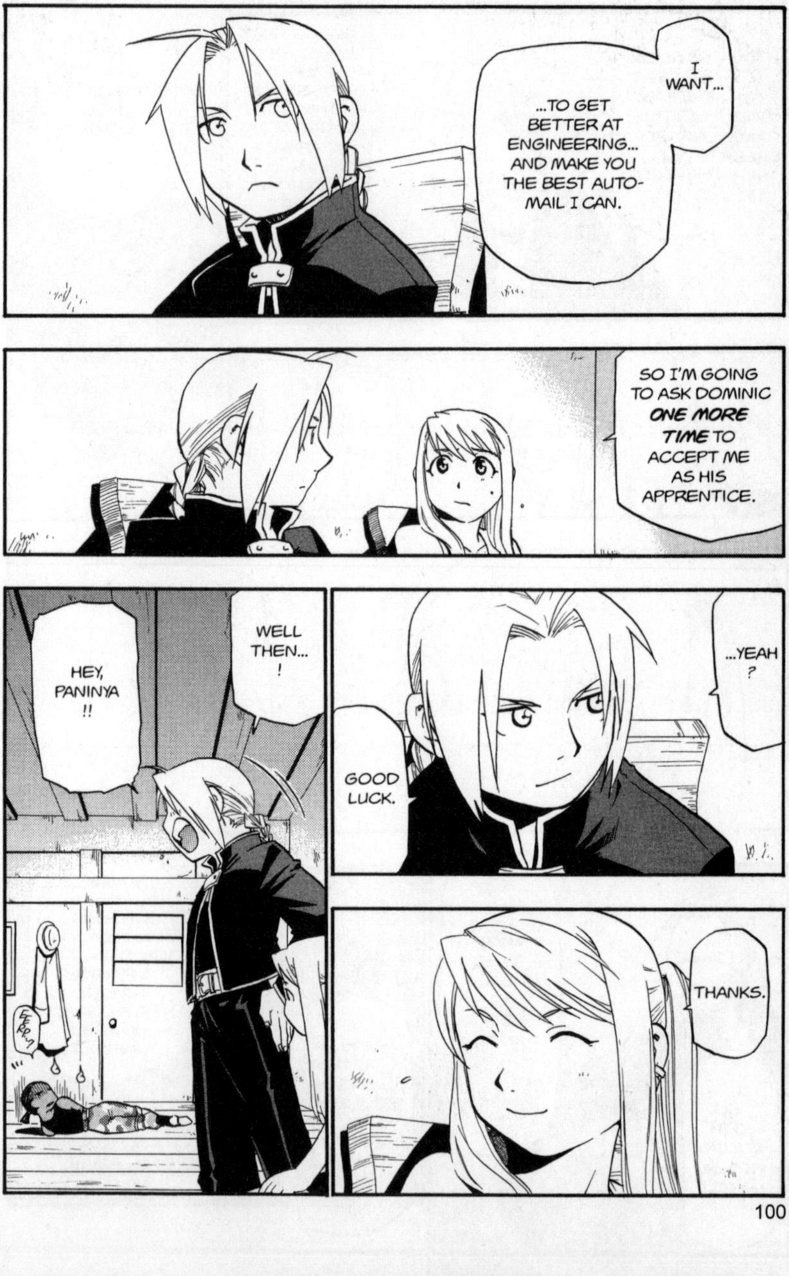
I WANT...
...TO GET BETTER AT ENGINEERING... AND MAKE YOU THE BEST AUTO-MAIL I CAN.
SO I'M GOING TO ASK DOMINIC ONE MORE TIME TO ACCEPT ME AS HIS APPRENTICE.
...YEAH?
GOOD LUCK.
THANKS.
WELL THEN...!
HEY, PANINYA!!
EERR...?

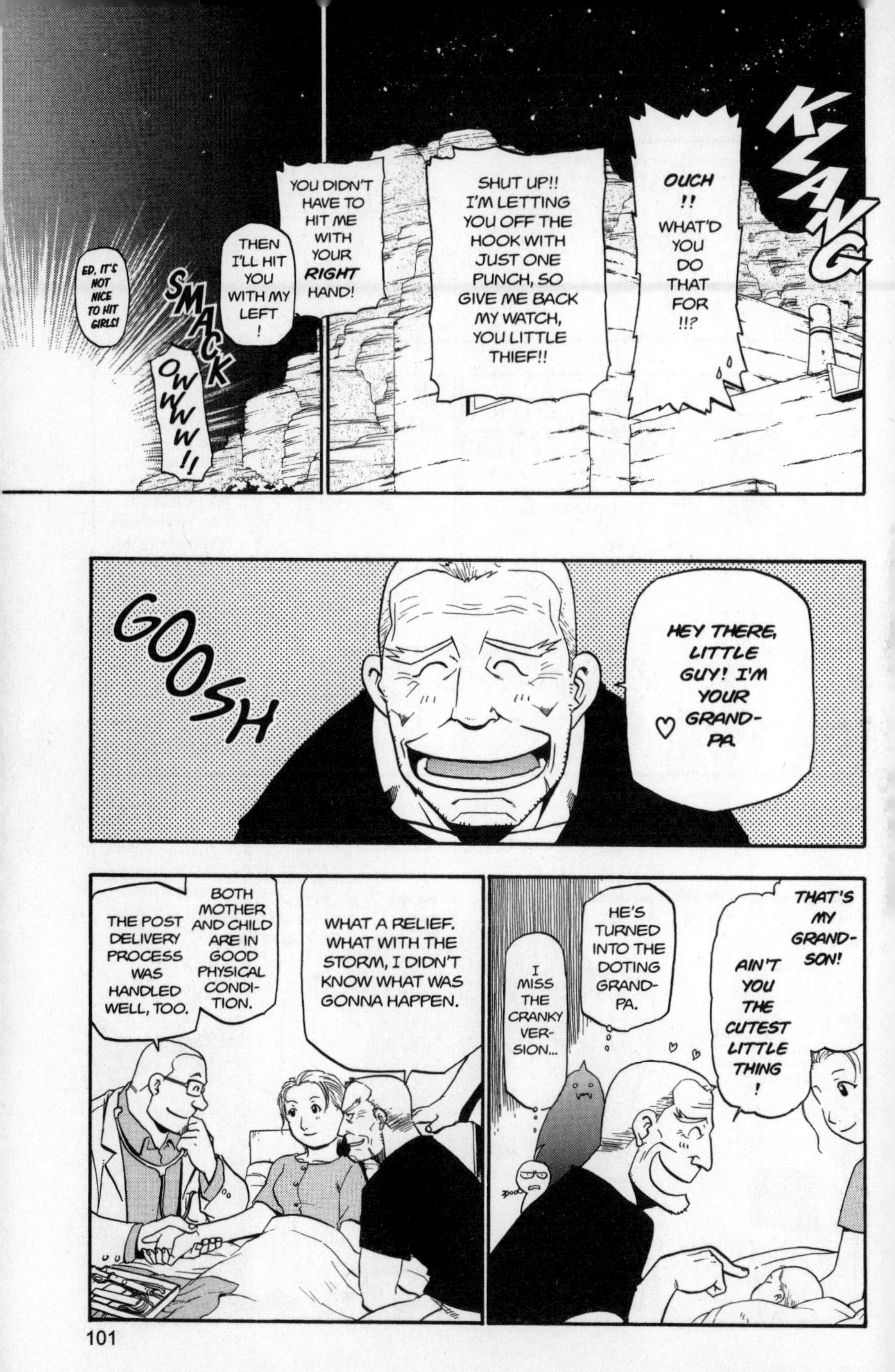
KLANG
OUCH!! WHAT'D YOU DO THAT FOR!!?
SHUT UP!! I'M LETTING YOU OFF THE HOOK WITH JUST ONE PUNCH, SO GIVE ME BACK MY WATCH, YOU LITTLE THIEF!!
YOU DIDN'T HAVE TO HIT ME WITH YOUR RIGHT HAND!
THEN I'LL HIT YOU WITH MY LEFT!
SMACK
OWWWW!!
ED, IT'S NOT NICE TO HIT GIRLS!
HEY THERE, LITTLE GUY! I'M YOUR GRAND-PA ♡
GOOSH
THAT'S MY GRAND-SON!
AIN'T YOU THE CUTEST LITTLE THING!
HE'S TURNED INTO THE DOTING GRAND-PA.
I MISS THE CRANKY VER-SION...
WHAT A RELIEF. WHAT WITH THE STORM, I DIDN'T KNOW WHAT WAS GONNA HAPPEN.
BOTH MOTHER AND CHILD ARE IN GOOD PHYSICAL CONDI-TION.
THE POST DELIVERY PROCESS WAS HANDLED WELL, TOO.

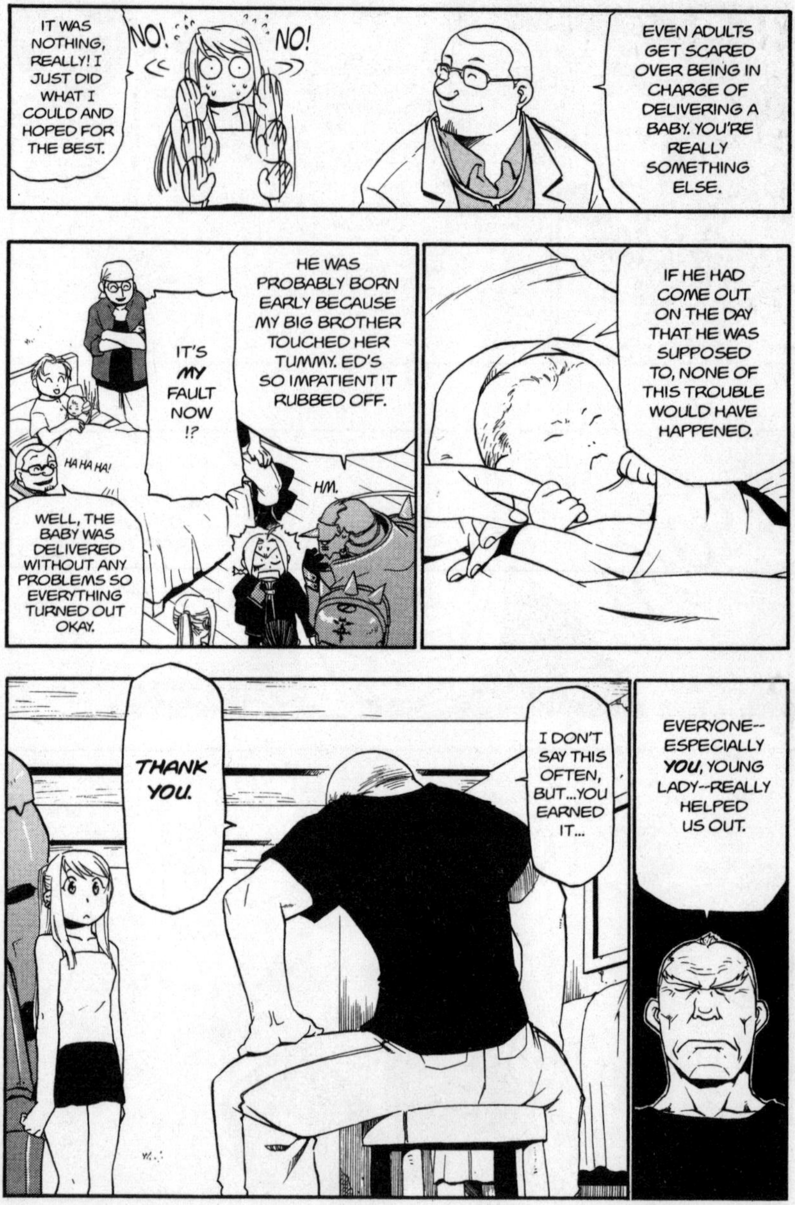
EVEN ADULTS GET SCARED OVER BEING IN CHARGE OF DELIVERING A BABY. YOU'RE REALLY SOMETHING ELSE.
NO!
NO!
IT WAS NOTHING, REALLY! I JUST DID WHAT I COULD AND HOPED FOR THE BEST.
IF HE HAD COME OUT ON THE DAY THAT HE WAS SUPPOSED TO, NONE OF THIS TROUBLE WOULD HAVE HAPPENED.
HE WAS PROBABLY BORN EARLY BECAUSE MY BIG BROTHER TOUCHED HER TUMMY. ED'S SO IMPATIENT IT RUBBED OFF.
IT'S MY FAULT NOW!?
HM.
HA HA HA!
WELL, THE BABY WAS DELIVERED WITHOUT ANY PROBLEMS SO EVERYTHING TURNED OUT OKAY.
EVERYONE--ESPECIALLY YOU, YOUNG LADY--REALLY HELPED US OUT.
I DON'T SAY THIS OFTEN, BUT...YOU EARNED IT...
THANK YOU.

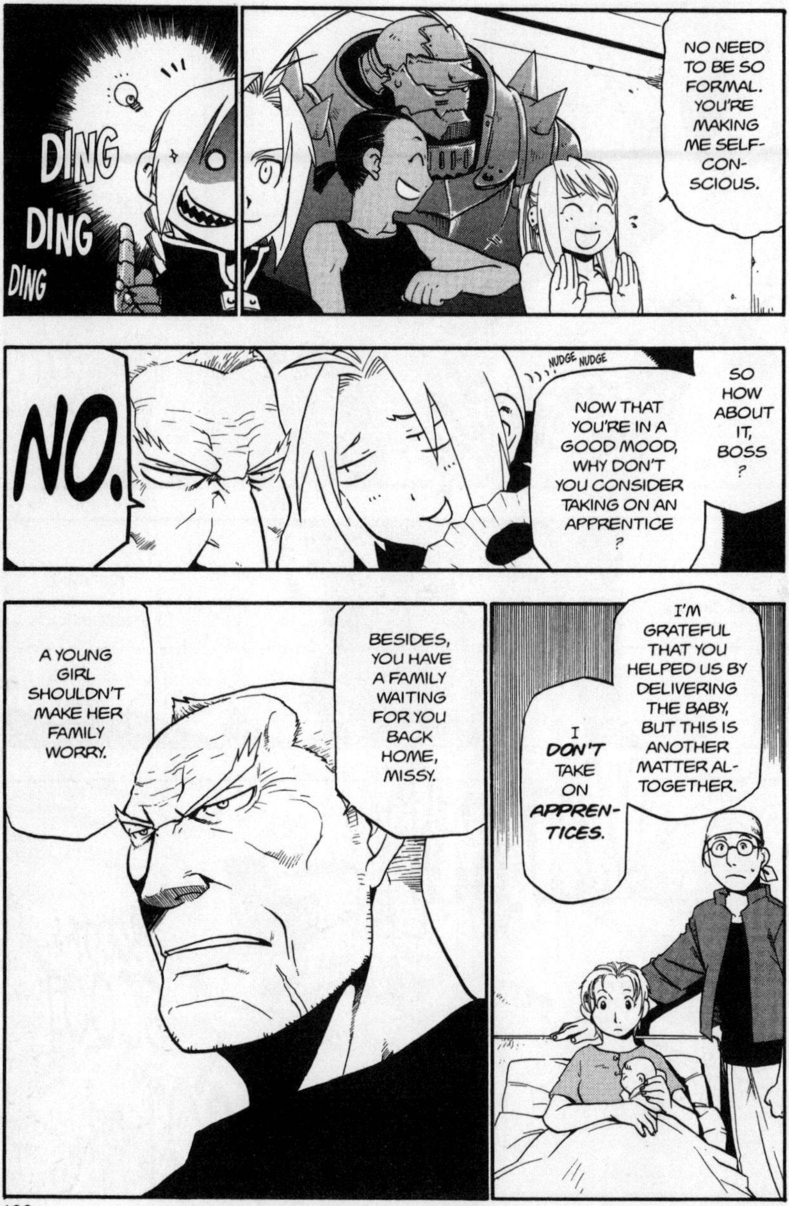
NO NEED TO BE SO FORMAL. YOU'RE MAKING ME SELF-CONSCIOUS.
DING DING DING
SO HOW ABOUT IT, BOSS?
NUDGE NUDGE
NOW THAT YOU'RE IN A GOOD MOOD, WHY DON'T YOU CONSIDER TAKING ON AN APPRENTICE?
NO.
I'M GRATEFUL THAT YOU HELPED US BY DELIVERING THE BABY, BUT THIS IS ANOTHER MATTER ALTOGETHER.
I DON'T TAKE ON APPRENTICES.
BESIDES, YOU HAVE A FAMILY WAITING FOR YOU BACK HOME, MISSY.
A YOUNG GIRL SHOULDN'T MAKE HER FAMILY WORRY.

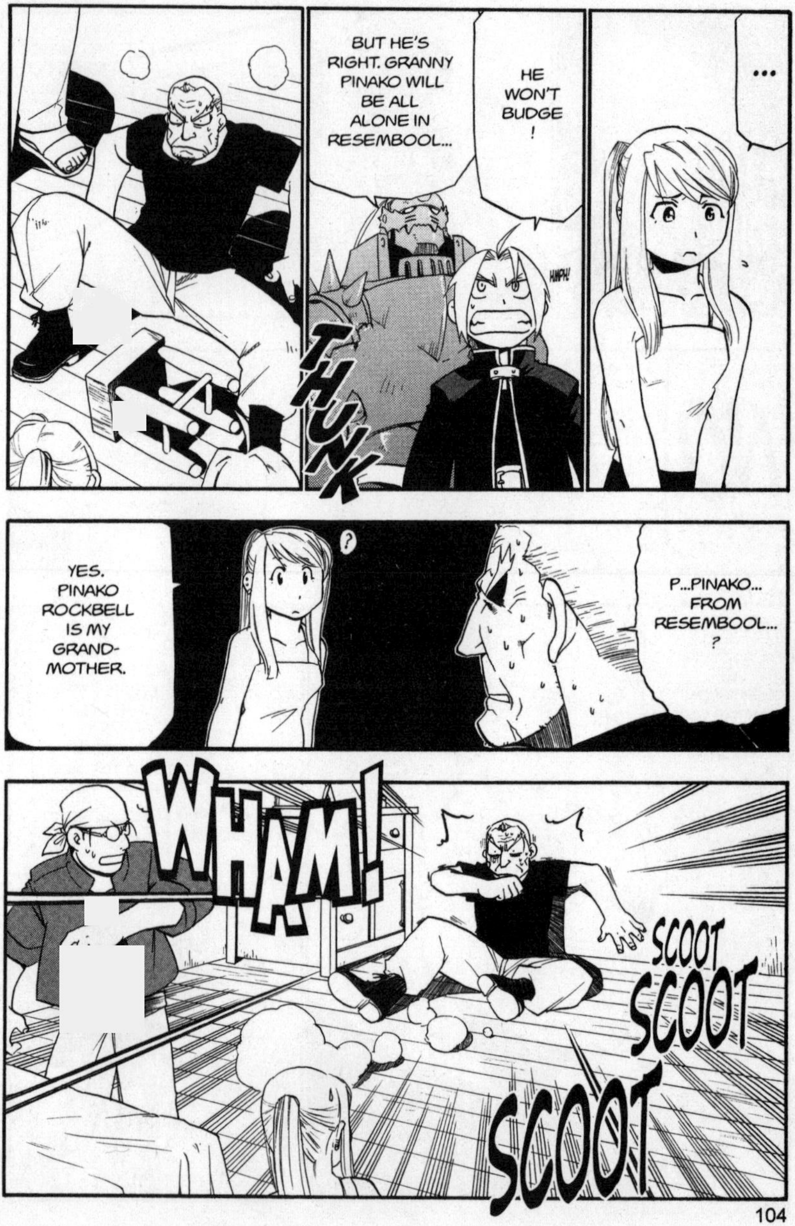
...
HE WON'T BUDGE!
BUT HE'S RIGHT. GRANNY PINAKO WILL BE ALL ALONE IN RESEMBOOL...
HMPH!
THUNK
P...PINAKO... FROM RESEMBOOL...?
?
YES. PINAKO ROCKBELL IS MY GRAND-MOTHER.
WHAM!
SCOOT
SCOOT
SCOOT

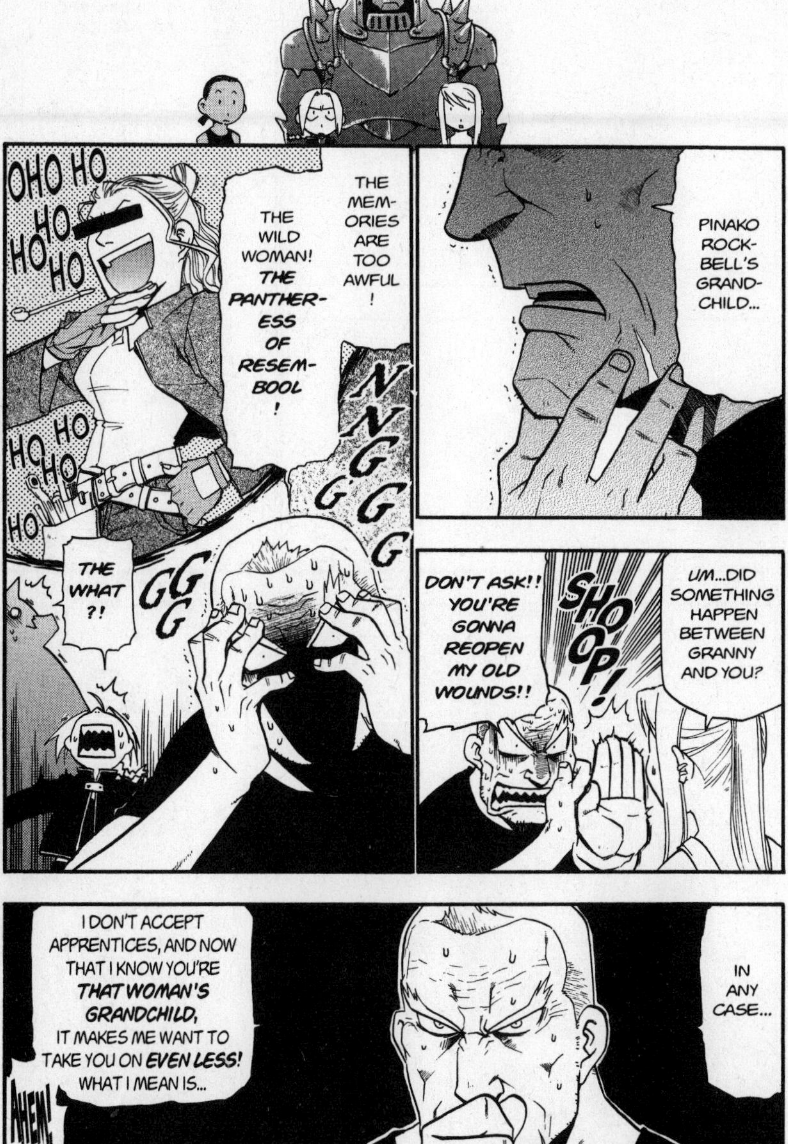
PINAKO ROCKBELL'S GRANDCHILD...
UM...DID SOMETHING HAPPEN BETWEEN GRANNY AND YOU?
SHOOP!
DON'T ASK!! YOU'RE GONNA REOPEN MY OLD WOUNDS!!
THE MEMORIES ARE TOO AWFUL!
THE WILD WOMAN! THE PANTHERESS OF RESEMBOOL!
OHO HO HO HO HO
NNGGGGGG
HO HO HO HO
THE WHAT?!
GGG
IN ANY CASE...
I DON'T ACCEPT APPRENTICES, AND NOW THAT I KNOW YOU'RE THAT WOMAN'S GRANDCHILD, IT MAKES ME WANT TO TAKE YOU ON EVEN LESS! WHAT I MEAN IS...
AHEM!

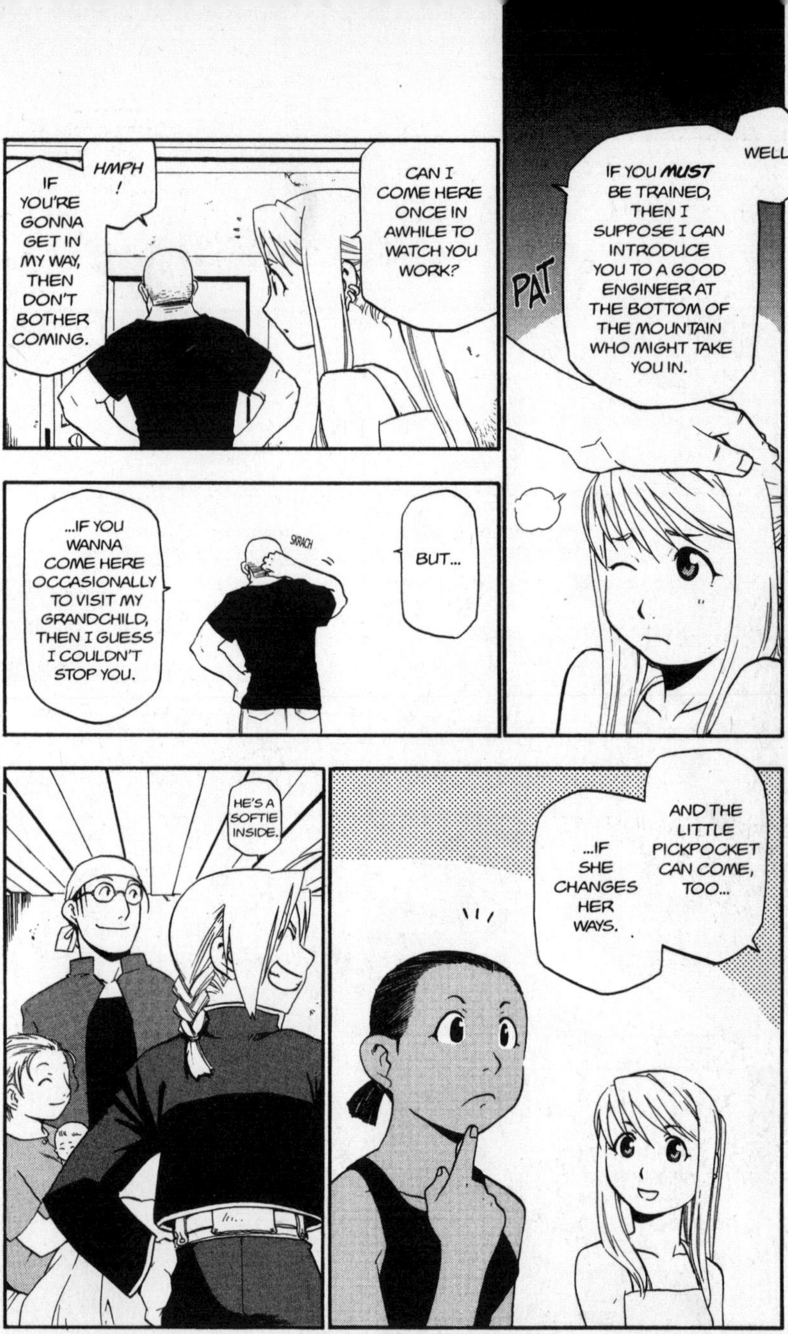
WELL...
IF YOU **MUST** BE TRAINED, THEN I SUPPOSE I CAN INTRODUCE YOU TO A GOOD ENGINEER AT THE BOTTOM OF THE MOUNTAIN WHO MIGHT TAKE YOU IN.
PAT
CAN I COME HERE ONCE IN AWHILE TO WATCH YOU WORK?
HMPH!
IF YOU'RE GONNA GET IN MY WAY, THEN DON'T BOTHER COMING.
BUT...
SKRACH
...IF YOU WANNA COME HERE OCCASIONALLY TO VISIT MY GRANDCHILD, THEN I GUESS I COULDN'T STOP YOU.
AND THE LITTLE PICKPOCKET CAN COME, TOO...
...IF SHE CHANGES HER WAYS.
HE'S A SOFTIE INSIDE.

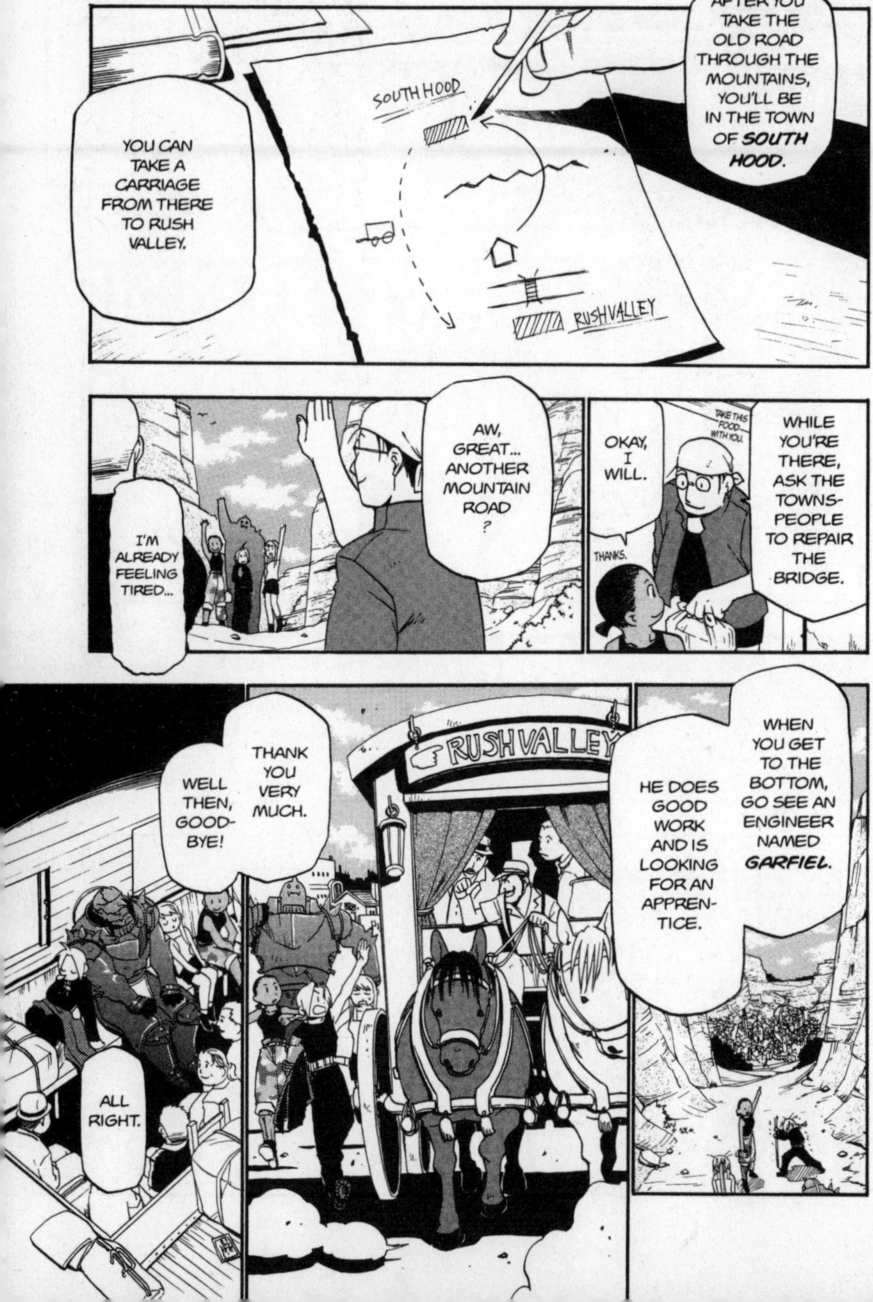
AFTER YOU TAKE THE OLD ROAD THROUGH THE MOUNTAINS, YOU'LL BE IN THE TOWN OF **SOUTH HOOD**.
SOUTH HOOD
RUSH VALLEY
YOU CAN TAKE A CARRIAGE FROM THERE TO RUSH VALLEY.
WHILE YOU'RE THERE, ASK THE TOWNS-PEOPLE TO REPAIR THE BRIDGE.
TAKE THIS FOOD WITH YOU.
OKAY, I WILL.
THANKS.
AW, GREAT... ANOTHER MOUNTAIN ROAD?
I'M ALREADY FEELING TIRED...
WHEN YOU GET TO THE BOTTOM, GO SEE AN ENGINEER NAMED **GARFIEL**.
HE DOES GOOD WORK AND IS LOOKING FOR AN APPREN-TICE.
RUSH VALLEY
THANK YOU VERY MUCH.
WELL THEN, GOOD-BYE!
ALL RIGHT.

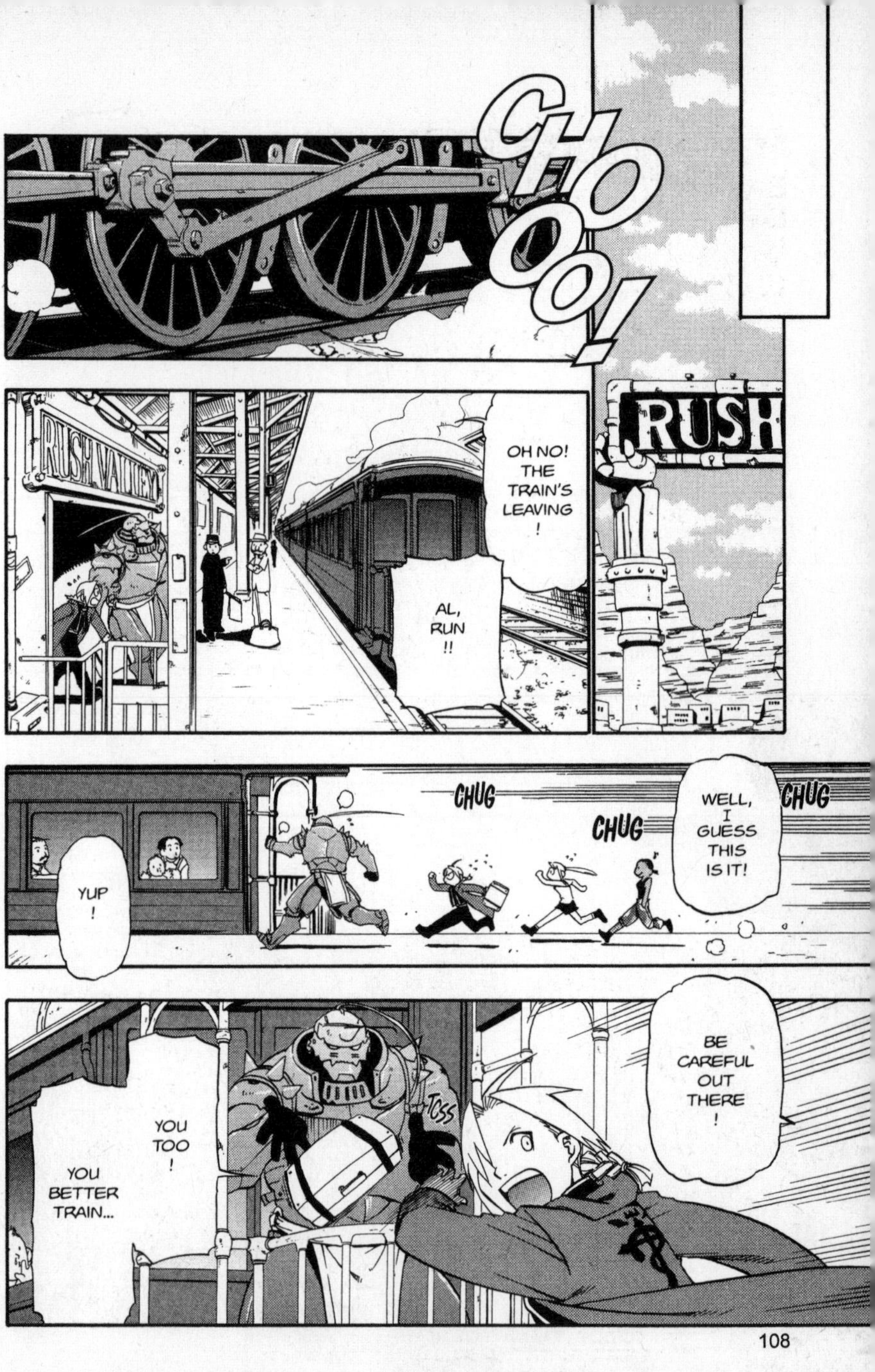
RUSH
CHOOOO!
RUSH VALLEY
OH NO! THE TRAIN'S LEAVING!
AL, RUN!!
WELL, I GUESS THIS IS IT!
CHUG
CHUG
CHUG
YUP!
BE CAREFUL OUT THERE!
TCSS
YOU TOO!
YOU BETTER TRAIN...

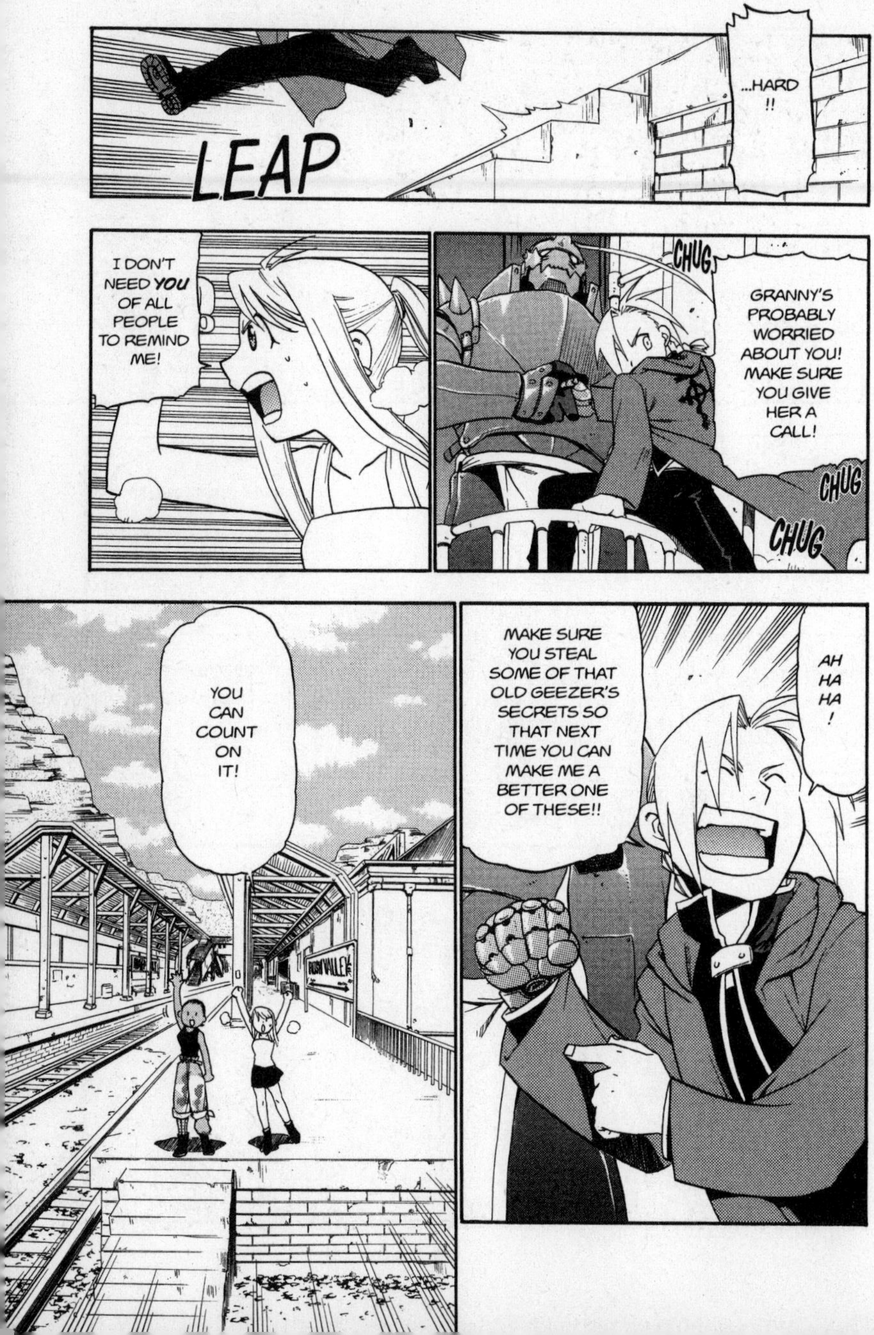
...HARD !!
LEAP
CHUG
...
GRANNY'S PROBABLY WORRIED ABOUT YOU! MAKE SURE YOU GIVE HER A CALL!
CHUG
CHUG
I DON'T NEED **YOU** OF ALL PEOPLE TO REMIND ME!
AH HA HA !
MAKE SURE YOU STEAL SOME OF THAT OLD GEEZER'S SECRETS SO THAT NEXT TIME YOU CAN MAKE ME A BETTER ONE OF THESE!!
YOU CAN COUNT ON IT!

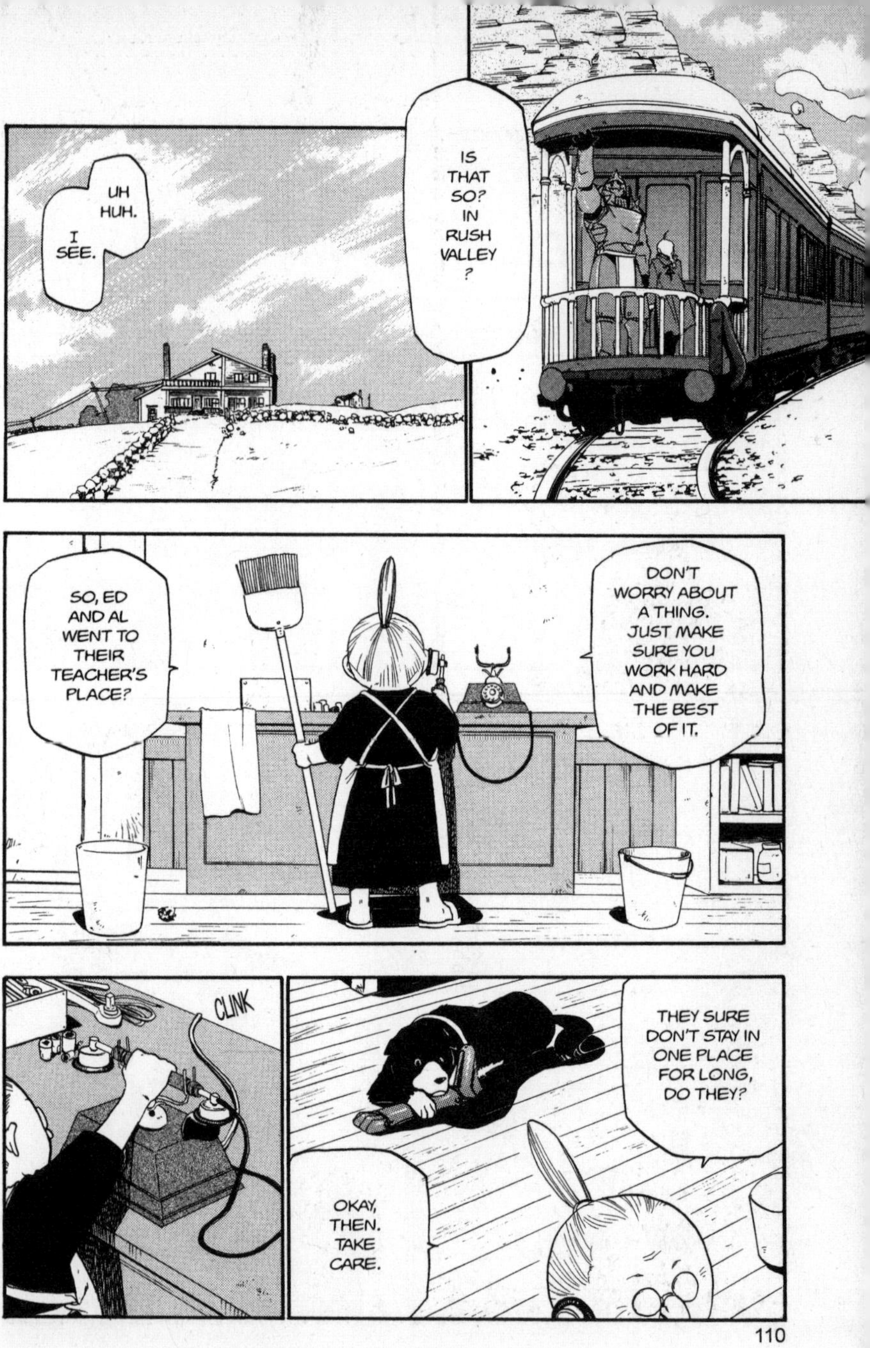
IS THAT SO? IN RUSH VALLEY?
UH HUH. I SEE.
DON'T WORRY ABOUT A THING. JUST MAKE SURE YOU WORK HARD AND MAKE THE BEST OF IT.
SO, ED AND AL WENT TO THEIR TEACHER'S PLACE?
THEY SURE DON'T STAY IN ONE PLACE FOR LONG, DO THEY?
OKAY, THEN. TAKE CARE.
CLINK

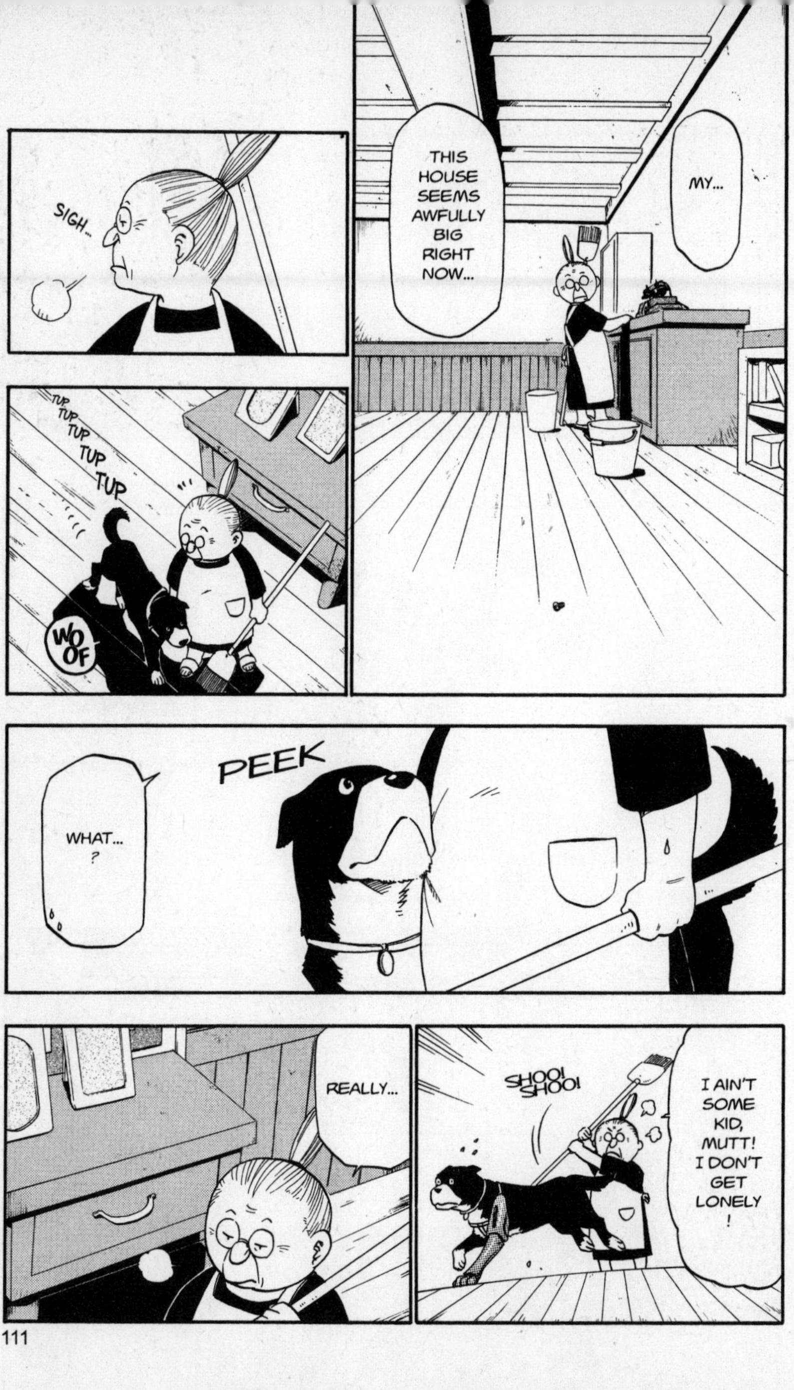
MY...
THIS HOUSE SEEMS AWFULLY BIG RIGHT NOW...
SIGH...
TUP TUP TUP TUP TUP
WOOF
PEEK
WHAT...?
I AIN'T SOME KID, MUTT! I DON'T GET LONELY!
SHOO! SHOO!
REALLY...

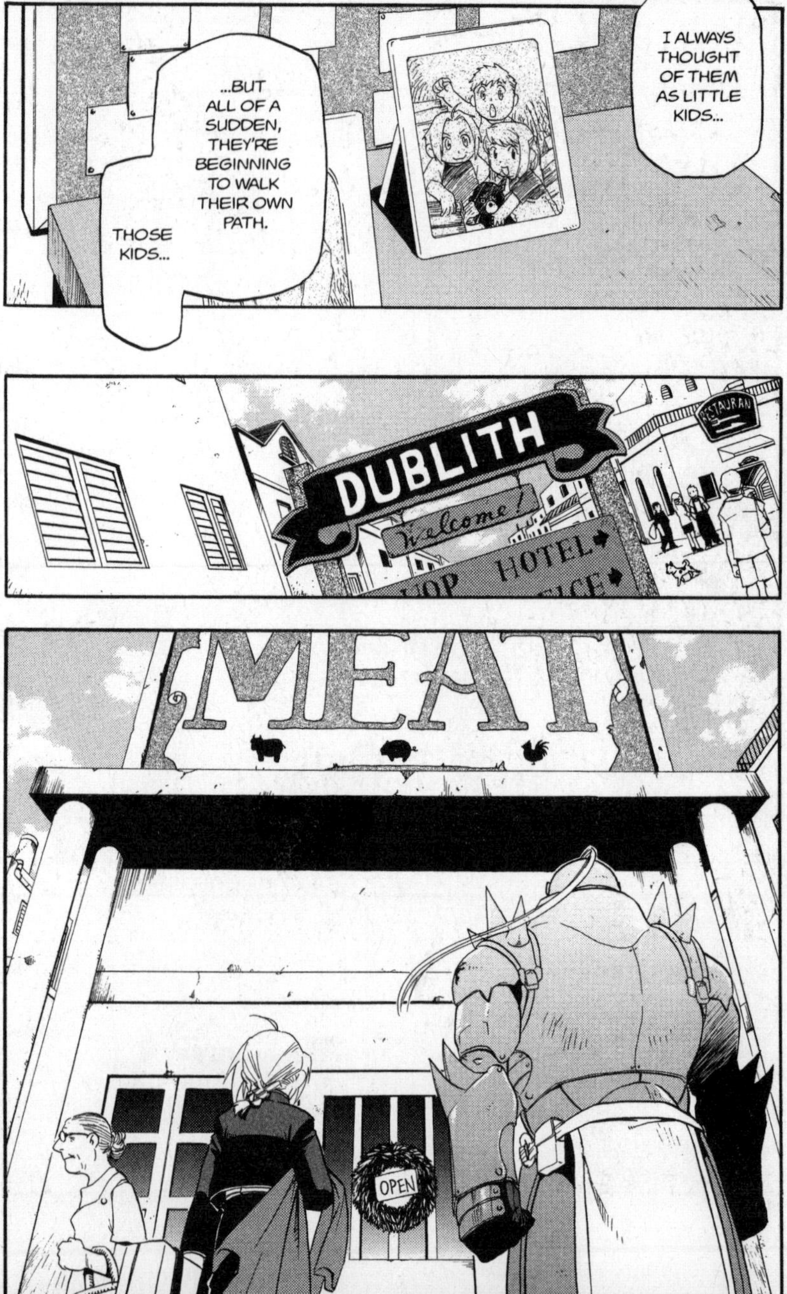
I ALWAYS THOUGHT OF THEM AS LITTLE KIDS...
...BUT ALL OF A SUDDEN, THEY'RE BEGINNING TO WALK THEIR OWN PATH.
THOSE KIDS...
DUBLITH
welcome!
HOTEL
RESTAURAN
MEAT
OPEN

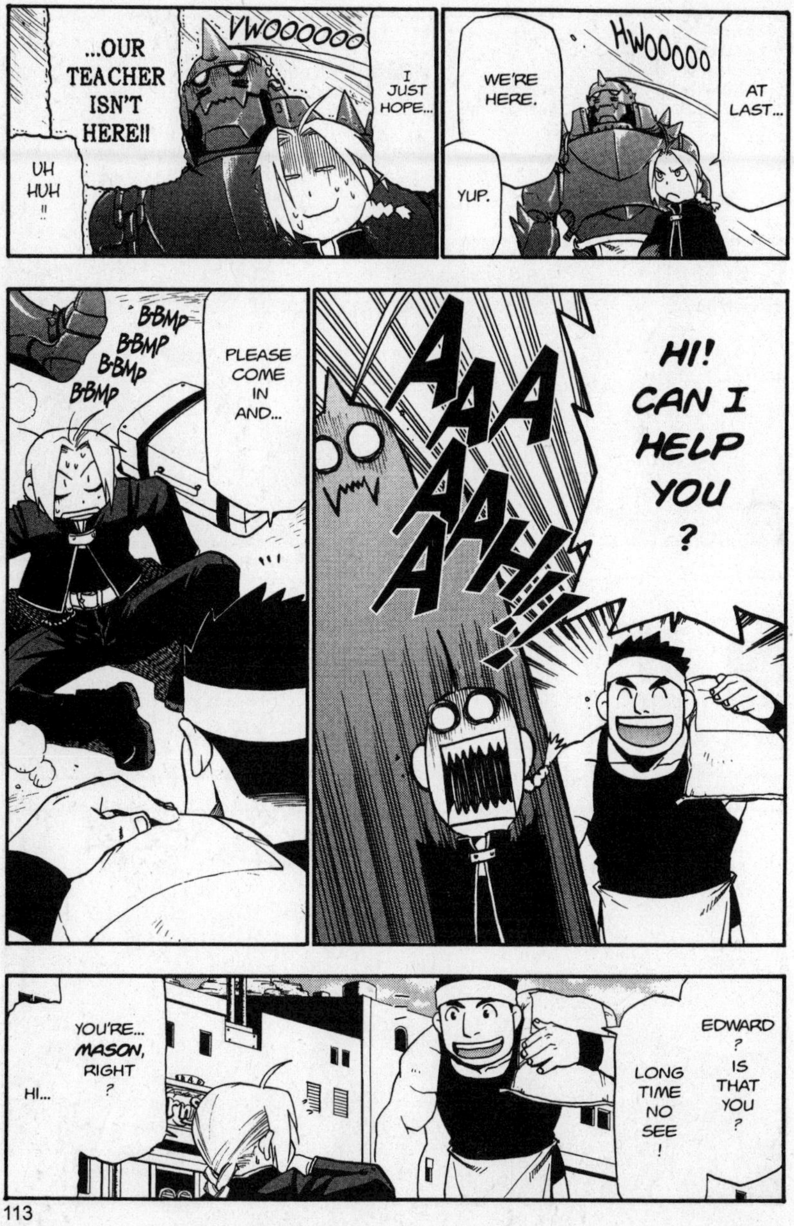
AT LAST...
HWOOOOO
WE'RE HERE.
YUP.
I JUST HOPE...
VWOOOOOO
...OUR TEACHER ISN'T HERE!!
UH HUH !!
HI! CAN I HELP YOU ?
AAAAAAH!!!
PLEASE COME IN AND...
B-BMP B-BMP B-BMP B-BMP
EDWARD ? IS THAT YOU ?
LONG TIME NO SEE !
...
YOU'RE... MASON, RIGHT ?
HI...

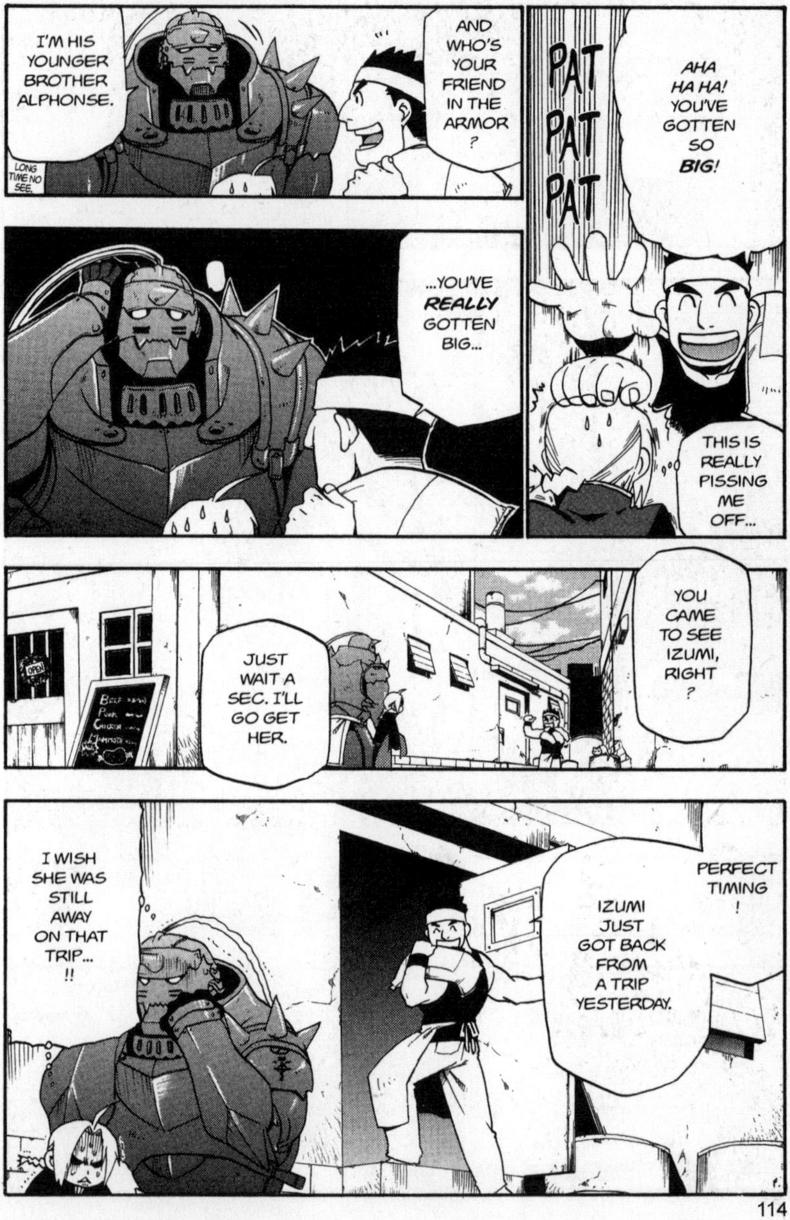
PAT PAT PAT
AHA HA HA! YOU'VE GOTTEN SO **BIG**!
THIS IS REALLY PISSING ME OFF...
AND WHO'S YOUR FRIEND IN THE ARMOR ?
I'M HIS YOUNGER BROTHER ALPHONSE.
LONG TIME NO SEE.
...YOU'VE **REALLY** GOTTEN BIG...
YOU CAME TO SEE IZUMI, RIGHT ?
JUST WAIT A SEC. I'LL GO GET HER.
OPEN
BEEF
PORK
CHICKEN
MAMMOTH
PERFECT TIMING !
IZUMI JUST GOT BACK FROM A TRIP YESTERDAY.
I WISH SHE WAS STILL AWAY ON THAT TRIP... !!

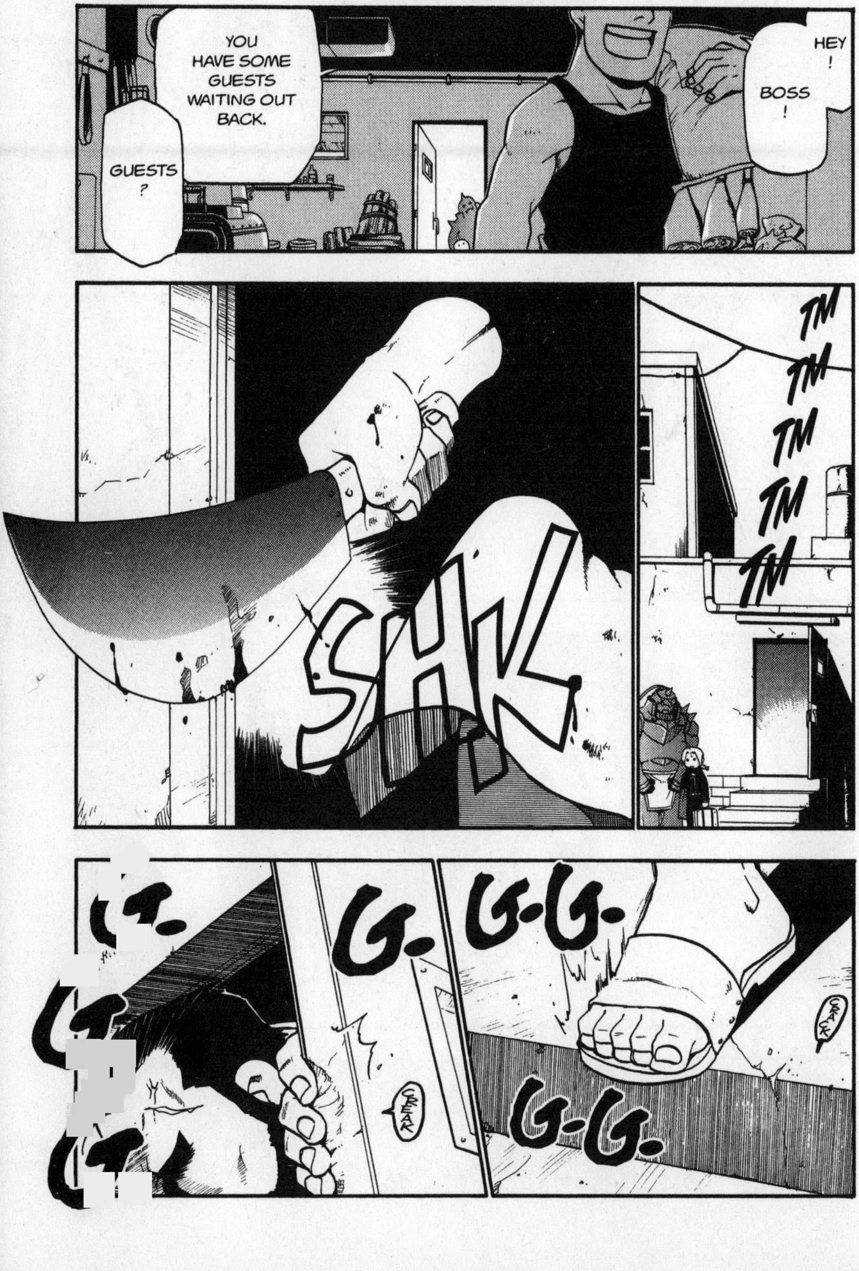
HEY! BOSS!
YOU HAVE SOME GUESTS WAITING OUT BACK.
GUESTS?
TM TM TM TM TM
SHK
G-G-G.
CRACK
G-G.
G.
CREAK

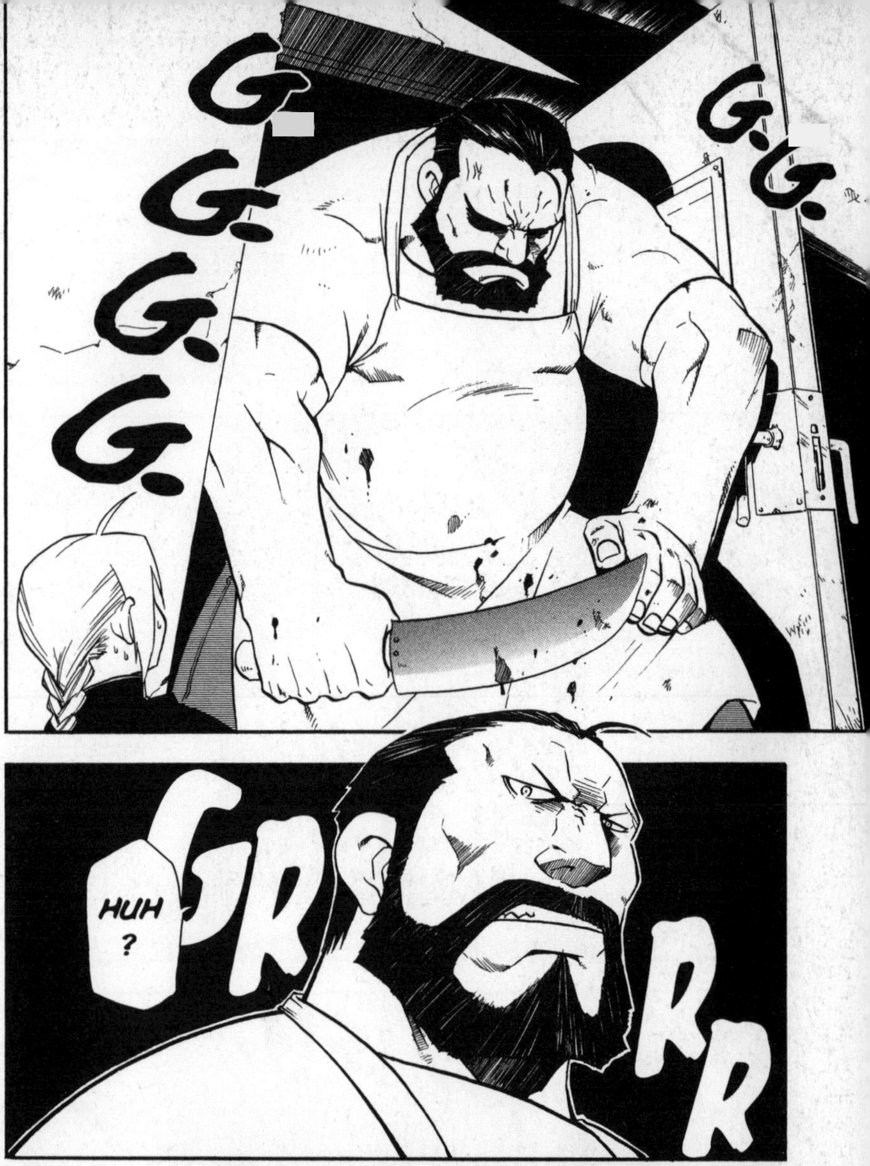
G.G.
G-G-G.G.
HUH ?
GR
RR
N...
NICE TO SEE YOU... AGAIN...

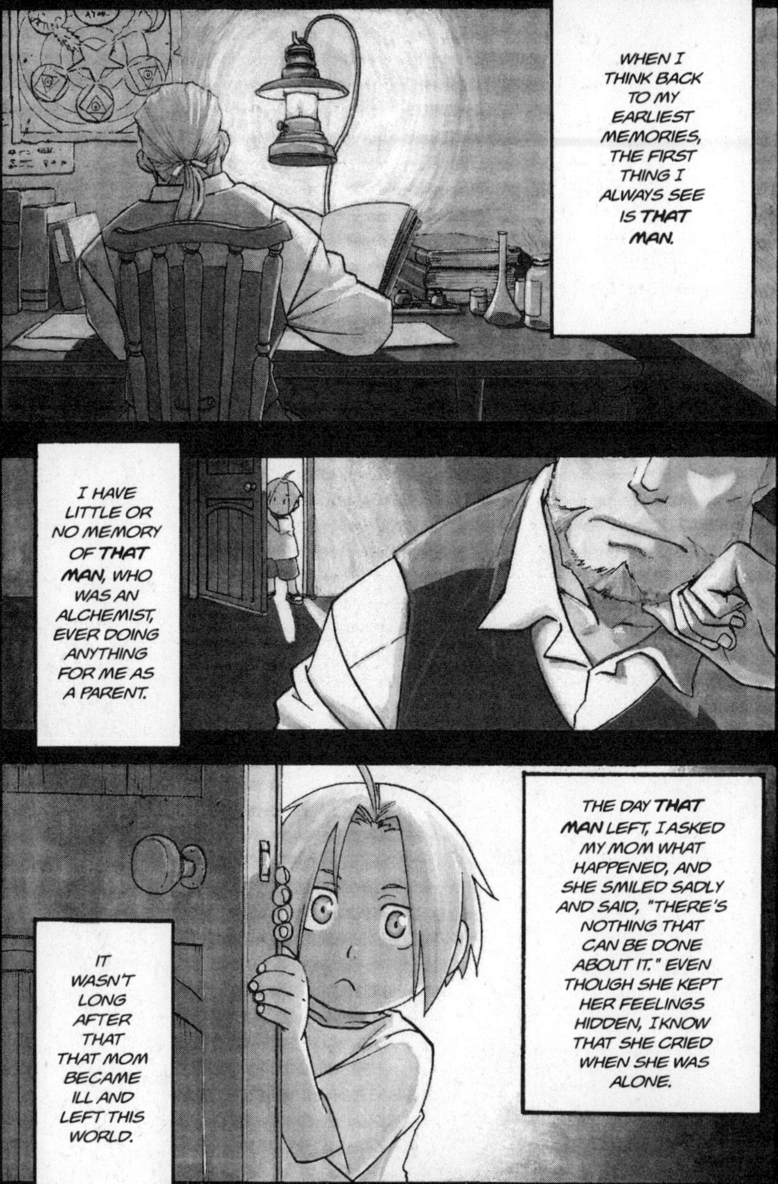
WHEN I THINK BACK TO MY EARLIEST MEMORIES, THE FIRST THING I ALWAYS SEE IS THAT MAN.
I HAVE LITTLE OR NO MEMORY OF THAT MAN, WHO WAS AN ALCHEMIST, EVER DOING ANYTHING FOR ME AS A PARENT.
THE DAY THAT MAN LEFT, I ASKED MY MOM WHAT HAPPENED, AND SHE SMILED SADLY AND SAID, "THERE'S NOTHING THAT CAN BE DONE ABOUT IT." EVEN THOUGH SHE KEPT HER FEELINGS HIDDEN, I KNOW THAT SHE CRIED WHEN SHE WAS ALONE.
IT WASN'T LONG AFTER THAT THAT MOM BECAME ILL AND LEFT THIS WORLD.

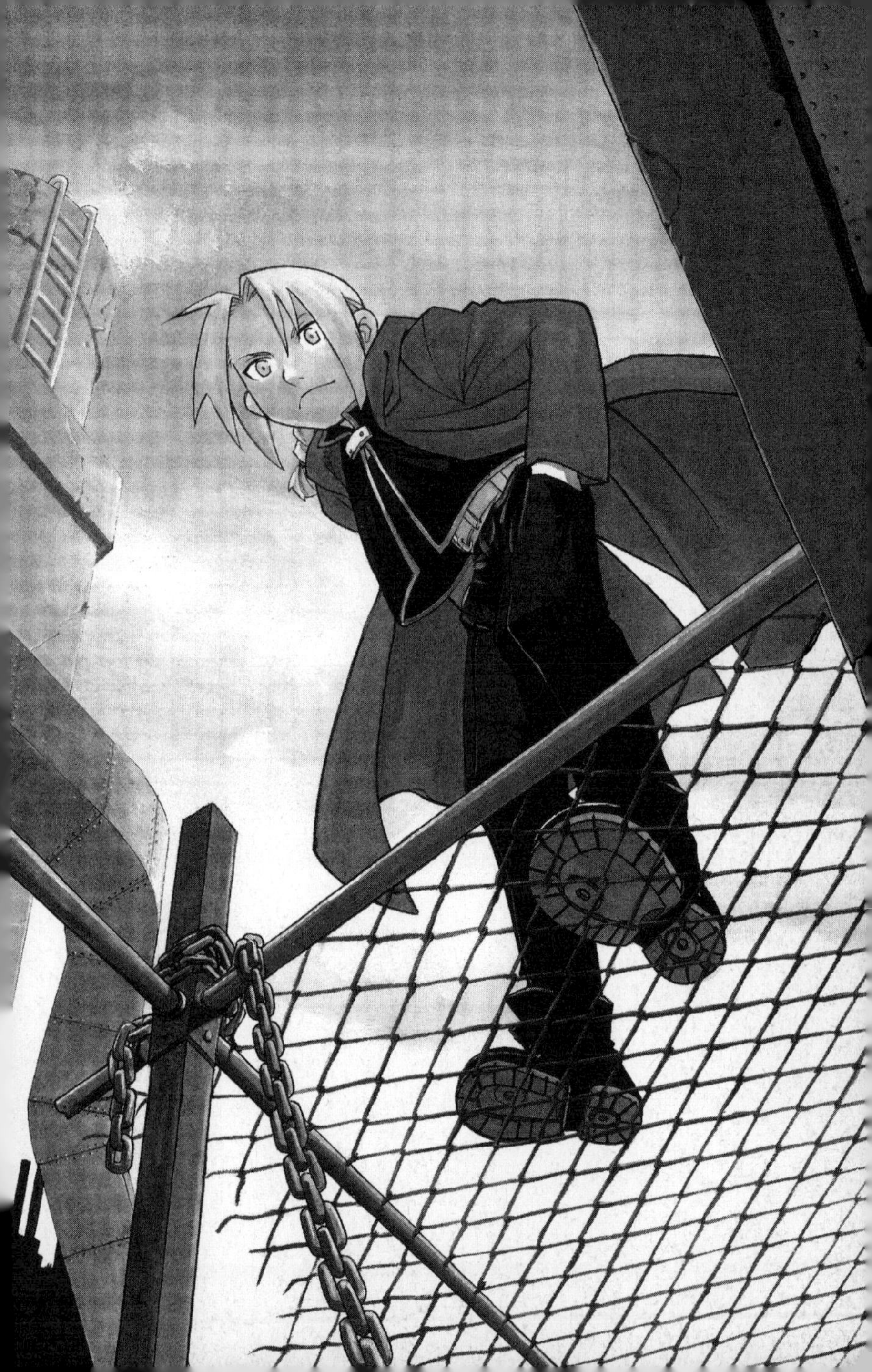

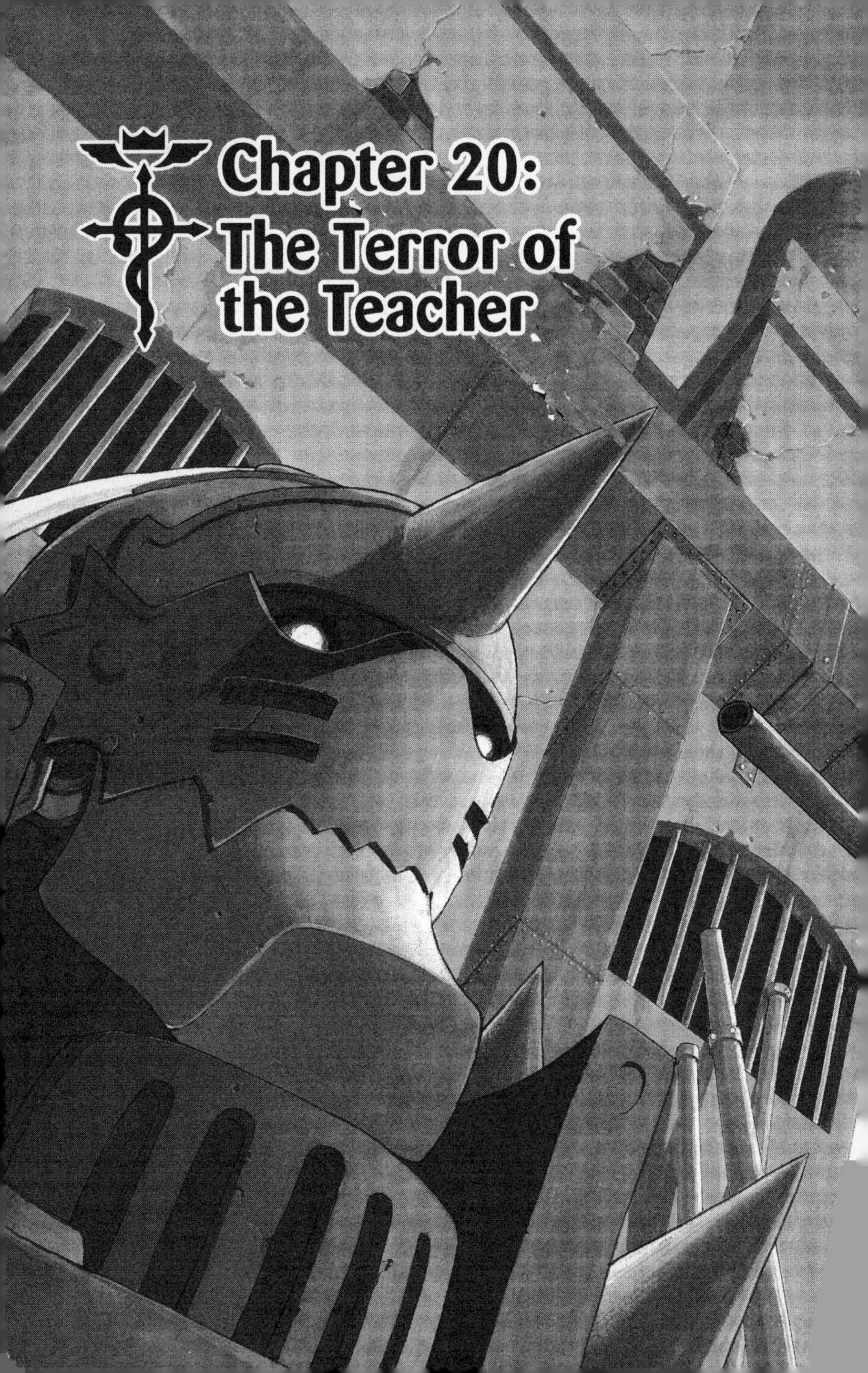
Chapter 20:
The Terror of the Teacher

FULLMETAL
ALCHEMIST

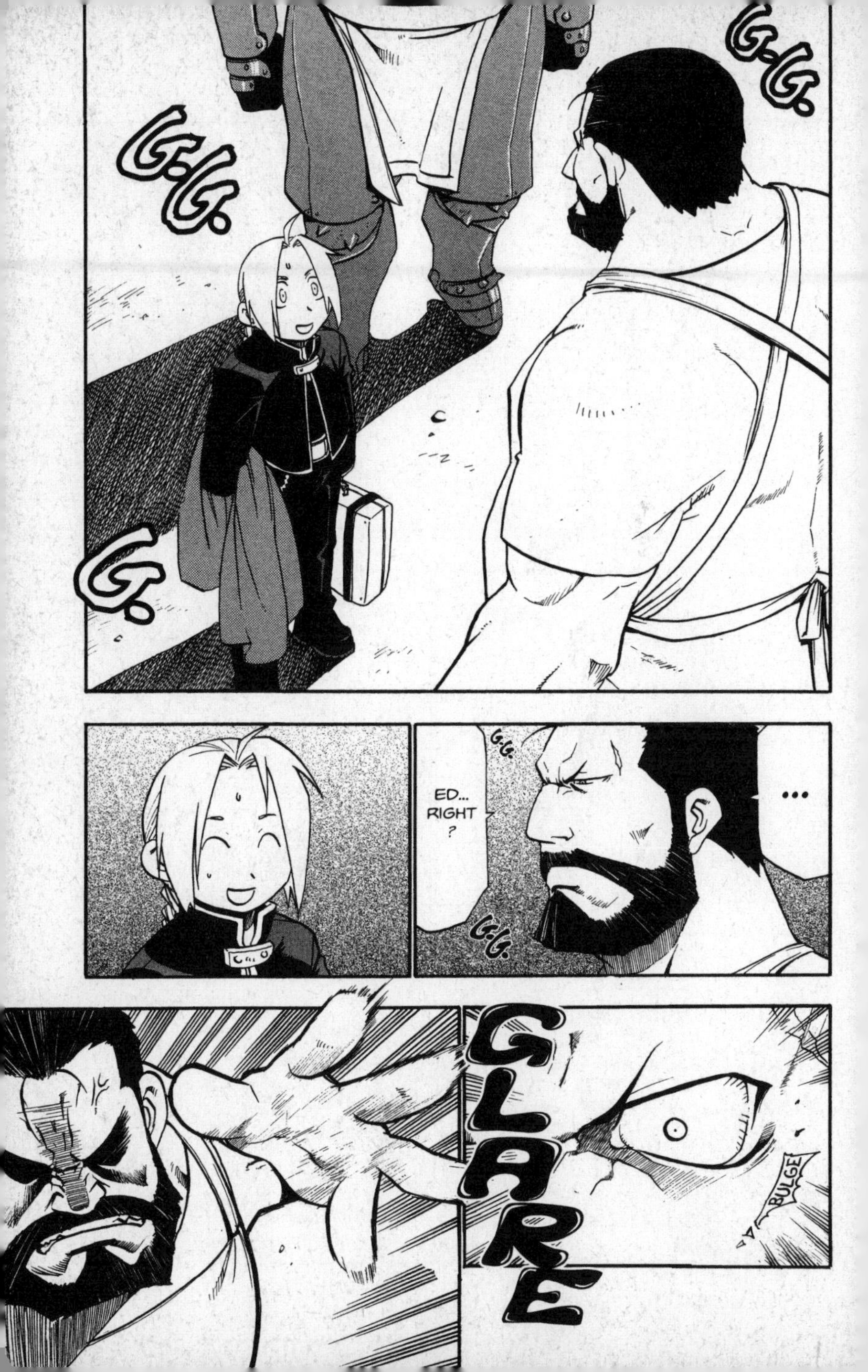
G-G.
G-G.
G.
G-G.
ED... RIGHT?
...
G-G.
GLARE
BULGE

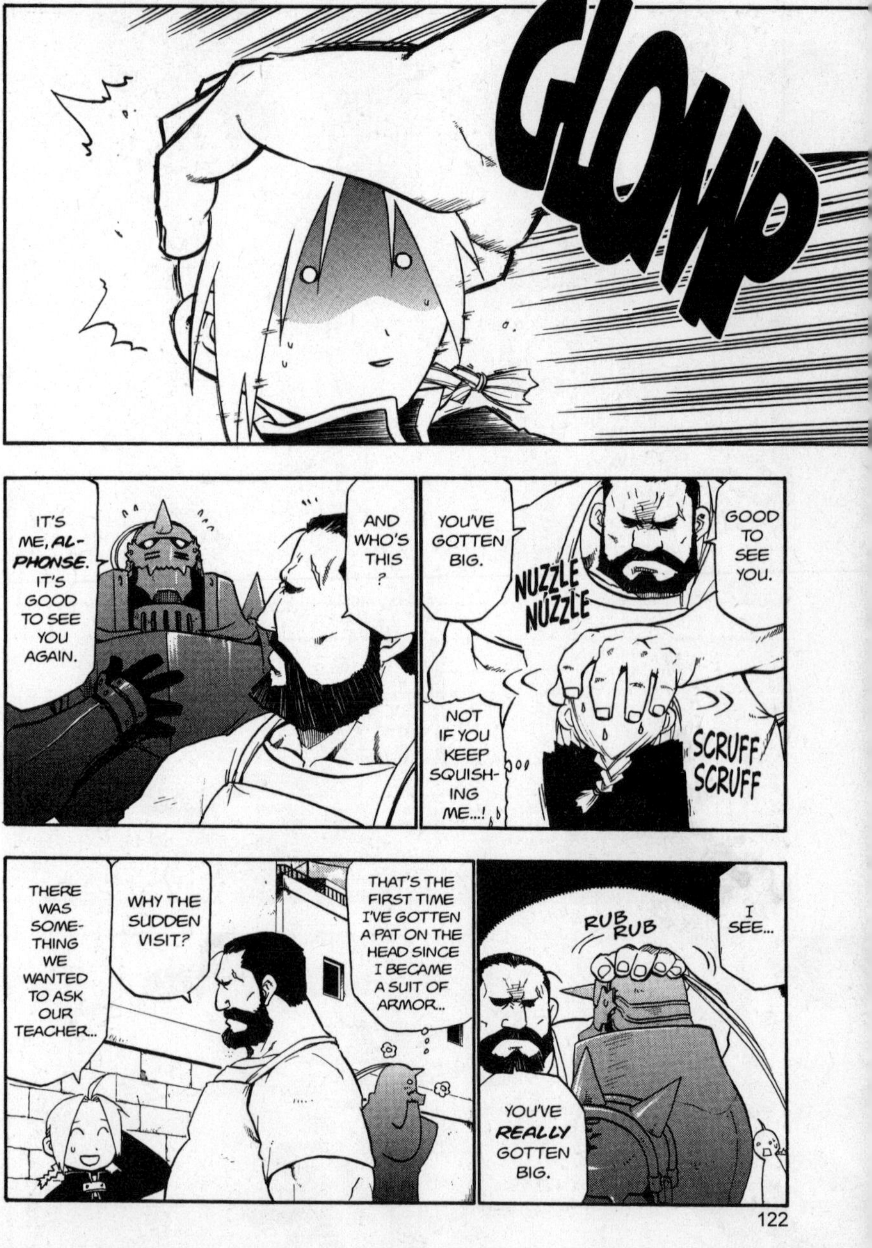
GLOMP
GOOD TO SEE YOU.
YOU'VE GOTTEN BIG.
NUZZLE NUZZLE
SCRUFF SCRUFF
NOT IF YOU KEEP SQUISHING ME...!
AND WHO'S THIS?
IT'S ME, ALPHONSE. IT'S GOOD TO SEE YOU AGAIN.
I SEE...
RUB RUB
YOU'VE REALLY GOTTEN BIG.
THAT'S THE FIRST TIME I'VE GOTTEN A PAT ON THE HEAD SINCE I BECAME A SUIT OF ARMOR...
WHY THE SUDDEN VISIT?
THERE WAS SOMETHING WE WANTED TO ASK OUR TEACHER...

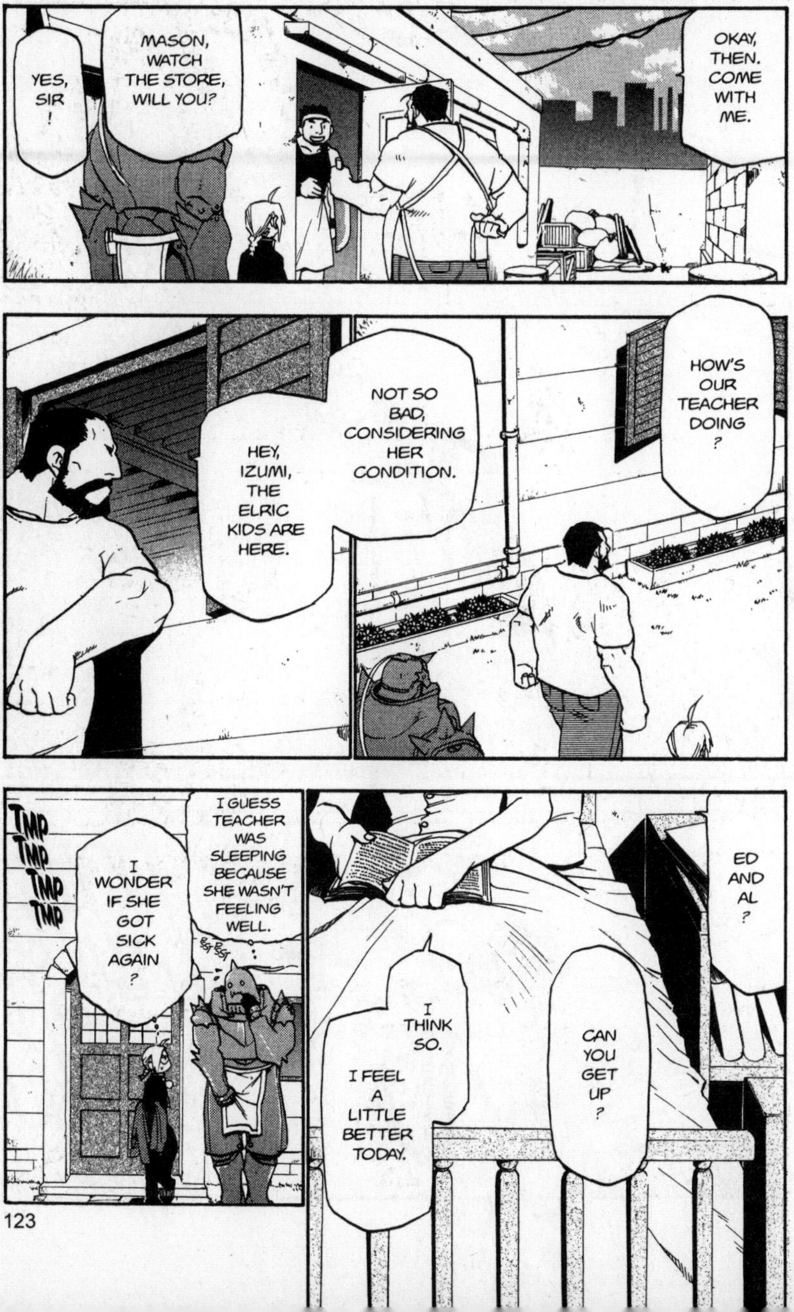
OKAY, THEN. COME WITH ME.
MASON, WATCH THE STORE, WILL YOU?
YES, SIR!
HOW'S OUR TEACHER DOING?
NOT SO BAD, CONSIDERING HER CONDITION.
HEY, IZUMI, THE ELRIC KIDS ARE HERE.
ED AND AL?
CAN YOU GET UP?
I THINK SO.
I FEEL A LITTLE BETTER TODAY.
TMP TMP TMP TMP
I GUESS TEACHER WAS SLEEPING BECAUSE SHE WASN'T FEELING WELL.
I WONDER IF SHE GOT SICK AGAIN?
PSST PSST

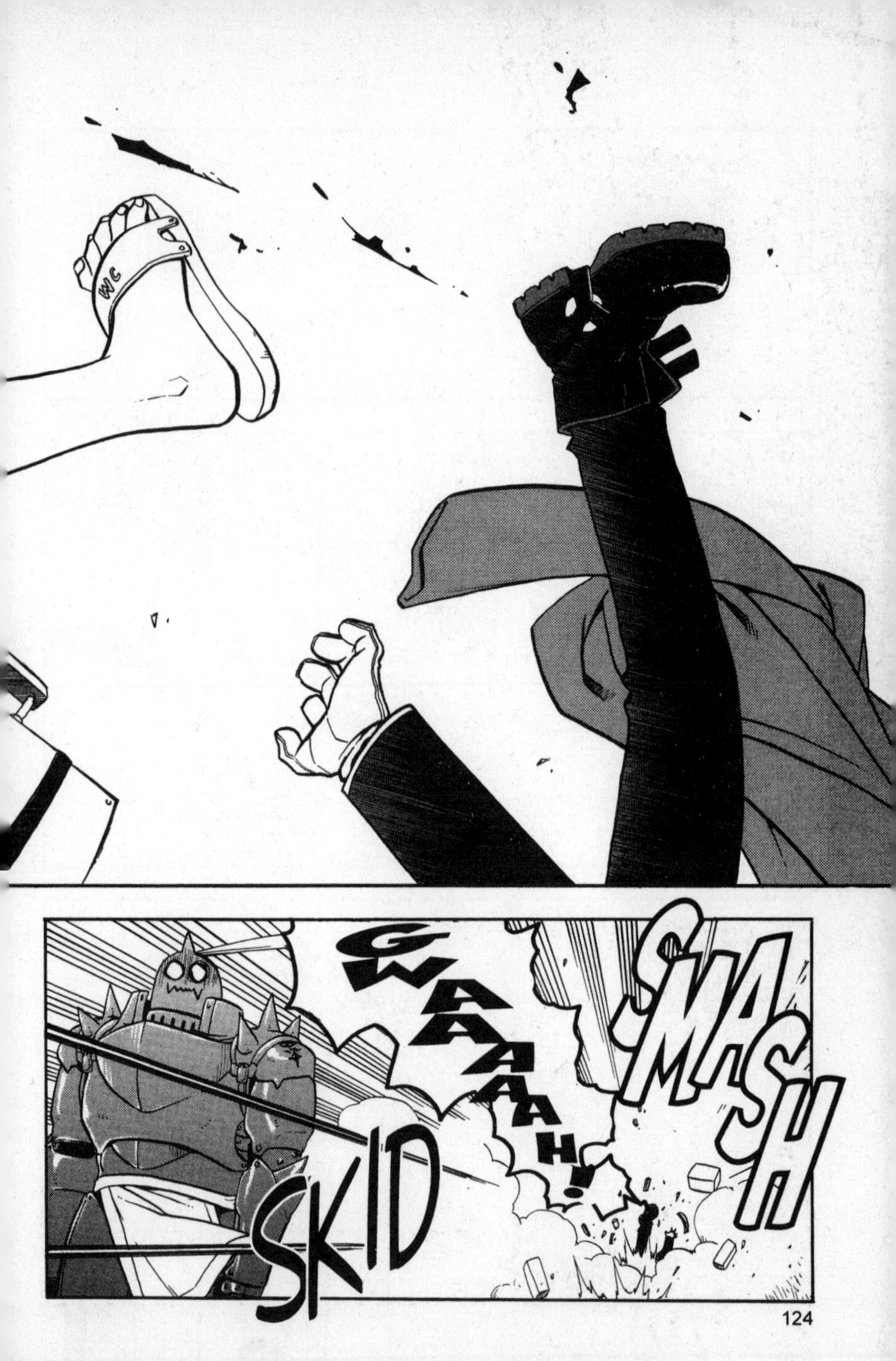
SMASH
GWAAAAAH!
SKID

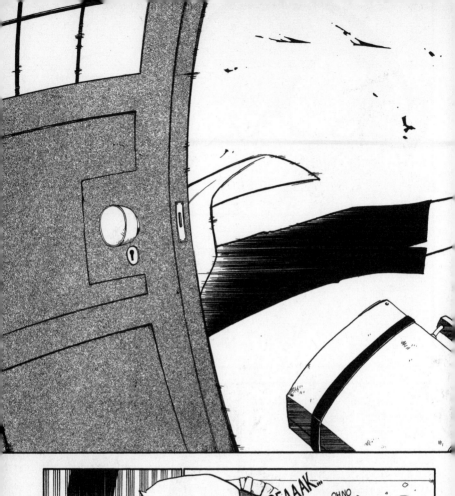

CREAAAK...

WELL, IF IT ISN'T MY FOOL OF AN APPRENTICE. I HEAR A LOT OF *RUMORS* ABOUT YOU TWO, EVEN OUT HERE IN DUBLITH.

OH NO OH NO

FSSS

SLAM

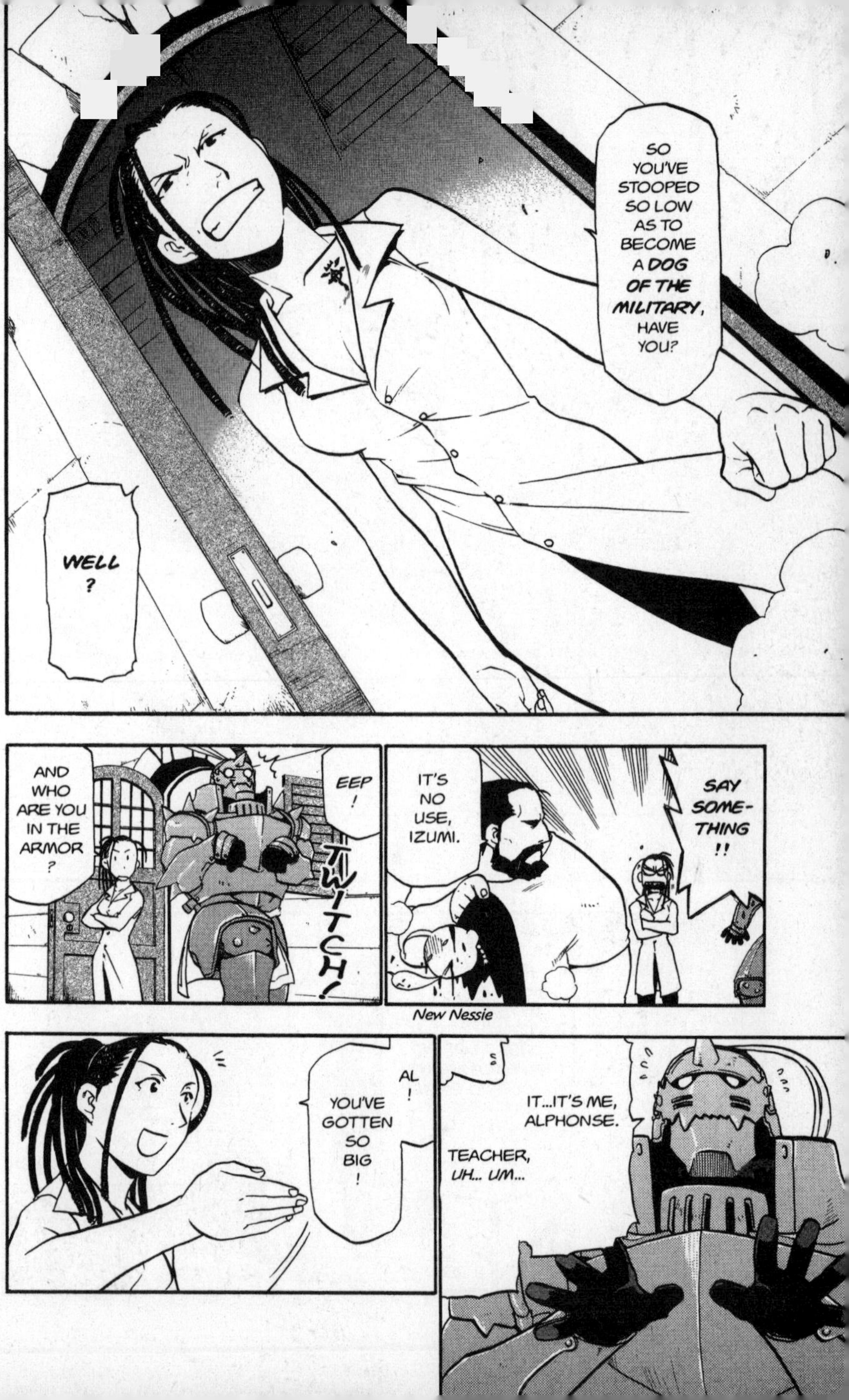
SO YOU'VE STOOPED SO LOW AS TO BECOME A DOG OF THE MILITARY, HAVE YOU?
WELL?
SAY SOME-THING!!
IT'S NO USE, IZUMI.
EEP!
TWITCH!
AND WHO ARE YOU IN THE ARMOR?
New Nessie
IT...IT'S ME, ALPHONSE.
TEACHER, UH... UM...
AL! YOU'VE GOTTEN SO BIG!

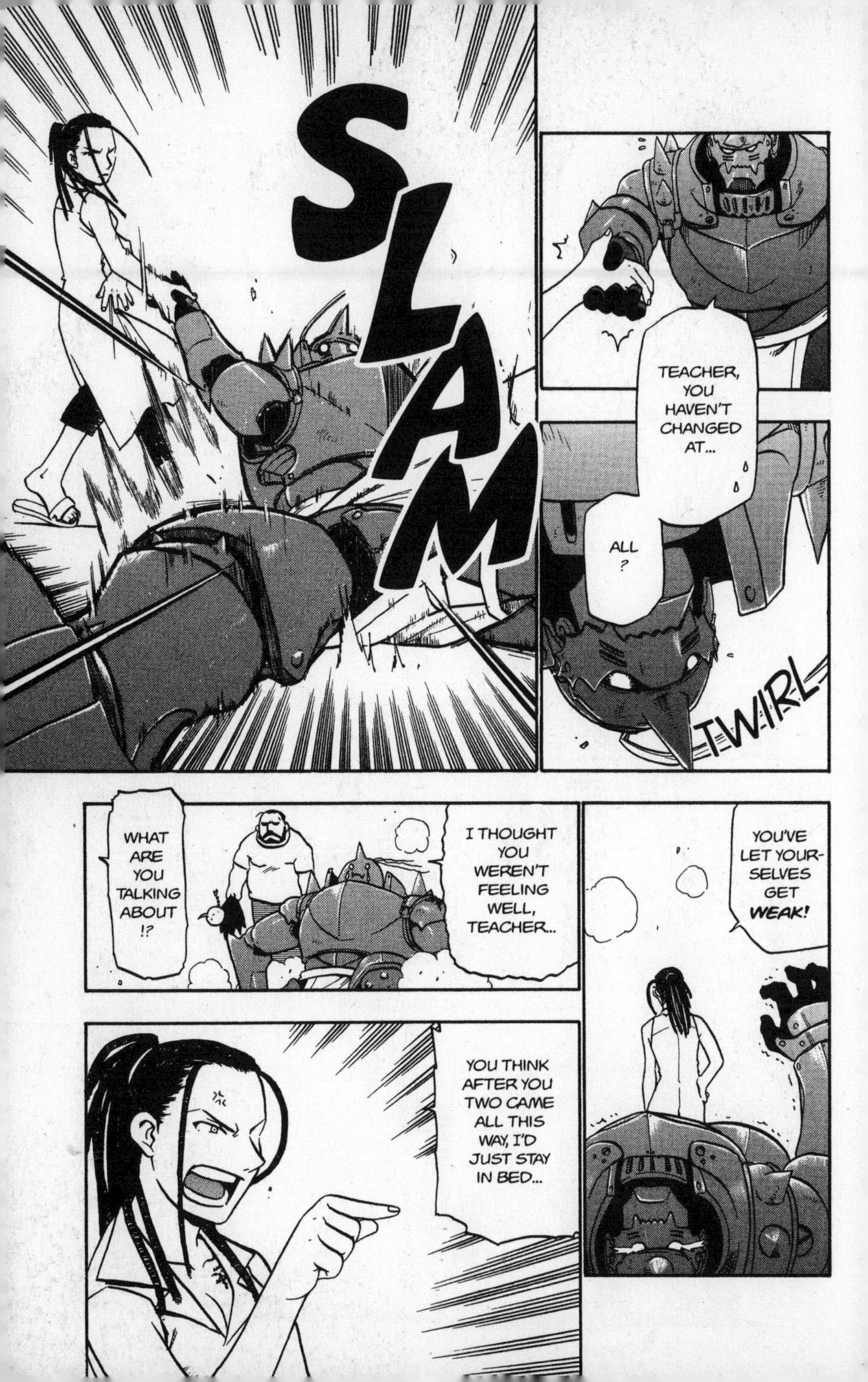
TEACHER, YOU HAVEN'T CHANGED AT...
ALL ?
TWIRL
SLAM
YOU'VE LET YOUR-SELVES GET WEAK!
I THOUGHT YOU WEREN'T FEELING WELL, TEACHER...
WHAT ARE YOU TALKING ABOUT !?
YOU THINK AFTER YOU TWO CAME ALL THIS WAY, I'D JUST STAY IN BED...

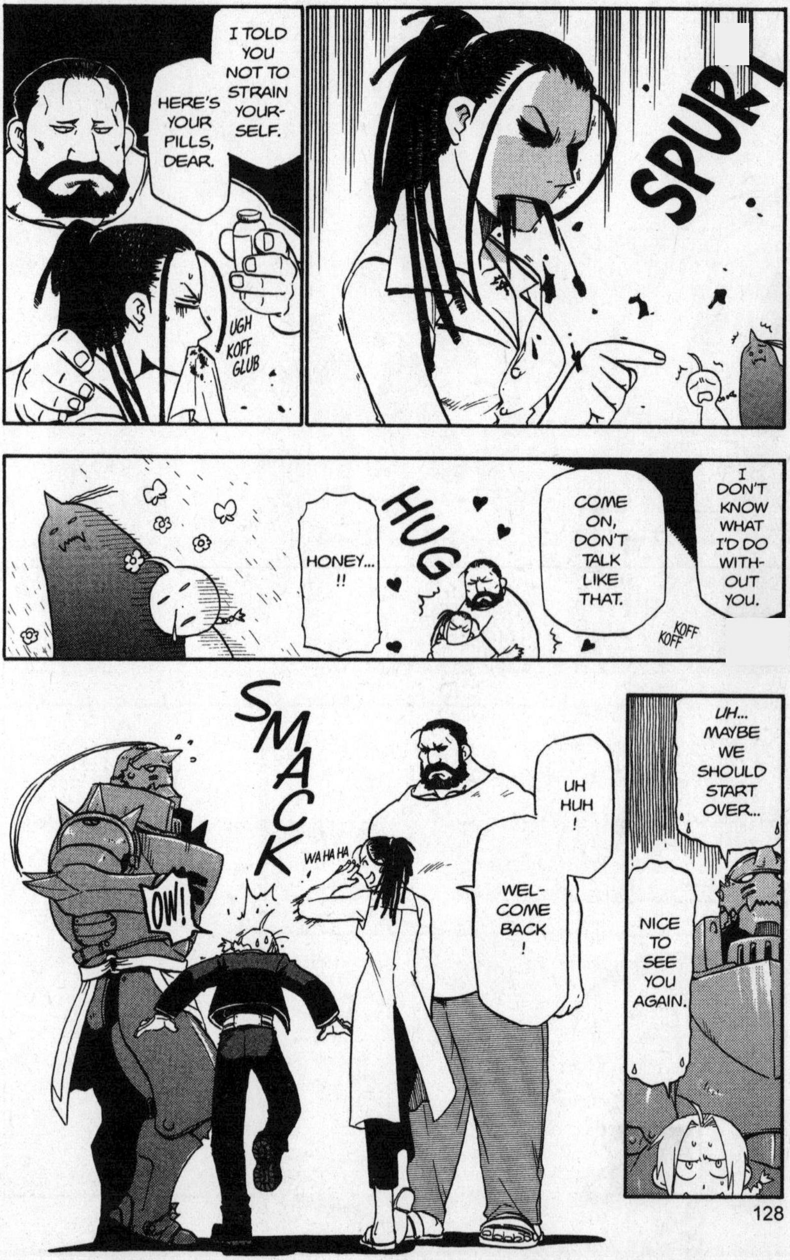
SPURT
I TOLD YOU NOT TO STRAIN YOURSELF.
HERE'S YOUR PILLS, DEAR.
UGH KOFF GLUB
I DON'T KNOW WHAT I'D DO WITHOUT YOU.
KOFF KOFF
COME ON, DON'T TALK LIKE THAT.
HUG
HONEY... !!
UH... MAYBE WE SHOULD START OVER...
NICE TO SEE YOU AGAIN.
UH HUH!
WELCOME BACK!
SMACK
WA HA HA
OW!

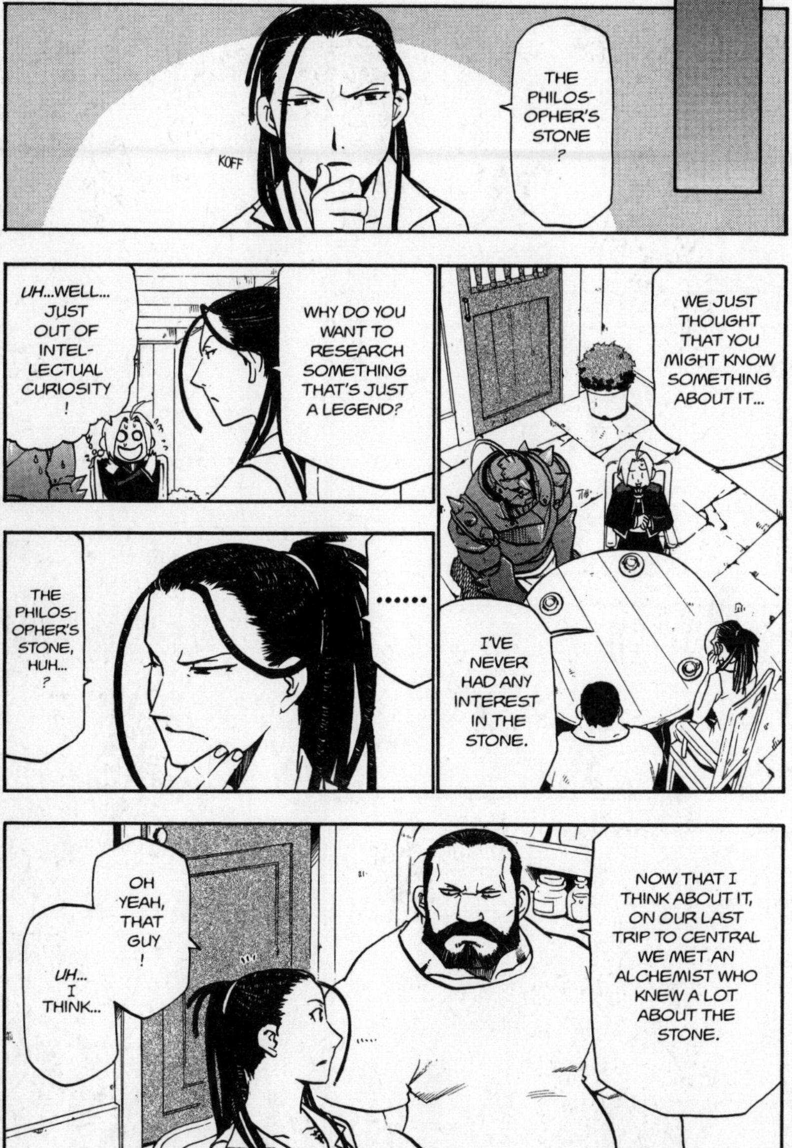
THE PHILOSOPHER'S STONE?
KOFF
WE JUST THOUGHT THAT YOU MIGHT KNOW SOMETHING ABOUT IT...
I'VE NEVER HAD ANY INTEREST IN THE STONE.
WHY DO YOU WANT TO RESEARCH SOMETHING THAT'S JUST A LEGEND?
UH...WELL... JUST OUT OF INTELLECTUAL CURIOSITY!
......
THE PHILOSOPHER'S STONE, HUH...?
NOW THAT I THINK ABOUT IT, ON OUR LAST TRIP TO CENTRAL WE MET AN ALCHEMIST WHO KNEW A LOT ABOUT THE STONE.
.....
OH YEAH, THAT GUY!
UH... I THINK...

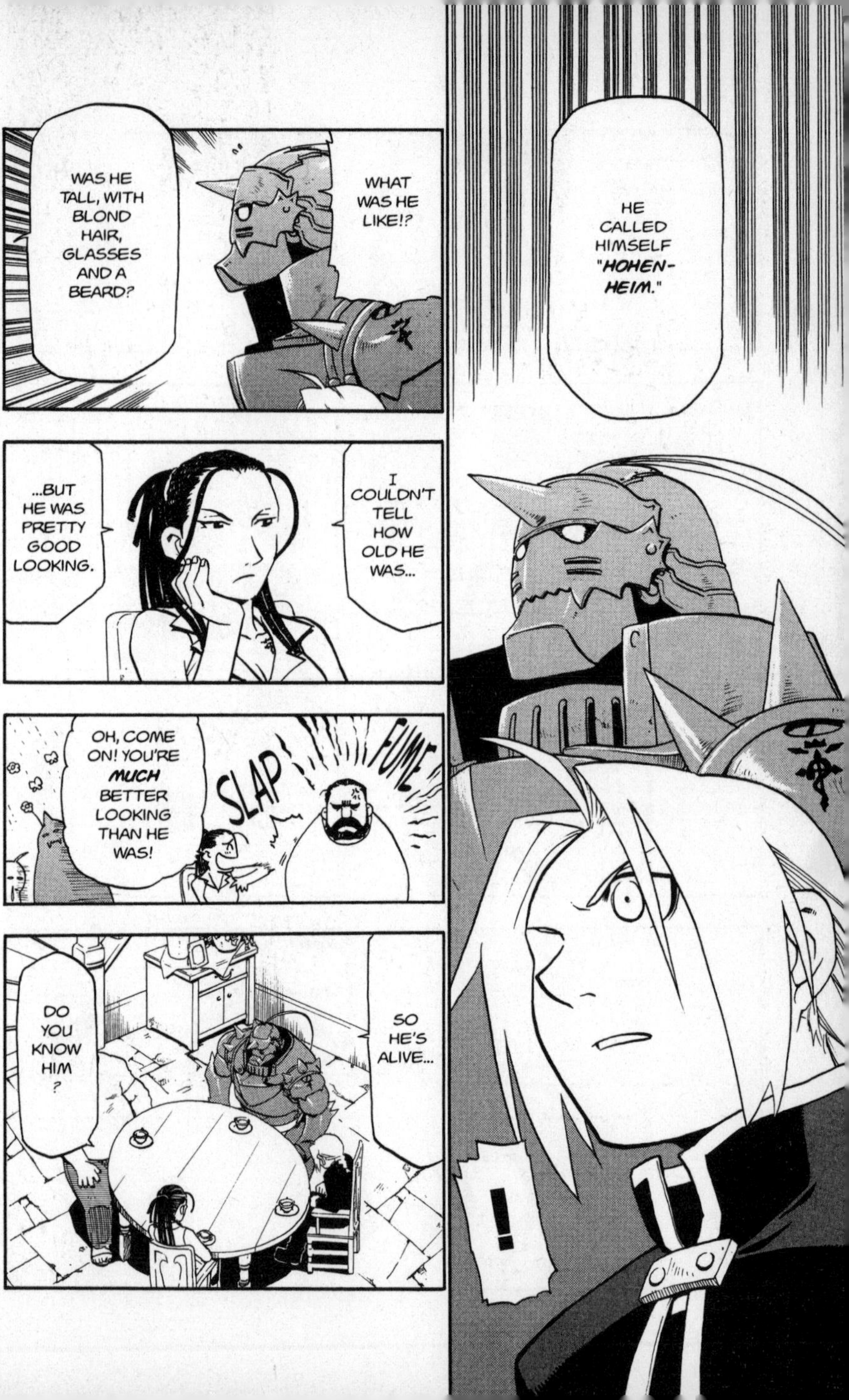
HE CALLED HIMSELF "HOHENHEIM."
!
WHAT WAS HE LIKE!?
WAS HE TALL, WITH BLOND HAIR, GLASSES AND A BEARD?
I COULDN'T TELL HOW OLD HE WAS...
...BUT HE WAS PRETTY GOOD LOOKING.
FUME
SLAP
OH, COME ON! YOU'RE MUCH BETTER LOOKING THAN HE WAS!
SO HE'S ALIVE...
DO YOU KNOW HIM?

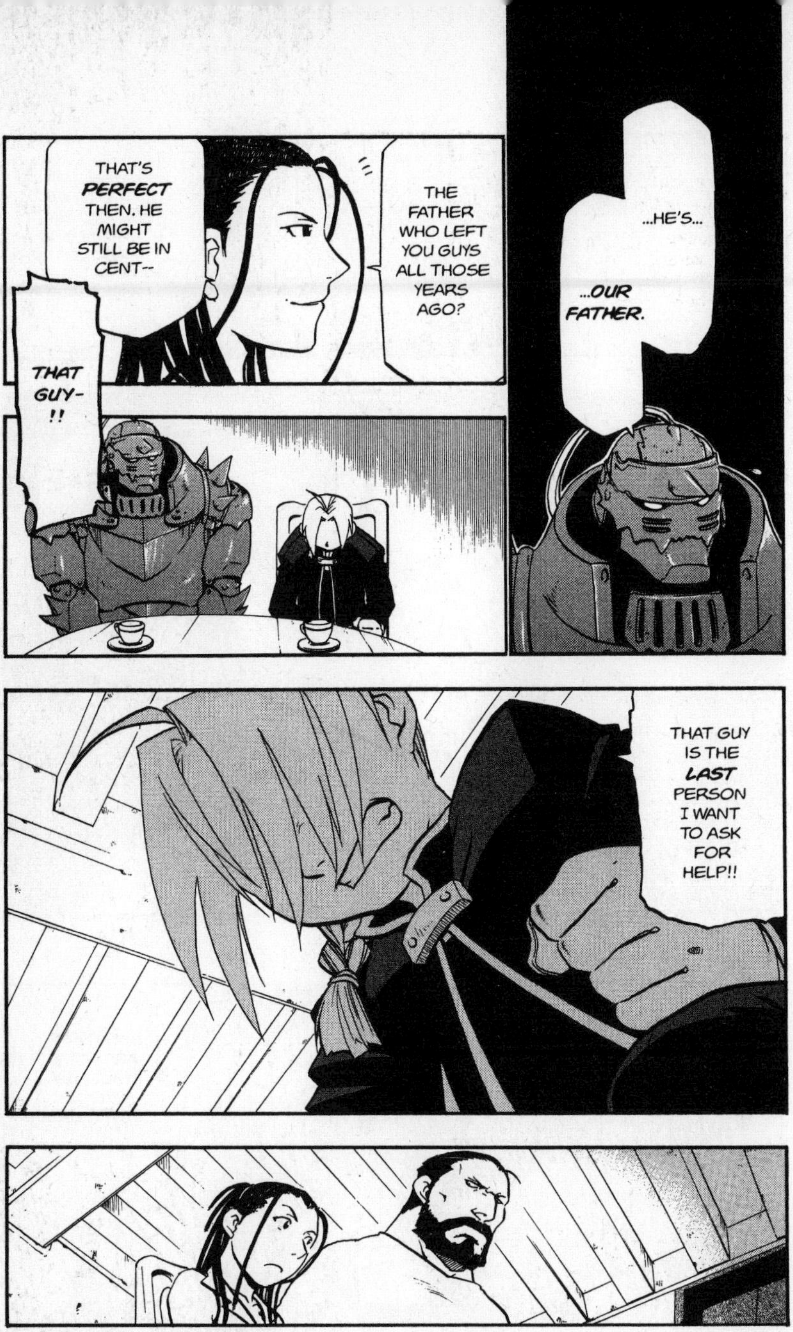
...HE'S...
...OUR FATHER.
THE FATHER WHO LEFT YOU GUYS ALL THOSE YEARS AGO?
THAT'S PERFECT THEN. HE MIGHT STILL BE IN CENT--
THAT GUY-!!
THAT GUY IS THE LAST PERSON I WANT TO ASK FOR HELP!!

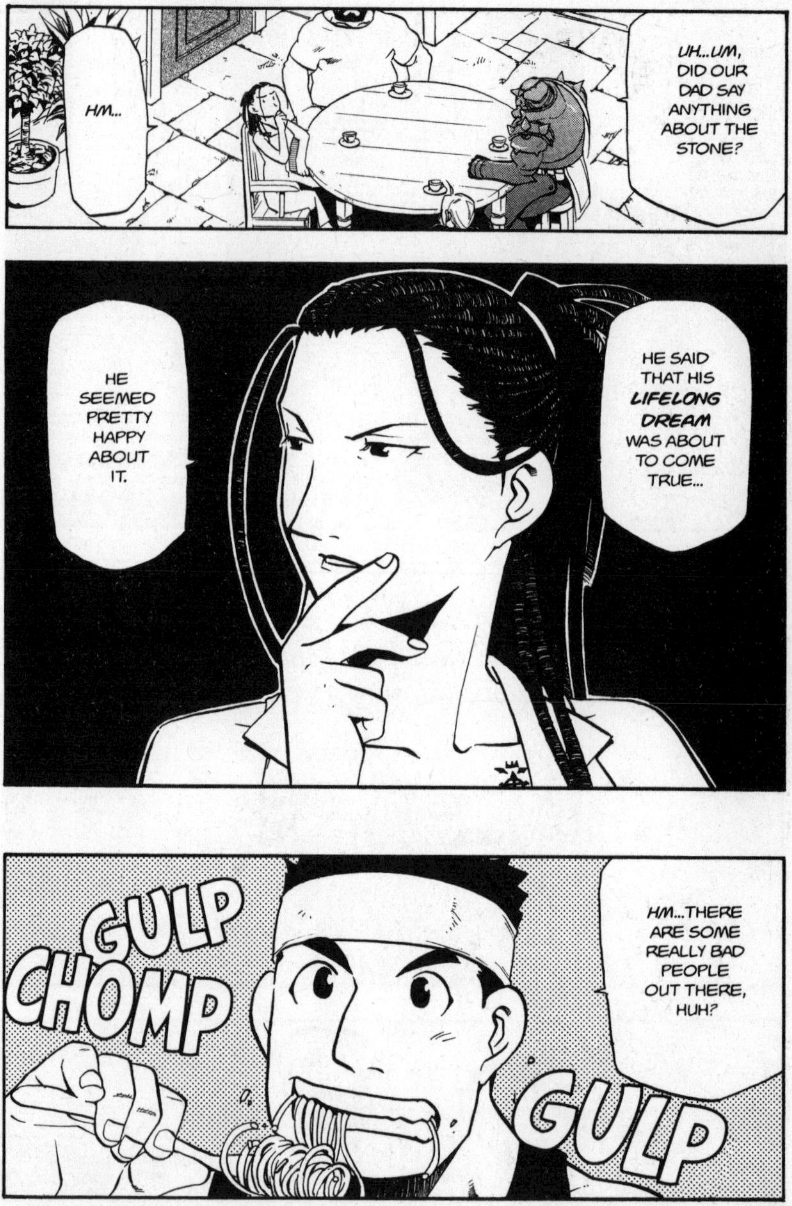
UH...UM, DID OUR DAD SAY ANYTHING ABOUT THE STONE?
HM...
HE SAID THAT HIS LIFELONG DREAM WAS ABOUT TO COME TRUE...
HE SEEMED PRETTY HAPPY ABOUT IT.
HM...THERE ARE SOME REALLY BAD PEOPLE OUT THERE, HUH?
GULP
CHOMP
GULP

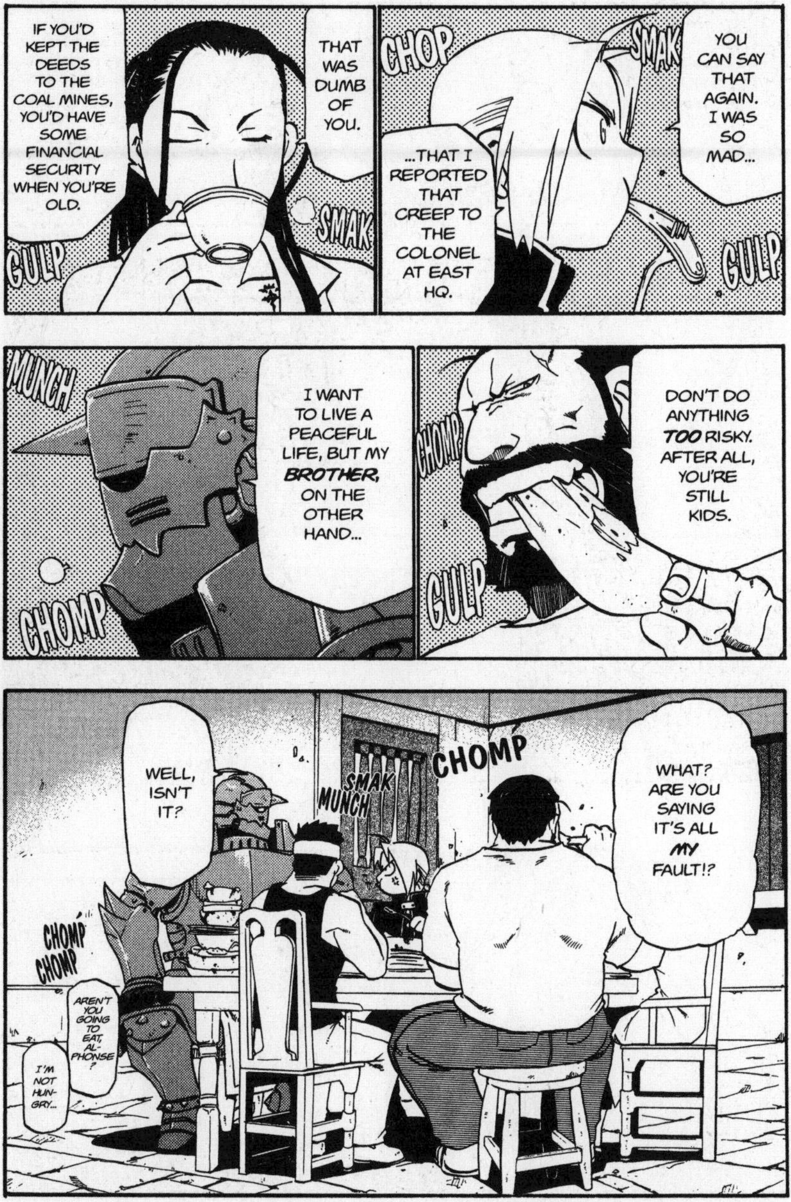
CHOP
SMAK
YOU CAN SAY THAT AGAIN. I WAS SO MAD...
...THAT I REPORTED THAT CREEP TO THE COLONEL AT EAST HQ.
GULP
THAT WAS DUMB OF YOU.
IF YOU'D KEPT THE DEEDS TO THE COAL MINES, YOU'D HAVE SOME FINANCIAL SECURITY WHEN YOU'RE OLD.
SMAK
GULP
DON'T DO ANYTHING *TOO* RISKY. AFTER ALL, YOU'RE STILL KIDS.
CHOMP
GULP
MUNCH
I WANT TO LIVE A PEACEFUL LIFE, BUT MY *BROTHER*, ON THE OTHER HAND...
CHOMP
WHAT? ARE YOU SAYING IT'S ALL *MY* FAULT!?
CHOMP
SMAK
MUNCH
WELL, ISN'T IT?
CHOMP CHOMP
AREN'T YOU GOING TO EAT, ALPHONSE?
I'M NOT HUNGRY...

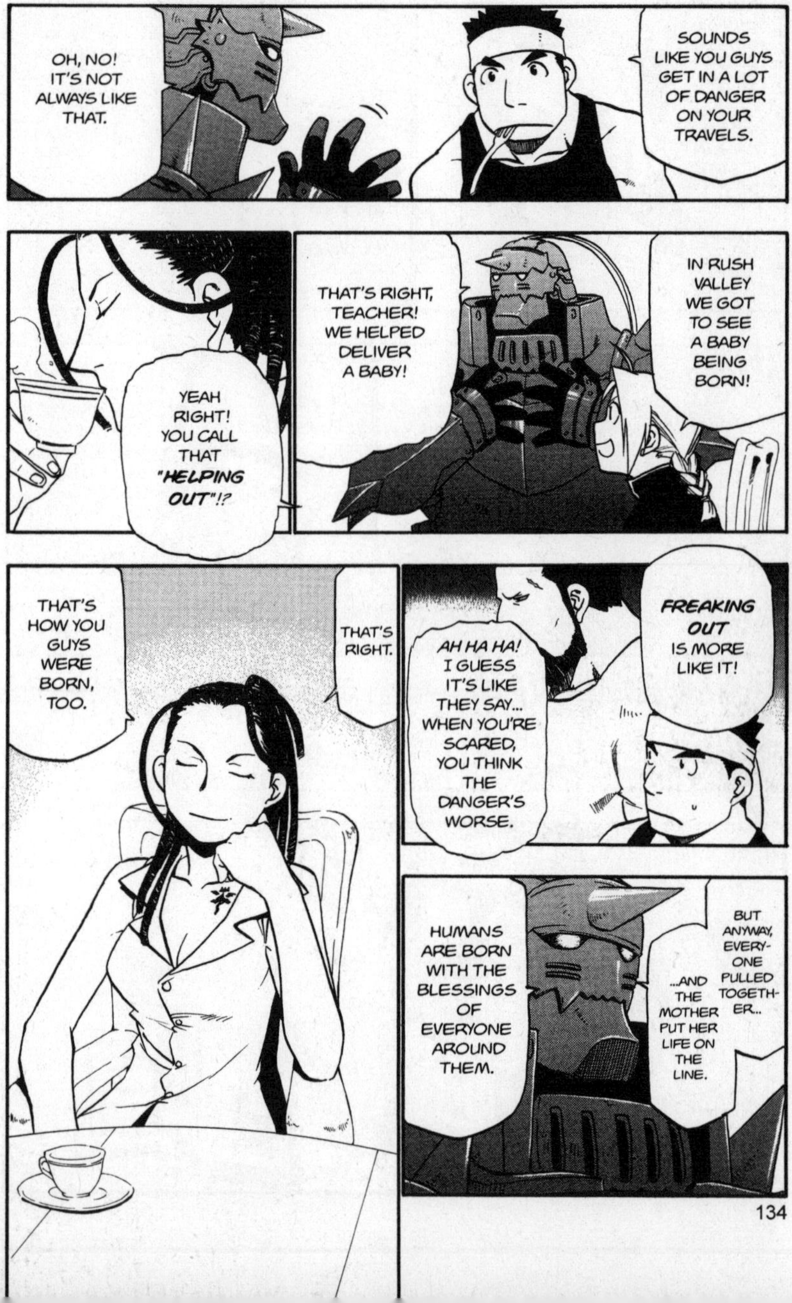
SOUNDS LIKE YOU GUYS GET IN A LOT OF DANGER ON YOUR TRAVELS.
OH, NO! IT'S NOT ALWAYS LIKE THAT.
IN RUSH VALLEY WE GOT TO SEE A BABY BEING BORN!
THAT'S RIGHT, TEACHER! WE HELPED DELIVER A BABY!
YEAH RIGHT! YOU CALL THAT "***HELPING OUT***"!?
FREAKING OUT IS MORE LIKE IT!
AH HA HA! I GUESS IT'S LIKE THEY SAY... WHEN YOU'RE SCARED, YOU THINK THE DANGER'S WORSE.
BUT ANYWAY, EVERY-ONE PULLED TOGETH-ER...
...AND THE MOTHER PUT HER LIFE ON THE LINE.
HUMANS ARE BORN WITH THE BLESSINGS OF EVERYONE AROUND THEM.
THAT'S RIGHT.
THAT'S HOW YOU GUYS WERE BORN, TOO.

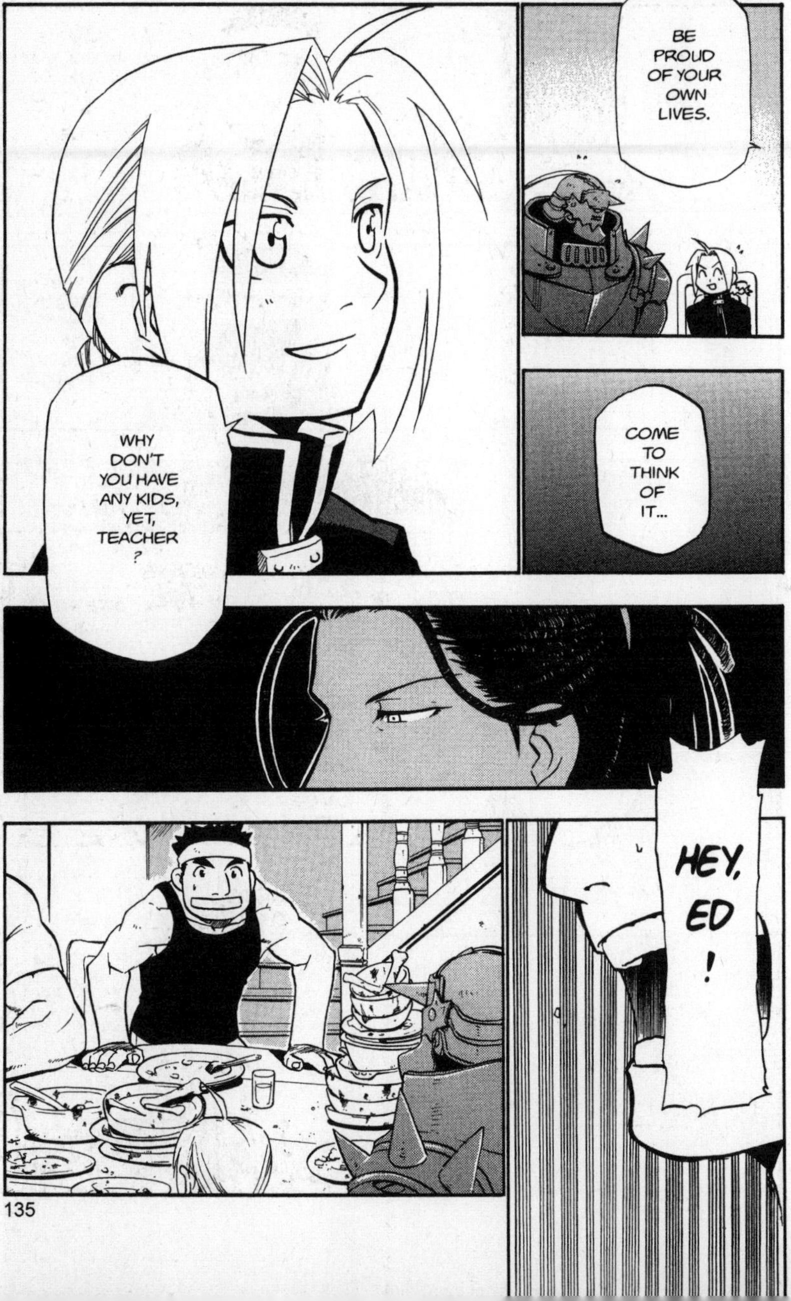
BE PROUD OF YOUR OWN LIVES.
COME TO THINK OF IT...
WHY DON'T YOU HAVE ANY KIDS, YET, TEACHER?
HEY, ED!

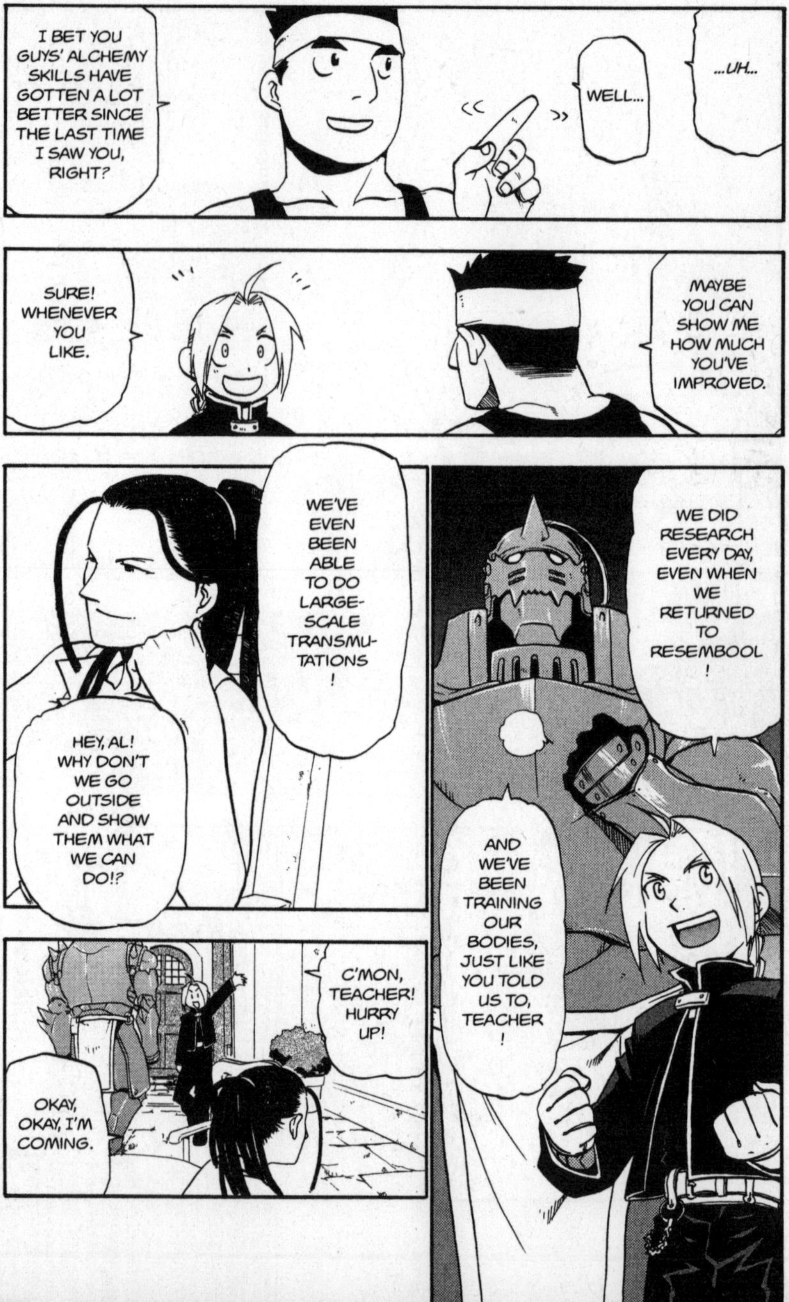
...UH...
WELL...
I BET YOU GUYS' ALCHEMY SKILLS HAVE GOTTEN A LOT BETTER SINCE THE LAST TIME I SAW YOU, RIGHT?
MAYBE YOU CAN SHOW ME HOW MUCH YOU'VE IMPROVED.
SURE! WHENEVER YOU LIKE.
WE DID RESEARCH EVERY DAY, EVEN WHEN WE RETURNED TO RESEMBOOL!
AND WE'VE BEEN TRAINING OUR BODIES, JUST LIKE YOU TOLD US TO, TEACHER!
WE'VE EVEN BEEN ABLE TO DO LARGE-SCALE TRANSMUTATIONS!
HEY, AL! WHY DON'T WE GO OUTSIDE AND SHOW THEM WHAT WE CAN DO!?
C'MON, TEACHER! HURRY UP!
OKAY, OKAY, I'M COMING.

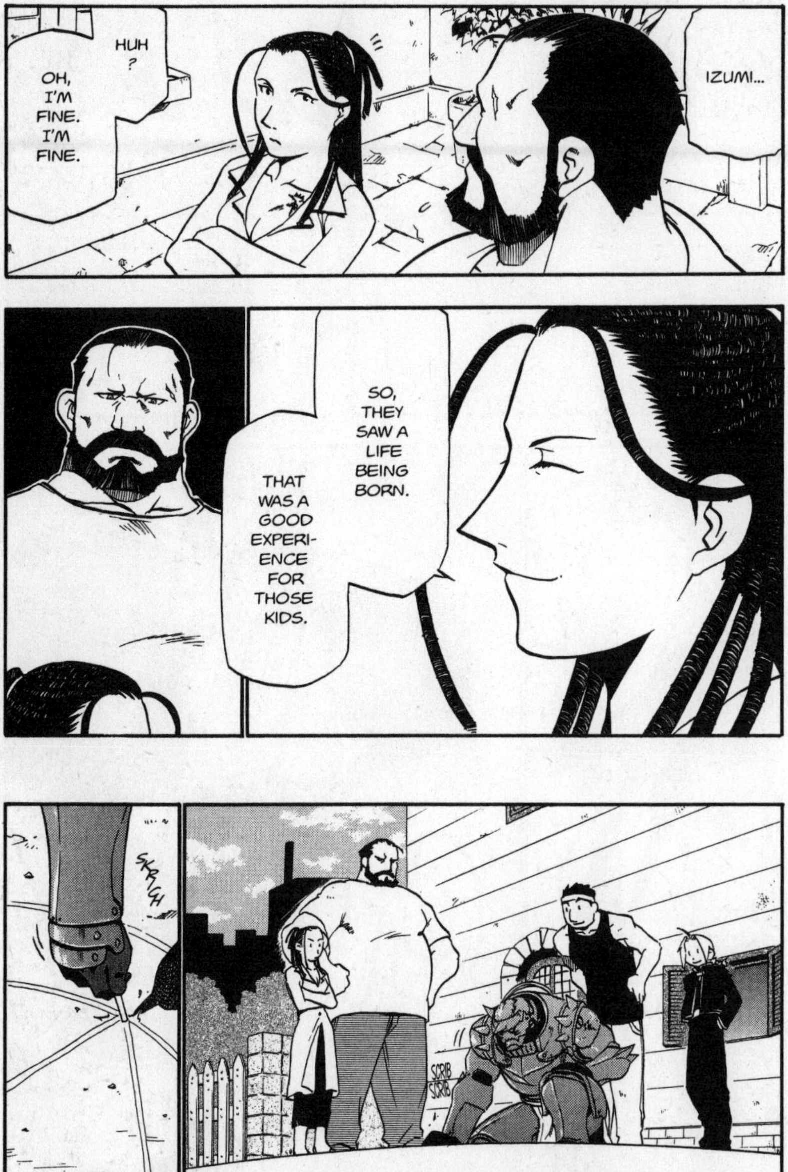
IZUMI...
HUH ?
OH, I'M FINE. I'M FINE.
SO, THEY SAW A LIFE BEING BORN.
THAT WAS A GOOD EXPERIENCE FOR THOSE KIDS.
SCRIB SCRIB
SKRICH

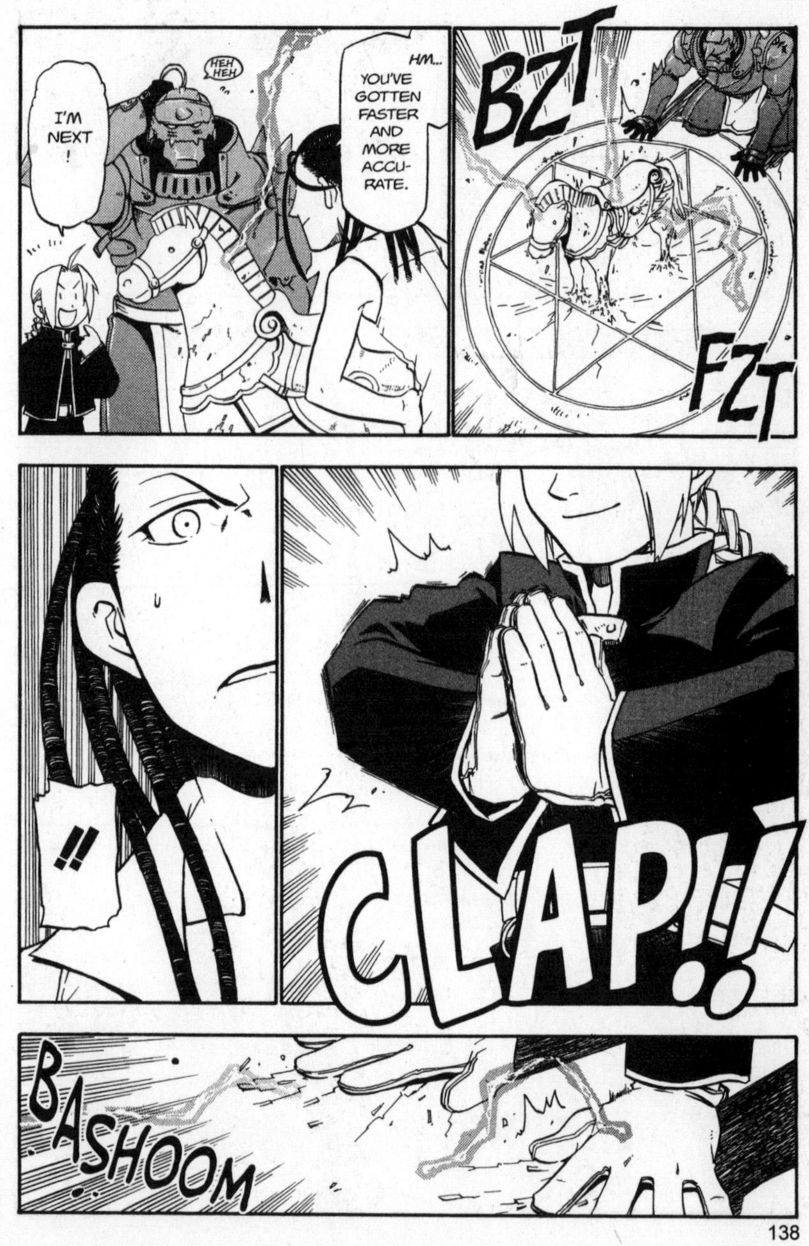
BZT
FZT
HM... YOU'VE GOTTEN FASTER AND MORE ACCU-RATE.
HEH HEH
I'M NEXT!
CLAP!!
!!
BASHOOM

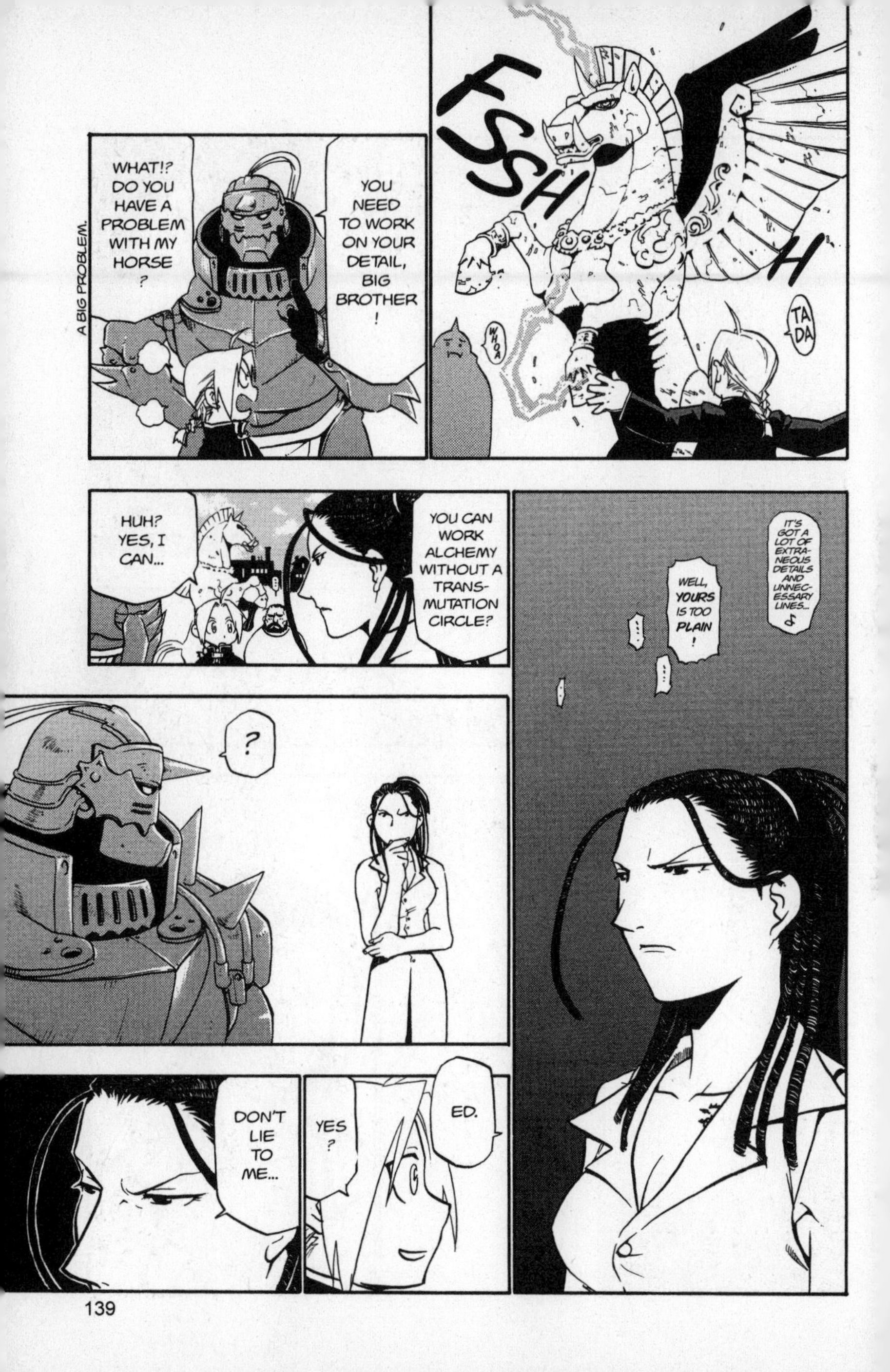
FSHH
TA DA
WHOA
YOU NEED TO WORK ON YOUR DETAIL, BIG BROTHER!
WHAT!? DO YOU HAVE A PROBLEM WITH MY HORSE?
A BIG PROBLEM.
IT'S GOT A LOT OF EXTRANEOUS DETAILS AND UNNECESSARY LINES...
WELL, YOURS IS TOO PLAIN!
...
...
YOU CAN WORK ALCHEMY WITHOUT A TRANSMUTATION CIRCLE?
HUH? YES, I CAN...
?
ED.
YES?
DON'T LIE TO ME...

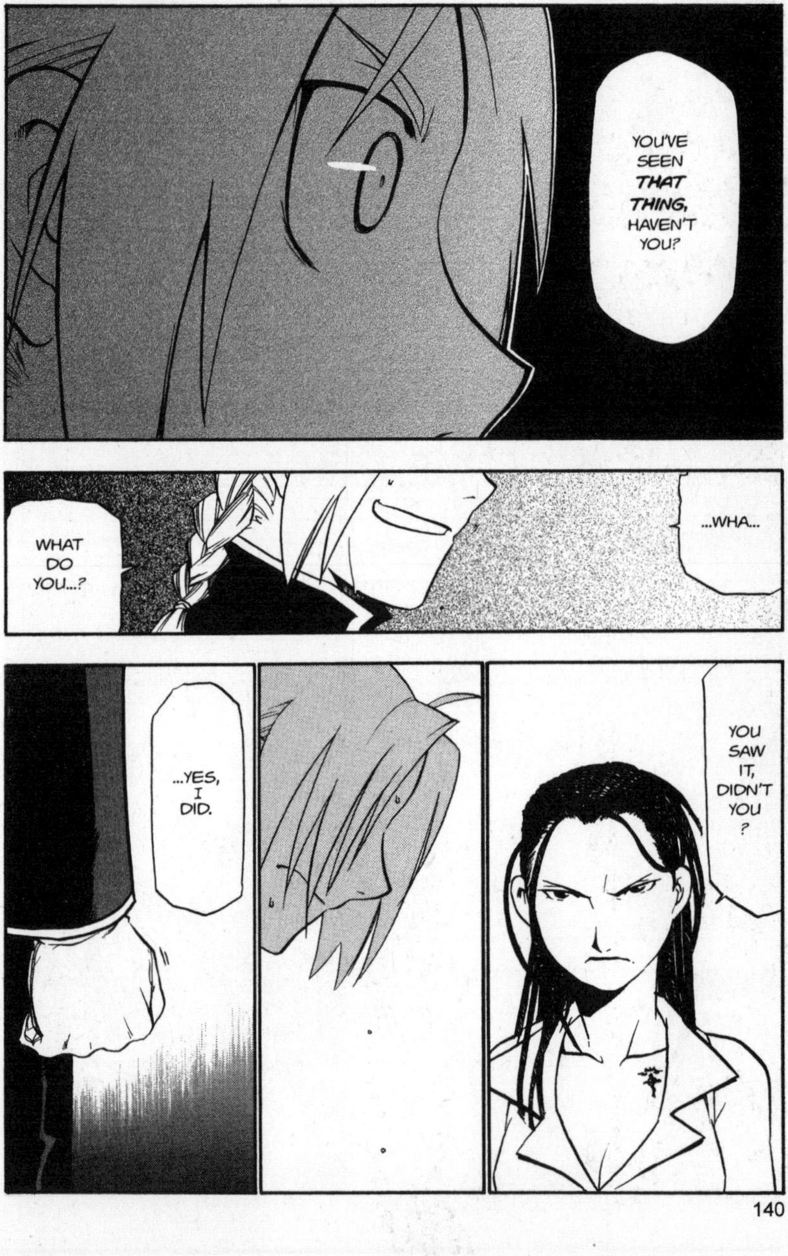
YOU'VE SEEN ***THAT THING,*** HAVEN'T YOU?
...WHA...
WHAT DO YOU...?
YOU SAW IT, DIDN'T YOU?
...YES, I DID.

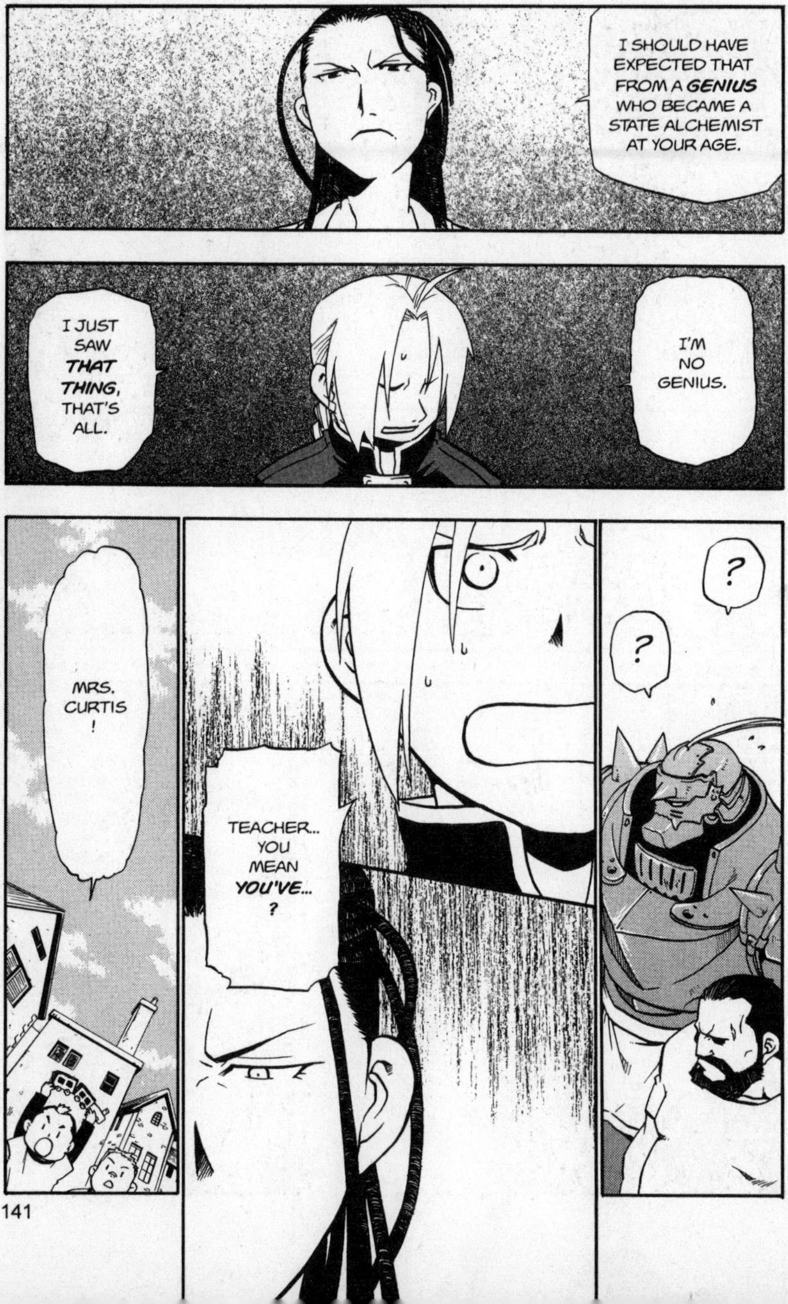
I SHOULD HAVE EXPECTED THAT FROM A **GENIUS** WHO BECAME A STATE ALCHEMIST AT YOUR AGE.
I'M NO GENIUS.
I JUST SAW **THAT THING**, THAT'S ALL.
?
?
TEACHER... YOU MEAN **YOU'VE...** ?
MRS. CURTIS!

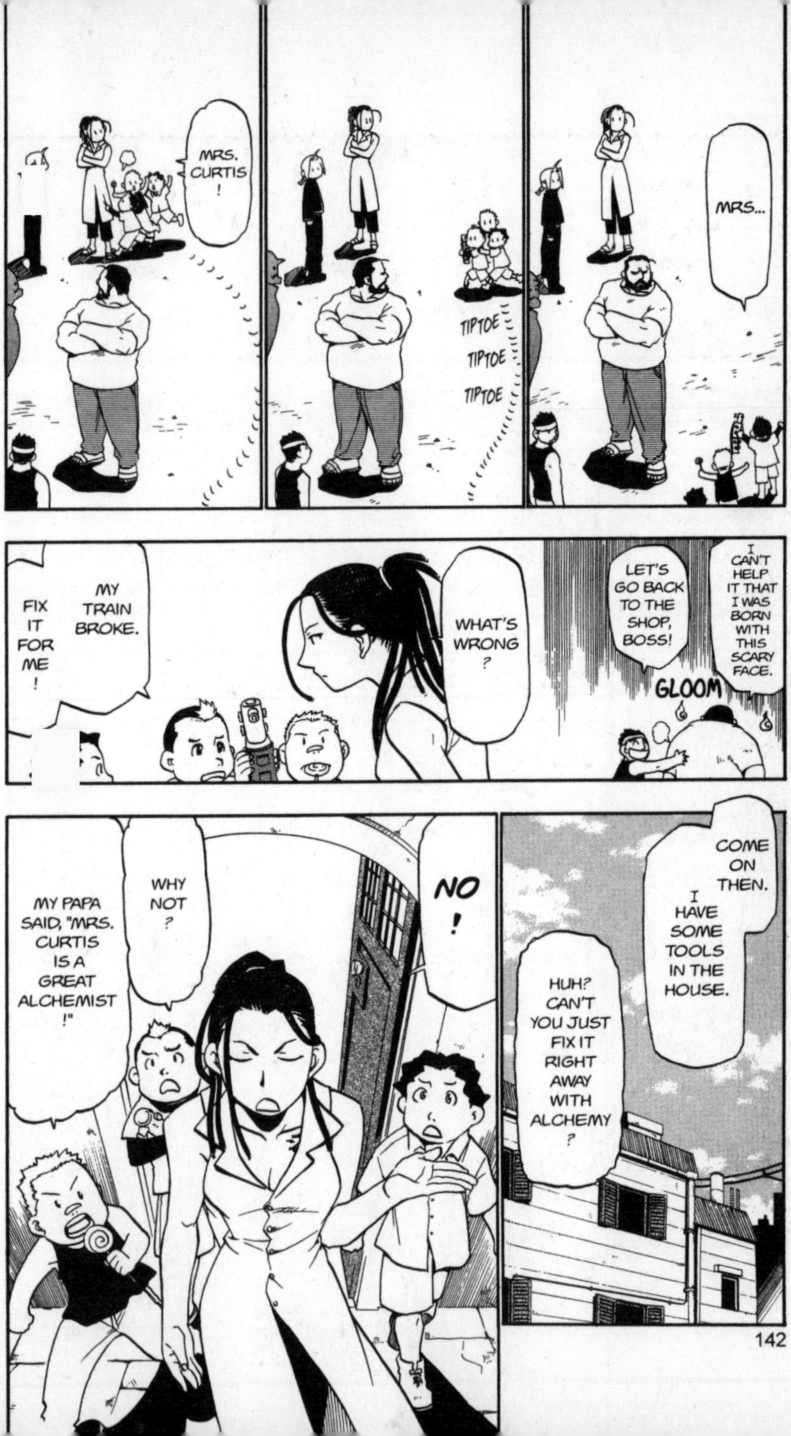
MRS...
TIPTOE
TIPTOE
TIPTOE
MRS. CURTIS!
I CAN'T HELP IT THAT I WAS BORN WITH THIS SCARY FACE.
LET'S GO BACK TO THE SHOP, BOSS!
GLOOM
WHAT'S WRONG?
MY TRAIN BROKE.
FIX IT FOR ME!
COME ON THEN. I HAVE SOME TOOLS IN THE HOUSE.
HUH? CAN'T YOU JUST FIX IT RIGHT AWAY WITH ALCHEMY?
NO!
WHY NOT?
MY PAPA SAID, "MRS. CURTIS IS A GREAT ALCHEMIST!"

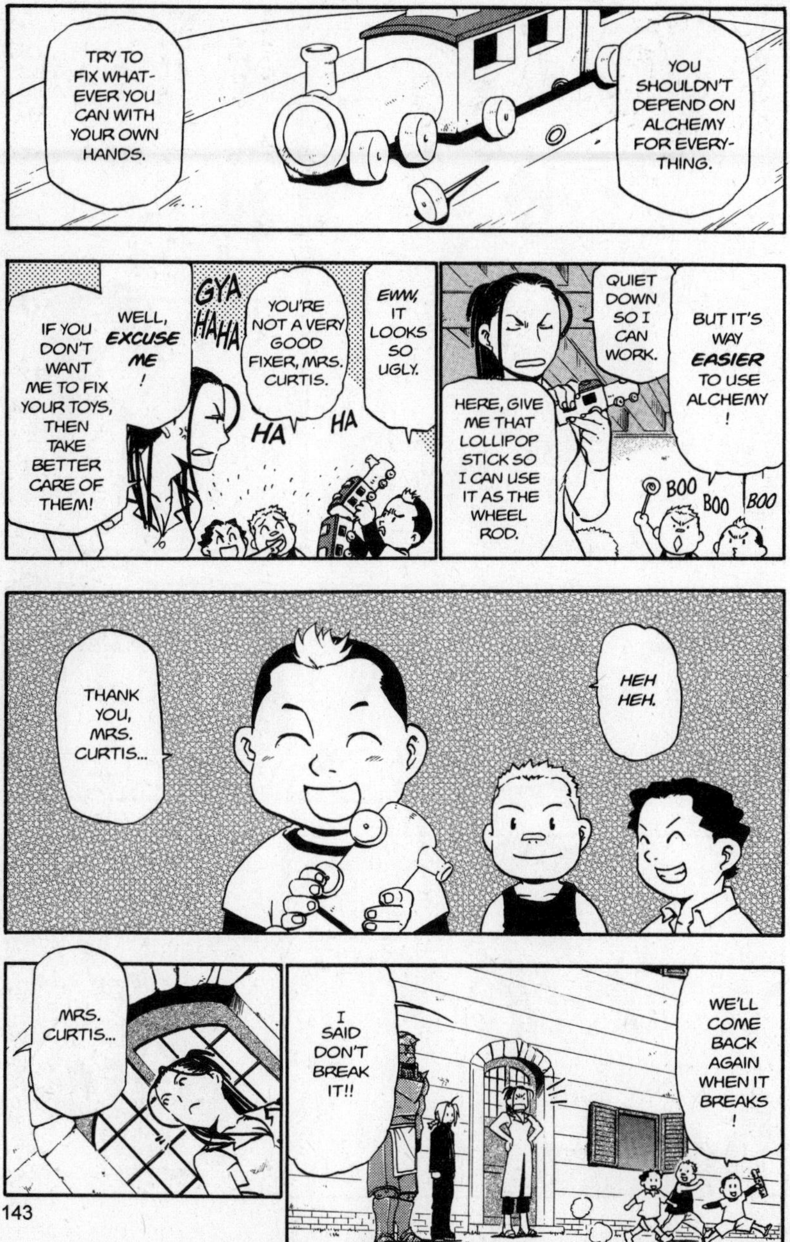
YOU SHOULDN'T DEPEND ON ALCHEMY FOR EVERYTHING.
TRY TO FIX WHATEVER YOU CAN WITH YOUR OWN HANDS.
BUT IT'S WAY **EASIER** TO USE ALCHEMY!
QUIET DOWN SO I CAN WORK.
HERE, GIVE ME THAT LOLLIPOP STICK SO I CAN USE IT AS THE WHEEL ROD.
BOO BOO BOO
EWW, IT LOOKS SO UGLY.
YOU'RE NOT A VERY GOOD FIXER, MRS. CURTIS.
GYA HAHA
HA HA
WELL, **EXCUSE ME**!
IF YOU DON'T WANT ME TO FIX YOUR TOYS, THEN TAKE BETTER CARE OF THEM!
HEH HEH.
THANK YOU, MRS. CURTIS...
WE'LL COME BACK AGAIN WHEN IT BREAKS!
I SAID DON'T BREAK IT!!
MRS. CURTIS...

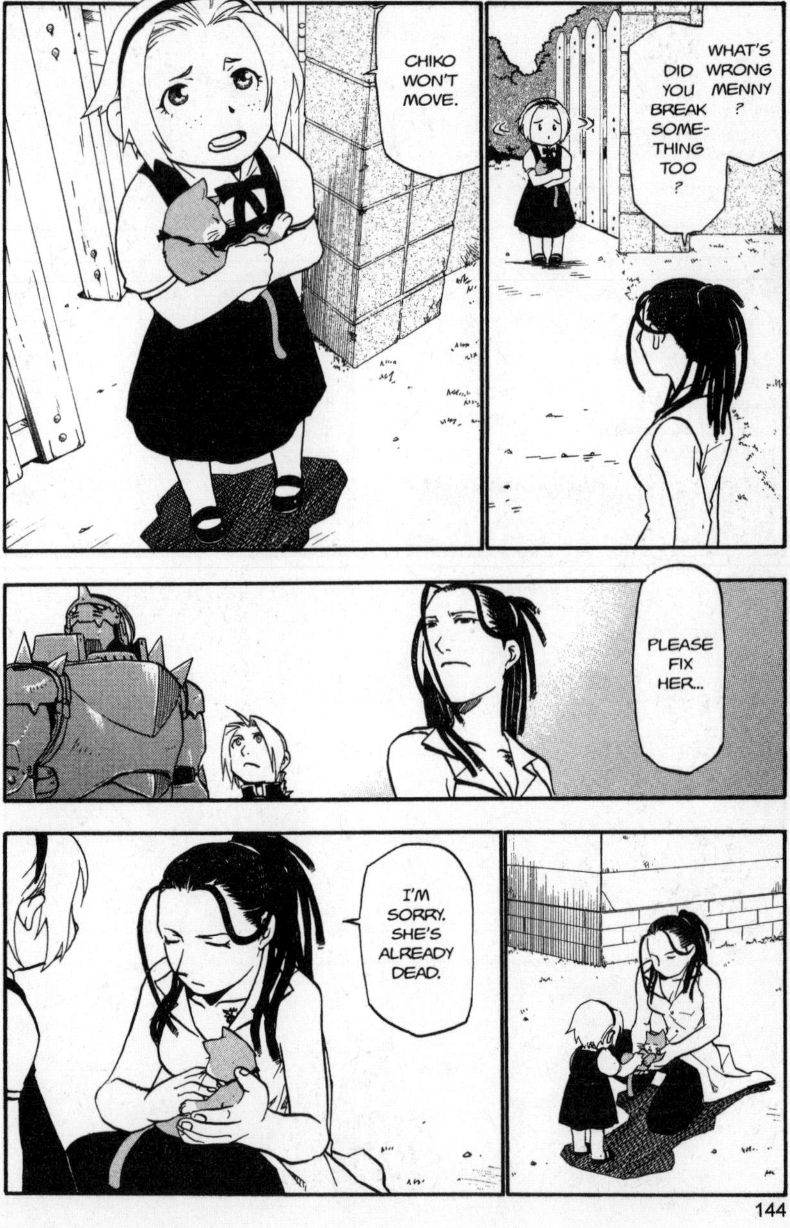
WHAT'S WRONG MENNY?
DID YOU BREAK SOMETHING TOO?
CHIKO WON'T MOVE.
PLEASE FIX HER...
I'M SORRY. SHE'S ALREADY DEAD.

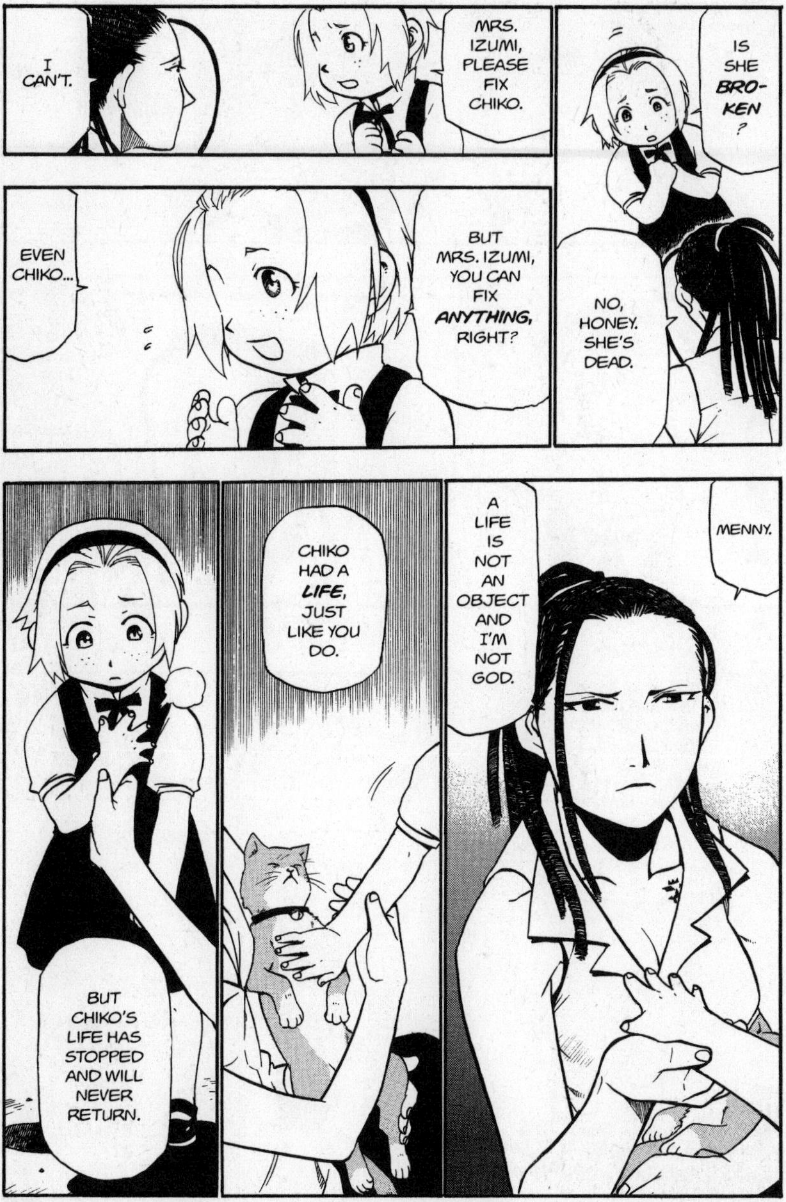
IS SHE BROKEN?
NO, HONEY. SHE'S DEAD.
MRS. IZUMI, PLEASE FIX CHIKO.
I CAN'T.
BUT MRS. IZUMI, YOU CAN FIX ANYTHING, RIGHT?
EVEN CHIKO...
MENNY.
A LIFE IS NOT AN OBJECT AND I'M NOT GOD.
CHIKO HAD A LIFE, JUST LIKE YOU DO.
BUT CHIKO'S LIFE HAS STOPPED AND WILL NEVER RETURN.

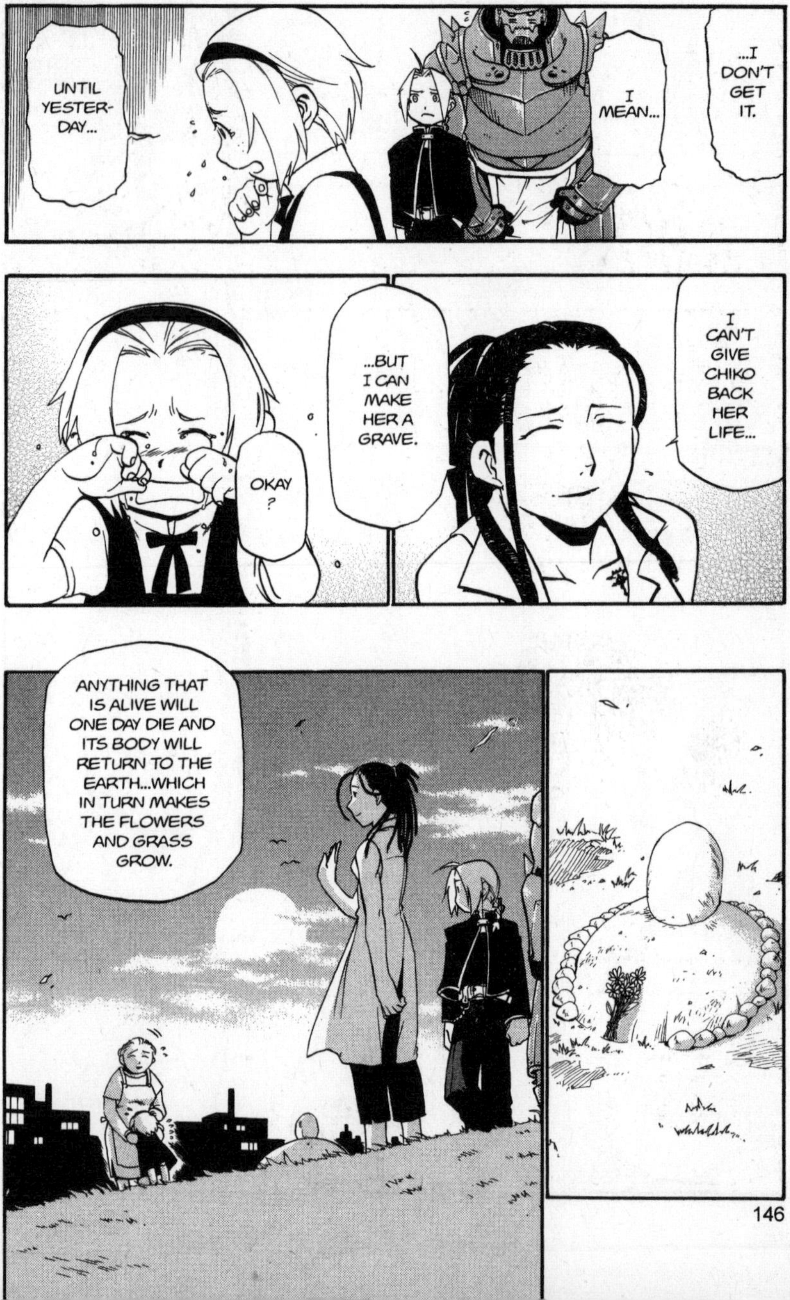
...I DON'T GET IT.
I MEAN...
UNTIL YESTER-DAY...
I CAN'T GIVE CHIKO BACK HER LIFE...
...BUT I CAN MAKE HER A GRAVE.
OKAY?
ANYTHING THAT IS ALIVE WILL ONE DAY DIE AND ITS BODY WILL RETURN TO THE EARTH...WHICH IN TURN MAKES THE FLOWERS AND GRASS GROW.

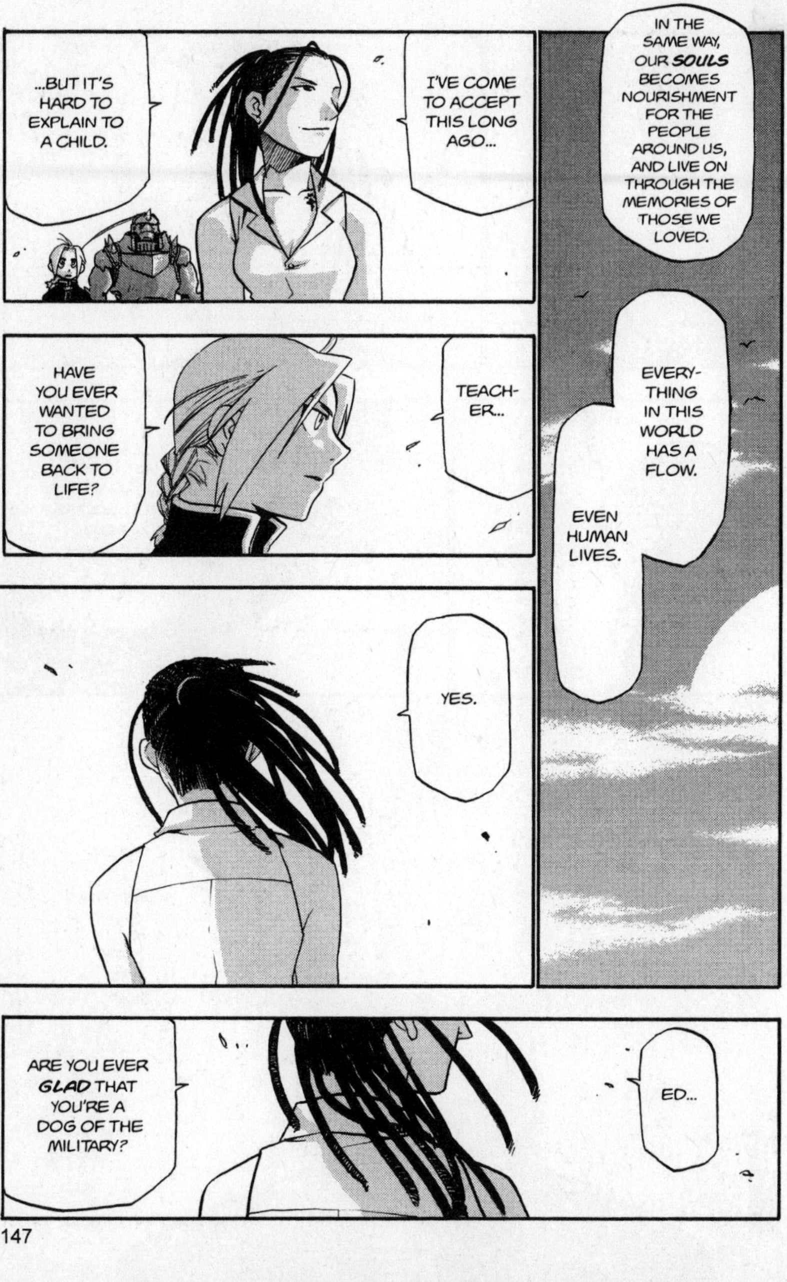
IN THE SAME WAY, OUR SOULS BECOMES NOURISHMENT FOR THE PEOPLE AROUND US, AND LIVE ON THROUGH THE MEMORIES OF THOSE WE LOVED.
EVERY-THING IN THIS WORLD HAS A FLOW.
EVEN HUMAN LIVES.
I'VE COME TO ACCEPT THIS LONG AGO...
...BUT IT'S HARD TO EXPLAIN TO A CHILD.
TEACHER...
HAVE YOU EVER WANTED TO BRING SOMEONE BACK TO LIFE?
YES.
ED...
ARE YOU EVER GLAD THAT YOU'RE A DOG OF THE MILITARY?

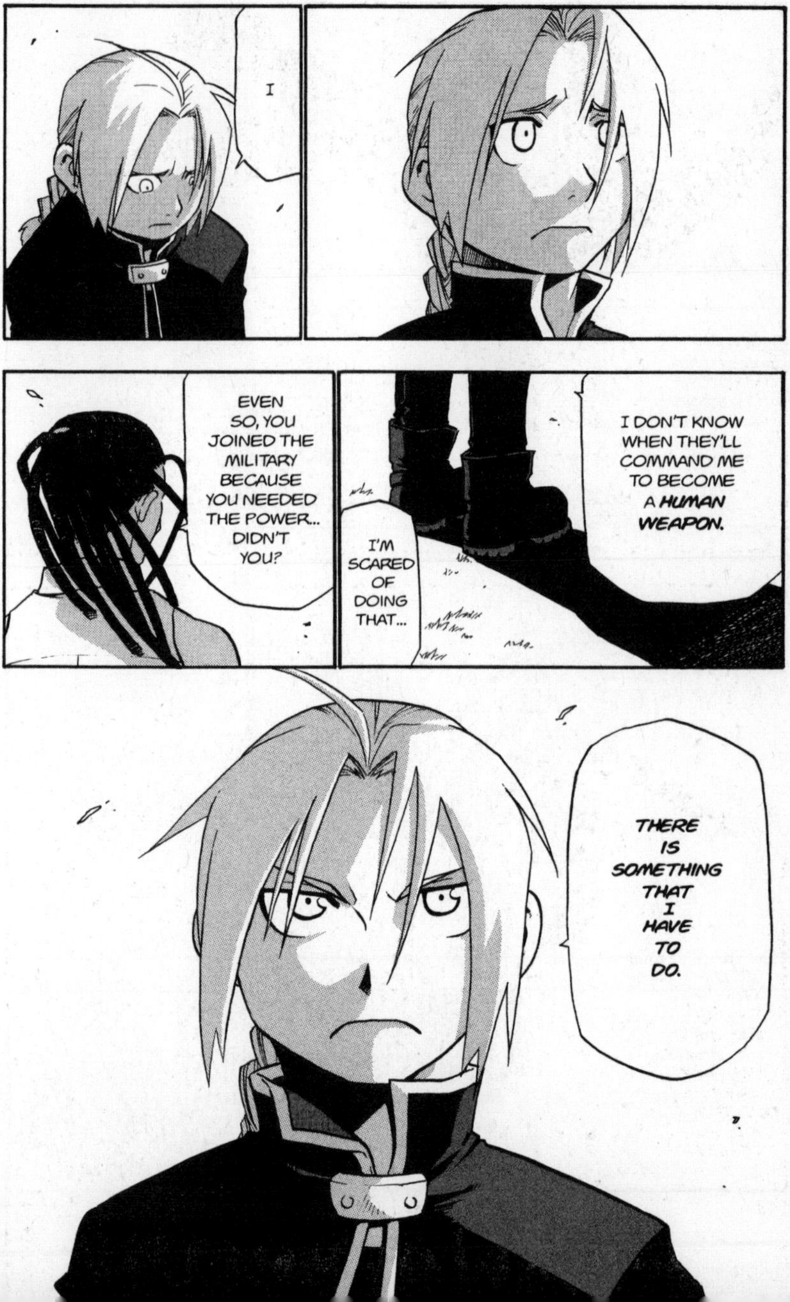
I
I DON'T KNOW WHEN THEY'LL COMMAND ME TO BECOME A **HUMAN WEAPON.**
I'M SCARED OF DOING THAT...
EVEN SO, YOU JOINED THE MILITARY BECAUSE YOU NEEDED THE POWER... DIDN'T YOU?
THERE IS SOMETHING THAT I HAVE TO DO.

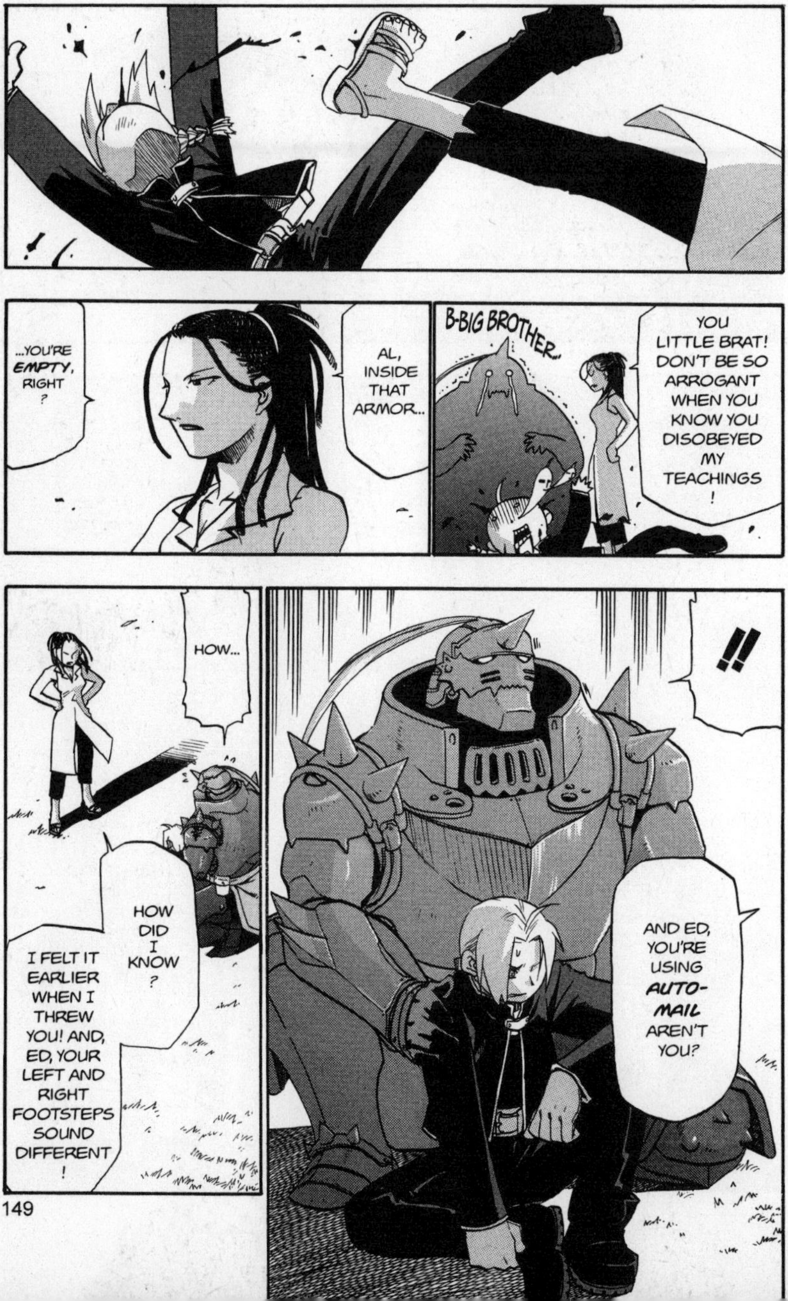
YOU LITTLE BRAT! DON'T BE SO ARROGANT WHEN YOU KNOW YOU DISOBEYED MY TEACHINGS!
B-BIG BROTHER...
AL, INSIDE THAT ARMOR...
...YOU'RE EMPTY, RIGHT?
!!
AND ED, YOU'RE USING AUTO-MAIL AREN'T YOU?
HOW...
HOW DID I KNOW?
I FELT IT EARLIER WHEN I THREW YOU! AND, ED, YOUR LEFT AND RIGHT FOOTSTEPS SOUND DIFFERENT!

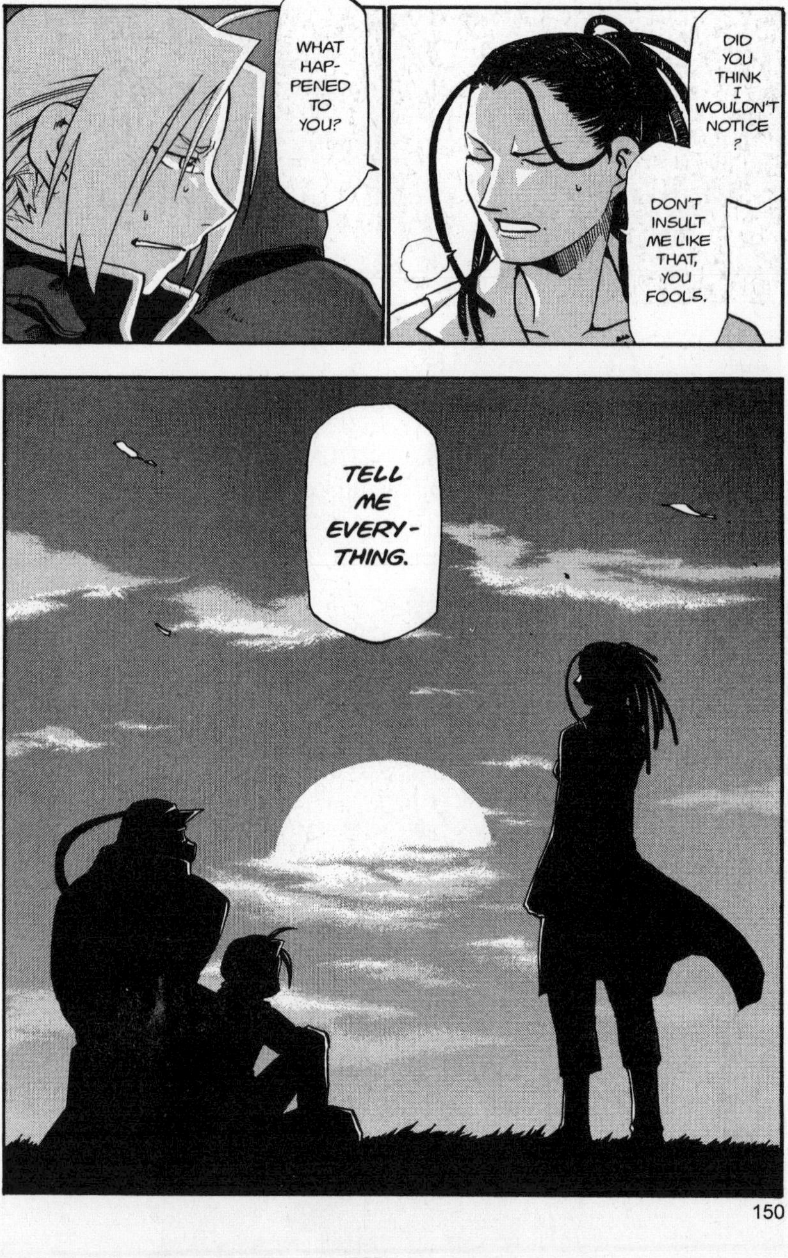
DID YOU THINK I WOULDN'T NOTICE?
DON'T INSULT ME LIKE THAT, YOU FOOLS.
WHAT HAP-PENED TO YOU?
TELL ME EVERY-THING.

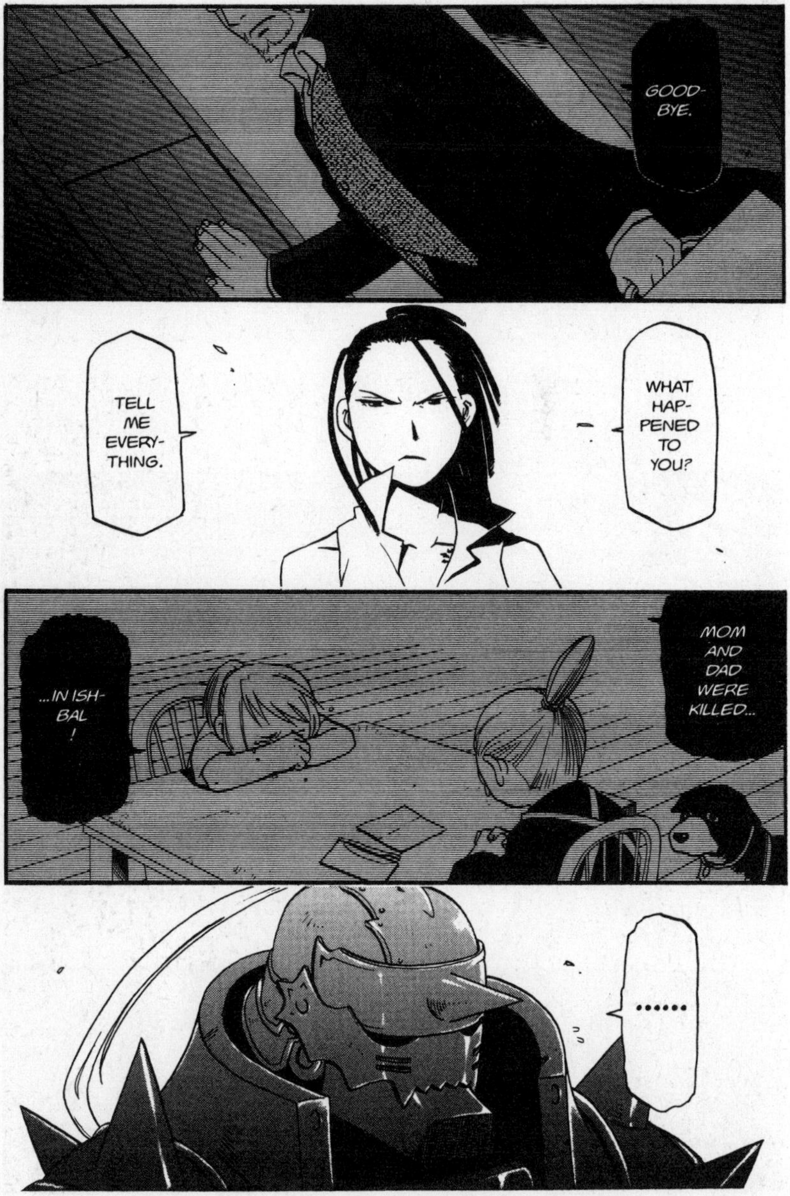
GOOD-BYE.
WHAT HAP-PENED TO YOU?
TELL ME EVERY-THING.
MOM AND DAD WERE KILLED...
...IN ISH-BAL!
......

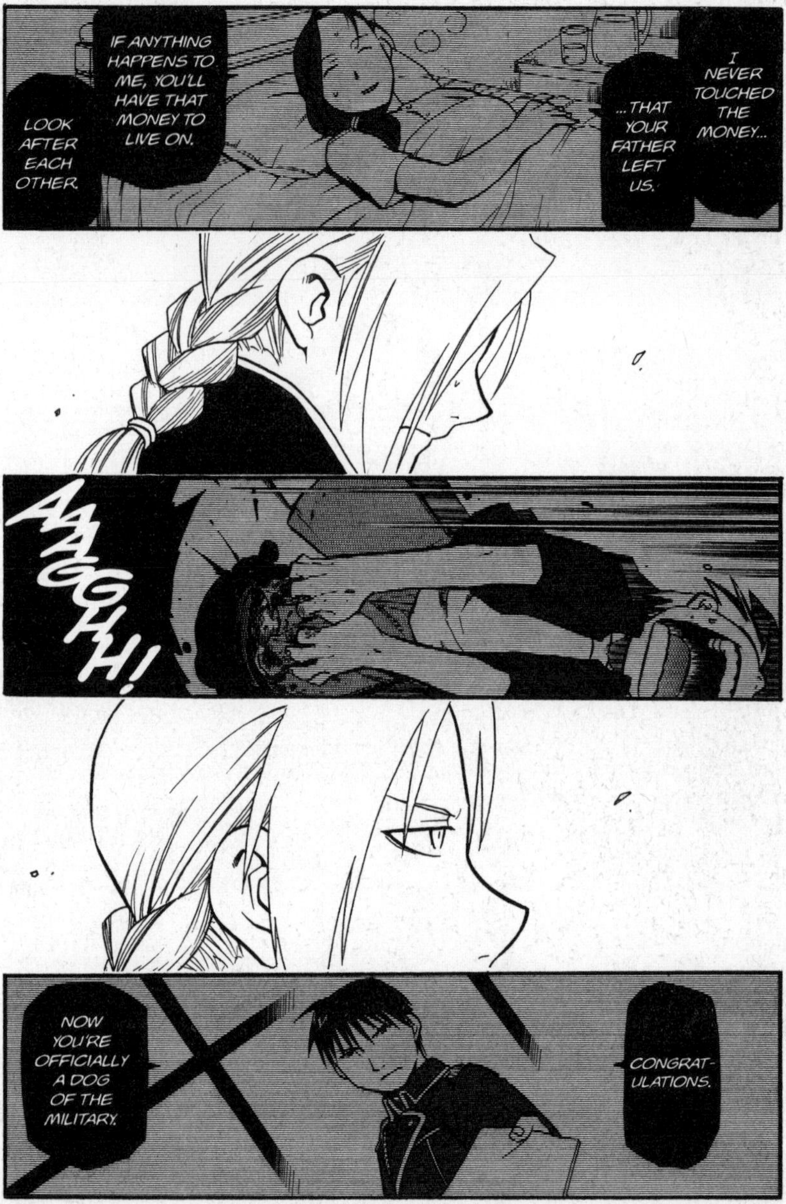
I NEVER TOUCHED THE MONEY...
...THAT YOUR FATHER LEFT US.
IF ANYTHING HAPPENS TO ME, YOU'LL HAVE THAT MONEY TO LIVE ON.
LOOK AFTER EACH OTHER.
AAAGGHH!
CONGRAT-ULATIONS.
NOW YOU'RE OFFICIALLY A DOG OF THE MILITARY.

Chapter 21: The Brothers' Secret

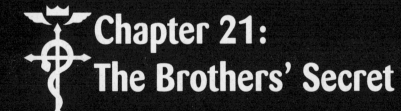

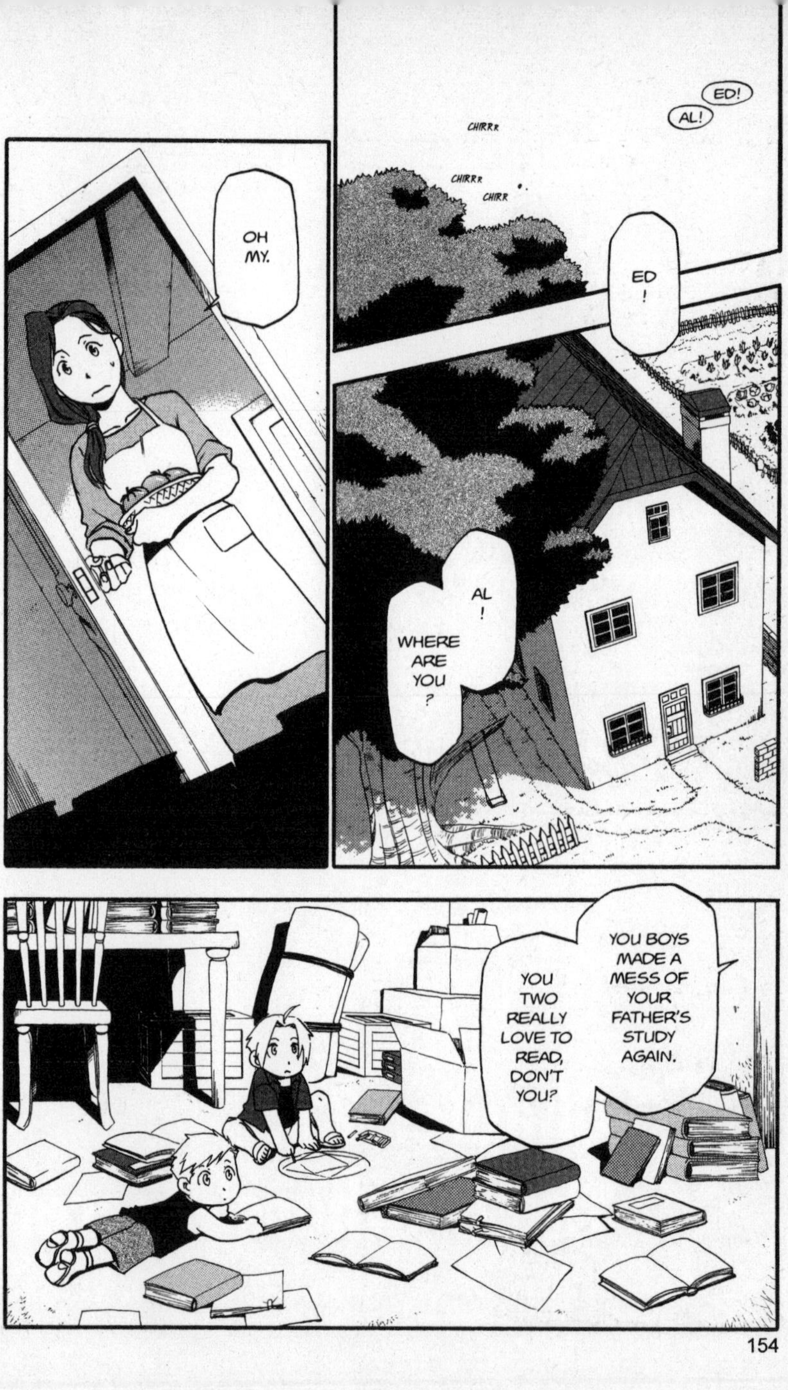
ED!
AL!
CHIRRR
CHIRRR
CHIRR
ED!
AL!
WHERE ARE YOU?
OH MY.
YOU BOYS MADE A MESS OF YOUR FATHER'S STUDY AGAIN.
YOU TWO REALLY LOVE TO READ, DON'T YOU?

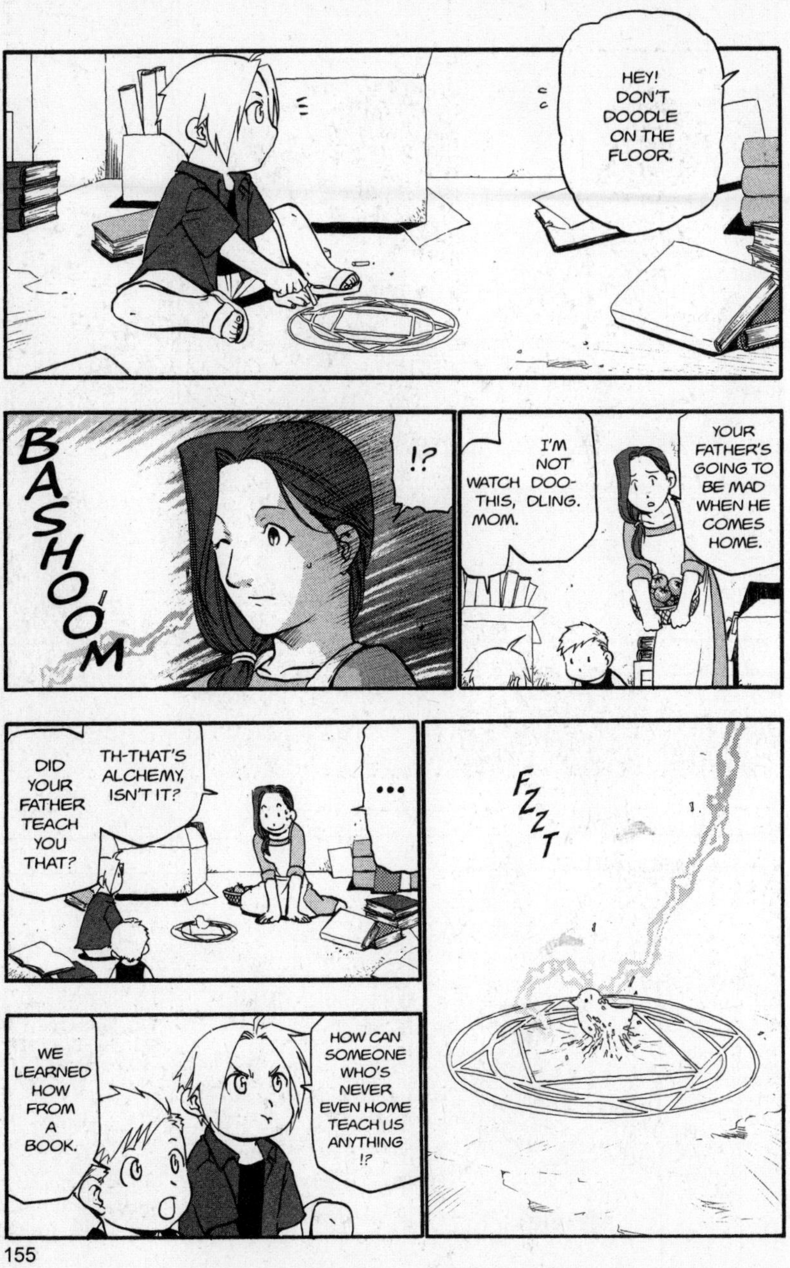
HEY! DON'T DOODLE ON THE FLOOR.
YOUR FATHER'S GOING TO BE MAD WHEN HE COMES HOME.
I'M NOT DOODLING.
WATCH THIS, MOM.
!?
BASHOOM
FZZT
...
TH-THAT'S ALCHEMY, ISN'T IT?
DID YOUR FATHER TEACH YOU THAT?
HOW CAN SOMEONE WHO'S NEVER EVEN HOME TEACH US ANYTHING!?
WE LEARNED HOW FROM A BOOK.

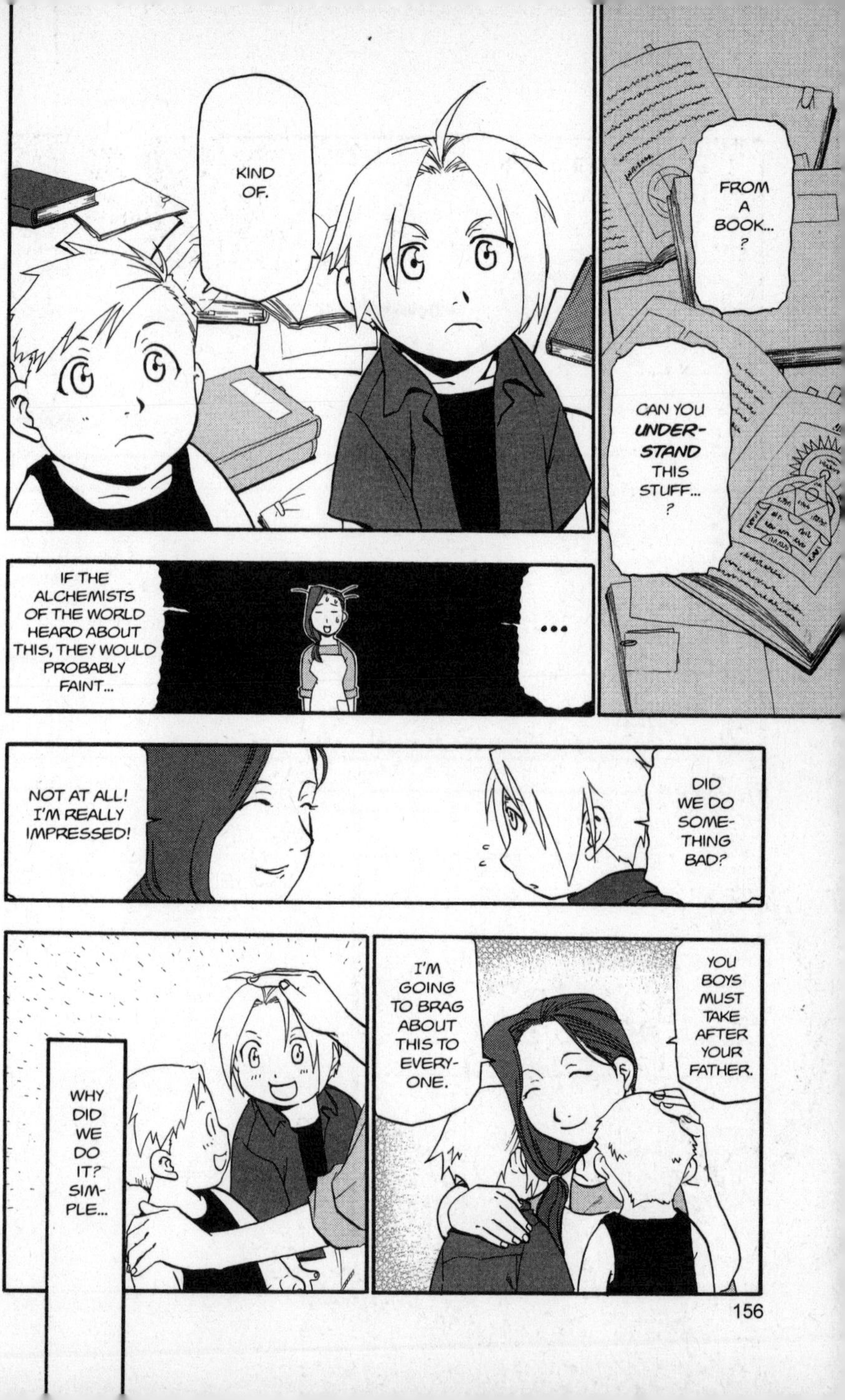
FROM A BOOK...?
CAN YOU UNDERSTAND THIS STUFF...?
KIND OF.
...
IF THE ALCHEMISTS OF THE WORLD HEARD ABOUT THIS, THEY WOULD PROBABLY FAINT...
DID WE DO SOME-THING BAD?
NOT AT ALL! I'M REALLY IMPRESSED!
YOU BOYS MUST TAKE AFTER YOUR FATHER.
I'M GOING TO BRAG ABOUT THIS TO EVERY-ONE.
WHY DID WE DO IT? SIM-PLE...

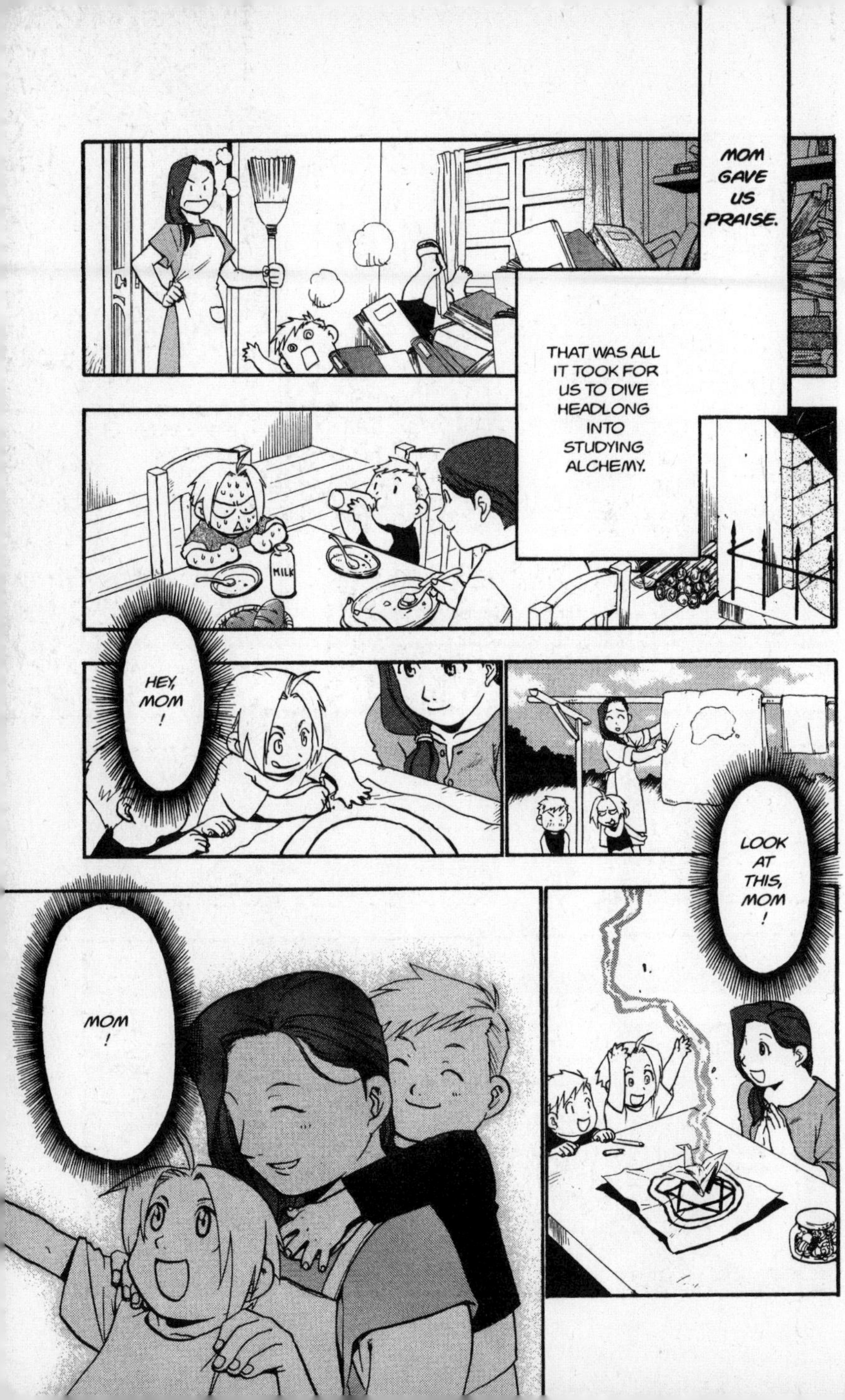
MOM GAVE US PRAISE.
THAT WAS ALL IT TOOK FOR US TO DIVE HEADLONG INTO STUDYING ALCHEMY.
HEY, MOM!
LOOK AT THIS, MOM!
MOM!

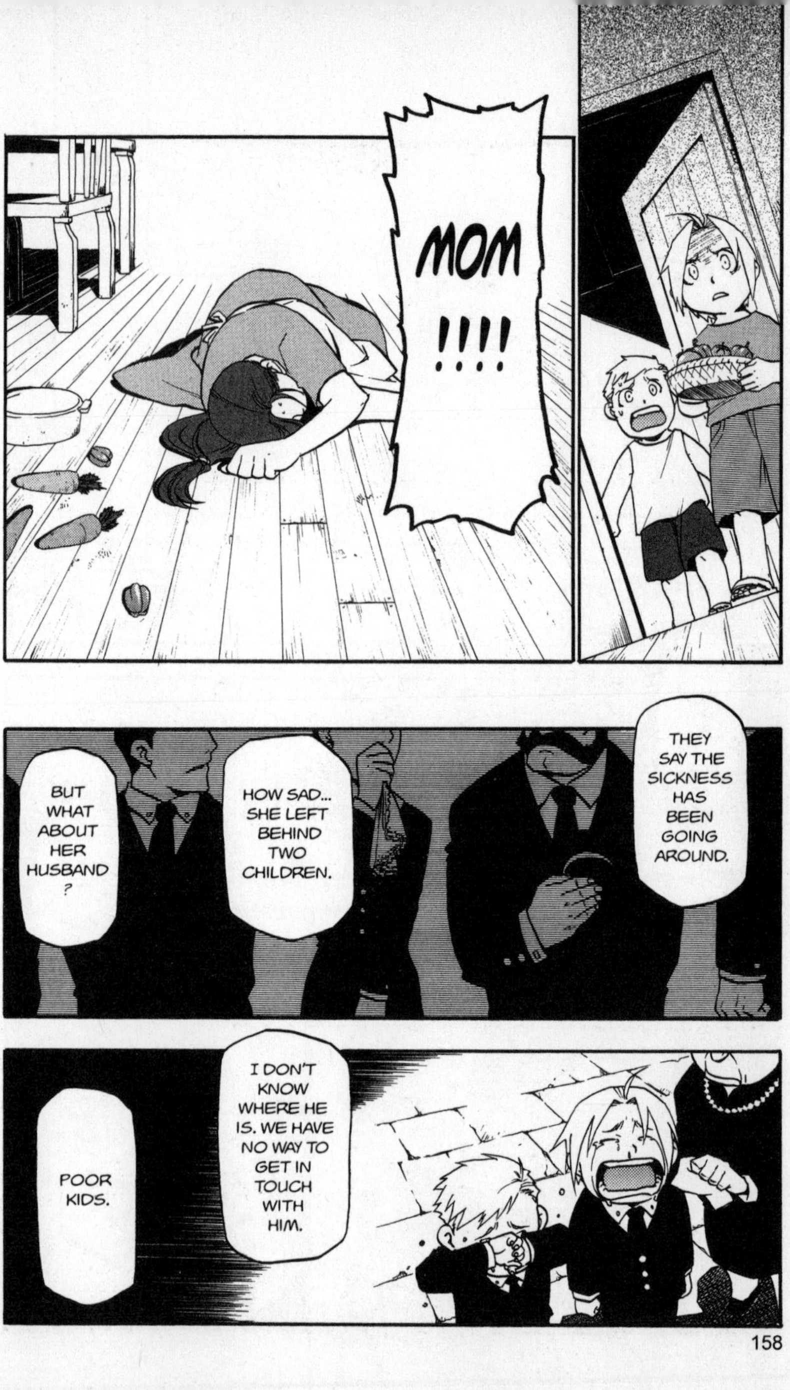
MOM !!!!
THEY SAY THE SICKNESS HAS BEEN GOING AROUND.
HOW SAD... SHE LEFT BEHIND TWO CHILDREN.
BUT WHAT ABOUT HER HUSBAND?
I DON'T KNOW WHERE HE IS. WE HAVE NO WAY TO GET IN TOUCH WITH HIM.
POOR KIDS.

I'M HUN-GRY.

BIG BRO-THER.

AND COLD.

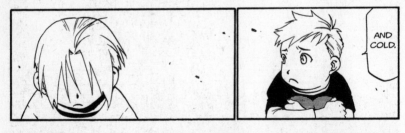

• • •

LET'S GO HOME.

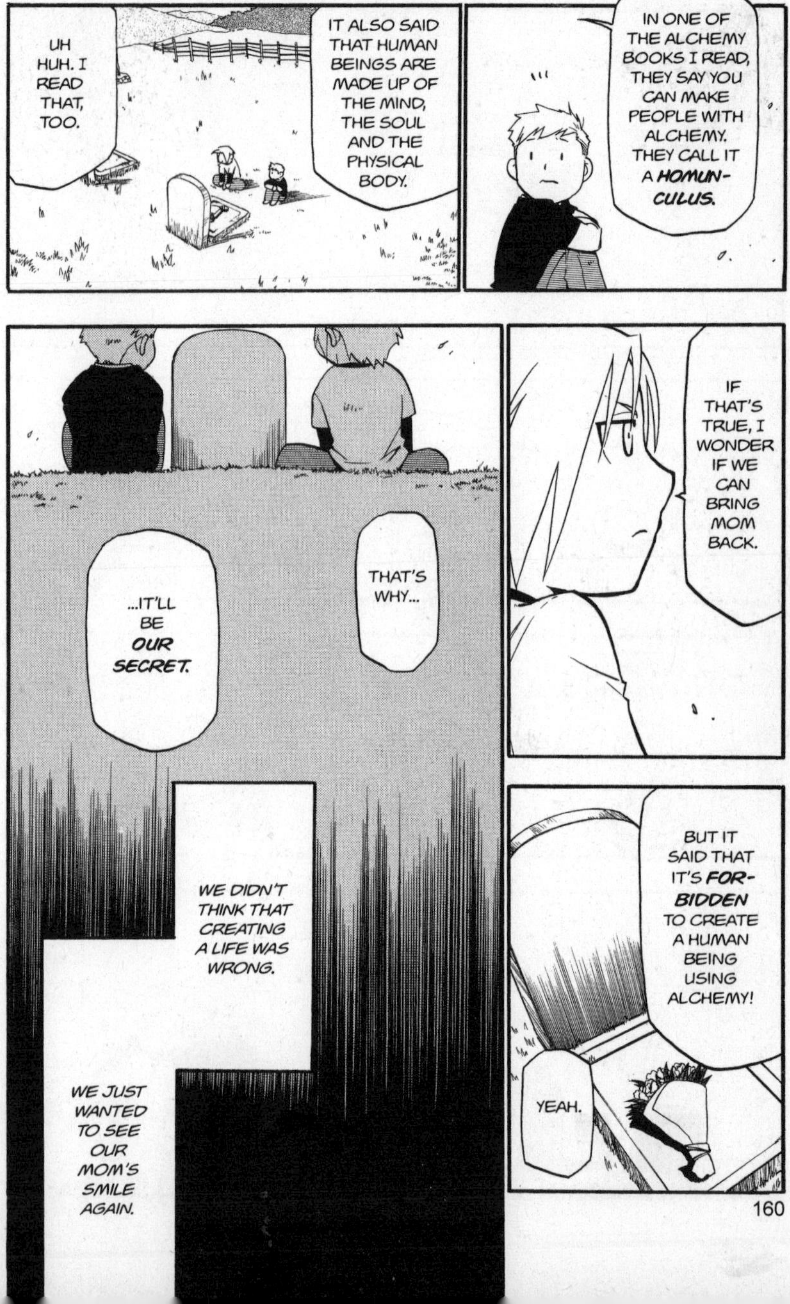
IN ONE OF THE ALCHEMY BOOKS I READ, THEY SAY YOU CAN MAKE PEOPLE WITH ALCHEMY. THEY CALL IT A HOMUNCULUS.
IT ALSO SAID THAT HUMAN BEINGS ARE MADE UP OF THE MIND, THE SOUL AND THE PHYSICAL BODY.
UH HUH. I READ THAT, TOO.
IF THAT'S TRUE, I WONDER IF WE CAN BRING MOM BACK.
BUT IT SAID THAT IT'S FORBIDDEN TO CREATE A HUMAN BEING USING ALCHEMY!
YEAH.
THAT'S WHY...
...IT'LL BE OUR SECRET.
WE DIDN'T THINK THAT CREATING A LIFE WAS WRONG.
WE JUST WANTED TO SEE OUR MOM'S SMILE AGAIN.

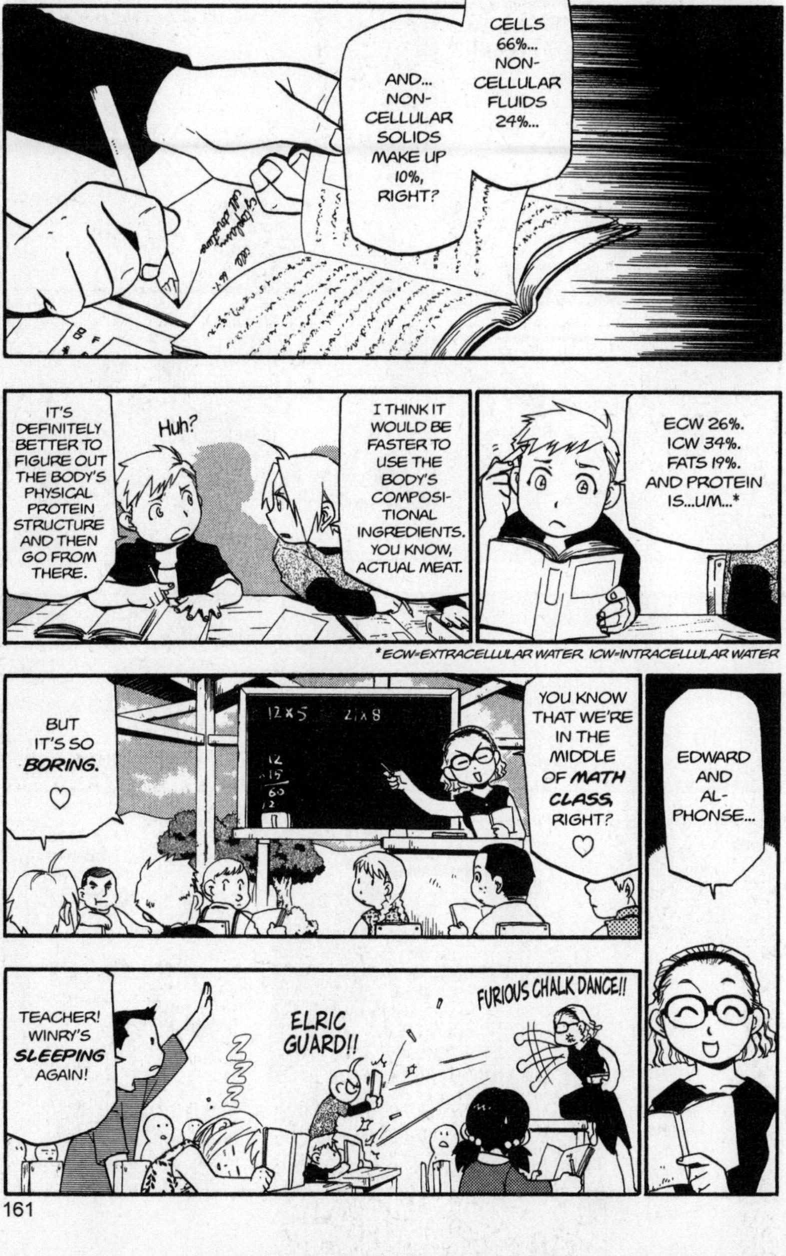
CELLS 66%... NON-CELLULAR FLUIDS 24%...
AND... NON-CELLULAR SOLIDS MAKE UP 10%, RIGHT?
ECW 26%. ICW 34%. FATS 19%. AND PROTEIN IS...UM...*
I THINK IT WOULD BE FASTER TO USE THE BODY'S COMPOSITIONAL INGREDIENTS. YOU KNOW, ACTUAL MEAT.
Huh?
IT'S DEFINITELY BETTER TO FIGURE OUT THE BODY'S PHYSICAL PROTEIN STRUCTURE AND THEN GO FROM THERE.
*ECW=EXTRACELLULAR WATER, ICW=INTRACELLULAR WATER
EDWARD AND AL-PHONSE...
YOU KNOW THAT WE'RE IN THE MIDDLE OF MATH CLASS, RIGHT? ♡
12×5 21×8
BUT IT'S SO BORING. ♡
FURIOUS CHALK DANCE!!
ELRIC GUARD!!
ZZZ
TEACHER! WINRY'S SLEEPING AGAIN!

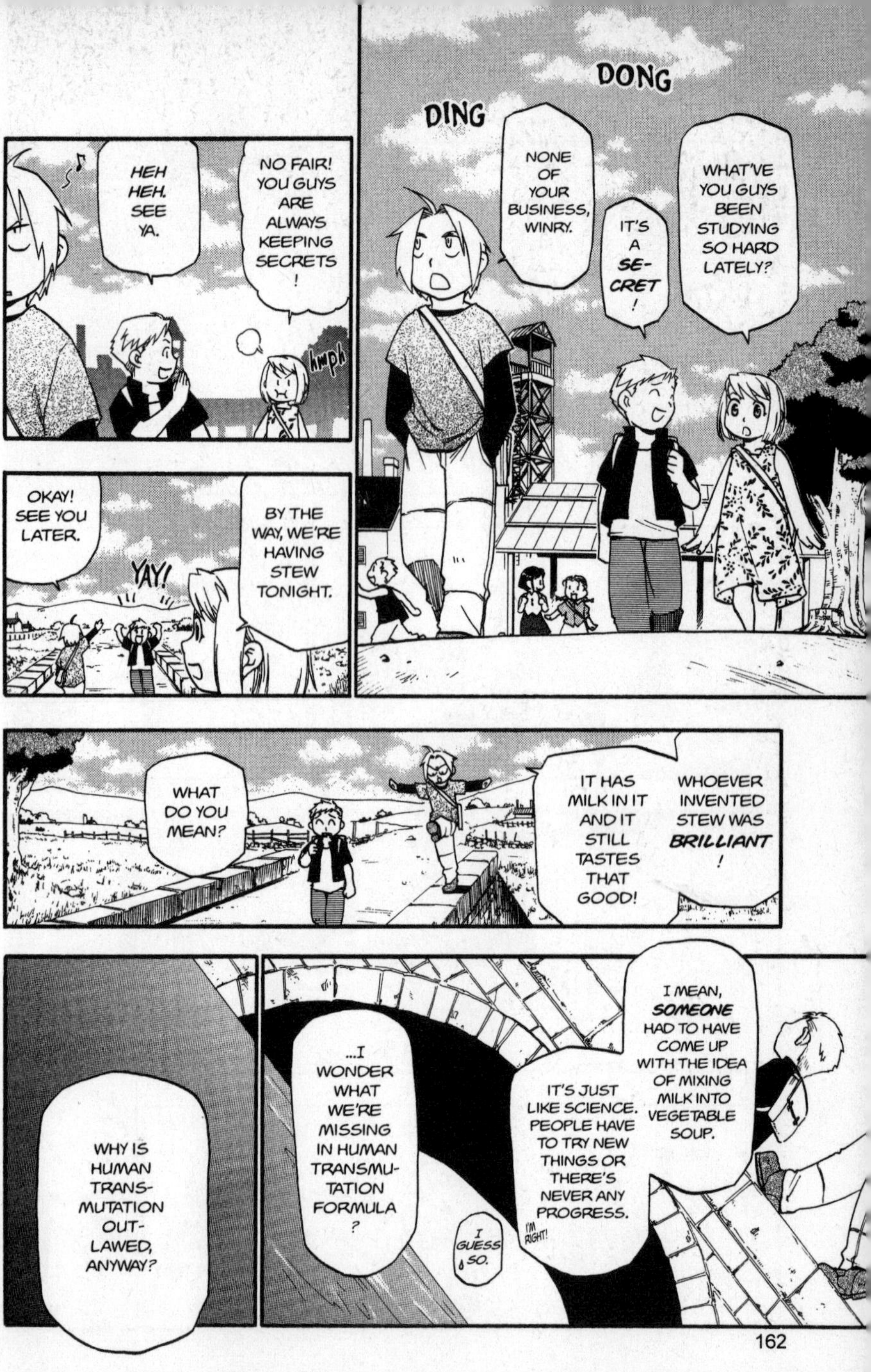
DONG
DING
WHAT'VE YOU GUYS BEEN STUDYING SO HARD LATELY?
IT'S A SE-CRET!
NONE OF YOUR BUSINESS, WINRY.
NO FAIR! YOU GUYS ARE ALWAYS KEEPING SECRETS!
HEH HEH. SEE YA.
hmph
BY THE WAY, WE'RE HAVING STEW TONIGHT.
YAY!
OKAY! SEE YOU LATER.
WHOEVER INVENTED STEW WAS BRILLIANT!
IT HAS MILK IN IT AND IT STILL TASTES THAT GOOD!
WHAT DO YOU MEAN?
I MEAN, SOMEONE HAD TO HAVE COME UP WITH THE IDEA OF MIXING MILK INTO VEGETABLE SOUP.
IT'S JUST LIKE SCIENCE. PEOPLE HAVE TO TRY NEW THINGS OR THERE'S NEVER ANY PROGRESS.
I'M RIGHT!
I GUESS SO.
...I WONDER WHAT WE'RE MISSING IN HUMAN TRANSMUTATION FORMULA?
WHY IS HUMAN TRANSMUTATION OUTLAWED, ANYWAY?

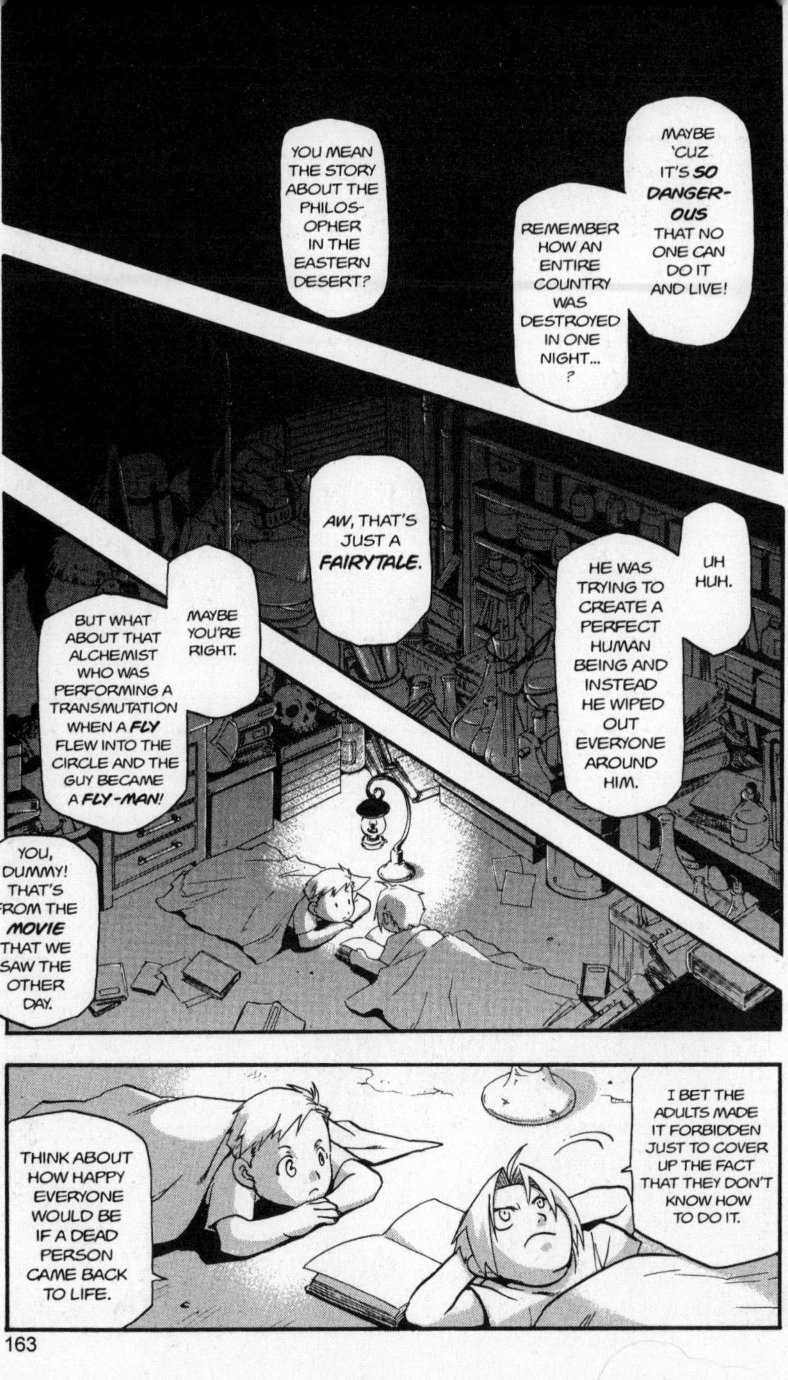
MAYBE 'CUZ IT'S SO DANGER-OUS THAT NO ONE CAN DO IT AND LIVE!
REMEMBER HOW AN ENTIRE COUNTRY WAS DESTROYED IN ONE NIGHT...?
YOU MEAN THE STORY ABOUT THE PHILOS-OPHER IN THE EASTERN DESERT?
UH HUH.
HE WAS TRYING TO CREATE A PERFECT HUMAN BEING AND INSTEAD HE WIPED OUT EVERYONE AROUND HIM.
AW, THAT'S JUST A FAIRYTALE.
MAYBE YOU'RE RIGHT.
BUT WHAT ABOUT THAT ALCHEMIST WHO WAS PERFORMING A TRANSMUTATION WHEN A FLY FLEW INTO THE CIRCLE AND THE GUY BECAME A FLY-MAN!
YOU, DUMMY! THAT'S FROM THE MOVIE THAT WE SAW THE OTHER DAY.
I BET THE ADULTS MADE IT FORBIDDEN JUST TO COVER UP THE FACT THAT THEY DON'T KNOW HOW TO DO IT.
THINK ABOUT HOW HAPPY EVERYONE WOULD BE IF A DEAD PERSON CAME BACK TO LIFE.

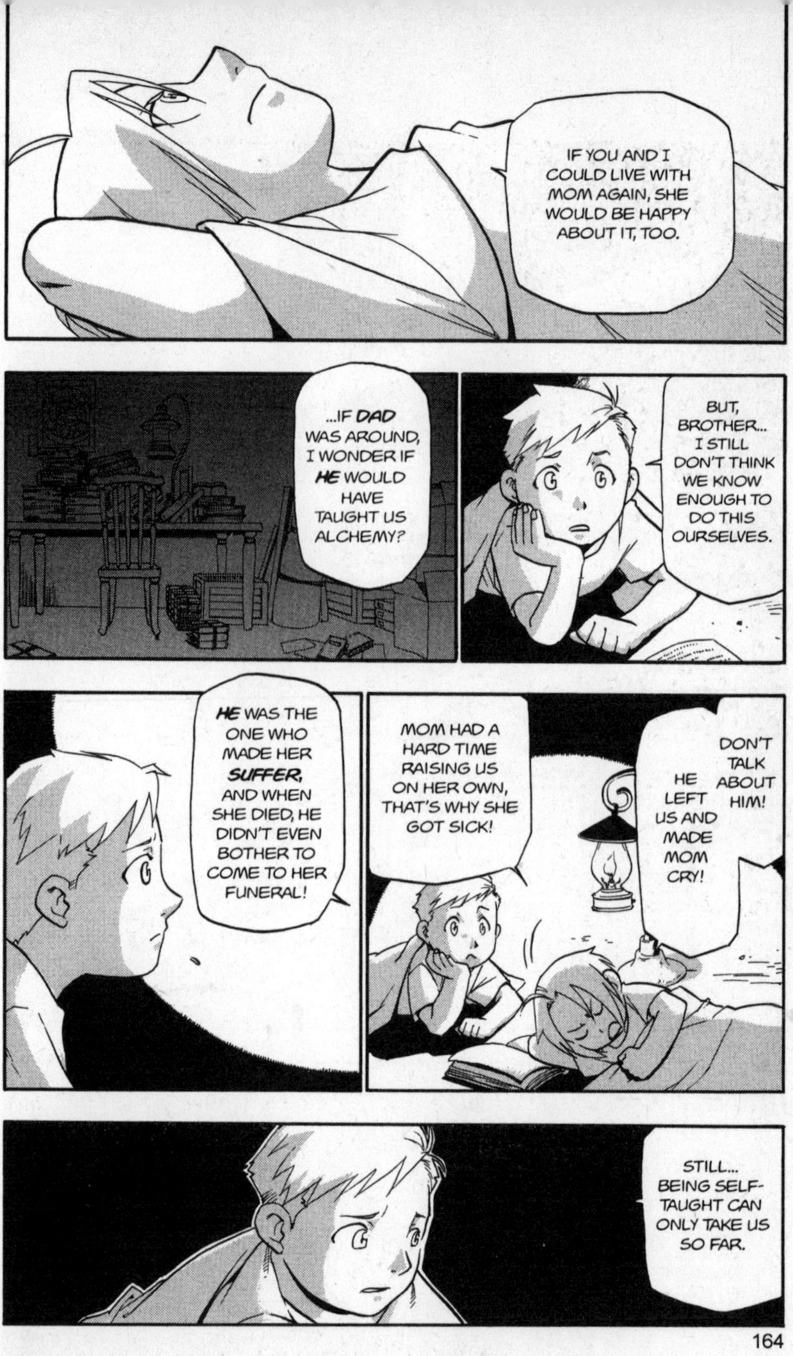
IF YOU AND I COULD LIVE WITH MOM AGAIN, SHE WOULD BE HAPPY ABOUT IT, TOO.
BUT, BROTHER... I STILL DON'T THINK WE KNOW ENOUGH TO DO THIS OURSELVES.
...IF DAD WAS AROUND, I WONDER IF HE WOULD HAVE TAUGHT US ALCHEMY?
DON'T TALK ABOUT HIM!
HE LEFT US AND MADE MOM CRY!
MOM HAD A HARD TIME RAISING US ON HER OWN, THAT'S WHY SHE GOT SICK!
HE WAS THE ONE WHO MADE HER SUFFER, AND WHEN SHE DIED, HE DIDN'T EVEN BOTHER TO COME TO HER FUNERAL!
STILL... BEING SELF-TAUGHT CAN ONLY TAKE US SO FAR.

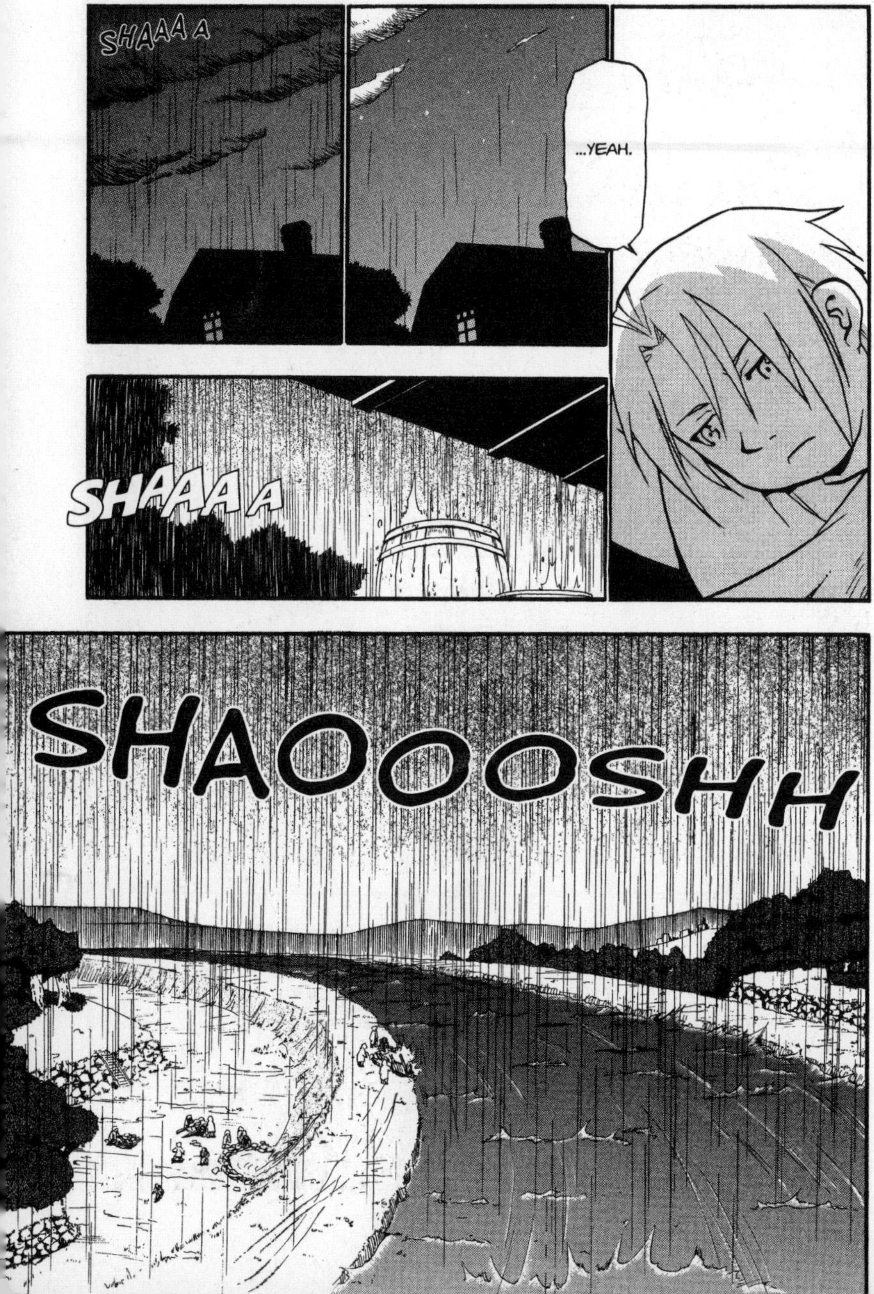
...YEAH.
SHAAAA
SHAAAA
SHAOOOSHH

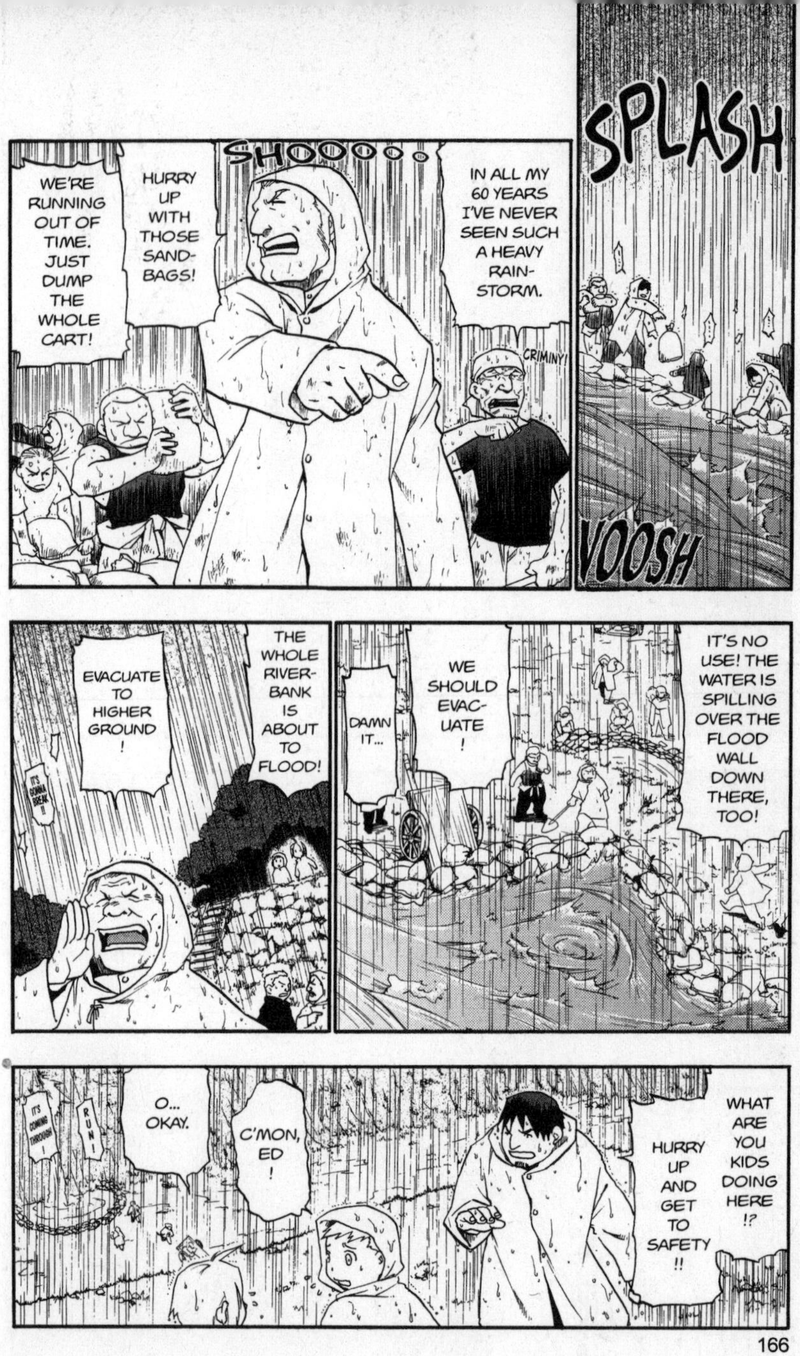
SPLASH
VOOSH
IN ALL MY 60 YEARS I'VE NEVER SEEN SUCH A HEAVY RAIN-STORM.
CRIMINY!
SHOOOOO
HURRY UP WITH THOSE SAND-BAGS!
WE'RE RUNNING OUT OF TIME. JUST DUMP THE WHOLE CART!
IT'S NO USE! THE WATER IS SPILLING OVER THE FLOOD WALL DOWN THERE, TOO!
WE SHOULD EVAC-UATE!
DAMN IT...
THE WHOLE RIVER-BANK IS ABOUT TO FLOOD!
EVACUATE TO HIGHER GROUND!
IT'S GONNA BREAK!!
WHAT ARE YOU KIDS DOING HERE!?
HURRY UP AND GET TO SAFETY!!
C'MON, ED!
O... OKAY.
RUN!
IT'S COMING THROUGH!

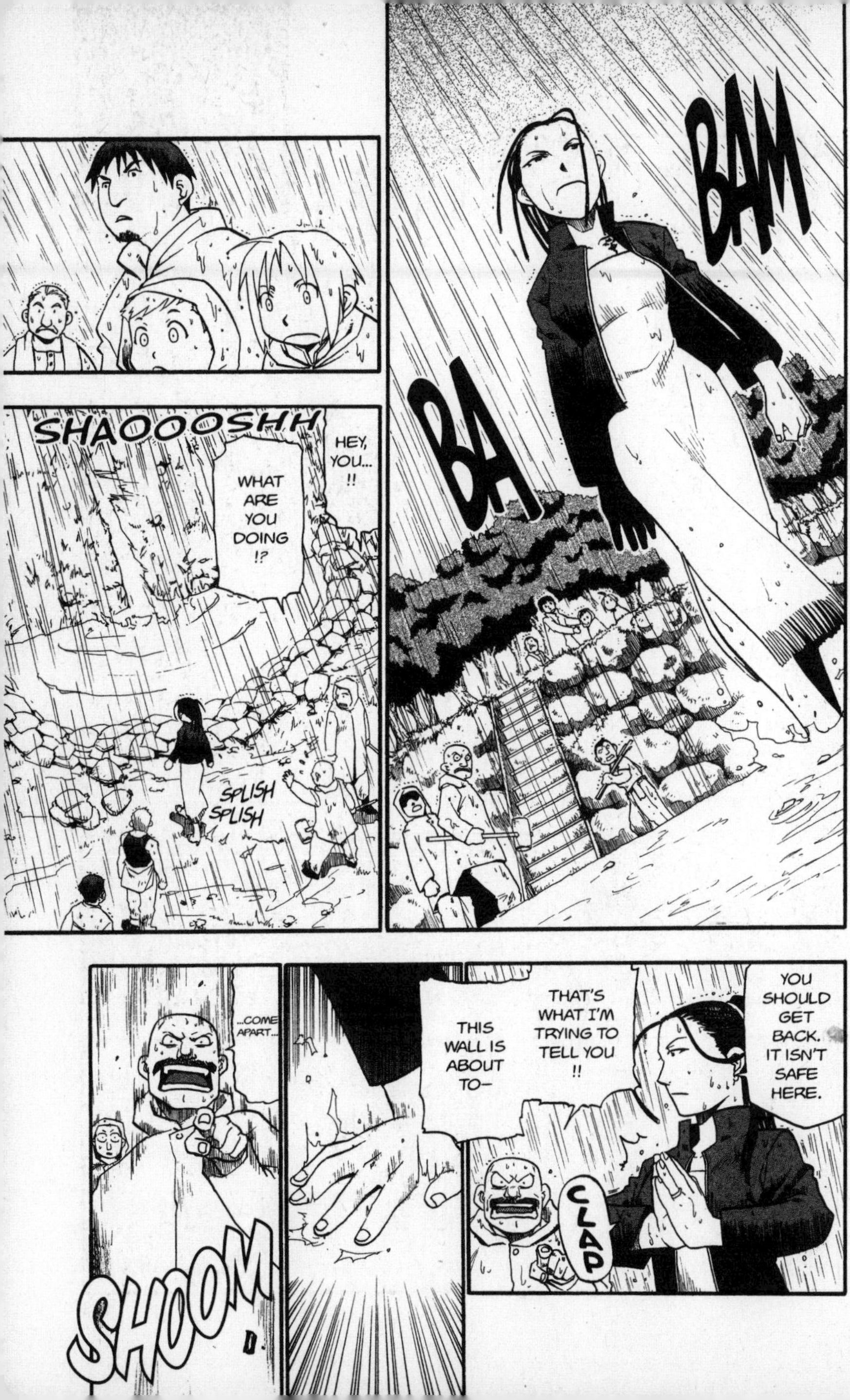
BAM
BA
HEY, YOU... !!
WHAT ARE YOU DOING !?
SHAOOOSHH
SPLISH SPLISH
YOU SHOULD GET BACK. IT ISN'T SAFE HERE.
THAT'S WHAT I'M TRYING TO TELL YOU !!
THIS WALL IS ABOUT TO—
CLAP
...COME APART...
SHOOM

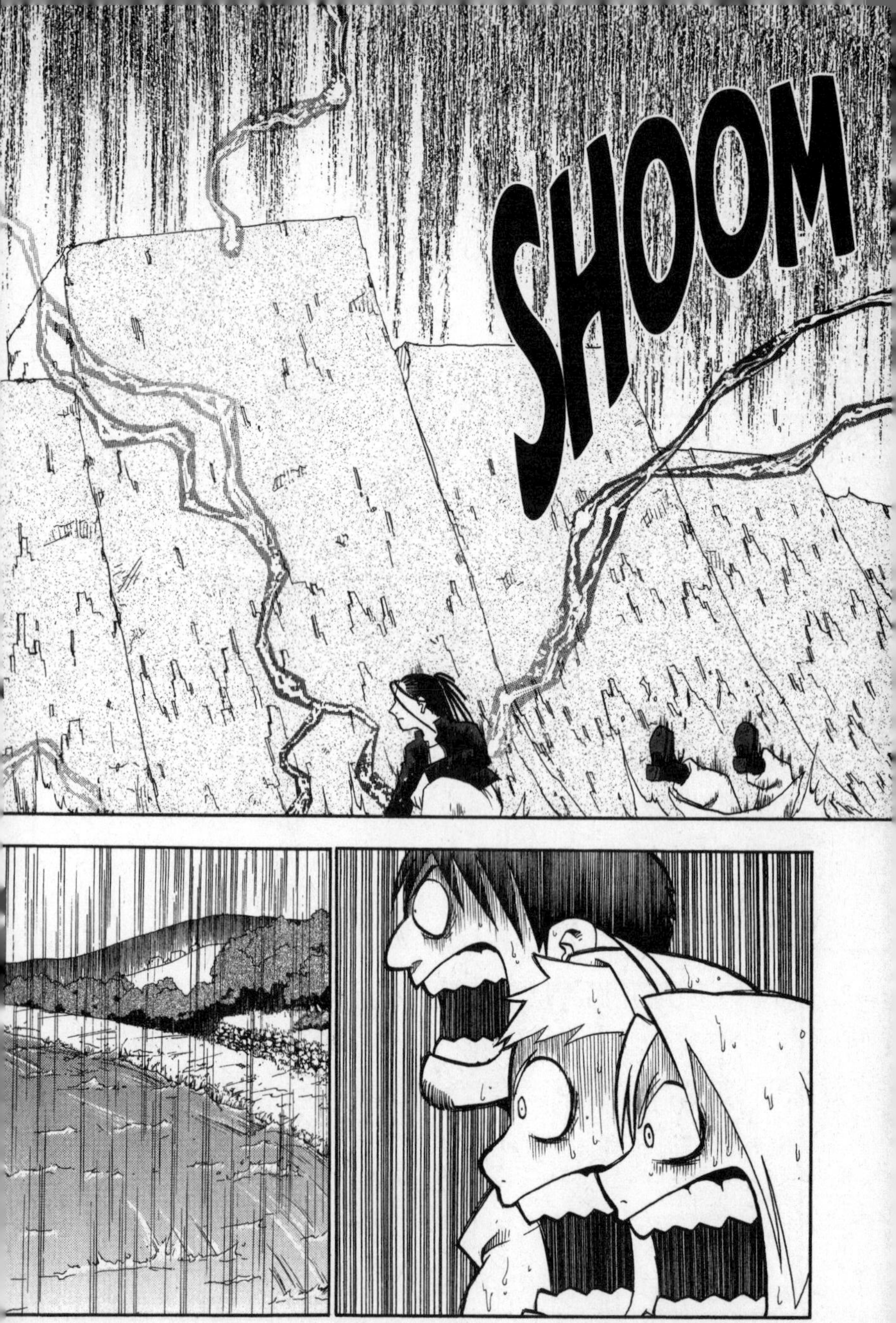
SHOOM

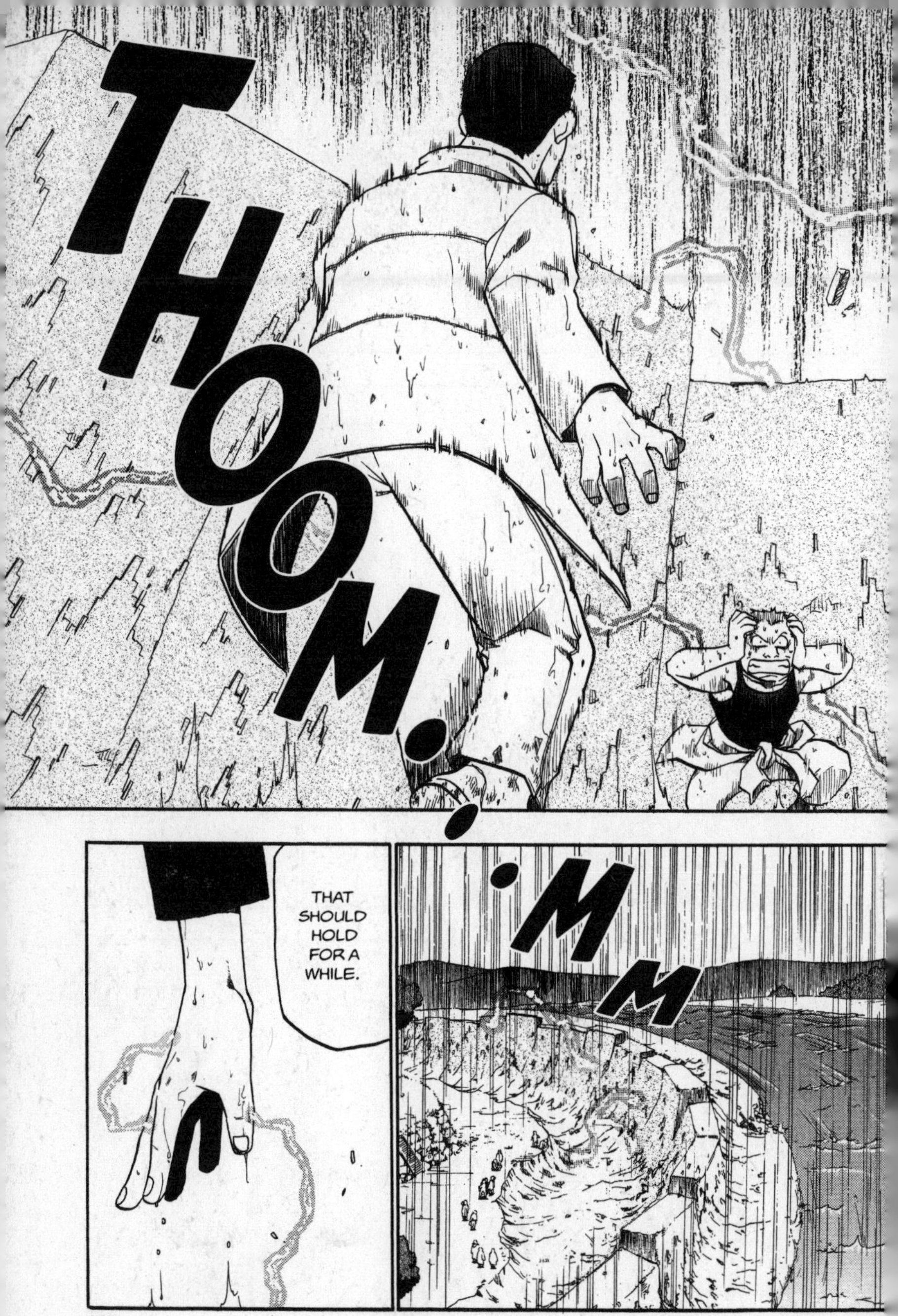
THOOM
MM
THAT SHOULD HOLD FOR A WHILE.

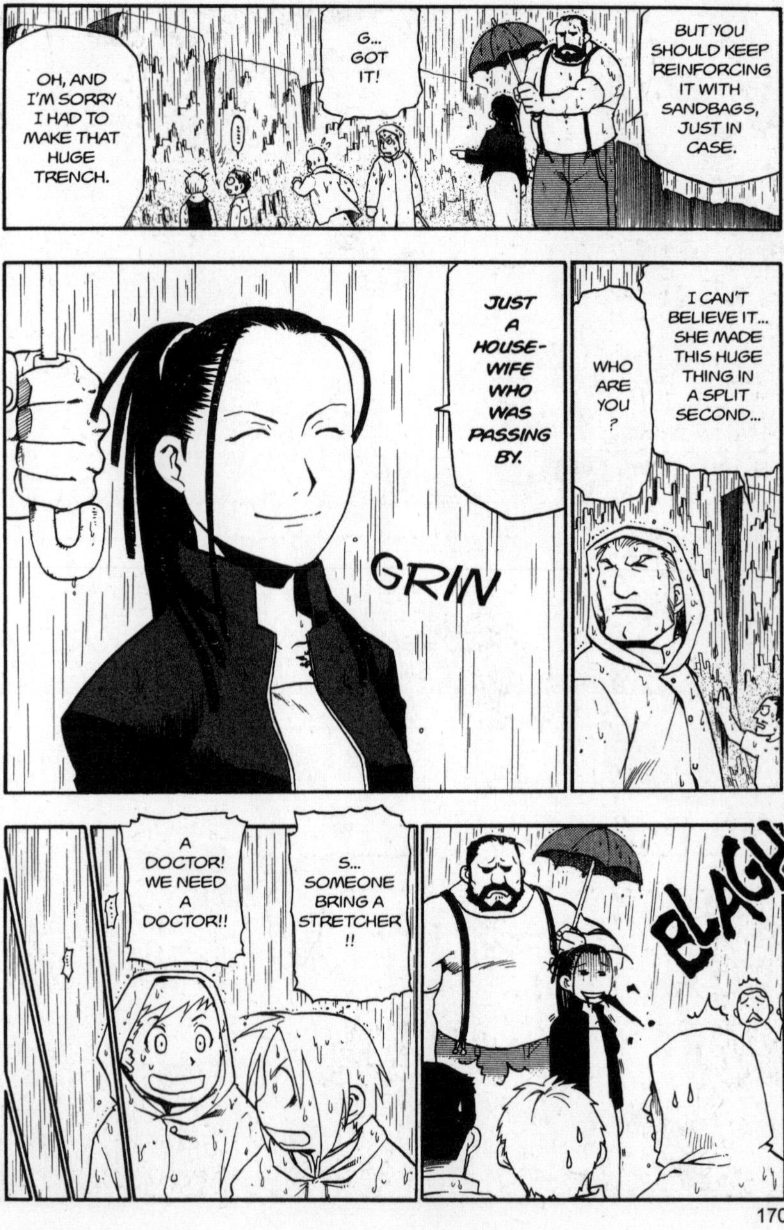
BUT YOU SHOULD KEEP REINFORCING IT WITH SANDBAGS, JUST IN CASE.
G... GOT IT!
OH, AND I'M SORRY I HAD TO MAKE THAT HUGE TRENCH.
I CAN'T BELIEVE IT... SHE MADE THIS HUGE THING IN A SPLIT SECOND...
WHO ARE YOU?
JUST A HOUSE-WIFE WHO WAS PASSING BY.
GRIN
BLAGH
S... SOMEONE BRING A STRETCHER!!
A DOCTOR! WE NEED A DOCTOR!!

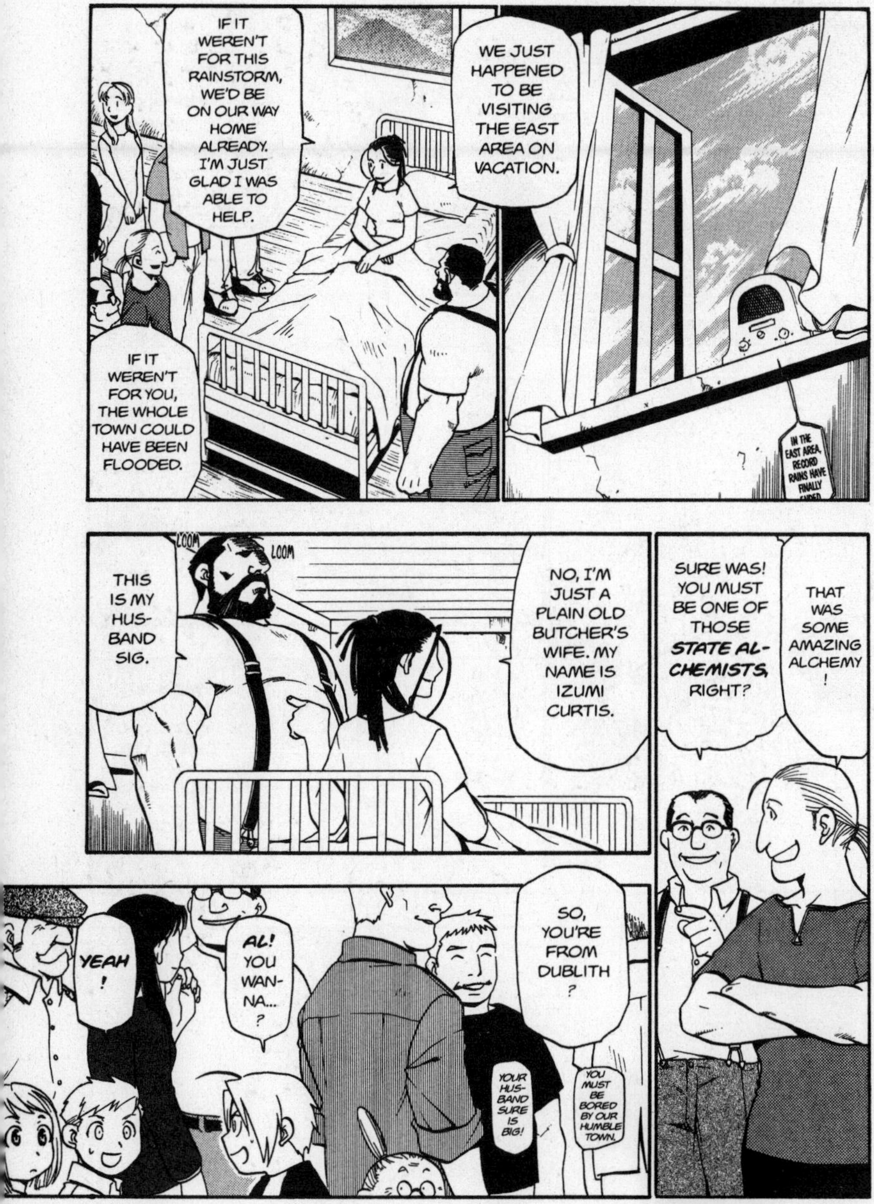
IN THE EAST AREA, RECORD RAINS HAVE FINALLY
WE JUST HAPPENED TO BE VISITING THE EAST AREA ON VACATION.
IF IT WEREN'T FOR THIS RAINSTORM, WE'D BE ON OUR WAY HOME ALREADY. I'M JUST GLAD I WAS ABLE TO HELP.
IF IT WEREN'T FOR YOU, THE WHOLE TOWN COULD HAVE BEEN FLOODED.
THAT WAS SOME AMAZING ALCHEMY!
SURE WAS! YOU MUST BE ONE OF THOSE ***STATE ALCHEMISTS,*** RIGHT?
NO, I'M JUST A PLAIN OLD BUTCHER'S WIFE. MY NAME IS IZUMI CURTIS.
LOOM
LOOM
THIS IS MY HUSBAND SIG.
YOU MUST BE BORED BY OUR HUMBLE TOWN.
SO, YOU'RE FROM DUBLITH?
YOUR HUSBAND SURE IS BIG!
AL! YOU WANNA...?
YEAH!

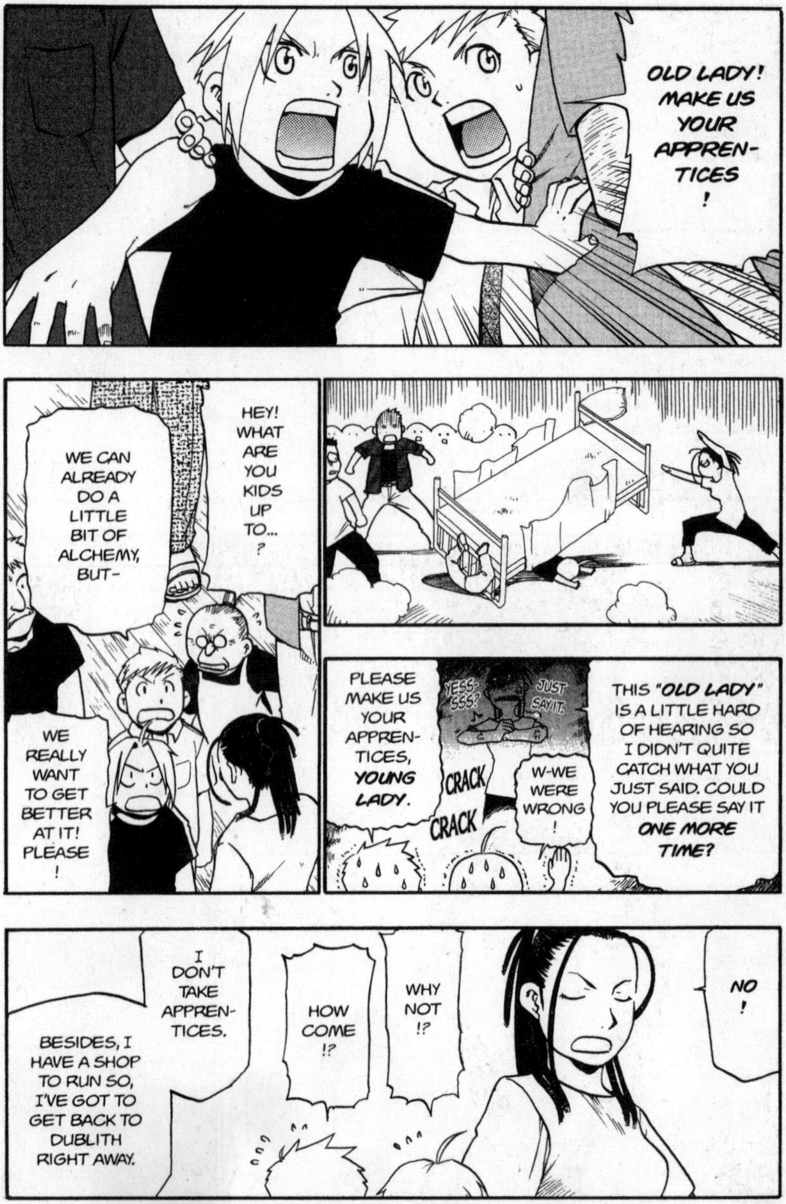
OLD LADY! MAKE US YOUR APPRENTICES!
THIS "OLD LADY" IS A LITTLE HARD OF HEARING SO I DIDN'T QUITE CATCH WHAT YOU JUST SAID. COULD YOU PLEASE SAY IT ONE MORE TIME?
JUST SAY IT.
YESSSSS?
W-WE WERE WRONG!
PLEASE MAKE US YOUR APPRENTICES, YOUNG LADY.
CRACK
CRACK
HEY! WHAT ARE YOU KIDS UP TO...?
WE CAN ALREADY DO A LITTLE BIT OF ALCHEMY, BUT-
WE REALLY WANT TO GET BETTER AT IT! PLEASE!
NO!
WHY NOT!?
HOW COME!?
I DON'T TAKE APPRENTICES.
BESIDES, I HAVE A SHOP TO RUN SO, I'VE GOT TO GET BACK TO DUBLITH RIGHT AWAY.

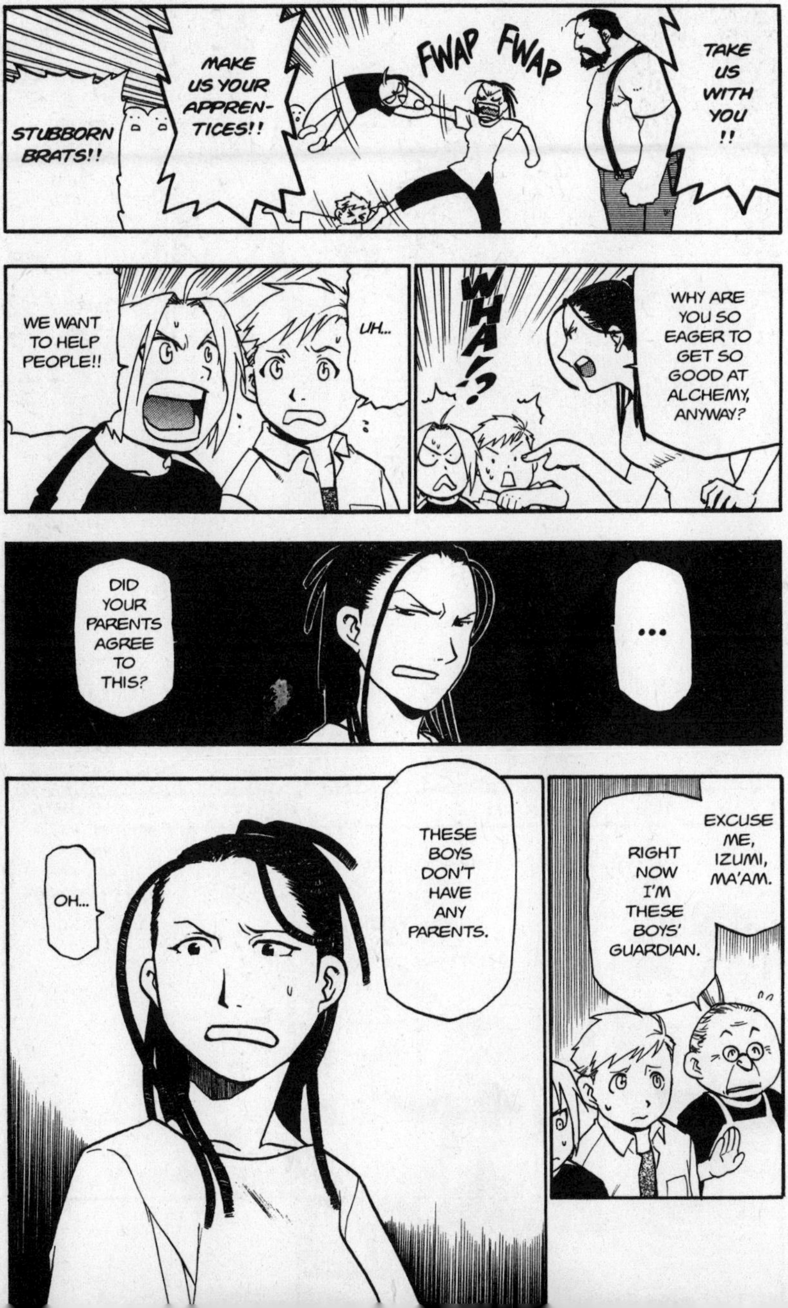
TAKE US WITH YOU!!
FWAP FWAP
MAKE US YOUR APPREN-TICES!!
STUBBORN BRATS!!
WHY ARE YOU SO EAGER TO GET SO GOOD AT ALCHEMY, ANYWAY?
WHA!?
UH...
WE WANT TO HELP PEOPLE!!
DID YOUR PARENTS AGREE TO THIS?
...
EXCUSE ME, IZUMI, MA'AM.
RIGHT NOW I'M THESE BOYS' GUARDIAN.
THESE BOYS DON'T HAVE ANY PARENTS.
OH...

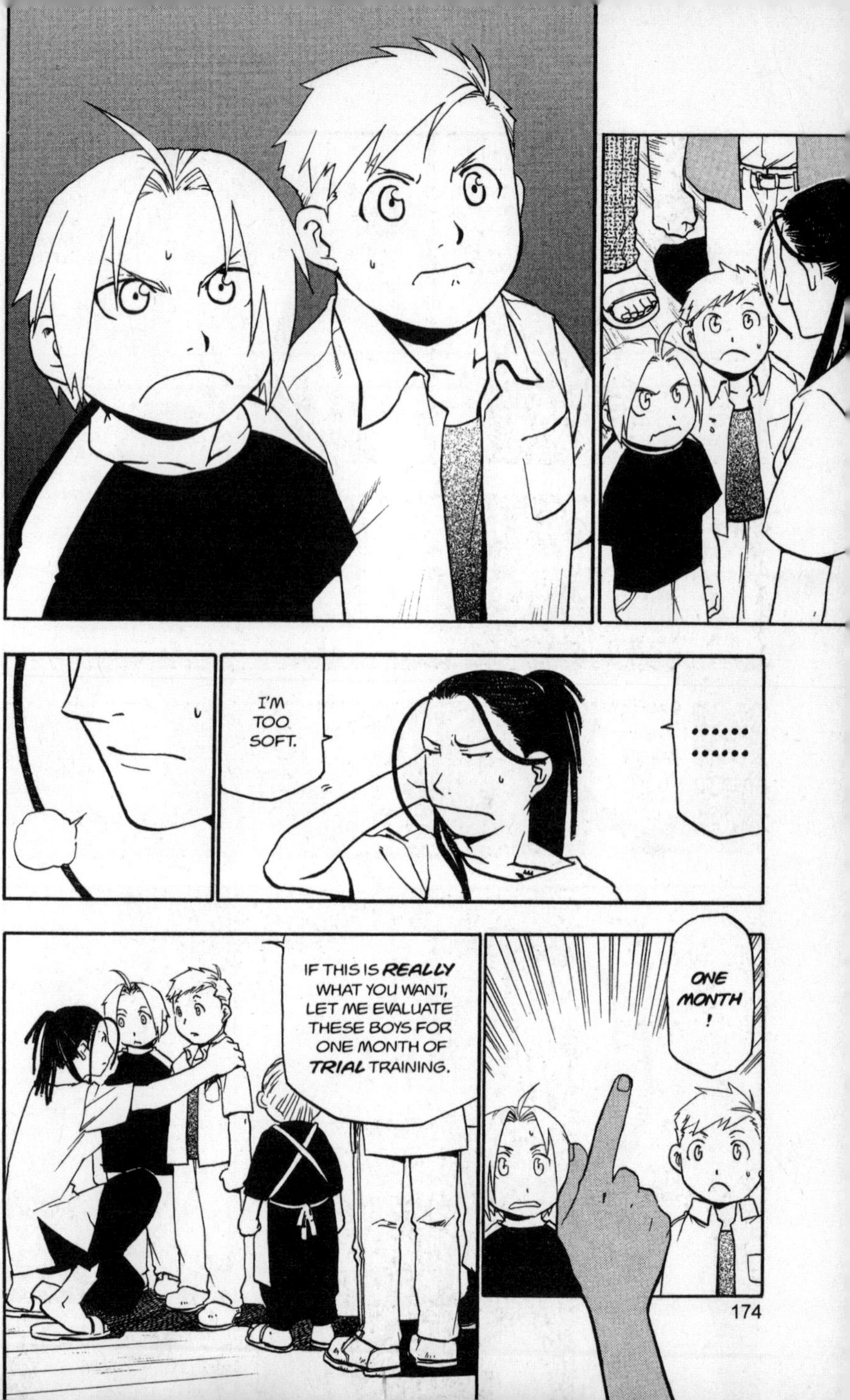
......
......
I'M TOO SOFT.
ONE MONTH!
IF THIS IS REALLY WHAT YOU WANT, LET ME EVALUATE THESE BOYS FOR ONE MONTH OF TRIAL TRAINING.

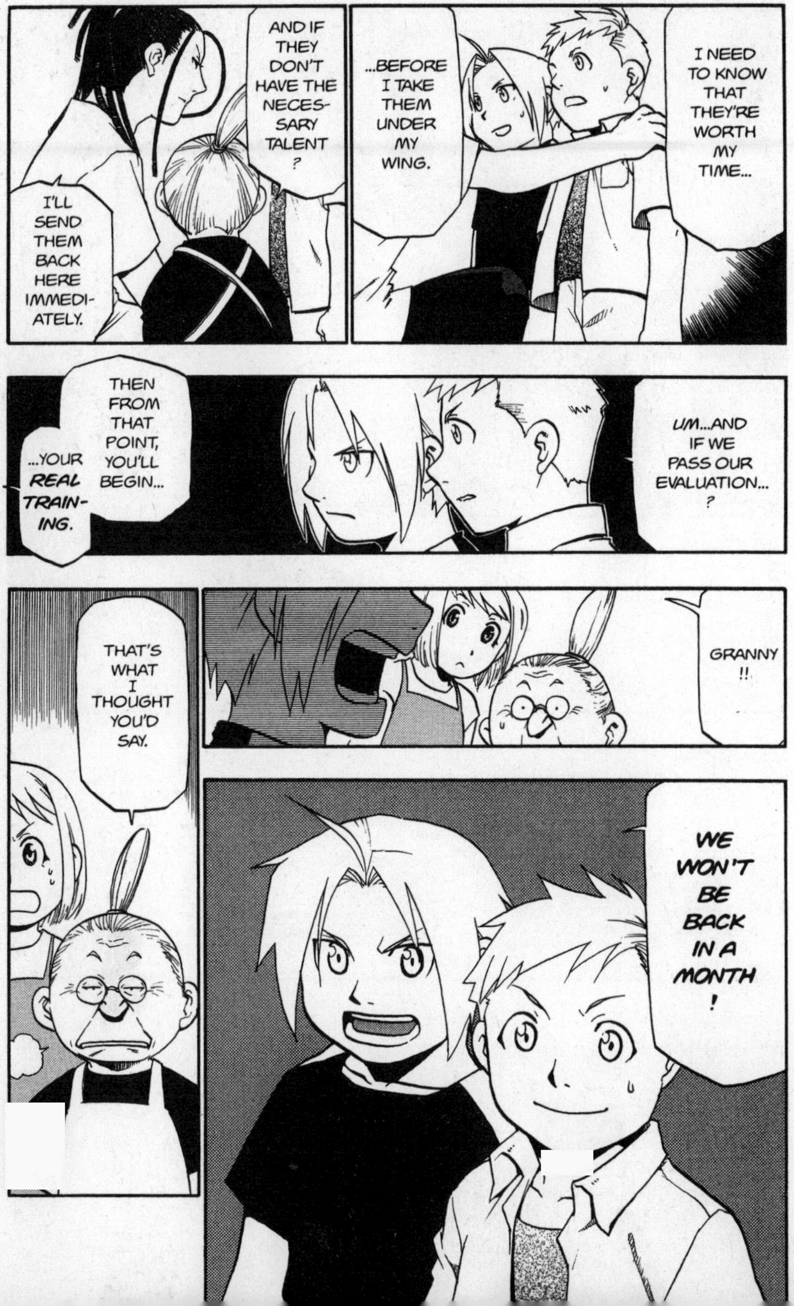
I NEED TO KNOW THAT THEY'RE WORTH MY TIME...
...BEFORE I TAKE THEM UNDER MY WING.
AND IF THEY DON'T HAVE THE NECES-SARY TALENT?
I'LL SEND THEM BACK HERE IMMEDI-ATELY.
UM...AND IF WE PASS OUR EVALUATION...?
THEN FROM THAT POINT, YOU'LL BEGIN...
...YOUR REAL TRAIN-ING.
GRANNY!!
WE WON'T BE BACK IN A MONTH!
THAT'S WHAT I THOUGHT YOU'D SAY.

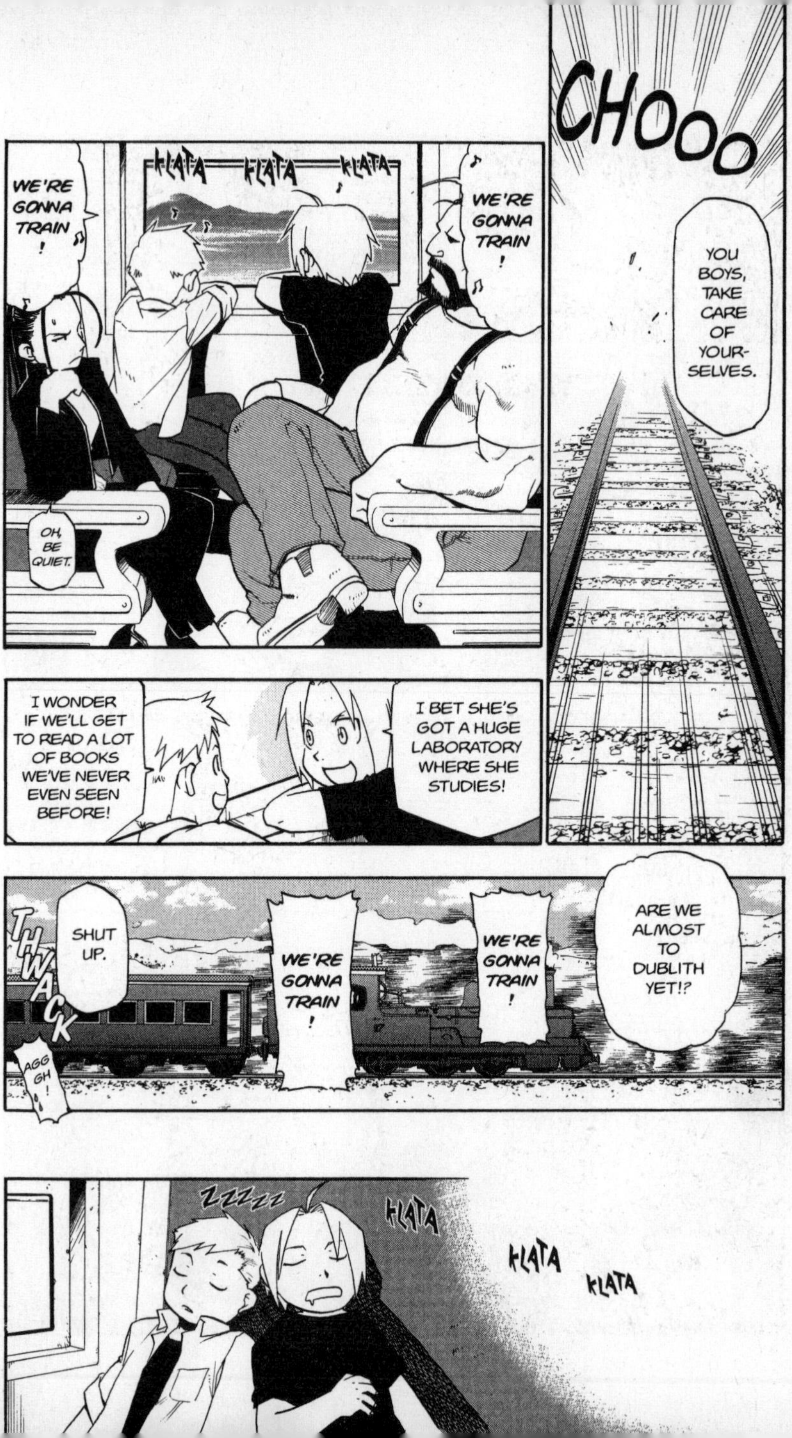
CHOOO
YOU BOYS, TAKE CARE OF YOURSELVES.
KLATA KLATA KLATA
WE'RE GONNA TRAIN!
WE'RE GONNA TRAIN!
OH, BE QUIET.
I BET SHE'S GOT A HUGE LABORATORY WHERE SHE STUDIES!
I WONDER IF WE'LL GET TO READ A LOT OF BOOKS WE'VE NEVER EVEN SEEN BEFORE!
ARE WE ALMOST TO DUBLITH YET!?
WE'RE GONNA TRAIN!
WE'RE GONNA TRAIN!
SHUT UP.
THWACK
AGGGH!
KLATA
KLATA
KLATA
ZZZZZ

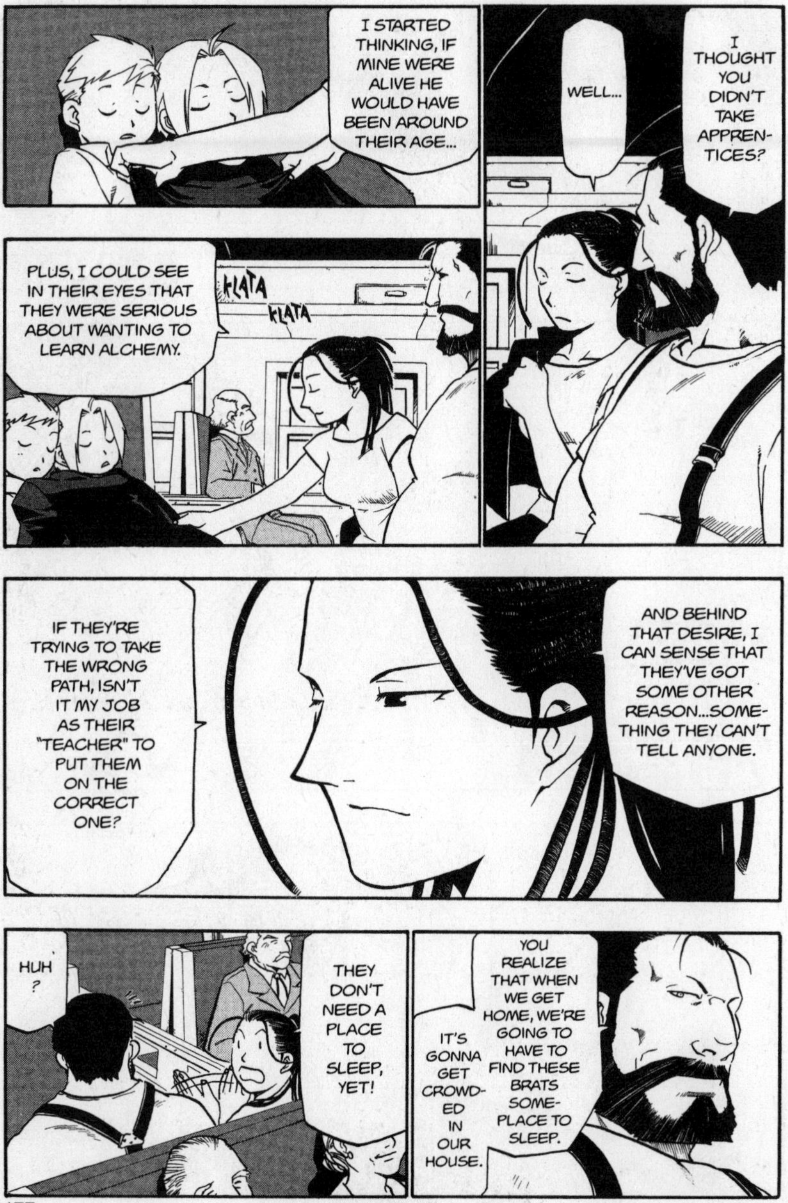
I THOUGHT YOU DIDN'T TAKE APPRENTICES?
WELL...
I STARTED THINKING, IF MINE WERE ALIVE HE WOULD HAVE BEEN AROUND THEIR AGE...
KLATA
KLATA
PLUS, I COULD SEE IN THEIR EYES THAT THEY WERE SERIOUS ABOUT WANTING TO LEARN ALCHEMY.
AND BEHIND THAT DESIRE, I CAN SENSE THAT THEY'VE GOT SOME OTHER REASON...SOMETHING THEY CAN'T TELL ANYONE.
IF THEY'RE TRYING TO TAKE THE WRONG PATH, ISN'T IT MY JOB AS THEIR "TEACHER" TO PUT THEM ON THE CORRECT ONE?
YOU REALIZE THAT WHEN WE GET HOME, WE'RE GOING TO HAVE TO FIND THESE BRATS SOMEPLACE TO SLEEP.
IT'S GONNA GET CROWDED IN OUR HOUSE.
THEY DON'T NEED A PLACE TO SLEEP, YET!
HUH?

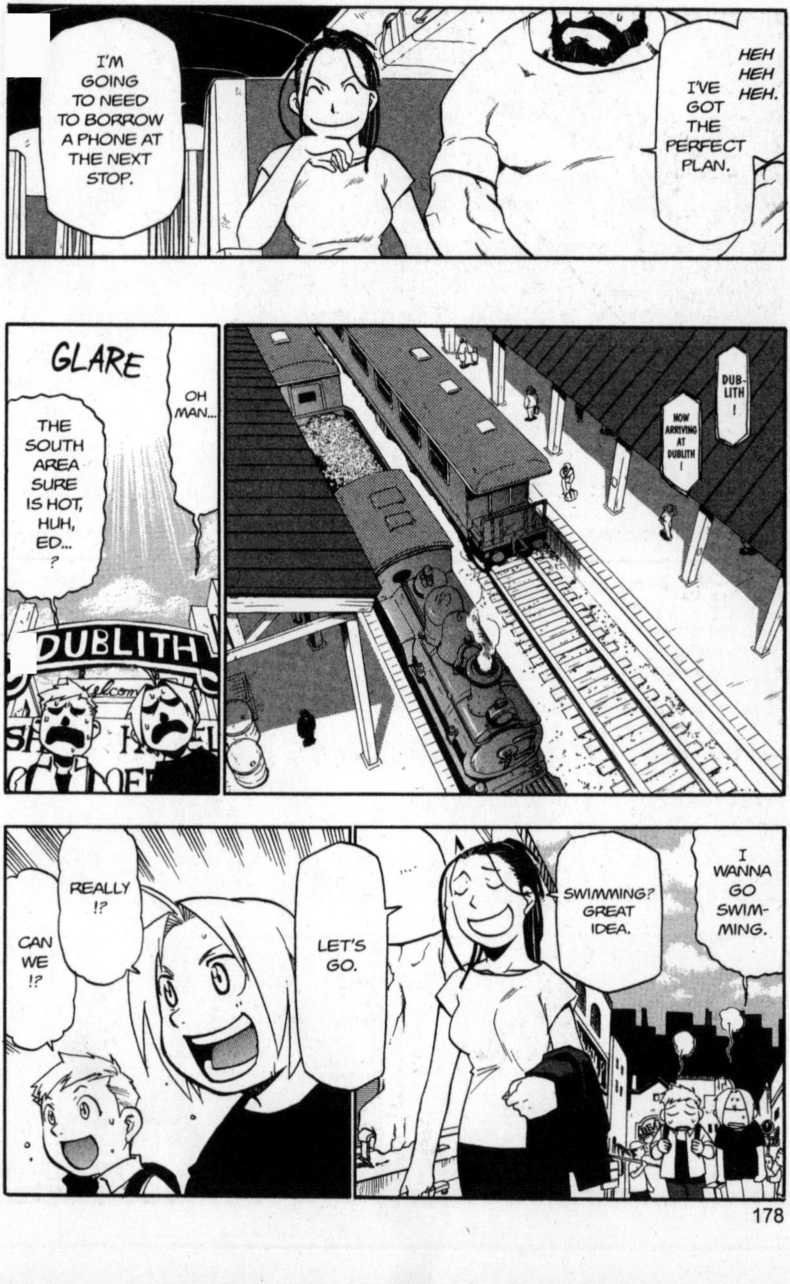
HEH HEH HEH.
I'VE GOT THE PERFECT PLAN.
I'M GOING TO NEED TO BORROW A PHONE AT THE NEXT STOP.
DUB-LITH !
NOW ARRIVING AT DUBLITH !
OH MAN...
GLARE
THE SOUTH AREA SURE IS HOT, HUH, ED... ?
DUBLITH
I WANNA GO SWIM-MING.
SWIMMING? GREAT IDEA.
...
LET'S GO.
REALLY !?
CAN WE !?

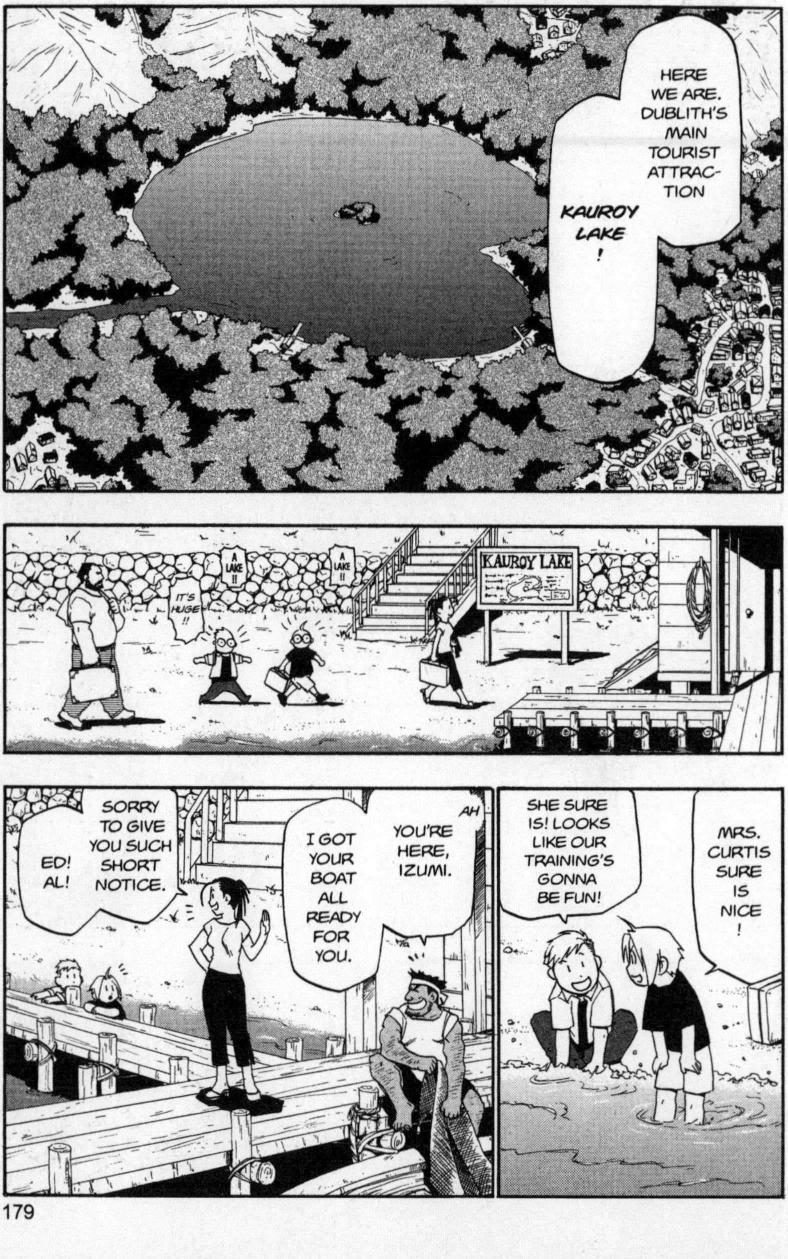
HERE WE ARE. DUBLITH'S MAIN TOURIST ATTRACTION
KAUROY LAKE!
KAUROY LAKE
A LAKE!!
A LAKE!!
IT'S HUGE!!
MRS. CURTIS SURE IS NICE!
SHE SURE IS! LOOKS LIKE OUR TRAINING'S GONNA BE FUN!
AH
YOU'RE HERE, IZUMI.
I GOT YOUR BOAT ALL READY FOR YOU.
SORRY TO GIVE YOU SUCH SHORT NOTICE.
ED! AL!

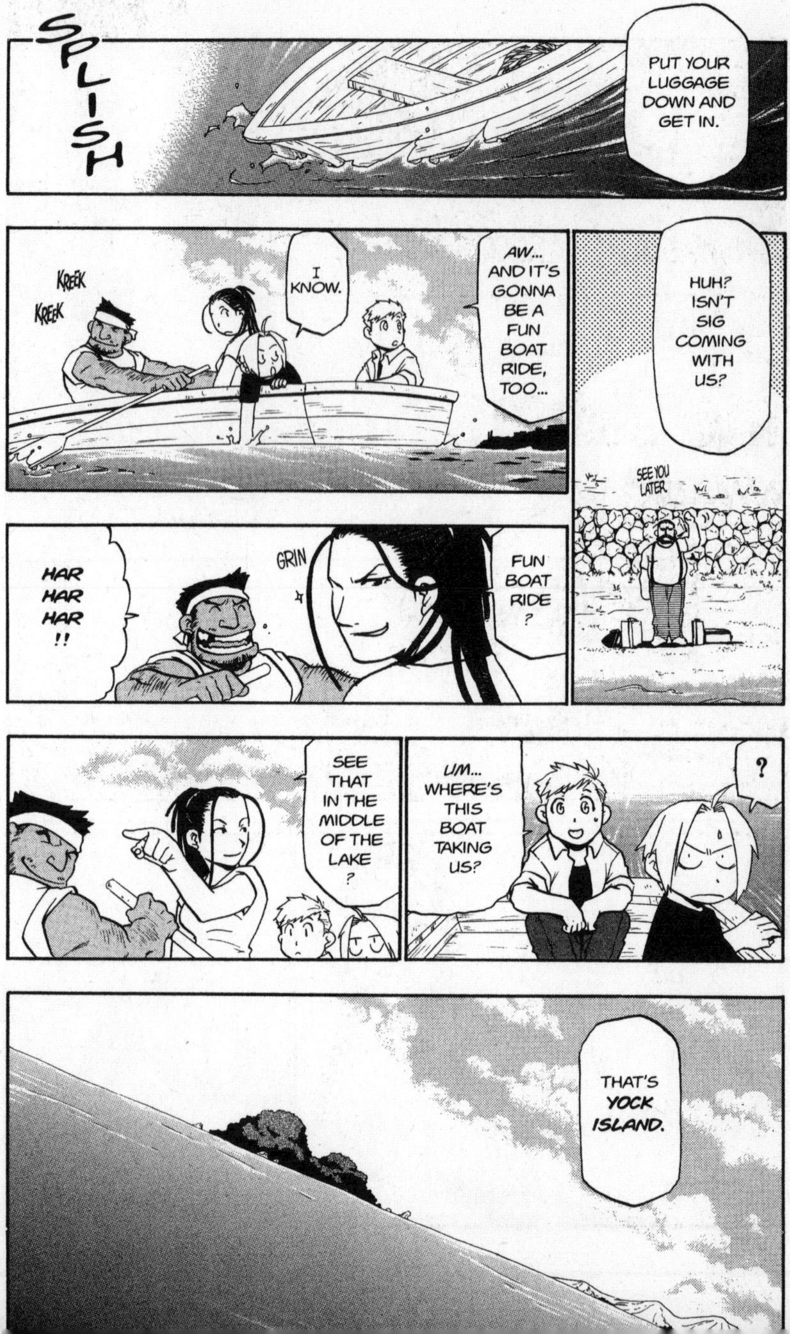
PUT YOUR LUGGAGE DOWN AND GET IN.
SPLISH
HUH? ISN'T SIG COMING WITH US?
SEE YOU LATER
AW... AND IT'S GONNA BE A FUN BOAT RIDE, TOO...
I KNOW.
KREEK
KREEK
FUN BOAT RIDE?
GRIN
HAR HAR HAR!!
?
UM... WHERE'S THIS BOAT TAKING US?
SEE THAT IN THE MIDDLE OF THE LAKE?
THAT'S YOCK ISLAND.

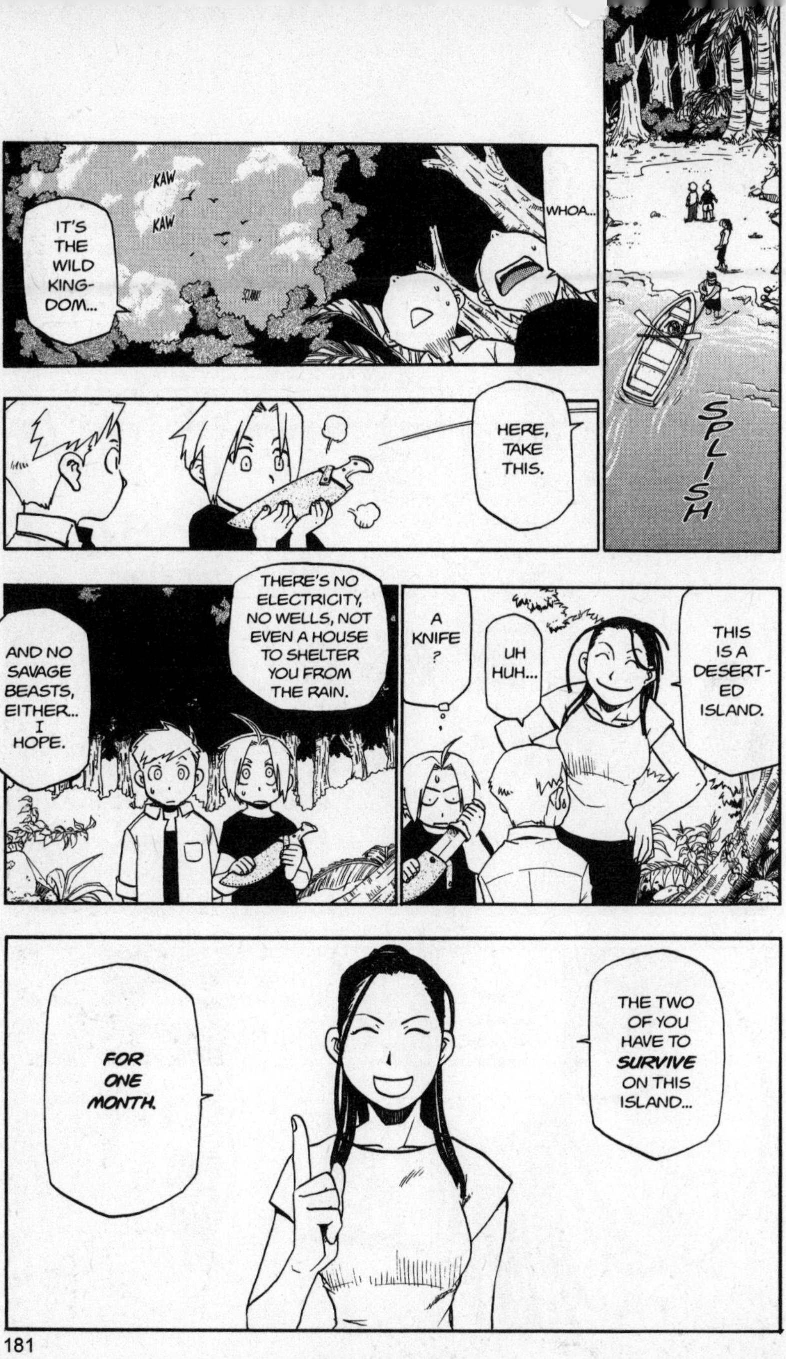
SPLISH
WHOA...
KAW
KAW
IT'S THE WILD KINGDOM...
HERE, TAKE THIS.
THIS IS A DESERTED ISLAND.
UH HUH...
A KNIFE?
THERE'S NO ELECTRICITY, NO WELLS, NOT EVEN A HOUSE TO SHELTER YOU FROM THE RAIN.
AND NO SAVAGE BEASTS, EITHER.. I HOPE.
THE TWO OF YOU HAVE TO **SURVIVE** ON THIS ISLAND...
FOR ONE MONTH.

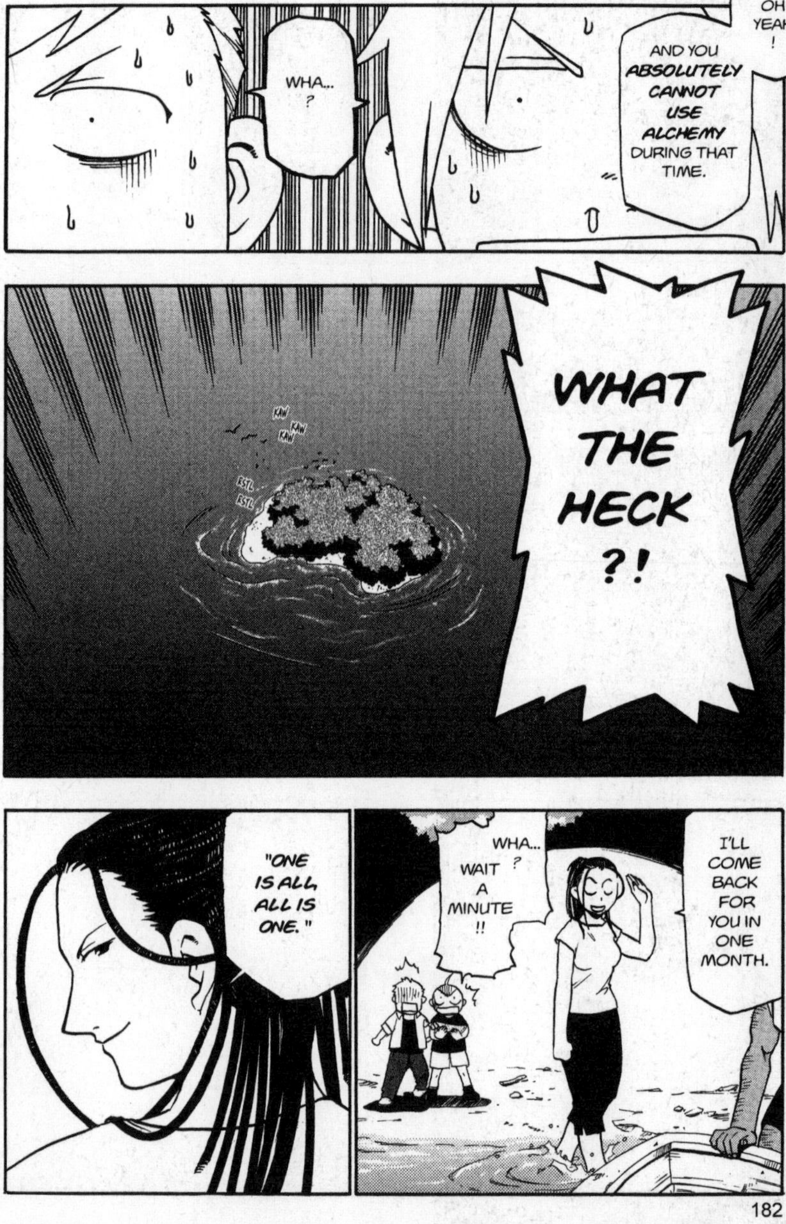
OH YEAH!
AND YOU ABSOLUTELY CANNOT USE ALCHEMY DURING THAT TIME.
WHA...?
WHAT THE HECK?!
KAW KAW KAW
RSTL RSTL
I'LL COME BACK FOR YOU IN ONE MONTH.
WHA...?
WAIT A MINUTE!!
"ONE IS ALL, ALL IS ONE."

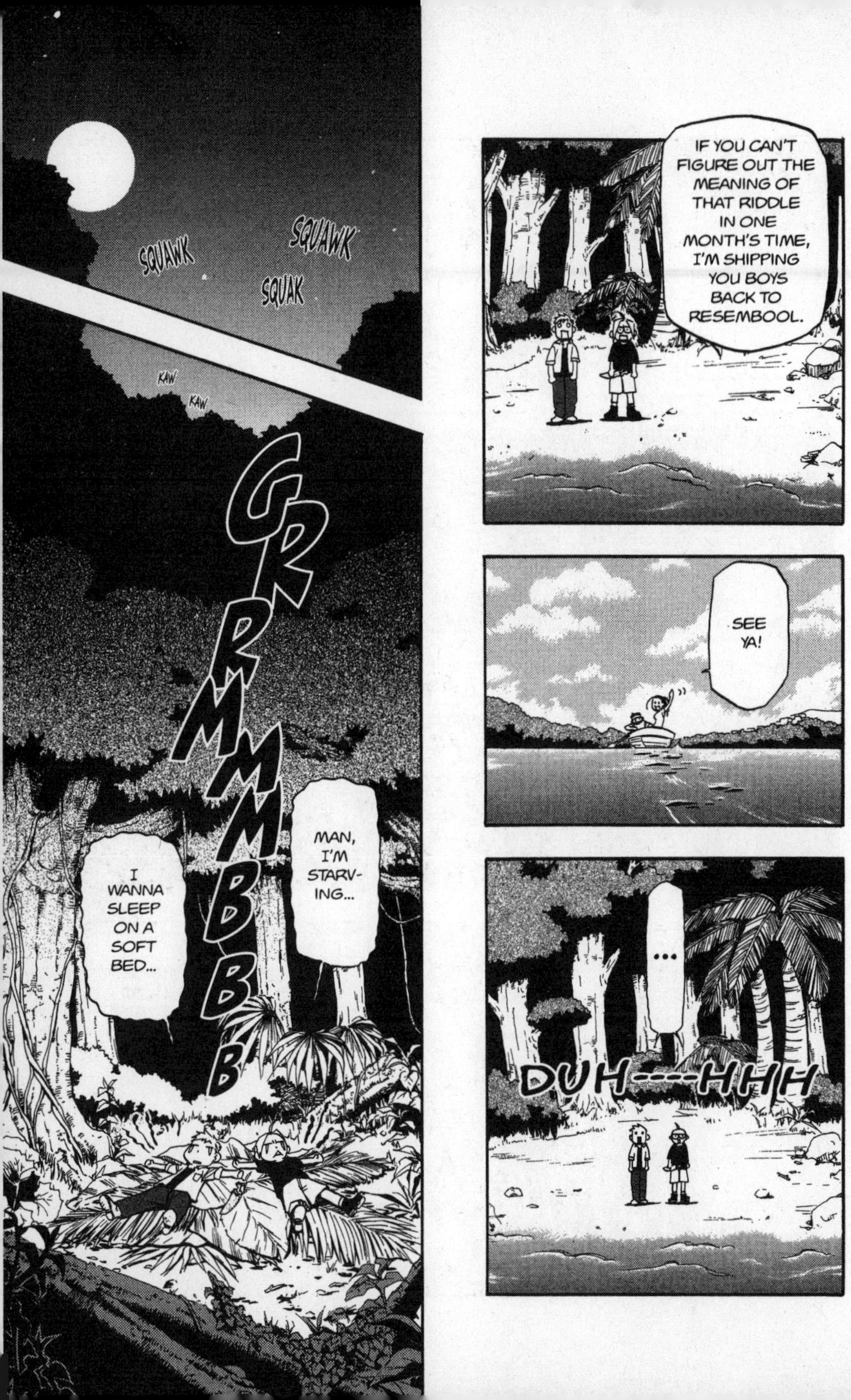
IF YOU CAN'T FIGURE OUT THE MEANING OF THAT RIDDLE IN ONE MONTH'S TIME, I'M SHIPPING YOU BOYS BACK TO RESEMBOOL.
SEE YA!
...
DUH----HHH
SQUAWK
SQUAWK
SQUAK
KAW
KAW
GRRMMMMBBB
MAN, I'M STARVING...
I WANNA SLEEP ON A SOFT BED...

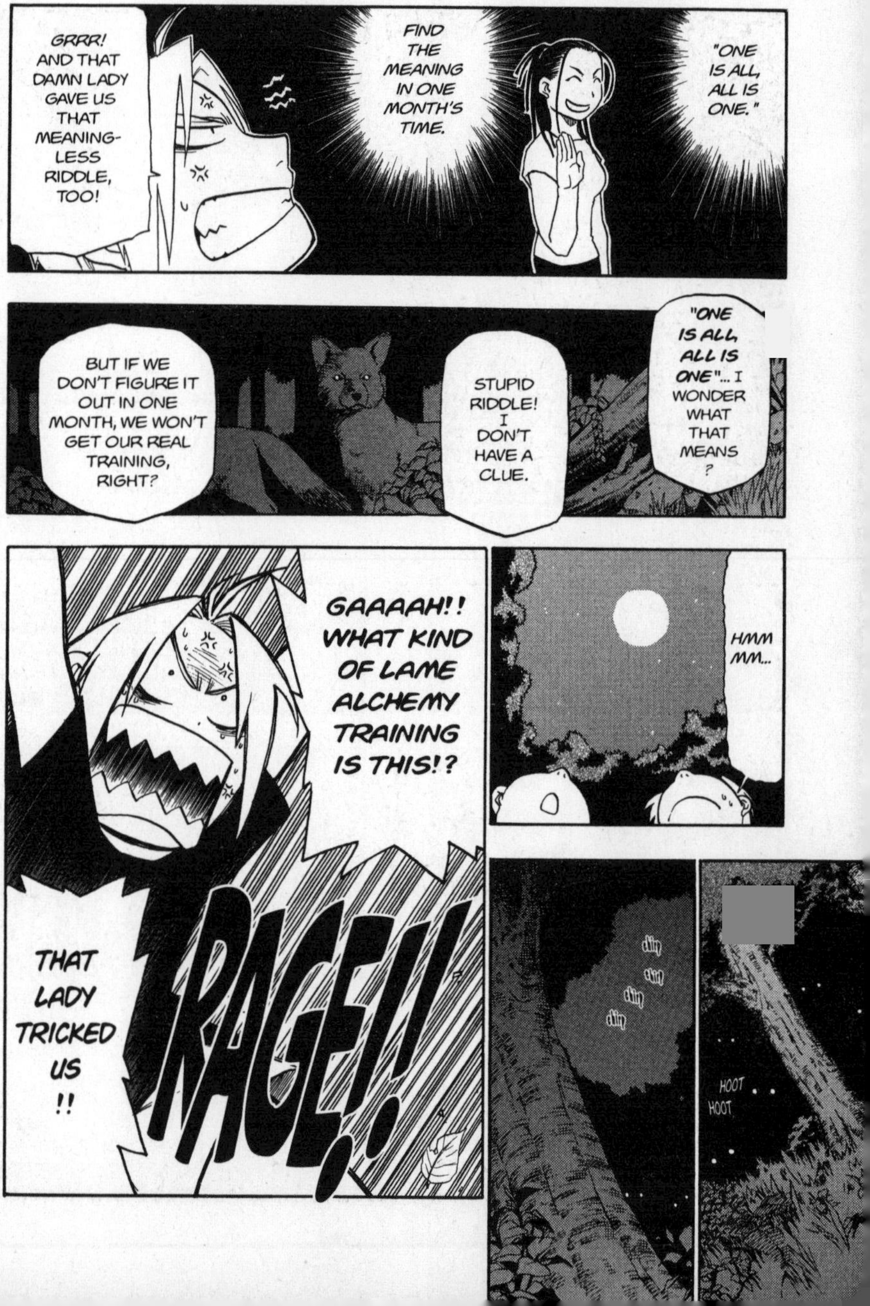
"ONE IS ALL, ALL IS ONE."
FIND THE MEANING IN ONE MONTH'S TIME.
GRRR! AND THAT DAMN LADY GAVE US THAT MEANINGLESS RIDDLE, TOO!
"ONE IS ALL, ALL IS ONE"... I WONDER WHAT THAT MEANS?
STUPID RIDDLE! I DON'T HAVE A CLUE.
BUT IF WE DON'T FIGURE IT OUT IN ONE MONTH, WE WON'T GET OUR REAL TRAINING, RIGHT?
HMMMM...
HOOT HOOT
dim dim dim dim
GAAAAH!! WHAT KIND OF LAME ALCHEMY TRAINING IS THIS!?
RAGE!!
THAT LADY TRICKED US!!

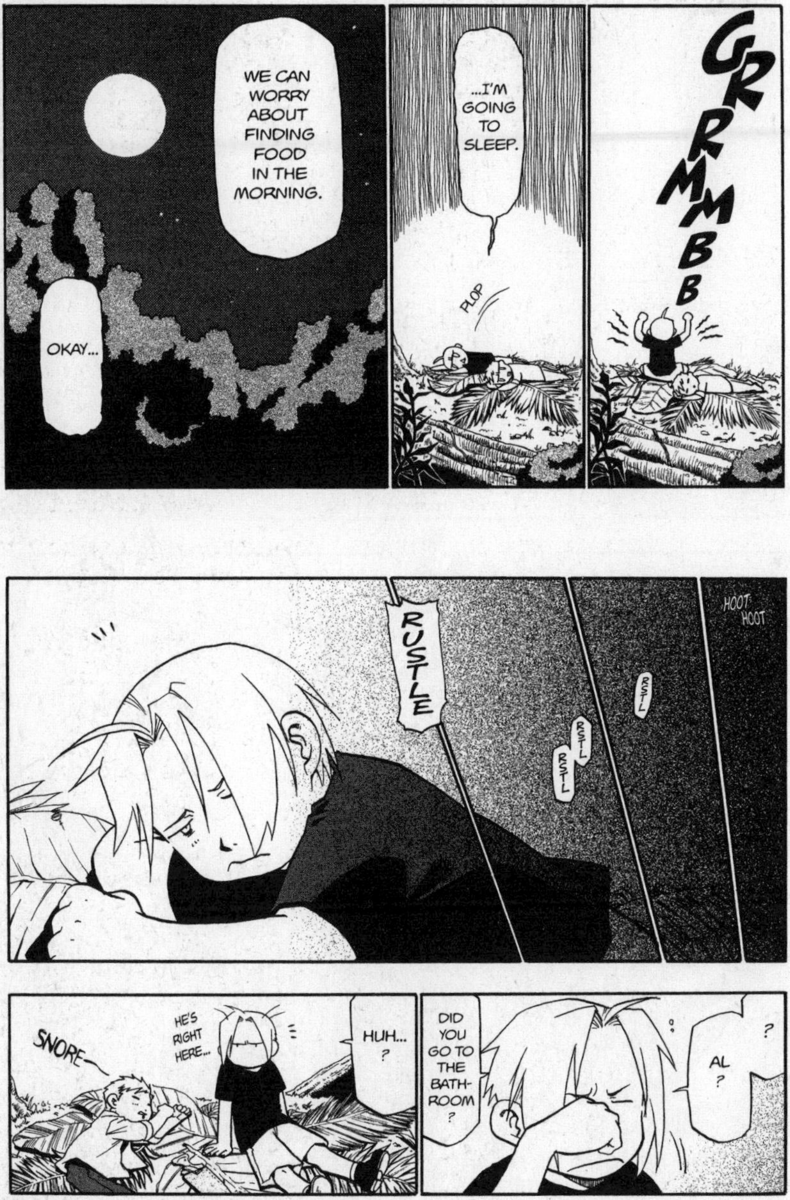
GRRMMBB
...I'M GOING TO SLEEP.
PLOP
WE CAN WORRY ABOUT FINDING FOOD IN THE MORNING.
OKAY...
HOOT HOOT
RSTL
RSTL
RSTL
RUSTLE
?
AL ?
DID YOU GO TO THE BATH-ROOM ?
HUH... ?
HE'S RIGHT HERE...
SNORE

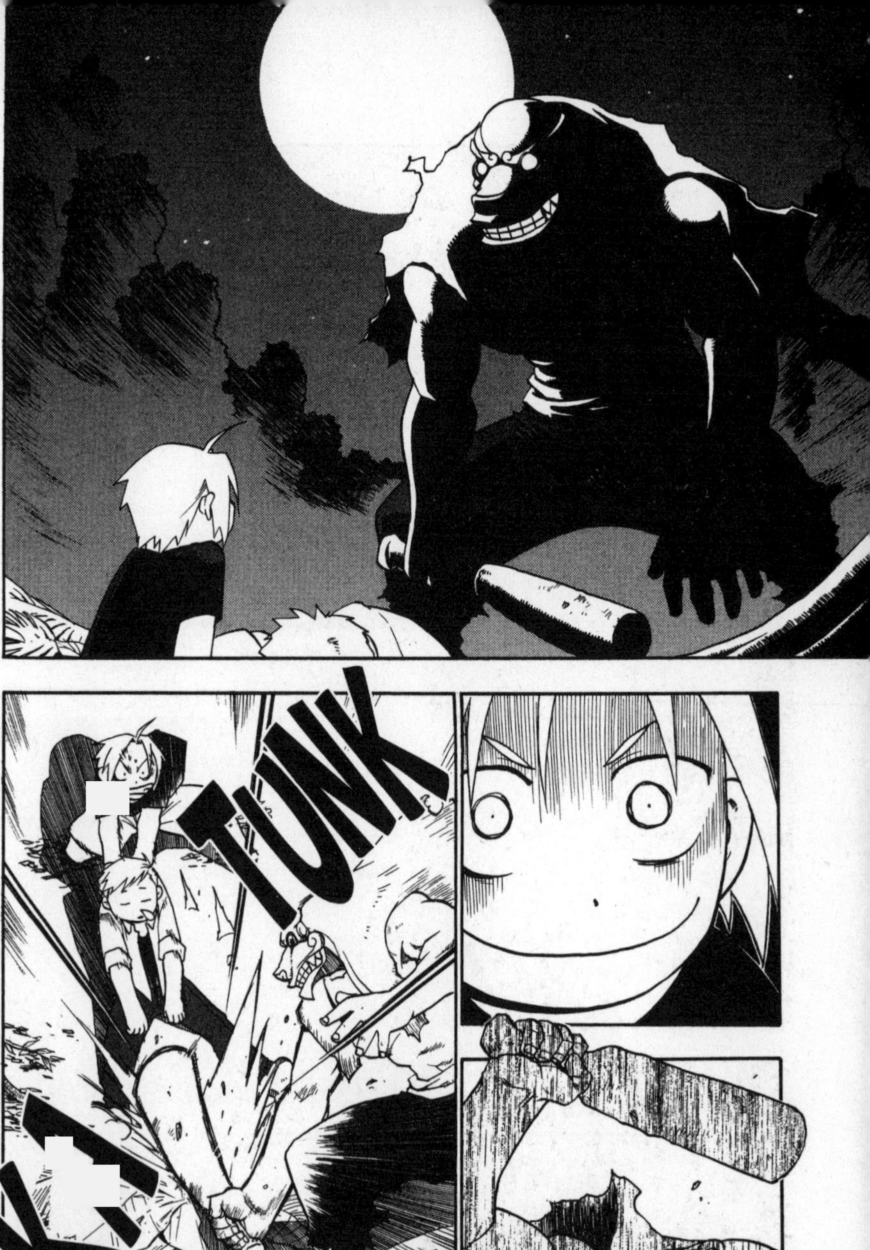
TUNK

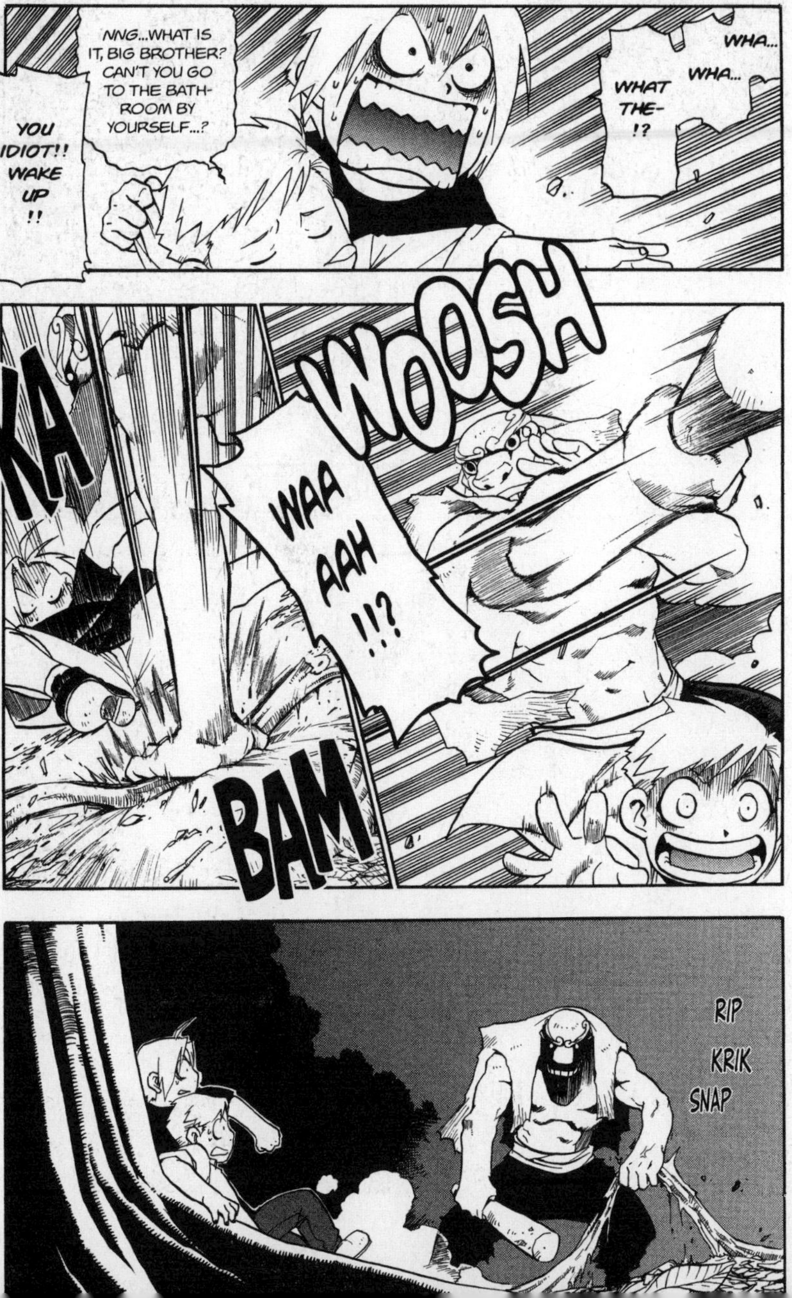
WHA... WHA... WHAT THE-!?
NNG...WHAT IS IT, BIG BROTHER? CAN'T YOU GO TO THE BATH-ROOM BY YOURSELF...?
YOU IDIOT!! WAKE UP!!
WOOSH
WAA AAH!!?
KA
BAM
RIP
KRIK
SNAP

THIS MANGA WAS ORIGINALLY PRINTED IN MONTHLY
SHONEN GANGAN, DECEMBER 2002 THROUGH APRIL 2003.

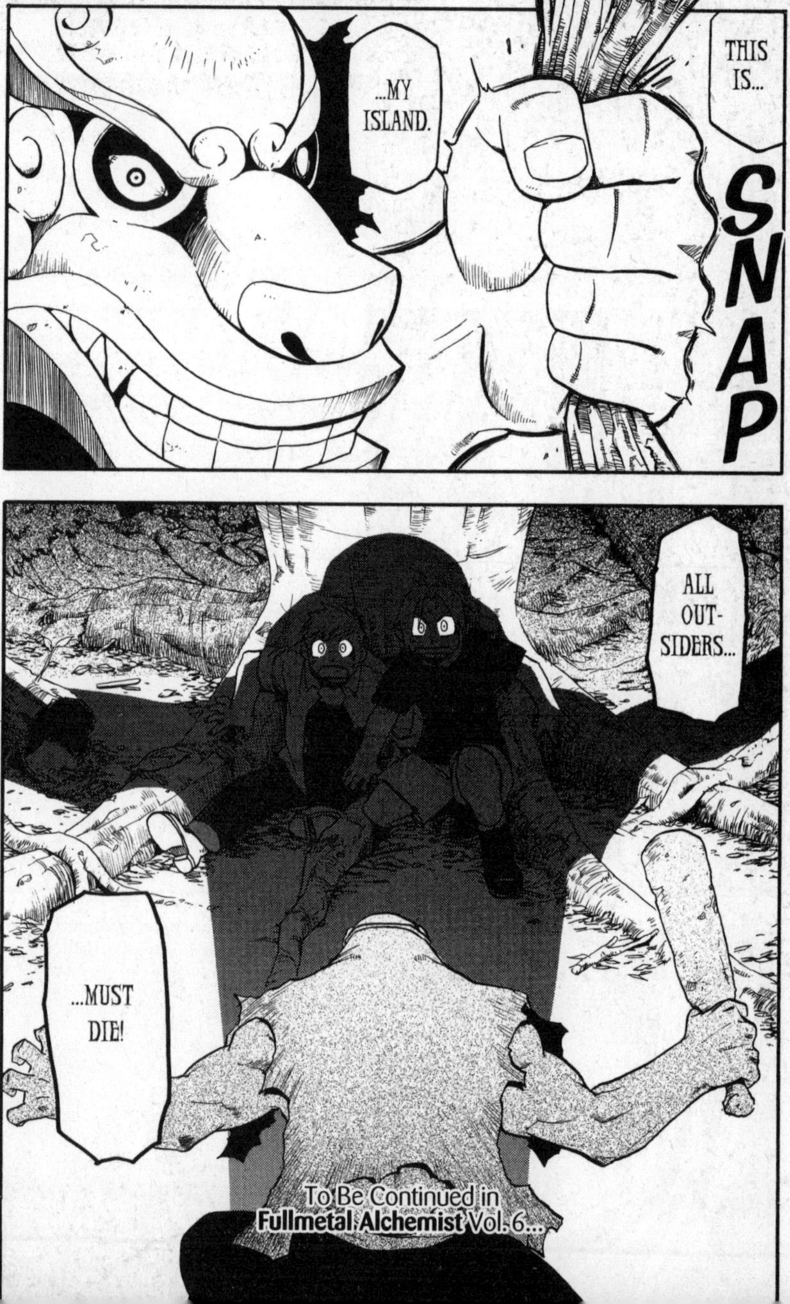
THIS IS...
SNAP
...MY ISLAND.
ALL OUT-SIDERS...
...MUST DIE!
To Be Continued in
Fullmetal Alchemist Vol. 6...

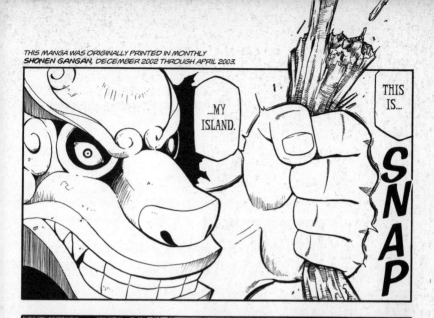

IT WAS A GREASE PEN, REMEMBER

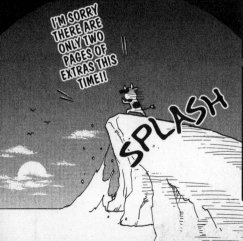

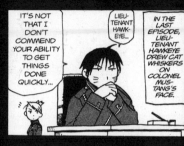

IN THE LAST EPISODE, LIEUTENANT HAWKEYE DREW CAT WHISKERS ON COLONEL MUSTANG'S FACE.
LIEUTENANT HAWKEYE...
IT'S NOT THAT I DON'T COMMEND YOUR ABILITY TO GET THINGS DONE QUICKLY...
...BUT I NEED TO LOOK MORE DIGNIFIED! THINK OF SOMETHING!
I SEE. LEAVE IT TO ME, SIR.
HE LOOKS WEIRD...
VERY WEIRD...
PSST PSST PSST

FULLMETAL ALCHEMIST 5

SPECIAL THANKS TO...

KEISUI TAKAEDA-SAN
SANKICHI HINODEYA-CHAN
JUN TOKO-SAN
MASANARI YUBEKA-SAN
JUNSHI BABA-SAN
NORIKO GUNJO-SAN
SHU HOZAKA-SAN
RIKA SUGIYAMA-SAN
YOICHI SHIMOMURA-SHI (MANAGER)

AND YOU!!

I'M SORRY THERE ARE ONLY TWO PAGES OF EXTRAS THIS TIME!!
SPLASH

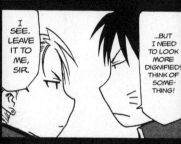

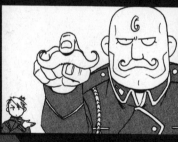

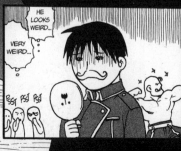

COW SHED DIARY

The Fierce Underwear Battle

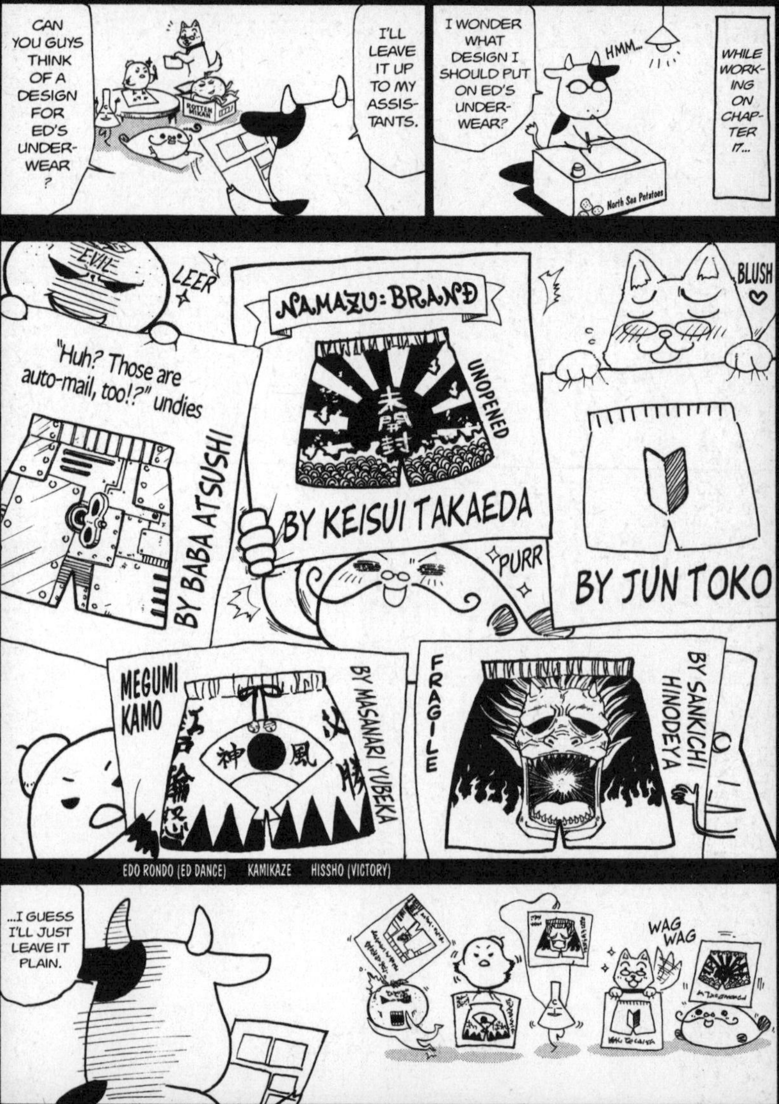

WHILE WORKING ON CHAPTER 17...
I WONDER WHAT DESIGN I SHOULD PUT ON ED'S UNDERWEAR?
HMM...
North Sea Potatoes
I'LL LEAVE IT UP TO MY ASSISTANTS.
CAN YOU GUYS THINK OF A DESIGN FOR ED'S UNDERWEAR?
ROTTEN MIKAN
BLUSH
BY JUN TOKO
NAMAZU-BRAND
UNOPENED
BY KEISUI TAKAEDA
PURR
EVIL
LEER
"Huh? Those are auto-mail, too!?" undies
BY BABA ATSUSHI
BY SANKICHI HINODEYA
FRAGILE
BY MASANARI YUBEKA
MEGUMI KAMO
EDO RONDO (ED DANCE) KAMIKAZE HISSHO (VICTORY)
WAG WAG
...I GUESS I'LL JUST LEAVE IT PLAIN.

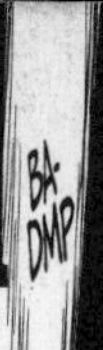
BA-DMP

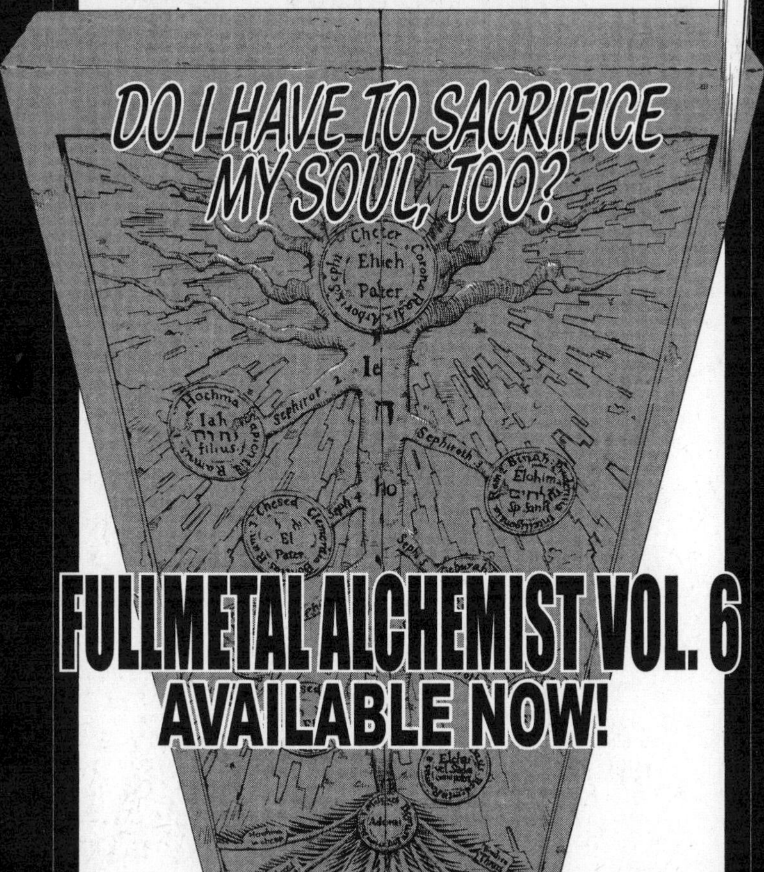

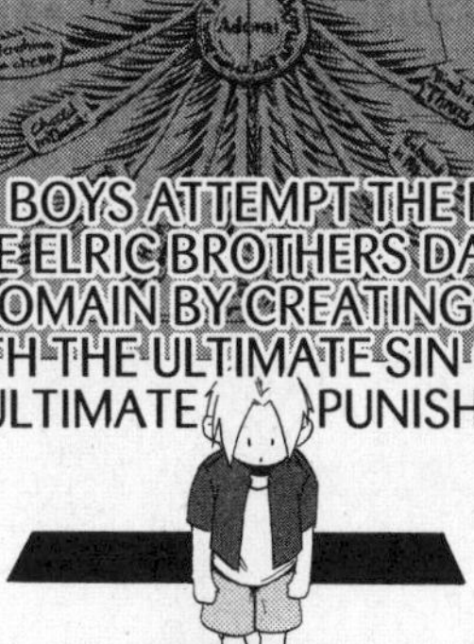

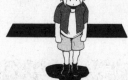

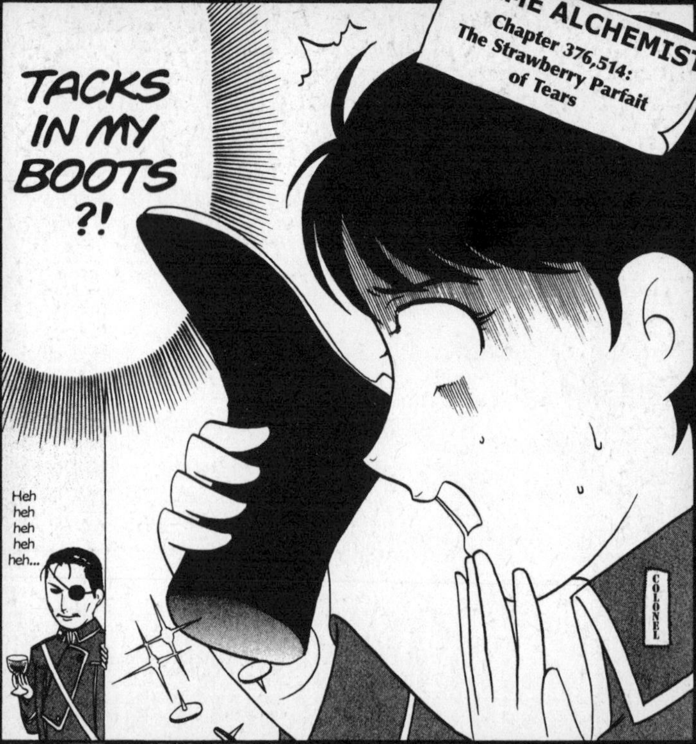
FLAME ALCHEMIST
Chapter 376,514: The Strawberry Parfait of Tears
COLONEL
TACKS IN MY BOOTS ?!
Heh heh heh heh heh...

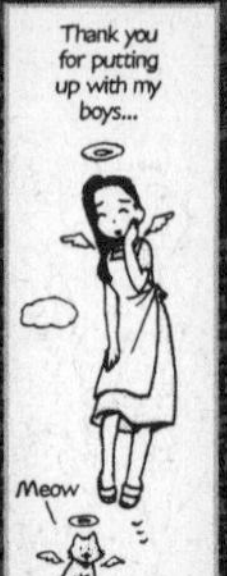
Thank you for putting up with my boys...
Meow

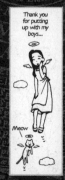

In Memoriam

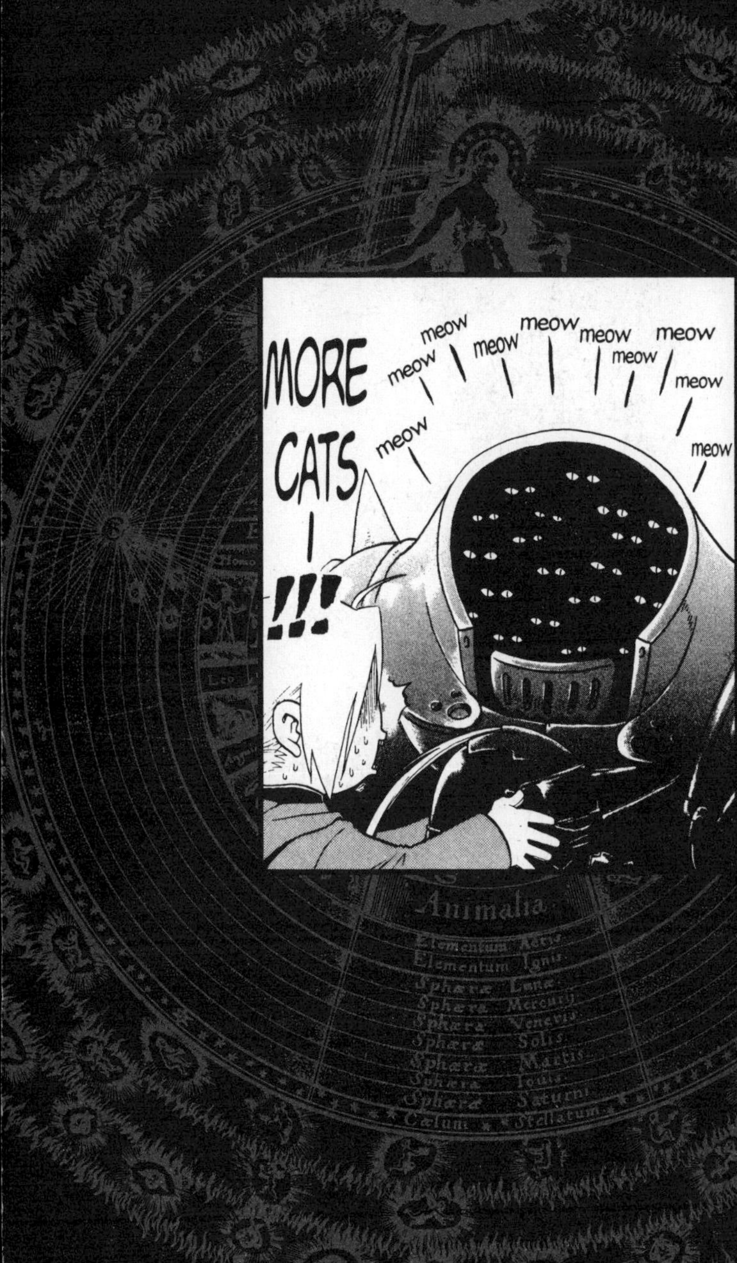
meow
meow
meow
meow
meow
meow
meow
meow
meow
meow
MORE CATS!!!

ᏉIᏃMᎯNᏀᎯ

Read manga anytime, anywhere!

From our newest hit series to the classics you know and love, the best manga in the world is now available digitally. Buy a volume* of digital manga for your:

iOS device (iPad®, iPhone®, iPod® touch)
through the **VIZ Manga app**

Android-powered device (phone or tablet)
with a browser by visiting VIZManga.com

Mac or PC computer by visiting VIZManga.com

VIZ Digital has loads to offer:

- 500+ ready-to-read volumes
- New volumes each week
- FREE previews
- Access on multiple devices! Create a log-in through the app
  so you buy a book once, and read it on your device of choice!*

To learn more, visit www.viz.com/apps

* Some series may not be available for multiple devices.
  Check the app on your device to find out what's available.

ratings.viz.com

viz.com/apps

BAKUMAN.

STORY BY TSUGUMI OHBA
ART BY TAKESHI OBATA

From the creators of *Death Note*

The mystery behind manga making REVEALED!

Average student Moritaka Mashiro enjoys drawing for fun. When his classmate and aspiring writer Akito Takagi discovers his talent, he begs to team up. But what exactly does it take to make it in the manga-publishing world?

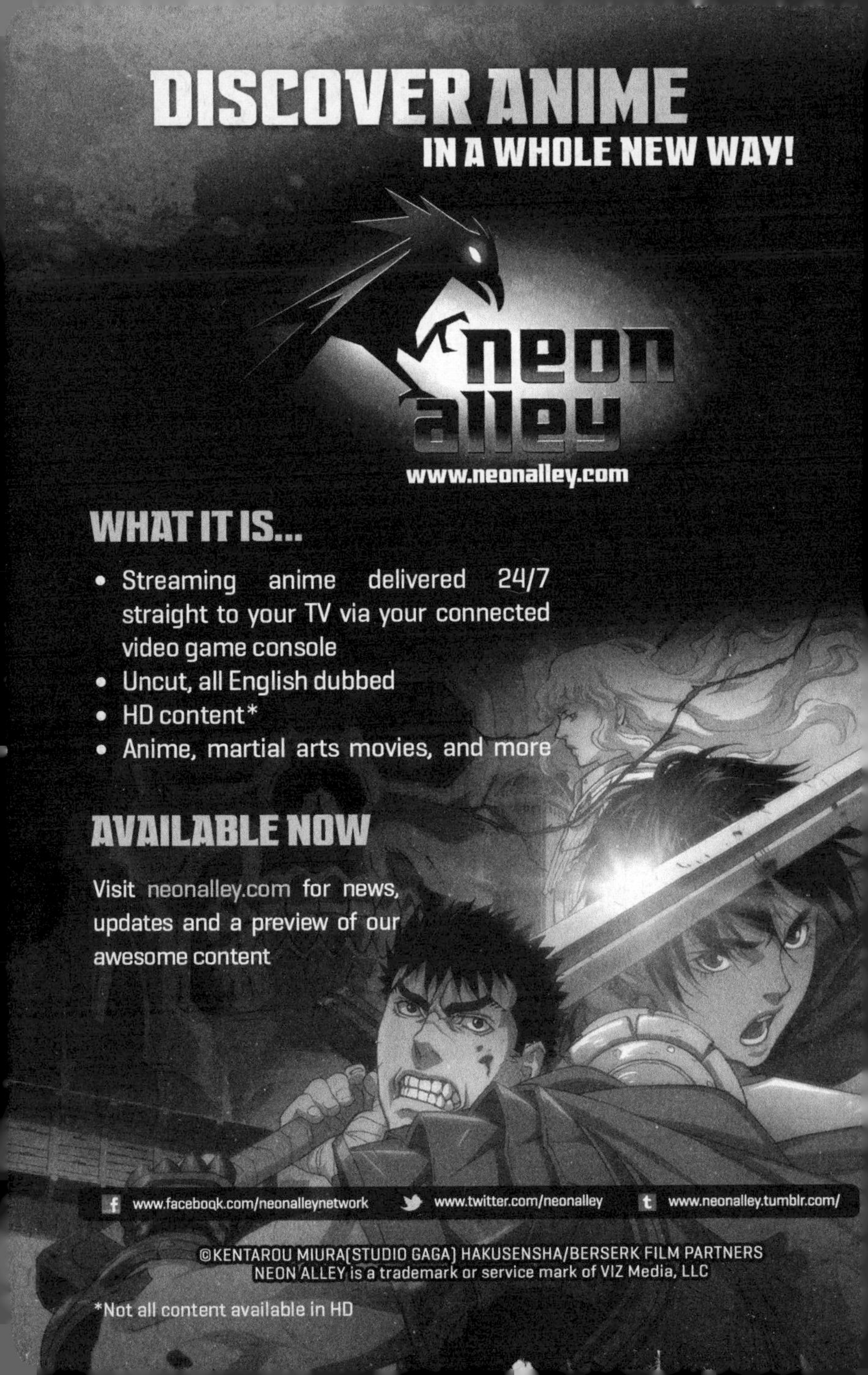
DISCOVER ANIME
IN A WHOLE NEW WAY!
neon alley
www.neonalley.com
WHAT IT IS...
• Streaming anime delivered 24/7 straight to your TV via your connected video game console
• Uncut, all English dubbed
• HD content*
• Anime, martial arts movies, and more
AVAILABLE NOW
Visit neonalley.com for news, updates and a preview of our awesome content
www.facebook.com/neonalleynetwork
www.twitter.com/neonalley
www.neonalley.tumblr.com/
©KENTAROU MIURA(STUDIO GAGA) HAKUSENSHA/BERSERK FILM PARTNERS
NEON ALLEY is a trademark or service mark of VIZ Media, LLC
*Not all content available in HD

Hey! You're Reading in the Wrong Direction!

This is the **end** of this graphic novel!

To properly enjoy this VIZ graphic novel, please turn it around and begin reading from **right to left.** Unlike English, Japanese is read right to left, so Japanese comics are read in reverse order from the way English comics are typically read.

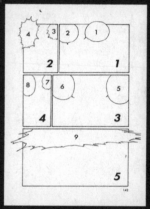

Follow the action this way

This book has been printed in the original Japanese